THE CHALLENGE OF
HUMANISTIC ECONOMICS

THE CHALLENGE OF HUMANISTIC ECONOMICS

MARK A. LUTZ
University of Maine at Orono
Department of Economics

KENNETH LUX, Ph.D.
Clinical Psychologist
Penobscot, Maine

Introduction by KENNETH BOULDING

THE BENJAMIN/CUMMINGS PUBLISHING COMPANY, INC.
Menlo Park, California • Reading, Massachusetts
London • Amsterdam • Dons Mills, Ontario • Sydney

Quotations on pages 129, 130, and 134 are from *Capitalism and Freedom,* by Milton Friedman. Copyright © 1962, The University of Chicago Press.

Quotation on pages 225–226 is from *British Factory—Japanese Factory* by Ronald Dore. Copyright © 1973, University of California Press. Reprinted by permission.

Quotations on pages 282, 283, 284, and 301 are from *Small Is Beautiful* by E. F. Schumacher. Copyright © 1973, Torchback Edition. Reprinted by permission of Harper & Row Publishers.

Figure on page 12 is from *Individual in Society* by Krech *et al.* Copyright ©. Used with permission of McGraw-Hill Book Co.

Quotations on pages 238–239 are reprinted from the March 28, 1977, issue of *Business Week* by special permission. Copyright © 1977, McGraw-Hill, Inc., New York, NY 10020. All rights reserved.

Figure on page 197 is from *Modern Social Policies in Britain and Sweden* by Hugh Helco. Copyright © 1974, p. 10, Yale University Press.

Quotations on pages 15 and 96 are from *Basic Economic Concepts,* 2nd edition, by Werner Sichel and Peter Eckstein, pp. 1, 142, 452–453. Copyright ©, Rand McNally College Publishing Company. Reprinted by permission.

Quotations on pages 267 and 268 are reprinted by permission of *The New Republic.* Copyright © 1974, The New Republic, Inc.

Quotations on pages 67 and 88 are from *Capitalism and Freedom,* by Milton Friedman. Copyright © 1962, The University of Chicago Press.

Quotation on page 305 is from *Toward a Steady State Economy* by H. Daly. W. H. Freeman and Co., 1973, pages 160–61. Original Source: University of Alabama, *Distinguished Lecture Series,* #2, 1971.

Copyright © 1979 by The Benjamin/Cummings Publishing Company, Inc.
Philippines copyright 1979 by The Benjamin/Cummings Publishing Company, Inc.

Library of Congress Cataloging in Publication Data

Lutz, Mark.
    The challenge of humanistic economics.

    1. Economics.   2. Economics—Moral and religious aspects.
3. Economics—Psychological aspects.   I. Lux, Kenneth, joint author.
II. Title.
HB72.L87   330.1   79–866
ISBN 0-8053-6642-3

ABCDEFGHIJ-MA-782109

The Benjamin/Cummings Publishing Company, Inc.
2727 Sand Hill Road
Menlo Park, California 94025

INTRODUCTION

In a day of sterile t-crossing and i-dotting in economics, and a generally hopeless feeling that all the answers to social questions are wrong, this book comes like a fresh blast out of the north Maine woods. The authors are young and I think are unashamedly romantic about the human race. Being somewhat a shamed romantic myself, I appreciate the unashamed variety. The authors may dress their romanticism up in Maslovian psychology and even slightly shunted-off-the-mainline economics, but the awful truth is that they believe in the human race, they think it has a lot of unexhausted potential, that there are still social inventions yet to make, and they unashamedly proclaim that a better world than the one we know now is not only possible but even quite likely. To this kind of romanticism I can only say "Amen," or if that sounds too pious, 2.9 cheers.

My one-tenth of a cheer reservation comes from two sources. One is a feeling that I have never quite been able to shake off, that there is something in the classical Christian doctrine of original sin, and this makes me have doubts about self-actualization according to Maslow. There is, or at least used to be, a small sect in the South called the "Two Seeds in the Spirit Predestinarian Baptists." I am too much of an Armenian Quaker to be a Predestinarian Baptist, but I always had a sneaking fondness for the two seeds in the spirit, one of which I presume is potential for good, and the other, potential for evil. Surely the idea that the self that can be actualized can only be good is unrealistic.

I have some doubts I must confess even about a hierarchy of physical needs, for outside the periods of famine, and apart from the need for advanced medical care, the vast majority of human beings at all times and places have been able to satisfy the minimum physical needs, the evidence being that they have stayed alive and reproduced their kind. George Stigler in 1945 discovered that a perfectly adequate, though probably inedible, diet for physical nutrition in the United States could be bought in 1944 for about sixty dollars a year. Even today this would be not much more than two hundred dollars, fantastically below anything that we like to think of in this country as a poverty level. This is not to deny the widespread incidence of malnutrition, protein deficiency, and inadequate medical care. A universal basic minimum in this regard is the first prerequisite for a tolerable earth, but this minimum cannot really be defined in physiological terms and we are into wants rather than needs before we know where we are. As we move up into the higher wants and the higher needs, the process of the learning of values becomes overwhelmingly important. One cannot even rule out the possibility of perverse genetics, little as we know about this. Hitler certainly actualized to the full an extremely disagreeable self, and the assumption which is sometimes made in this book, that self-actualization will lead to altruism, at least needs careful examination.

Nevertheless, the conclusions of the authors may be better than their reasons for them. The human mind is enormously flexible. Beyond a primitive genetic base, our values are largely learned. The critique of false values is just as legitimate as the critique of our fallacious images of fact. There is indeed an evolutionary process which can lead us to the learning of values and preferences which are "better" than those of the past, and in this process there are ups and downs, often very deep downs, like Hitler's Germany, or Stalin's Russia, or present day Cambodia. But there is also a certain basic irreversibility, in that when we "wise up," either in our images of fact or of value, we hardly ever "wise down" again to where we were before. If this is Tennysonian Locksley Hall optimism—"Yet I doubt not through the ages one increasing purpose runs, And the thoughts of men are widen'd with the process of the suns"—so be it. It is something which I share with the authors of this volume.

My other qualm about the thesis of this volume is that I think the human race has a much stronger desire for freedom in many of its innumerable meanings than the authors of this volume recognize. Some of these demands for freedom may not even be very respectable, like the demand for freedom from responsibility and even for the freedom to be a fool. There is an almost infinite variety in the human species and the danger of all reformers is that they tend to make it over in their own image. Thus, the failure of producers' cooperatives (the authors' analysis of this is one of the best things in the book) is not only a result of a defect in financial organization, it is also a result of a widespread distaste for responsibility, a demand for "an honest day's work for an honest day's pay" (and it is no damn business of my employer what I do when I get home). An active labor market and working for pay, even without much control of the conditions of work, is something which is genuinely liberating to certain human spirits.

This is not to deny that there is an important niche in social life for workers' cooperatives, participatory democracy, and all these delights and that this niche can be expanded by appropriate technical devices. This is all to the good, but it is a great mistake to mistake a niche for the ecosystem, and the division of labor between those who like to take responsibility and those who do not is by no means adverse to general human welfare.

The hatred of competition, which again up to a point may be justified, is part of the same syndrome of the fear of freedom. Competition can easily degenerate into pathological conflict and malevolence, negative-sum games, arms races, and a nightmare of descending spirals that lead to Belfast, Lebanon, Zaire or Cambodia. It is very important to be able to identify and defend ourselves against these degenerative processes. But competition is also consistent with benevolence. In a certain sense it is the only source of advancement. Cooperation is a purely instrumental good. It is probably even easier to cooperate for evil purposes than it is for good ones. Monopoly always hovers on the edge of injustice and frequently falls over into it. My mainline economics, therefore, reasserts itself and I must defend competition as on the whole healthy and necessary.

That this book will stir controversy is evident from this introduction. The controversy that it will create, however, is precisely what we need to rescue us from mainline stagnation and radical cant. In a certain sense this book is written for economists, and I know of no economists who would fail to benefit from reading it and taking it seriously. Its message, however, is much wider, for this book has a message for everybody who is concerned about the future of the world and with a little judicious skipping, non-economists should not find it too difficult. It will be, and should be, criticized severely. It will annoy the radicals I am sure as much as it will annoy the mainliners, but it deserves to be read widely and taken seriously.

Kenneth E. Boulding
Distinguished Professor of Economics
University of Colorado at Boulder

Dedicated to E. F. Schumacher, the gentle giant of humanistic economics.

PREFACE

We wrote this book to present to the student of economics, both lay and professional, a point of view or school of thought that we feel has increasing relevance for our times. But, as can be seen from Kenneth Boulding's introduction, this viewpoint seems bound to raise controversy. This controversy is probably necessary and all to the good. We feel that out of it will come an understanding and appreciation for a new direction in economics.

We are an economist and a psychologist who were both galvanized by the same idea—the value of building economics on a foundation of humanistic psychology—rather than the old psychology that economics had so long relied on, the psychology of utilitarianism. Our idea grew and gained its own momentum until it finally materialized into its present form. The primary thesis of this book is that economics as a science should promote human welfare by recognizing and integrating the full range of basic human values.

This text does not easily fall into standard classifications. It is meant to be a new and different approach that will make what is too frequently considered a dismal science glow with vitality. Rather than demonstrating that conventional economics is wrong, we are interested in widening its scope.

The first half of this book explains what we mean by humanistic (need-based) economics and how it differs from its utilitarian (want-based) counterpart. The second half explores the applicability of the book's main thesis by examining postwar developments in the United States, Europe, and the Third World. Some of the more obscure, or at least subtle, concepts of modern economics such as revealed preference theory, lexicographic orderings, and Pareto optimality have been covered for the beginning student. We recognize that this is an unconventional feature of a book on this level, but we are convinced that such a presentation is long overdue. In any case, the entire book has been written assuming no prior knowledge of economics or any other social science. All concepts have been worked up from the beginning.

This book is ideally suited as supplementary reading for an introductory course in microeconomics, or as one of several texts in other undergraduate courses, such as Economic Issues, Modern Economic Thought, Comparative Economic Systems, Social Economics, Institutional Economics and Political Economy.

ACKNOWLEDGEMENTS

For sharing our editorial labors, without which this book would probably still be several years away from completion, our deep felt thanks go to Gail Morrow. Her help was indispensable.

We also thank, for the much welcomed humanistic investment in the book from the first outline of a draft to the finished version of the manuscript, R. H. Lutz.

Additionally, we would like to thank the referees, including Kenneth Boulding, E. K. Hunt, Larry D. Singell, Margaret H. Simeral, James F. Willis, and Benjamin Ward, who did much to add value to the finished product. Special thanks go to Nicholas Georgescu-Roegen for his personal attention to several topics in this book, particularly some of the material in the appendices. Last, but not least, on both an emotional and a practical level, help has been forthcoming from the other Lutz and Lux, our wives, Margie and Katy, and our families. We are grateful for their support as well as their infinite patience.

Mark A. Lutz
Kenneth Lux

CONTENTS

PART ONE
INTRODUCTION

Chapter One

HUMANISM AS A CONCEPT: ITS EMERGING SIGNIFICANCE IN PSYCHOLOGY AND ECONOMICS

INTRODUCTION

What kind of world do we want?

This is a question of values. It asks, what are the values that govern our society, and what should they be? It is a perfectly reasonable question, which, in one form or another, concerns most people today. Therefore it seems rather surprising that economists, of all people, have generally excluded this question from their field for almost a century. Rejecting the question of values, most economists have limited themselves to what they believed was a purely objective position of describing what is, that is, how economic systems work. They claimed to make no value judgements and recommend no prescriptions. This was supposed to be the domain of politics, not economics. Now this attempt at objective description sounds admirable, and in a science like physics it *may be* possible. But a science about people is fundamentally different from a science about things, and if you confuse the two you tend to treat people as if they were things, and this in effect becomes the first value judgement. If it is the case that a social science cannot get away from value judgements then the danger comes, not from making value judgements, but from being unaware of what those values are that are operating. Humanism in economics gives attention to values and shows what part they can and should legitimately play in the field.

But this is not the essence. Humanism in economics goes behind values to something even more fundamental, from which our values actually derive, and this is human needs. *Needs* is a concept so simple and so basic that its significance can easily be overlooked, but once we have recognized it, our economics may never be quite the same. Conventional, mainstream economics has not been able to adequately deal with values because it has not seen economics in terms of needs. But, you may ask, if it has not seen needs as the focus of economics, what *has* been its focus? The answer is *wants*, and, as we will show later in this chapter, the difference between wants and needs marks the turning point in economics from its non-humanistic to its humanistic varieties. We believe that the number of economists who are turning their attention to needs instead of wants is on the increase today, and will continue to grow

HUMANISM AS A CONCEPT

Humanism occupied a central position among the Hebrew prophets and Greek philosophers, yet it is only within the last five centuries that the idea has experienced a revival. In 1510 the Dutchman, Desiderius Erasmus, wrote a book with the delightful title *In Praise of Folly*. This was near the beginning of the Renaissance, a period when Europeans, whose thinking and culture had been dominated for a thousand years by church and theological doctrine, began to reawaken to the world around them, and to reach out in new directions. In his book Erasmus satirized the foibles of his culture, which seemed so limited and artificial, referring to "the God Latin, the crabbed learning, the barren subtlety, and the needlessly elaborate theology of the schoolmen."[1] The *schoolmen* was the name given to those schooled in academic and theological argumentation.

The concept of humanism has gone through many changes and usages since its beginning in the Renaissance, and today it can mean a great variety of things. It is even used to refer solely to the study of Greek literature. But, for our purposes, certain interrelated meanings of the concept of humanism are relevant.

The first point is that humanism puts *the person in the center of study*. A classic humanist phrase in this regard is, "The proper study of mankind is man." Another is, "Man is the measure of all things." (*Man* is a generic term that, of course, includes women and men.)

Related to this is the belief that people are most meaningfully seen as living in a social world. They are continuously surrounded by a dense web of *interpersonal relationships*, of which they themselves are a part, acting and reacting. To study a human being devoid of the all-important social context may be similar to studying the behavioral characteristics of chimps by observing one animal in lonely confinement. A caged and isolated chimp hardly gives us the picture of the real life of chimpanzees.

The next point involves a belief about the nature of the person, or what we call human nature. Humanism rejects the idea that the person is a blank slate who has no inner nature and exists only as raw material for the forces of society to design and shape. Humanism also rejects the belief that, if there is a human nature, it is only one of selfishness and acquisitiveness. Humanists believe that altruism and the qualities of giving are at least as fundamental to human nature. It is, in fact, necessary to make a distinction between the lower and the higher human tendencies, for without this distinction we have eliminated values, since we do not have a scale of comparison, and without values we have stripped human beings of one of their prime characteristics. So for humanists both the positive and the negative, the higher and the lower, make up the whole human being. Later in this chapter we will describe how these different tendencies relate to each other.

Another characteristic of humanism is the emphasis on growth and the development of human potentialities. Growth is the emergence in people of what is positive and creative in them, their increasing discovery of who they are, and the continuing refinement of their values and preferences. In short, it is the unfolding of the higher.

The focus on growth takes us to our final point, and that is that a society or a culture is a dynamic process. Like the individual, it is always growing and evolving. This means that time, and changes over time, are vital elements in understanding human behavior and human institutions. This is in contrast to the belief that society is best seen as static, so that all changes are understood to occur in a limited and regular sequence, much like the workings of an engine. Humanism tends to see life as having a special quality that makes it more than just a complicated machine, and that reveals new possibilities, rather than just a new arrangement of the parts, with the passage of time.

THE EMERGENCE OF HUMANISM IN PSYCHOLOGY

In the early 1960s a conception of man that was given the name *humanistic* began to emerge in the field of psychology. The Journal of Humanistic Psychology was established in 1961. It was quickly followed by the formation of the American Association for Humanistic Psychology, and in 1971 a Division of Humanistic Psychology was set up in the American Psychological Association. This conception of man has gained increasingly widespread recognition and influence and is seen as a major viewpoint in contemporary psychology. Among the founding figures of this modern revolution in psychology have been some of the leading psychologists of our time. These include Carl Rogers and Abraham Maslow, as well as, perhaps somewhat more peripherally, people such as Fritz Perls and Erich Fromm.

Humanism emerged as a "third force" in psychology as an alternative to the previously dominating traditions of behaviorism on the one hand and Freudian psychology on the other. To understand the significance of this development we need to see it in its historical context, one that is common to both psychology and economics.

Utilitarianism

All of the social sciences, including psychology and economics, developed out of eighteenth- and nineteenth-century attempts to understand human nature through the concepts and attitudes formed in the natural sciences, such as physics and biology.

An important basis of this approach was the philosophical position known as *utilitarianism*, first formulated by the Englishman, Jeremy Bentham (1748–1832). Utilitarianism is the idea that people do the things they do because these actions are useful to them (have utility) in the sense of bringing them happiness or pleasure. Here, in a famous phrase, is how Bentham expressed it, "Nature has placed mankind under the governance of two sovereign masters, pain and pleasure. It is for them alone to point out what we ought to do, as well as to determine what we should do."[2] The importance of this doctrine for the study of the person is that it allowed the newly budding social scientists largely to sidestep the classic human issues of ethics and justice, or values, by stating that what is good is also pleasurable, and what is bad is painful. Therefore all those complicated questions of good and bad, right and wrong, could be reduced to the matter of pleasure and pain. (The basis is also laid here for the eventual study of animal behavior as a parallel to human behavior.)

A second feature of utilitarianism which appealed to the early social scientists was the comparison made between the operations of the mind or brain and those of a calculator. According to Bentham, the person was a "felicity computer" who calculated the amount of pleasure and pain in each possible action and took that direction that promised the maximum pleasure or least pain.

Physics and Positivism

The human being as a calculator under the sway of the forces of pleasure and pain—how very much it resembles a physical body whose movements through space reflect the forces of attraction and repulsion! It is no wonder that such a picture was persuasive to those thinkers of the nineteenth century who were so impressed with the success of Isaac Newton's physics. There seemed no reason to doubt that the path to certain and absolute knowledge lay in emulating what physics had done, and using as many of its ideas as possible. The philosophy of finding definite or positive knowledge, as physics supposedly had, was given the name *positivism* by Auguste Comte, and as a way to knowledge it was readily embraced by all the social sciences.

Newton developed a world view that positivism took as its guiding model. It was the model of the universe as a giant machine, something on the order of a cosmically scaled clockworks. As Fontenelle, an eighteenth-century admirer of Newton put it, "I esteem the universe all the more since I have known it is like a watch. It is surprising that nature, admirable as it is, is based on such simple things."[3]

For anyone who was influenced by Newtonian physics and the positivistic outlook it was a relatively short step to conceive of man as a machine just like the physical universe of which he was a part. In fact this development of the idea that man can best be understood as a machine had been in progress for at least one hundred years. In the early 1700s La Mettrie said: "Let us conclude boldly, then, that man is a machine, and that there is only one substance, differently modified, in the whole world."[4]

What are the characteristics of this machine that is man? We can state them as another pair of "isms," which fit very nicely into the package of a positivistic philosophy. One is *materialism*. The universe consists of material things, matter, stuff, and so does man. The intangibles like mind, thought, and spirit do not really count, or may not even exist. When we understand all the principles of physics and chemistry we will understand all the principles that make man tick. (The word *tick* here is quite apropos in the context of positivism!)

Our second "ism" is *determinism*, which states that all human behavior is determined by outside forces or stimuli. This is analogous to the movement of the gear of a clock which is determined by the movements of the other gears, the flywheel, the tension of the spring, and so forth. In other words, the behavior of a human being is a mechanical, automatic, and inevitable reaction to forces and causes outside the person's conscious control. The idea of human purpose, intention, thought, plan, or anything related to what we might think of as the spirit of man, is seen as false and illusory. Man in this strict framework is part of the lawful course of nature, just as the rising and falling of the tides are, or the molting of animal fur in the spring.

The Traditional Psychologist and Humanistic Psychology Humanism arose in psychology in order to correct what it saw as the distortions that this historical and philosophical background had introduced into traditional psychology. This tradition resulted in two forces, as we have already mentioned, behaviorism and Freudianism. Humanism entered psychology as a third force, since it stood in opposition to two main deficiencies that both of the traditional psychologies shared. One was that they were excessively rooted in the old-fashioned conception of science that depended on the mechanical determinism of Newton. The second was that their methods of study led to too pessimistic a picture of man, a picture grounded in the hedonism of the utilitarians.

Problems with Physics as a Model

The problem with psychology's being dependent on an eighteenth- and nineteenth-century scientific frame of reference is twofold. One was that physics itself had changed dramatically since the nineteenth century, and Newtonian mechanical determinism was no longer even adequate as a world-view *in physics*. The second was that the positivistic attempt to apply directly the concepts of physics to human beings might be mistaken at the outset, whether or not it uses a physics that is up-to-date.

The publication of Einstein's special Theory of Relativity in 1905, followed a decade later by his general theory, showed that the Newtonian mechanistic picture of the physical world was only true as a limited case, and as a general theory was inadequate. The renowned philosopher Alfred North Whitehead summed up the state of affairs in 1925:

> ☐ The progress of science has now reached a turning point. The stable foundations of physics have broken up. . . . The old foundations of scientific thought are becoming unintelligible. Time, space, matter, material, ether, electricity, mechanism, . . . all require reinterpretation. What is the sense of talking about a mechanical explanation when you do not know what you mean by mechanics?[5]

The breakup of the Newtonian world-view by Einstein led to a further reformulation of physics by two other scientific giants of this century, Max Planck originating the concept of the quantum, and Werner Heisenberg with his Uncertainty Principle. The change that these two ideas brought about throughout physics is well summed up by Sir James Jeans, "Today there is a wide measure of agreement, which on the physical side of science approaches almost to unanimity, that the stream of knowledge is heading toward a non-mechanical reality; the universe begins to look more like a great thought than like a great machine."[6]

The tables have been turned on the mechanical determinists. They believed the universe was like a machine and that man was a miniature copy of the same principle. Instead, it was discovered by some of *the leading physicists themselves* that we are not machines, and the universe is more likely to copy us than we are to copy it. An illustration can be found in Heisenberg's explanation of indeterminacy or uncertainty in physics. "Natural science," he said, "does not simply describe and explain nature; it is a part of the interplay between nature and ourselves." Thus "we cannot observe the course of nature without disturbing it."[7]

If this is true in the inanimate world of physics, how much more true must it be in the animate *and* social world of man. This leads directly to the second part of the problem: the attempt to base the study of psychology on the concepts of physics, regardless of what kind of physics.

For the humanists the direct application of physics to psychology is subject to a fundamental and fatal error. When the physicist observes nature he or she is observing something different from himself or herself; an animate conscious being, the physicist, is observing an inanimate non-conscious phenomenon, say, the motion of gases in a sealed chamber. There is the most fundamental difference in kind between these two entities: the physicist, a person, a subject, and the gases, a thing, a static object. The laws that the physicist might devise to describe the world of objects are pertinent to that kind of world and those phenomena. But when a psychologist or an economist observes another person, it is a case of like observing like. The investigator and his or her subject are of the same nature. Therefore in the case of psychology and the other social sciences there exists, not a subject-object relationship, but a subject-subject relationship. From this it follows that the kinds of theories physicists construct ought to be largely inappropriate to the kinds of theories that psychologists and other social scientists need. The whole concept of "law" which had been useful to the physicist (and is much less useful today) may be totally inadequate for the study of man. According to the humanists it was the retaining of the subject-object point of view from physics that led behaviorists to the absurd conclusion that consciousness and purpose were either non-existent or, at best, irrelevant.

The second problem with the traditional psychologies is their pessimism. In a general sense, this pessimism is the logical outcome of joining the utilitarianism of pleasure and pain with the mechanistic world-view of nineteenth-century physics. Not much of an inspiring or ennobling image of the person is left when he or she has been fundamentally described as a mechanical pleasure computer.

THE CONCEPTS OF HUMANISTIC PSYCHOLOGY

Growth and Needs

The central concept of humanistic psychology, upon which all of the other concepts rest, is that of human growth through a series of needs. This refers to the development and increasing maturation of the self, that inner sense of who one is and what one feels and thinks. In a healthy person this growth takes place throughout life, and is continually moving towards higher levels of self-realization or *self-actualization*, to use Abraham Maslow's term for this process.[8]

The growth of the human being towards self-actualization represents the attainment of full human potential. Maslow has listed the growth necessities in their order of priority for the human being as the needs of physiology (food, clothing, shelter), safety and security, belongingness (meaningful social relationships), esteem (a sense of self-worth), and finally, self-actualization itself.

While each person naturally grows and evolves in a unique way, all the above-mentioned items or circumstances are necessary if this personal evolution is to be realized. It might be said that the uniqueness of individuals lies in how they go about meeting their basic needs, but not in whether they have or don't have these needs. The humanistic psychologists have seen them as characteristic of the human species.

The Hierarchical Nature
of Human Needs

Psychologists have long recognized that when the fundamental, basic needs, such as the physiological, are not satisfied they will exert a pressure on the person that will tend to override all other possible concerns and needs. Thus, even though self-esteem, for example, is one of the basic human needs, it remains well in the background if the need for security is unsatisfied.

The converse of this is equally important. Once a basic need is satisfied, then a higher basic need emerges to the forefront of attention and interest. Therefore, by satisfying one area or category of need, the person is able to become involved with the needs that exist at a higher level of development. In other words, human needs manifest themselves in a series of stages, and you have to get through one stage before you can go on to the next. These stages can be seen as priorities, so that a more crucial priority must be heeded before another priority can claim attention. This can be seen to define the process of growth. It has been summarized by Maslow in the following phrase: "Man does not live by bread alone—*if* he has enough bread."

Thus, the various basic human needs can be arranged in a hierarchical order in terms of their necessity for growth and development. The lower needs have to be satisfied before the higher ones. A depiction of this hierarchy, based on Maslow's work, is shown in Figure 1-1. Let us review these needs.

The most basic needs are physiological. We have to survive, and for this we need a minimum of food, water, shelter, and clothing, etc. If not sufficiently satisfied, according to Maslow, these needs will dominate the organism, "pressing all its capacities into their service and organizing these capacities so that they may be most efficient in their service." Relative gratification, on the other hand, submerges them, making room for the next higher set of needs to dominate one's personality. Concern with hunger and other material necessities will now turn into concern with safety and security.

Safety and security needs provide a transition from the physiological area of need to the social area. On a physiological level

FIGURE 1-1   MASLOW'S HIERARCHY OF NEEDS (VALUES)

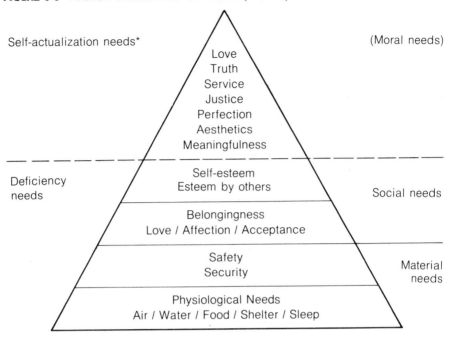

Self-actualization needs*

(Moral needs)

Love
Truth
Service
Justice
Perfection
Aesthetics
Meaningfulness

Deficiency
needs

Self-esteem
Esteem by others

Social needs

Belongingness
Love / Affection / Acceptance

Safety
Security

Material
needs

Physiological Needs
Air / Water / Food / Shelter / Sleep

*Self-actualization needs are of equal importance (not hierarchical).

security means that one can expect to meet one's physiological needs into the foreseeable future. This then blends into the more socially oriented need that one is safe from threat or loss due to the actions of others. All in all, safety and security relates to the feeling of having basic survival needs met, and of being protected. Together with the physiological needs they constitute the *material* needs.

The third cluster of needs revolves around the social area, and is what can be called the need for belongingness. This means being part of a family, community, and society at large, and forming close and meaningful interpersonal relationships.

Maslow spoke about a fourth area of need that also has a strong social focus. This is the need for esteem, which is the need to feel respected, to feel worth something, to have basic dignity as a person. Here we move more clearly into the area of work, and the need to feel that one is productive, and that there is value in what one is doing. We will often refer to the needs of belongingness and esteem as the basic *social* need.

Maslow's studies led him to use the term *deficiency needs* to describe these first four categories of need. He used the term because deprivation in these areas produces illness, very much like the idea of a deficiency disease, such as the absence of certain vitamins. A distinguishing characteristic of a deficiency need is that it is *psychologically* inactive, or latent, in a healthy person. Of course, everyone always needs food, shelter, etc., but the point is that these don't occupy as much consciousness when they are routinely satisfied. Nevertheless, these lower needs can become temporarily dominant as a result of deprivation.

The most basic deficiency needs, such as that for food and water, are cyclical or episodal; they are quieted upon being satisfied, but after a period of time they again press for satisfaction. This is why the safety and security need is closely tied to an adequate fulfillment of the physiological needs. They cannot be satisfied once and for all, but need the assurance of being able to be satisfied in the future. In the same way, once each of the subsequent human needs are met they tend to decrease in importance for the organism, and the way is made for the next need to emerge. This is illustrated in Figure 1-2, which also shows the course of development of the whole hierarchy of needs.

FIGURE 1-2   THE DEVELOPMENT OF NEEDS (VALUES)

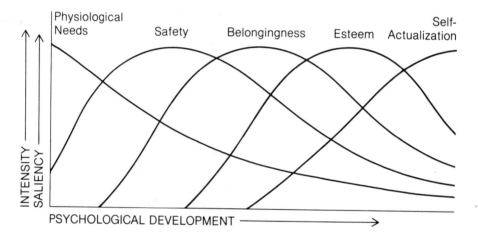

Self-Actualization   When all the deficiency or lower needs are met the person does not stop growing. On the contrary, at this point the person has the possibility of entering into the most fulfilling phase of human development, which Maslow termed *self-actualization*. These are needs for creative development, and are the paramount needs in the life of a mature and healthy adult.

A major characteristic of growth needs, in contrast to the deficiency needs, is that their gratification leads to an *increase* rather than a decrease in their strength. This is illustrated by the constantly rising line for self-actualization in Figure 1-2. For example, when a person is able to produce something creative, say, through painting, this generates even further interest in artistic expression. Similarly, the desire for truth is never satisfied but builds upon itself to produce a further and deeper search. These needs tend to be continued and ever-present, in an upward and future-oriented development. They carry a person to the heights of what it means to be fully human. This striving for the good and the beautiful can also be seen as a *moral* need.

It will be noted in Figure 1-1 that there is not a hard and fast line between the deficiency needs and self-actualization, with the need for esteem being a borderline need. Note also in the diagram that the lower needs are object-oriented and materialistic, and the higher needs become more socially oriented and more abstracted from objects. This distinction parallels the classic distinction between the material and the spiritual.

What are the qualities of the highly self-actualized person? Research discussed in the work of Maslow and Rogers indicates that they tend to be creative, spontaneous yet disciplined, non-power-seeking; they tend to recognize the worth and value of others; their attitudes are highly democratic rather than authoritarian; they prefer decentralized organizational structures; and they prefer cooperative rather than competitive relationships with others. [9]

The above is a sampling of a whole list of qualities that are indicative of the self-actualized person. It is not exhaustive, and really cannot be, but it does serve to give the flavor of what a person is like who seems to have reached some of the higher levels of human development. In a word, this is a picture of the fully mature human being.

Correctly Interpreting the Theory There is a possible weakness in Maslow's theory that stems, not so much from what it directly describes, but from what it seems to suggest or imply. This is the implication that only the rich and economically successful can be creative or self-actualized. Such an implication is obviously false. There are many great artistic and scientific works created under conditions of poverty. Maslow himself would not deny this. What he would say is that at sufficiently extreme levels of deprivation most higher levels of activity become increasingly unlikely.

In terms of social policy Maslow's theory applies even though there can be individual exceptions (because fortunately the human being has the ability to rise above all manner of limitations); *fulfilling lower needs is the best guarantee of promoting human development.*

There is one other aspect of the phenomenon of the deprived, yet creative, individual that helps us get a deeper insight into the hierarchy of needs. It is that a higher-order need, once experienced, diminishes the value that is given to a lower need. This means that once people experience the joy of creative or socially meaningful activity they tend to have less interest in pursuing material wealth or the accumulation of goods.

Needs and Values

Previously we said that humanistic economics was concerned with values. At this point we should mention that values and needs are closely related, one being easily translatable into the other. We might even say that they are synonyms. If someone has a need for a particular object or experience we can say that that person values that object or experience. And, conversely, one values that for which one senses a need. If a person has been scrambling for a living all his or her life, and has never had the opportunity to experience the need for esteem or dignity, then there will be no value placed on those things. "Bread" will generally be the highest value for a person in that situation.

As the person grows and develops there is a shift of needs or values from the materially oriented values to values more concerned with discovery, creativity, love, and so forth. This shift in values represents a corresponding shift in the self. The maturing person grows from qualities that are often considered ego-building or egotistical, such as wealth, power, and status, to qualities that move beyond egotism and towards authentic selfhood.

Authentic selfhood. This is all well and good, but what happens when a person doesn't grow? So far we have painted a picture of the person that might appear pretty rosy. The person is seen to fulfill one need and then move on to another, seemingly moving in an uninterrupted fashion to ever higher levels of human fulfillment. But such a rosy image can hardly be said to fit the state of humanity in general. Does this contradict the theory of growth and self-actualization that humanists have proposed? No, it doesn't. As a matter of fact, humanists believe that it is only such a theory that can adequately enable us to understand and correct the widespread social deficiencies that we observe around us. Humanistic economics devotes itself to this very purpose.

Fixation: The Blockage of Growth

Here humanism borrows a concept from Freudian psychology, but adapts it for its own purposes. When there is a barrier to growth, for whatever reason, this means that a certain need category cannot adequately be fulfilled. When this occurs people become *fixated* at a lower need level than that for which they are developmentally ready. This fixation involves an excessive involvement and preoccupation with the objects and experiences of the lower level, since the higher level, which is the gateway to their future growth, has been blocked off.

For most purposes fixations can be said to manifest themselves as materialism or egotism. The former involves excessive involvement with objects, and the latter with status and power. Insecurity, lack of belongingness, or lack of esteem are some of the prime generators of these disorders of growth.

Materialism and egotism develop because the overall self-actualization drive is frustrated and thus gets channelled back into the lower needs, rather than being able to naturally fulfill itself through the higher needs. This is like a short circuiting of energy, the energy of growth, so that the lower needs become overloaded. When the consumption of objects becomes overloaded with this developmental energy we have materialism. When social position and role become similarly overloaded we have egotism. These two growth disorders can also go hand-in-hand. It all depends on which higher needs are prevented from being fulfilled.

PSYCHOLOGY AND ECONOMICS

First of all, it is necessary to realize that in order for economics to apply to people at all it has to assume a psychology. It does so either explicitly or implicity. As the well-known economist, John S. Gambs, put it, "Psychology is like the foundation of a house. The importance of a foundation in a building is undisputed, but when the whole is completed, the supporting masonry is often invisible, unadmired, undiscussed, and unmentioned. It plays forever a determining role, however."[10] How modern economics has constructed its present psychology will be fully explored in Chapter 3, Economic Man. For now we would like to introduce two concepts, basic to conventional economics, which illustrate what kind of psychology this is. Then we will contrast this psychology with humanistic psychology and show the new economic understanding that springs out of assuming this new psychology.

The first concept is *diminishing marginal utility*. Marginal utility comes from the notions of utilitarianism, and for our present purposes can be taken to mean present or future satisfaction to be gotten from a commodity or service. *Diminishing* marginal utility is the familiar observation that an individual's satisfaction diminishes the more he or she consumes additional amounts of a particular good or service. Here is a standard textbook explanation of this concept:

> □ Diminishing marginal utility is an expression of the "variety is the spice of life" philosophy of most individuals—that people prefer to have one or a few of a lot of different goods and services rather than a great many of only a few goods and services. For example, diminishing marginal utility suggests that an individual will derive more satisfaction from eating a first apple than a second apple, which in turn provides more satisfaction than a third apple, and so on—where all the apples are eaten at one sitting. . . . Exceptions to diminishing marginal utility are only infrequently observed.[11]

First of all, it is clear from this presentation that real-world behavior, and thus a psychology, is involved. It attempts to be a description of how people really function.

The same thing applies to the second economic concept we wish to discuss, and that is *opportunity cost*. This is a simple, easily understood idea that is seen to have almost universal applicability. Its meaning is that the cost of any particular action is the opportunity given up to engage in any other action. Here too we will refer to a conventional textbook explanation to show how this concept is understood:

> ☐ The real cost of any action (going to a movie, buying a pair of jeans, manufacturing a lawnmower, moving to Halifax, raising beef cattle, building a hardware store, taking out an insurance policy) is the value of the alternative opportunity that must be sacrificed in order to take the action.

The book then goes on to make the following point:

> ☐ The theory of supply in economics is not essentially different from the theory of demand. Both assume that decision-makers face alternatives and choose among them, and that their choices reflect a comparison of the benefits anticipated from the alternatives. The logic of the economizing process is the same for producers as it is for consumers.[12]

With these two concepts we now have sufficient basis to describe the essence of human behavior as conventional economics has conceived it.

The human being is confronted by an array of different commodities in the world, each of which offers him or her a certain amount of utility or benefit. The person then calculates the opportunity cost of engaging in each activity compared to the others and comes up with that activity or consumptive behavior that has the lowest opportunity cost, and thus the greatest satisfaction. The process is sometimes referred to as a cost/benefit analysis. Since there is diminishing marginal utility, or satisfaction, involved in any consumption—variety is the spice of life—the individual leaves this particular activity, and then makes a new opportunity cost analysis, since conditions do change, which leads him or her to go on to a new activity. And so it goes.

Is this a plausible picture of how people behave? We would say that in a number of respects it is, and thus it is not surprising that it has persisted in economics for almost a hundred years. We should also point out that it is a psychology that is very close to behaviorism, which follows from the fact that both conventional economics and behaviorism share the same philosophical background in utilitarianism and Newtonian physics. Therefore, the fact that humanistic psychology has uncovered serious deficiencies in behaviorism indicates that there are serious problems with conventional, utilitarian economics. To these we now turn.

In that disarmingly simple textbook explanation of diminishing marginal utility that we previously quoted lies what we believe is a key to unravelling the flawed tapestry of conventional economics. It is in the dictum "variety is the spice of life." This is put forth as the explanation of why there is *diminishing* marginal utility, such as in the eating of apples. We need also to say that this phrase is not unique to this particular textbook, but is the typical way the explanation is phrased in the field of conventional economics. We picked this textbook precisely because of the clarity of its presentation of basic economic concepts.

If one spends a few moments thinking about that example carefully, a remarkable discovery may emerge. True, there is definite wisdom in the saying that variety is the spice of life, and there is no quarrel with that in itself. But is that the major reason why there is less satisfaction gotten from eating the second apple than from the first, and so on? Of course not. Common sense easily tells us that the person is less *hungry* after the first apple, and that is why the second apple is less satisfying. This is quite obvious. Hunger is really the point, not that successive apples somehow get less interesting. It is correct that boredom, or conversely, a need for variety, plays its part in life, but it is certainly not the primary factor in the explanation of eating. To the variety-spice theme we will return a little later. What we need to do now is ask ourselves this: Why in the world does conventional economics avoid the obvious explanation here in favor of a more far-fetched one?

The answer we think lies in the idea of need—as in human need. Conventional economics goes to great lengths, as we have just seen, to avoid talking about needs. Instead it talks about what are called "wants," and this is why the variety is seen as relevant. A want is seen in conventional economics as simply what a person chooses, or appears to prefer, what maximizes his or her utility or satisfaction. As far as economics is concerned, one want is as good (or as bad) as another. Wants are seen as randomly strung out, side by side, on a one-dimensional plane, like a series of pick-up sticks, and it is of no consequence to the science which wants are chosen. So if a person eventually stops eating apples and goes on to something else, it is not because a need has been fulfilled but because his or her wants have changed. The person is seen moving from want to want with the randomness of the wind, and it might just as well be that variety is behind it all.

Having said this, we now need to ask ourselves why economics has avoided talking about needs. The answer lies in recognizing what happens as soon as you begin talking about needs—a hierarchy very naturally emerges. And a hierarchy means an ordering according to relative importance. So talking about needs naturally leads to a scale of relative values. Such a scale of values or needs does not necessarily depend upon using the specific categories that Maslow has settled upon, or even using categories that are at the same level of generality as Maslow's. Talking about needs leads to an ordering of those needs according to relative importance, and that is the critical point.

For example, here is part of a list proposed by the late nineteenth-century economist, Karl Menger: water, food, clothing, shelter, coach (transportation), tobacco.[13] The list is given in the order of importance that Menger himself proposed for these needs—water being the most important, and tobacco the least. You may find yourself agreeing or disagreeing with the exact ordering of needs as Menger proposes them, but you can easily accept that such an ordering is basically on the right track.

Economists were not comfortable with what Menger was trying to do with his list of needs, and soon rejected the whole attempt. Two arguments, or two levels of an argument, were offered for doing so. The first was that the listing of needs in order of importance is a value premise, and such premises should not be a part of science. Ethics, perhaps yes, but science, no. For justification, conventional economics could point to what we just said about Menger's hierarchy: People may disagree as to what the exact ordering would be. Isn't it the case that each person has his or her own ordering of needs? After all, one person's meat is another person's poison. How can we say anything about people in general, which is what economics tries to do?

This argument is not very convincing. Once the economist accepts that there is an ordering of importance of needs, the question of differences in needs between people is relatively unessential, and we feel that the economist *must* accept that there is an ordering of needs among people. To do otherwise is to, once again, fly in the face of common sense. Let us keep with Menger's list as an example. His first item of importance is water and the last is tobacco. Between the two it is clear that water is the more important of the two. No doubt about it. Without water you couldn't live, and even with the strongest tobacco habit in the world you could certainly stay alive without it. So when it comes to the issue of the importance of needs we have a very clear-cut determinant, and that is *life*. The more necessary for life, or life supporting, a particular good, service, or experience is, the more important it is. It is as simple as that. An economics that has no theoretical way of making a distinction between the importance of supplying water and the importance of supplying tobacco hardly seems relevant to a living organism, let alone a human development.

Now, of course, not every comparison between two commodities will yield as easy a judgement as to which is the more life supporting, and the more complex and abstract the commodity the more difficult the judgement becomes, and at some point the issue will boil down to merely a question of individual taste. But from the perspective of the broad outline of human needs the basics would appear to be fairly unarguable. Certainly, just because some comparisons are difficult, it does not mean that all need comparisons should be abandoned. Maslow never tired of emphasizing that "the organism itself dictates hierarchies of values, which the scientific observer reports rather than creates." He felt it was necessary to emphasize this, "because so many still consider that values can never be more than the arbitrary imposition upon data of the writer's own tastes, prejudices, intuitions, or other corporeal or unprovable assumptions,"[14] and he devoted much of his work to show that the higher needs are evolutionary and ontogenetically based. We return to this issue in Chapter 9.

Keep in mind that what Maslow has come up with in his study of values, in terms of an ordering, is not very esoteric. He talks about five classes of needs that he lists under the headings *physiological, safety, belongingness, esteem,* and *self-actualization.* One could argue with some of the particular classifications, say, for example, that the separation of belongingness and esteem into two separate categories is unnecessary. Perhaps it would be better to see them both as making up a more general category of social needs. But this kind of change does not refute the overall process that Maslow has described. Does someone want to deny that social needs are intrinsic to life, for example? Or that the body must be kept alive first, before social needs can be turned to? Maslow's hierarchy is eminently sensible, which goes hand-in-hand with its being scientific. To not recognize some kind of basic human grants and evolution as scientific is akin to the medieval schoolmen refusing to look through Galileo's telescope.

The second argument, while not entirely unconnected from the first, takes place in a more passionate arena than the more purely philosophical discussion of what constitutes science. This is the arena of politics, and here is where the going gets touchy. That economics involves issues with political import is of no surprise, and we need to recall that the initial name of the science was *political* economy.

The particular issue involved here is that of inequality of income and wealth between individuals, and the whole area of poverty. For it turns out that if one accepts that there is a hierarchy of needs, with some needs being crucial and necessary for the maintenance of a decent life, or of life itself, then a case can be made for policies that lead to a more equal distribution of wealth, enough at least so that everyone's most basic needs can be met. As we will later show, a humanistic economics leads to this conclusion. The scientific stance that the humanist takes leads him or her to believe that it is against the best interests of social development for the rich to get richer while the poor remain poor. Conventional economics, while perhaps having some human sympathies with this position, has felt that it could not be reached on scientific grounds, and that the science could draw no conclusions as to the value of narrowing the income gap between rich and poor. This whole argument has an interesting and important history which we will examine more closely in Chapter 4. For now it is only necessary to point out that when we start talking about needs rather than wants the science of economics begins to move in a new direction.

We had mentioned before that conventional economics becomes un-ravelled when we pull out the key pieces. Nowhere is this more dramatically revealed than in the concept of utility itself.*

As we have explained, utility is the idea that there is a certain *amount* of satisfaction obtained from each act of consumption, and that this satisfaction functions like a quantity, allowing us to say something like consuming item x is twice as satisfying as consuming item y, or only that consuming item x is *more* satisfying than item y, regardless of how much the difference is.

When we look at economics from the perspective of human needs, we discover the basic fallacy of utilitarian thinking. Put most directly it is that need satisfaction is a qualitative phenomenon, not a quantitative one. What this means, and this is a critical point to be grasped, is that the satisfaction of a need in one category is not comparable with the satisfaction of a need in another category. To phrase the matter in slightly more technical terms, there is no com-mensurability or additivity between needs in different categories. This is a fundamental implication of a concept of a hierarchy of needs. For example, the satisfaction of being well-fed is not comparable in terms of more or less satisfaction to the satisfaction of good social compan-ionship. They are two different kettles of fish, if you'll pardon the metaphor. Even within the same category of need, such as the physiological, this can often be true. There is no real way to compare the utility gotten from a glass of water and a piece of bread. When you are thirsty only the water will do; when you are hungry, only the bread.

This is a fundamental critique of the idea of utility, or any prefer-ence notion, which tries to apply a common scale of satisfaction across different needs. Any need-based economics makes the point that satis-faction is related to an active or prepotent need, and thus any scaling of common satisfaction across needs is, in principle, false. The utility of food is of a completely different order than the utility of social relation-ships. The satisfaction of a particular *kind* of need is its own unique experience related to that need, and not comparable to the satisfaction of another *kind* of need. The word *kind* is used here to point out the qualitative nature of need satisfaction. We know that conventional economics, as well as modern life, appears to turn everything into numbers, what Guenon has called "the reign of quantity,"[15] and we know that there is something wrong with this. Here, through the

---

*Some mainstream economists would claim that utility has already been aban-doned in economics, but a glance at any textbook would show this hardly is the case. In any event, our argument applies to any utility-related concept. This matter, as well as the so-called 'revealed preference' approach, will be further discussed in Chapter 3.

---

analysis of humanistic economics, we are able to put our finger on one of the conceptual roots of this disturbing development. The various needs cannot be added up; they don't have the same measuring stick. Conventional utility theory treated human needs as if they could be, and utility was the measuring stick.

Implications for Opportunity Cost

Human growth consists of the growth or maturation of people's needs through a series of stages. At any point in a person's development (or a society's, for that matter), he or she is most involved in, and draws deepest satisfaction from, the goods, services, and experiences of a particular stage. The satisfaction of needs relating to other stages are always "second best," since the needs of those stages are either completely absent or of secondary importance. In terms of the fulfillment of a need there can be no satisfactory substitutes not related to that need. Here, once again, is how Maslow puts it: "the basic human needs resist all blandishments, substitutions, bribes and alternatives; nothing will do for them but their proper and intrinsic gratifications . . . for the love hungry, there is only one genuine, long-run satisfier, i.e., honest and satisfying affection. For the sex-starved, food-starved, or water-starved person, only sex, food or water will ultimately serve."[16]

An implication of the above is that in the fulfillment of a prepotent need there is no such clear-cut and easily calculable thing as opportunity cost. When people are able to satisfy prepotent needs they are not losing out on anything. According to the concept of utility, one measure of satisfaction is gained by giving up another—opportunity cost. Humanistic economics says that this need not happen. When a prepotent need is satisfied the satisfaction of a higher need is not given up because those needs are not yet active; the satisfaction of a lower need is not given up because those needs, by definition, are less prepotent.

It is true that life presents us with decisions all the time. But these decisions are between needs (or values), not between relative satisfactions. It is only when a person, through a given act, cannot meet his or her most prepotent need that such an act has an opportunity cost. The opportunity forfeited is always an opportunity to grow or to satisfy a higher need. When people are able to satisfy their highest active needs, nothing is given up.

Wants, as the economist understands the term, can now be technically defined as the various preferences within a *common* category or level of need. It is within this framework that opportunity cost makes sense. Should I get a Chevrolet or a Toyota? That is a question of opportunity cost. Should I go to the State University or a private college? That is a question of opportunity cost. Conventional economics reduces all choices to one common plane. Should I get a Chevrolet, get a Toyota, go to the State University, or go to a private college? All these choices have now been transformed into wants because they are now all related to fulfilling the same goal, the increase of utility. A car may do it just as well as a college education. The concept that different sets of these items relate to different orders of need has been obliterated. The concept of utility, in this way, allows all choices to be flattened down to a single plane of wants.

When Variety is the Spice of Life

What happens when an individual, for one reason or another, is not able to satisfy his or her prepotent need? Then the gateway to growth, which lies in the fulfillment of that need, is blocked. When this happens behavior is then trapped in a one-dimensional plane, the plane of the lower need. A person can no longer move up, in a developmental sense, only outward, and fixation results. Instead of growing, one can only *increase*. All development now turns to overweight, perhaps literally as well as figuratively. It is at this point that "variety is the spice of life" becomes a relevant operating procedure. You eat an apple not because you need it, but because there is nothing better to do. But apples do not sustain your interest, so you quickly move on to something else; you "prefer to have one or a few of a lot of goods and services rather than a great many of only a few." The variety-spice conception is, in fact, a perfect expression for an economics that has no philosophy of human growth, an economics of wants, not needs. This is economics of a flat existence. Best to "spice it up," give it some taste.

WHAT IS HUMANISTIC ECONOMICS: TOWARDS A DEFINITION

We began the previous paragraph by asking the question, what happens when an individual, for one reason or another, is not able to satisfy his prepotent need? That little phrase "for one reason or another" is of the essence for humanistic economics. This kind of economics takes as most important the study of those reasons, the conditions and circumstances that promote or impede human and social growth. We can bring this meaning more clearly into focus through an example that illustrates the difference between the two kinds of economics, mainstream and humanistic.

A certain amount of what can be called economic behavior may be observed in a prison camp. If the prison camp is rather loosely structured, then a fairly wide range of such behavior may be found. Some individuals will trade their cigarettes for another person's food. Depending on supply, a certain number of cigarettes will be worth a certain amount of bread or vegetables, and so forth. Work time and tasks that needed to be performed in the camp may also be exchanged for commodities. In the context of this prison camp a miniature economic society could be said to exist. Economists could, and have, studied such societies as economies. They could set up supply and demand curves that describe the interchange of goods and services, and study how the laws of economics function here like everywhere else, or in what particular ways they are different, how changes in certain variables affect changes in opportunity costs, etc.

But the conventional economic approach is not equipped with the concepts and perspective to recognize that *this is a prison camp*. That most dominating fact, overhanging all exchanges and opportunity costs, falls completely outside the scope of its analysis. Thus, it cannot deal with the most pressing growth need of this population, which is to get out of prison. All the cigarettes, food, beer, and even radios they can consume will not meet the most salient needs of this particular population. This can only be recognized and analyzed by an economics that is able to deal with the particular social and institutional frameworks that determine the satisfaction or frustration of human needs. In this case the obvious institutional framework prohibiting growth is that of a prison camp, and this is precisely what the humanistic economist would want to observe.

Having given this example, we are now ready to advance a more formal definition of humanistic economics. *Humanistic economics is a scientific framework for the theoretical understanding, as well as design of appropriate institutional arrangements pertaining to, the processes of production, distribution, and consumption that will enable optimal satisfaction of the hierarchy of human needs.*

This definition catches the essential element of humanistic economics: the relationship between human need satisfaction and economic activity. Humanistic economics is directed by its underlying value premise of human *life* and its quality. Instead of the conventional emphasis on wealth and wants it focuses on development and needs. In short, humanistic economics is preoccupied with vital values, rather than monetary wealth.

In the following chapter we attempt to demonstrate the relative importance accorded to vital values in the historical evolution of both utilitarian and humanistic economics.

Maslow's work on human needs appears ideally suited for a systematic, although preliminary, conceptualization of the quality dimension in life. We recognize that his concept of self-actualization constitutes just one of many views of the good life and how to attain it; yet all of the humanistic approaches, either explicitly or implicitly, are based on some kind of need hierarchy of their own. They all recognize a "higher" and a "lower" quality of life.

The choice of Maslow's hierarchy permits us to examine more rigorously some of the important principles of modern economics from a humanistic perspective. To do this it will prove helpful to familiarize ourselves with the historical roots of modern economic thought. For a better understanding of the present, it is always useful to look to history.

References

1. Coates, William H., White, Hayden V., and Schapiro, J. Salwyn. *The Emergence of Liberal Humanism*. New York: McGraw Hill, 1966, p. 40.

2. Miller, George A. *Psychology: The Science of Mental Life*. New York: Harper and Row, 1962, pp. 230–31.

3. Matson, Floyd W. *The Broken Image*. New York: George Braziller, 1964, p. 29.

4. Matson, Floyd W. *The Broken Image*. New York: George Braziller, 1964, pp. 29–30.

5. Whitehead, Alfred North. *Science and the Modern World*. New York: Macmillan (Mentor Books), 1925, p. 23.

6. Koestler, Arthur. *The Roots of Coincidence*. New York: Random House, 1972, p. 58.

7. Heisenberg, Werner. *Physics and Philosophy*. London: Allen and Unwin, 1963, p. 75.

8. Maslow, Abraham. *Motivation and Personality*. New York: Harper and Row, 1970.

9. Maslow, Abraham. *Motivation and Personality*. New York: Harper and Row, 1970, Chapter 11.

10. Gambs, John. *Beyond Supply and Demand*. New York: Columbia University Press, 1946, pp. 27–28.

11. Sichel, Werner, and Eckstein, Peter. *Basic Economic Concepts*. Chicago: Rand McNally, 1974, pp. 128–29.

12. Heyne, Hall. *The Economic Way of Thinking*. 2nd ed. Chicago: SRA Inc., 1976.

13. Menger, Karl. *Principles of Economics*. Glencoe, Illinois: The Free Press, 1950.

14. Maslow, Abraham. *Motivation and Personality*. New York: Harper and Row, 1970, p. 97.

15. Guenon, Rene. *The Reign of Quantity and the Signs of the Times*. Baltimore: Penguin Books, 1972.

16. Maslow, Abraham. *Motivation and Personality*. New York: Harper and Row, 1970, p. 62.

Chapter Two

THE HISTORY OF ECONOMICS FROM A HUMANISTIC PERSPECTIVE

INTRODUCTION

The beginning student of economics is rarely made aware of how the science has developed over time. Instead, most textbooks start with a short description of what economics is today, leaving the reader to assume that this is what economics always was, is, and will be. Within this assumption, one textbook states that "the central concern of economics is expressed in the concept of scarcity. It recognizes that human wants are virtually infinite, but that resources—labor, land and natural resources, and machines—are limited. This is the essence of 'the economic problem.' "[1]

But such a conception has not always been the core of the science. Before the late 1800s economics had a rather different definition, and had already changed its face many times. For this reason we must assume that economics is nothing other than what economists and the times deem it to be: there is nothing "scientific" about the modern definition and, like its various predecessors, it is likely to change again.

The entire history of the science can be seen as a painful struggle to gain its identity, and today this struggle is far from settled, as the many competing schools of thought readily confirm. There is neoclassical, or mainstream, economics, neo-Marxian economics, Cambridge economics, institutional economics and Austrian economics, to list the more important ones in order of their academic preponderance in the United States and Canada. All have their ideas of the relative importance of the basic questions to be asked, and all operate with alternative basic assumptions about the economic process and what constitutes human nature. All analyze problems somewhat differently and come up with different answers to certain problems.

What about humanistic economics? It, too, has some adherents today, but it was once much stronger. In fact, if humanistic economics is defined as human needs oriented, its history extends back to the Greek philosophers, notably Plato as he expressed himself in *The Republic*. And of course the name of the science came from the Greek word for economy, *oekonomia*, which means "the rule of the household"; in more general terms, management of the estate. But management was interpreted in the broadest possible terms, referring to the proper care of the body and mind, as well as objects. Similarly, the Greeks also wrote about *political* economy, referring to the proper management of the city (state). The goal of the science was not to accumulate wealth or to possess the strongest army, but simply to make possible the good life and a happy citizenry. This is what political economy has generally meant, even for Adam Smith, the father of economics.

Plato wrote his *Republic* to describe an ideal state. The entire book is concerned with human needs and their satisfaction. "The first and chief of our needs is the provision of food for existence and life. The second is housing and the third is raiment and that sort of thing."[2] To most readers, statements like this may sound trivial, but the modern economist has been talking a very different language, as this chapter will progressively show.

In the Middle Ages, emphasis shifted to describing (or *prescribing*) a just society in the service of spiritual values. Prices had to only reflect the human labor involved in production, wages had to enable subsistence, and interest in loans was deemed unnecessary, unjust, and even sinful.

One of the most interesting economics books written at that time was Thomas More's *Utopia*, published in 1516.* In the first half of the book we find a brilliant critique of the social and economic order in Tudor England, particularly as it was affected by the birth pangs of the enclosure movement, which was the initial intrusion of the commercial profit motive into the static feudal society and caused a sudden onslaught of human misery, crime, and a new kind of inequality and poverty.

The second part proposed an alternative model of an economic system, one based on human needs and aiming at enabling every member of society to attain the highest state of happiness, in Maslowian terms: self-actualization.

A hundred years after *Utopia*, political economy was for the first time subordinated to serving more worldly ends. It was to be an

---

*Space precludes a survey of *Utopia*, but any student interested in humanistic economics will not regret having read this time-honored book. Since the original was written in Latin, each English translation reads differently. We recommend the Paul Turner version, of the Penguin Classics series.

instrument to help the King to more *power*, which was at that time equated with the ability to command a lavishly equipped standing army. That task required an impressive treasury, so the economists of the Court got busy concerning themselves with the nature and causes of the wealth of nations, meaning hard cash or gold bullion at the disposal of the King. It is with these *mercantilist* economists that people and their needs had for the first time to take a back seat and preference was given to the hunger for power, a disease that characterized the monarchies in those days.

ADAM SMITH (1723–90)

It was exactly in protest to this mercantilist thought that the science took a new turn. Its undisputed exponent and leader was the Englishman, Adam Smith. With him political economy now meant the "science of a statesman or legislator" to pursue the objects of "enriching both the people and the sovereign." Adam Smith reverted halfway to the earlier humanistic tradition: political economy continued to remain narrowly concerned with material values, but he recognized that what counted was not the King and his treasury, but the material interests of the people at large. As such he represents the true father of the discipline as it is being taught today in most universities.

Adam Smith's *An Inquiry into the Wealth of Nations* was published in England in 1776, the year that revolution was brewing in the colonies. In the book, Smith advocated that a government could best advance the wealth of the nation by letting the "natural" play of economic self-interest proceed without restraint and interference by the government, by which he meant the agencies of the King. This was the policy that the French had referred to as *laissez-faire*, meaning "let it happen."

Now, interestingly, Smith's doctrine has been taken since his time to apply to the economic action of any kind of government, overlooking the fact that, for Smith, government meant monarchy; democratic and popular representative government was only on the threshold of existence. With his concept of laissez-faire, Smith referred to the desirability of limiting the parasitic effect of the King and his feudal retinue on the productive efforts of the nation at large. The great enemy for Smith was not regulation per se, since regulation in the interests of the people was mostly unheard of, but the monopolistic influence of a government composed of the aristocratic and wealthy.

The question that supporters of the Crown posed to Smith's idea was this: If the monarchy was not to serve as the economic regulator of society, to preserve order and prevent chaos, what was? Smith's answer was a rather mystical one, his famous *invisible hand*. Here, in his first great book, *The Theory of Moral Sentiments*, he explains this concept:

☐ The produce of the soil maintains at all times nearly that number of inhabitants which it is capable of maintaining. The rich only select from the heap what is more precious and agreeable. They consume little more than the poor; and in spite of their natural selfishness and rapacity, though they mean only their own conveniency, though the sole end which they propose from the labours of all the thousands whom they employ be the gratification of their own vain and insatiable desires, they divide with the poor the produce of all their improvements. They are led by *an invisible hand* to make nearly the same distribution of the necessaries of life which would have been made had the earth been divided into equal portions among all its inhabitants; and thus, without intending it, without knowing it, advance the interest of the society, and afford means to the multiplication of the species. When Providence divided the earth among a few lordly masters, it neither forgot nor abandoned those who seemed to have been left out in the partition.[3]

How interesting! The effect of the invisible hand is "to make nearly the same distribution of the necessaries of life which would have been made had the earth been divided into equal proportions among all its inhabitants." *That* is how we are to know it is operating, when there has been a nearly equal division of the necessities of life. This is quite different from the way the concept is ordinarily taken. The invisible hand is generally seen to refer to the workings of natural law, just as much as the action of gravitation is a natural law, and has no suggestion of the guidance of a universal moral order. Let the forces of self-interest and competition reign, it is said, and the invisible hand will be seen to operate for the good of all. Interfere with competition and you upset the operation of the invisible hand. Yet, if the invisible hand is the hand of "Providence" (Smith's capitalization), its effects are seen in an equitable and just distribution of goods.

As Smith well recognized, the existence of "moral sentiments" in a society is what allows for the operation of the invisible hand of Providence:

☐ All the members of human society stand in need of each other's assistance, and are likewise exposed to mutual injuries. Where the necessary assistance is reciprocally afforded from love, from gratitude, from friendship, and esteem, the society flourishes and is happy. All the different members of it are bound together by the agreeable bands of love and affection, and are, as it were, drawn to one common centre of mutual good offices.

Society, however, cannot subsist among those who are at all times ready to hurt and injure one another. The moment that injury begins, the moment that mutual resentment and animosity takes place, all the bands of it are broken asunder, and the different members of which it consisted, are, as it were, dissipated and scattered abroad by the violence and opposition of their discordant affections.[4]

How ignored is this part of Smith in the mainstream textbook. Some economists would claim that Smith abandoned many of his ideas in the earlier *Theory of Moral Sentiments* when he wrote *The Wealth of Nations*. But this is not borne out by its history. The book went through six editions in Smith's lifetime, the last one in the final year of Smith's life. Nor is there any evidence that Smith ever repudiated the book. Adam Smith's mission, and a difficult one it was, was to try to discern the operation of moral principles in an increasingly amoral world. It seems to us that Smith would be appalled at a later economics which would assume that morality was completely beside the point, and state this belief in Smith's own name!

Anybody who reads *The Wealth of Nations* will be impressed by the underlying themes of optimism and harmony that run through all its chapters. An economic system based on private property and free exchange and markets was seen as the only "natural" way of economic organization. And if it were natural, how could it be anything else than good and harmonious? More to the point, if we leave things to Mother Nature, won't they improve by themselves? Self-interest—only held in check by competition—will lead to accumulation, an increasingly productive labor force, and more and more material wealth for workers, employers and landowners alike. All the economy needs is a good dose of trust in its natural soundness and some time to reward the faithful.

However, despite Smith's hopeful theorizing, the unvarnished truth was that England by the first half of the nineteenth century was a gloomy place for the bulk of its inhabitants. The working day was sixteen hours, a far cry from Thomas More's ideal of six. Armies of pauper children, ages ten years and older, spent their lives in the factory and slept in supervised dormitories at night. Increasingly, man became only another input into the fast-developing industrial machine, and goods was the output of the process. As Robert Heilbroner so pointedly puts it, there was "a social climate in which practices of the most callous inhumanity were accepted as the natural order of events and even more important, as nobody's business."[5] The outlook for the future was not particularly reassuring.

The well-known economists of the period, Jean Baptiste Say, David Ricardo and Thomas Robert Malthus, publishing their respective texts in the first two decades of the nineteenth century, attempted to elaborate and further develop the discipline that Adam Smith had initiated. This was the age of what is now called classical economics. But in their hands a subtle change was introduced into Adam Smith's original idea of political economy. Political economy was increasingly, and more explicitly, seen as a natural science attempting to uncover the natural laws. Ricardo and Malthus, especially, were preoccupied with the detection of the (presumably immutable) laws of the distribution of wealth. They believed that, with the exception of landlords, everybody in society was drifting more and more towards mere subsistence. Little could be done about this prospect; it was natural and inevitable.

The Count Sismondi was the first to throw his weight against the stream of conventional economic thought. Ironically, he had gained a reputation as an ardent supporter of Adam Smith and his *Wealth of Nations*, the ideas of which he promulgated on the Continent by his first book, *La Richesse Commerciale*, in 1803. Why the sudden reversal? During the ensuing decade Sismondi had found that Smith's optimistic outlook could not be reconciled with the deteriorating and harsh realities of the day. After repeated visits to England he wrote:

> ☐ In this astonishing country (Great Britain), which seems to be submitted to a great experiment for the instruction of the rest of the world, I have seen production increasing whilst enjoyments were diminishing. The mass of the nation here, no less than philosophers, seems to forget that the increase of wealth is not the end in political economy, but its instrument in procuring the happiness of all. I sought for this happiness in *every* class, and I could nowhere find it.[6]

Sismondi, as an economist, could not ignore the suffering which the increasingly successful quest for industrial wealth brought to the majority of the people. Out of this disenchantment and disillusionment with conventional political economy, an alternative vision was born. In 1819 he published his *New Principles of Political Economy*, in which he urged economists to follow him "in the name of those calamities which . . . at the present day, afflict so large numbers of our brethren, and which *the old principles of this science teach us neither to understand nor to prevent.*"[7]

Sismondi was the first well-known economist to turn his back on the doctrine of laissez-faire. The invisible hand, so dearly praised by the followers of Adam Smith, had produced a new and miserable clan: the industrial workers, who were not helped by wealth. Quite the contrary. Similarly, the invisible hand seemed to move in an erratic manner, producing periodic crises of overproduction and high unemployment. Sismondi was one of the very first to discover the business cycle. He attempted to show its cause in growing inequality which was resulting in a mounting deficiency of purchasing power of the increasingly large working class.[*]

Sismondi's Vision

The object of economics should be "Man," not wealth, thought Sismondi. Wealth is only relevant to the extent that it enables "participation of all citizens in the pleasures which it represents."

Sismondi took human needs and their satisfaction as the first (and

---

[*]"By the concentration of fortunes in the hands of a small number of owners, the internal market is all the time shrinking, and industry is more and more reduced to looking for outlets in foreign markets."[8]

only) goal of economic activity. Having little interest in abstract theorizing, Sismondi saw it to be the task of the economist to make possible an optimum quality of life for everybody.

The economic vision of Sismondi can quite easily be explained by reference to our Maslowian framework of hierarchy of needs. It implied, first and foremost, satisfaction of physiological needs. "The first attention of society must be given to the securing of its material interests, of its subsistence; and we wish to endeavor to discover what path must be followed in order that the material wealth which labor creates may procure and maintain the greatest well-being for all. . . ." And immediately he added this:

> □ . . . more than any of our forerunners, we consider political economy in its relation with the soul, and with the intellect. But subsistence is necessary to life, and with life, to all the moral developments, all the intellectual developments, of which the human race is susceptible. Society, as well as individuals, must consider bodily wealth before anything else, must provide in the first place for its wants and its developments; for without the vigour which this health supplies, without the leisure, which only begins when these wants are satisfied, the health of the mind is impossible.[9]

As the primary mechanism for improving the lot of the working class he advocated legislation to shorten the working days, to abolish child labor and to redistribute wealth by progressive taxation. The visible hand of government could be used to create security by requiring employers to provide for their workers in case of layoffs, illness, and old age. Such a scheme would give entrepreneurs an incentive not to seek higher profits and wealth at the expense of diminishing human welfare. Finally, he cautioned against the prevailing faith and encouragement of industrialization; instead he believed in policies that would enable peasant proprietorships and small rural business to survive.

All this turned out to be too far removed a vision to come true; industrialization and urbanization continued their rapid pace in France as elsewhere. Sismondi was painfully aware of that before he died in 1842. One of his last entries in his diary conveys the immense suffering that this growing realization evoked:

> □ I cry, take care, you are bruising, you are crushing miserable persons who do not even see from whence comes the evil which they experience, but who remain languishing and mutilated on the road which you have passed over. I cry out, and no one hears me: I cry out and the car of the Juggernaut continues to roll on, making new victims.[10]

JOHN STUART MILL (1806–73)

Among the classical economists following the tradition of Adam Smith, Jean Baptiste Say and David Ricardo, humanism asserted itself most powerfully in the writings of John Stuart Mill. His book *The Principles of Political Economy* (1848) remained a leading text throughout the second half of the nineteenth century, and it continued to be assigned at the prestigious Oxford University as late as 1919.

Mill was a classical economist and shared some of the traditional attitudes of the economists who immediately preceded him, such as Ricardo, but he broke with them in a significant way. He made a distinction between what he called the *laws of production* and the *laws of distribution*. The laws of production of goods, he held, "partake of the character of physical truths. There is nothing optional or arbitrary about them." In this belief he shared the deterministic and supposedly scientific attitude of Ricardo, Malthus and Say. As for the distribution of wealth, this depends on the "laws and customs of society." They are solely within the realm of "human institution." So, given his definition, political economy is now the study—among other things—of appropriate institutions to promote human development.

In a famous statement Mill declared that he was "not charmed with the ideal of life held out by those who think that the normal state of human beings is that of struggling to get on; that the trampling, crushing, elbowing, and treading on each other's heels, which form the existing type of social life, are the most desirable lot of human kind, or anything but the disagreeable symptoms of one of the phases of industrial progress."

Instead he foresaw a society "in which, while no one is poor, no one desires to be richer, nor has any reason to fear being thrust back, by the efforts of others to push them forward."[11] This is the classic humanist sentiment that we have encountered all the way back to Plato. Mill came to believe that one of the "prime necessities of human well-being" is the "internal culture of the individual, the cultivation not only of his reason and conscience but of his aesthetic nature." This would be achieved, in the main, by the development of large-scale education. As one observer notes, "For Mill the cultivation of altruism and the proper direction of egoism is a function of education, both individual and collective."[12]

Here again we see an almost identical statement to Maslow's in regard to higher values and the redirection of egoism towards altruism. Like all humanists, Mill explicitly recognized that altruistic or non-selfish motives were a necessary and real part of human nature.

Mill and Utilitarianism

In the history of ideas Mill is seen as one of the developers of the utilitarian philosophy, along with his teacher, Jeremy Bentham. But Mill was to become critical of the strongly hedonistic overtones that were present in Bentham's conception of utility, and the predominant focus that it gave to materialistic pursuits. For Mill, Bentham's philosophy "does not pretend to aid individuals in the formation of their own character"; and it "overlook(ed) the existence of about half of the whole number of mental feelings which human beings are capable of, including all those of which the direct objectives are states of their own mind." And furthermore, Bentham never recognized man "as a being capable of pursuing spiritual perception as an end; of desiring, for its own sake, the conformity of his own character to his standard of excellence, without hope of good or fear of evil from other sources than his own inward consciousness."[13] So the humanistic criticism of the utilitarian conception that we advanced in the first chapter is foreshadowed in Mill's uneasiness with Bentham's use of the idea.

After Mill, the age of the classical economists is almost at its end. At this point we discern economics branching off in three directions. One is that taken by Karl Marx, another we see as humanistic economics proper, and the third is neoclassical economics, which forms the basis of today's mainstream economics. As we look at each of these we will be better able to see the characteristics that make for humanism in economics. The chapter concludes with Thorstein Veblen's humanistic critique of the image of man fashioned by neoclassical economics, "Rational Economic Man."

KARL MARX (1818–83)

1848 was a big year in world history and in economics. Tumultuous political changes were happening in Europe. Mill published the first edition of his *Principles of Economics,* and a relatively small, pamphlet-sized document was put out by two social and economic theorists named Friedrich Engels and Karl Marx. They called it *The Communist Manifesto.*

Today, over 125 years later, it is probably still not possible to discuss Marx's place in economics with dispassion and objectivity (if such a thing is ever possible). So we don't claim these virtues for the following presentation. But we will claim that we are approaching Marx, not from the standpoint of capitalism or socialism, but from the standpoint of humanism, an economic point of view that lies outside the usual arena of these two isms. When we do this, we find that a curious mixture of both humanism and non-humanism exists in Marx's thought, and herein lie some of the reasons for the consternation that Marx produces.

These two sides of Marx seem to be divided by the year 1845, shortly before he wrote the *Manifesto,* and before his most definitive work, *Das Kapital.* Marx's work before that year seems to clearly express a philosophical humanism or humanistic socialism, while the work following that year forms the body of thought that he calls *scientific socialism.* It is interesting to learn that the most important of Marx's pre-1845 writings, called *The Economic and Philosophic Manuscripts,* written in 1844, was never published during his lifetime, but was first published in the late 1920s. When a friend in 1893 urged Engels to have it published he reportedly replied, "Marx had also written poetry in his student years, but it could hardly interest anybody."[14] Theoreticians in the Soviet Union used to call Marx's earlier work his "pre-Marxist" writings.

What happened in 1845 to cause such a drastic change? The major event seemed to be that Marx started working closely with Engels at that time, whereas previously they had only a passing contact. Before going on to examine just what this change was between the humanistic and the "scientific" Marx, we should mention that not all scholars agree with this interpretation. Tucker, for example, in a chapter entitled, "Two Marxisms or One?" concludes that there is only one.[15] Tucker bases his belief on Marx and Engels' own statements that there is only one continuous and consistent Marx. But we feel that the difference in Marx's writings speaks for itself, regardless of what he and Engels profess to the contrary. Nevertheless, Tucker's work is first-rate and we respect his difference of opinion.

The Early Marx

Marx majored in philosophy and was strongly influenced by the humanist thought of Hegel, and then Feuerbach. The very roots of Marx's thought are found in Hegel's masterpiece *The Phenomenology of Mind* (1803), where Hegel interprets history as a process of progressive consciousness or self-realization of the Spirit, or God. In the hands of his interpreter, Feuerbach, Hegel was "turned upside down," as it is put. Instead of the Spirit's self-realization, going beyond the fetters of the material world, it was Man's self-realization in a material world. In essence, Feuerbach despiritualized or materialized Hegel's spiritual humanism.

It was to be this domain of *material dialectics* that Karl Marx chose as his framework of history. He too accepted the notion of interpreting history as progress towards ultimate self-realization, but he pointed his finger at the economic institutions of a particular epoch, at how they formed social classes, and at the relationship between those classes.

It was the time of the rapidly expanding factory system. Its primary input was human labor, its output commodities to be sold in the marketplace. The young philosopher sympathized with the new working class and its mounting deprivation of human dignity and freedom. The wage laborer, by having to sell his labor power on the newly created "labor market" to the factory owner, not only loses control of his labor but at the same time also has to sell part of himself. During the production process he becomes "alienated" (or estranged) from his product, as well as from his fellow workers and himself. As Marx puts it, "labor is external to the worker, i.e., it does not belong to his essential being; in his work, therefore, he does not affirm himself but denies himself."[16]

It is here that the concept of alienation first enters economics. The whole history of capitalism becomes a mere step towards a new system that would enable more self-realization and less alienation of the individual. As we will see in Chapter 8, the concept of alienation or human estrangement is of paramount importance in contemporary humanist thought of all persuasions, particularly as it applies to the quality of work.

No one doubted that the young Marx was a social philosopher with a primarily humanistic bent. Most of the quotations in support of the humanist Marx—among others by such well-known humanist socialists as Erich Fromm—are taken from his earliest writings, in particular his *Economic and Philosophic Manuscripts*. There the reader will encounter the outlines of an economy of human needs and their thwarting by the capitalist institutions of competitive markets, money, and private ownership of the "means for production" or factories. Capitalism failed and was therefore historically doomed because it blocked human self-realization. Political economy, by its very orientation towards pecuniary wealth, was equally off-base and doomed. Nothing could be more suggestive of the young Marx's positive humanism as the following quote from the *Manuscripts:*

> ☐ It will be seen how in place of the *wealth* and *poverty* of political economy come the *rich human being* and rich *human* need. The *rich human being* is simultaneously the human being *in need of* a totality of human life-activities—the man in whom his own realization exists as an inner necessity, as *need*.[17]

The Later Marx

The last forty years of Marx's work culminated with publication of his major book *Das Kapital* ("This Is Capitalism") where he discusses in minute detail his discovery of the "scientific" laws of motion which are propelling the capitalist system to its eventual collapse. The "innate tendencies" or laws of capitalism were anchored in the mutual interaction of technological change and the parallel changes in the division of labor and the employer-employee relationship.

The entire process pivots on the *law of the falling rate of profit*, which is brought about by the competitive pressure on all entrepreneurs to replace labor by machines in order to keep costs down. Yet in Marx all profits are simply the result of exploiting labor and, since machines cannot be exploited, replacing men with machines automatically brings about successively smaller profit margins for the capitalist class. As a result, Marx predicts, there will be economic crises recurring periodically and with increasing vigor until they trigger the final revolution and expropriation of the expropriators.

Other "laws" are the tendency of *increasing immiseration* of the working class and of *increasing concentration* in ownership of the means of production. It goes without saying that scholars disagree sharply on whether these laws have actually been materialized in capitalist development, this in spite of a full hundred years having elapsed since their postulation. Marxists, on the whole, believe that they have,* while non-Marxists feel that they have not. The reader should decide for himself or herself.

From the perspective of this chapter, the extent to which Marx's predictions about capitalism are correct is not the crucial issue. The crucial issue is, in what way does the Marx of *The Communist Manifesto* and *Das Kapital*, in his preoccupation with "the material laws of capitalist production" working with "iron necessity towards inevitable results," lose his humanism?

While there are several aspects to the answer, we believe it hinges on the fact that you can't have self-realization if you have no self, and in his concept of class Marx abandons the self. So, for example, we read in the *Manifesto* that "Man who belongs to no class has no reality and subsists only in the misty realm of philosophical fantasy."[19] Workers are "real" if they are seen as members of the working class, and entrepreneurs and landlords are only "real" as capitalists. The cornerstone of the 1844 *Manuscripts*, the concept of individual alienation or self-realization, hardly appears in the lengthy volumes of *Das Kapital*. Neither do we find much of moral criticism there. In that work, Marx made every effort not to prescribe, but to restrict his scientific economics to the domain of describing. Similarly, the order of the post-capitalist economy is left to the reader's imagination. The elaboration of such a dream-come-true was of little concern to the scientist.

Both Marx and Engels prided themselves on having developed this new scientific socialism, ready to replace the traditional moral kind with this appeal to the intellect rather than the heart. No doubt it was this new scientific twist that sold Marxism to so many intellectuals around the world. But, by the same token he advanced the perspective of an abstract, cold-blooded analysis. As one writer put it, this "on occasion provided future Marxists with an excuse for viewing history as an automatically functioning mechanism whose most important concepts are not living men but dead objects—instruments of labor, machines, object relations."[20] The inner split analyzed in the *Manuscripts* as human self-alienation is now social antagonism and conflict manifested in an ever more fierce class struggle. Only when the expropriat-

---

*A notable exception in the Marxist camp is the British scholar, Ronald Meek, who flatly states: "Now it is a simple fact that most of Marx's 'laws of motion of capitalism' have *not* revealed themselves on the surface of economic reality, at any rate during the last quarter century and at any rate in the advanced capitalist countries."[18]

ing class will have been expropriated, clearing the paths for a new *classless* society, will a fulfilled life for the working man be possible at last.

So the class struggle takes the place of previous emphasis on the individual process of self-realization. The class division is to later Marxian economics what alienation is to earlier Marxian philosophy, and each sees history as a process of eventually overcoming its own version of the dichotomy.

The importance of the notion of the class struggle to Marxian economics is universally agreed upon. Marx himself left no doubt about that: "Where the class struggle is pushed aside, as a disagreeable 'coarse' phenomenon, nothing remains of socialism but 'the true love of humanity' and empty phraseology of justice."[21] But it is exactly this "coarse" doctrine of class antagonism that drives a wedge between Marxian economics and humanistic economics.

Class Struggle Versus Values Struggle A humanistic perspective helps illuminate the shortcoming of the class concept as Marx and Engels used it. In *Das Kapital* Marx, losing his earlier faith in the generic wholeness of humanity, now pictures individuals as quasi-soldiers fighting a civil war for material goods, political power and social privilege. Individual wholeness and morality are unobtainable in a split and immoral social system. Nobody has any real choice, there is no freedom to rise above oneself, and it is of course precisely this lack of freedom which is the very basis of human predictability and historical "laws." Capitalists are driven by endless greed and the motive of profit maximization, workers by their need to survive and improve their increasingly deteriorating economic lot. The consciousness of both worker and employer is forged by class interest. The full range of individual needs and values is reduced and projected into the domain of group economic self-interest.

But the generic wholeness of humanity means that the identification with humanity or society is of a higher order than the identification with a particular subgroup of society. That is why there are so many exceptions to the "rule" that people identify with what should be their narrow economic and class interests. Here is how the economic historian, Karl Polanyi, puts it (in a book highly critical of capitalist market society): "The fate of classes is much more often determined by the needs of society than the fate of society is determined by the needs of classes."[22]

From the perspective of humanistic economics what really is at the heart of history is not a class struggle but, more basically and fundamentally, an individual values struggle. If individuals hold similar values they can naturally be seen as members of a class. If those values are material they can be seen as members of an economic class. But the bedrock of human action of all kinds is Man and his or her individual needs. A statement by Alexander Solzhenitsyn is apt here: "The line between good and evil does not run through ideologies, philosophies, classes or nations, but through every human heart."

Once the most elementary survival needs have been satisfied in society, demands will arise for social action to assure security. In a democratic society, such demands can be satisfied through social ameliorative action, and reform need not stop there. Humanist thinkers, starting with Sismondi, fully realized the potential for reforming the capitalist system without the need for violent revolution. And the history of advanced capitalism, particularly in Western Europe, bears them out, as we will show in the third part of this book.

However, if democratic institutions are too weak to enable social reform, i.e., political actualization of widely felt human needs, if society is fixated at a certain level of social development through brutal force of an entrenched and powerful elite, Marxian class struggle may provide the only answer to social *and* individual integration. It is for this reason the Marxian analysis may be much more valid in some parts of the world, e.g., South America, and even Eastern Europe, than elsewhere. Marxian class theory is a special case applying selectively to the problems facing the world today. But for a more general and a more humanistic economics we must turn to Ruskin, and above all to his disciple, John Hobson.

JOHN RUSKIN (1819–1900)

In any history of economics viewed from a humanistic perspective, John Ruskin must occupy one of the foremost places of honor. He lived in England as a contemporary of Marx, but in spite of the similarity of interests and geographical proximity, neither seems to have been aware of the other.

Ruskin's mentor was the great English author, Thomas Carlyle, who as a student started his career by translating Sismondi's first pages of humanistic economics from French into English at Edinburgh, and ever after remained highly critical of political economy—which he christened contemptuously as the "dismal science," professing a "pig philosophy." But it was really his student, Ruskin, who directly and systematically dealt with political economy and its inner logic, even though his thoughts on the subject are scattered through a number of books, some of them dealing primarily with art, others with architecture. But it is in *Unto This Last* (1862) and *Munera Pulveris* (1871) that we find the substance of his economic thinking. The first is essentially a critique of the method and scope of what he called "vulgar" political economy and the second may be seen as his alternative reconstruction of the science. Perhaps most important, from our humanistic perspective, is Ruskin's forceful critique of economic method. The basic problem is this:

☐ The social affections, say the economist, are accidental and disturbing elements in human nature; but avarice and the desire of progress are constant elements. Let us eliminate the inconstants, and considering the human being merely as a covetous machine, examine by what laws of labor, purchase and sale, the greatest accumulative result in wealth is attainable. Those laws at once determined, it will be for each individual afterwards to introduce as much of the disturbing affectionate element as he chooses, and to determine for himself the result on the new conditions supposed.[23]

Now Ruskin grants this method would be perfectly logical and successful "if the accidents afterward to be introduced were of the same nature as the powers first examined." But in the social problem, this is not so; by no means. The disturbing elements are of a different quality than the constant ones: "they alter the essence of the creature under examination the moment they are added; they operate, not mathematically, but chemically, introducing conditions which render all our previous knowledge unavailable."[24]

It is this early recognition of what we consider to be the primary problem of modern economics, and to which we will devote Chapter 3, which turns the eloquent writer and artist into a first-rate economist as well.

He continues: "I neither impugn nor doubt the conclusion of the science, if its terms are accepted. I am simply uninterested in them, as I should be of a science of gymnastics which assumed that men had no skeletons." Similarly, on the assumption that Man is all skeleton, modern political economy "found an ossifiant theory of progress on this negation of a soul; and having shown the utmost that may be made of bones, and constructed a number of interesting geometrical figures with death's heads and humeri, successfully proves the inconvenience of the reappearance of a soul among these corpuscular structures."[25] In brief, Ruskin flatly defies the modern political economy to make any intelligent statements "on advantageous code of social action" as long as it works with a fragmented and reduced concept of Man.

Turning to his chief constructive theoretical contributions, we will restrict ourselves to his emphasis on the human life in determining value and wealth as well as his stress on creative value of work.

Like Sismondi, Ruskin's political economy is aimed at his concept of life, both "healthy and happy," and not abstract wealth; but he went further in claiming that "there is no wealth, but life," As a result, commodities only had value to the extent that they "avail life." or satisfy basic human needs. Proper distribution and consumption is as important to valuation as is the cost of production. Ruskin implicitly rejects the notion of value being equivalent to exchange value, since market scarcity reflects demand representing "capricious desires" rather than pure utility or basic needs. Production of effectual value, or wealth, always involves two components: "first, the production of a thing essentially useful; then the production of the capacity to use it."[26] It is in this second element of wealth where Ruskin adds significantly to Sismondi. Human capacity to use and appreciate the output of an economy is to a large extent determined by the nature of work. The laborer should make good and beautiful things, which "will recreate him," rather than bad and ugly things, which will "corrupt him" or "break him in pieces," in a sense "kill him." So much labor blinds the thoughts and the eyes, blunts the hopes, steals the joys, and blasts the souls of workers. Wasting labor by depriving it of creativity is a grave inefficiency in a human economy. For these reasons Ruskin was not a friend of machine production. By stifling creativity and disintegrating physical skills and imaginative energy, as well as displacing labor, the increasing stock of capital goods tends to produce growing quantities of riches instead of better qualities of life.

John Ruskin, unfortunately, had very little direct influence on classical economics. The scholars of his days, with the exception of John Stuart Mill, chose to acknowledge him by not dealing with his unorthodox and perhaps uncomfortable criticism. Yet Ruskin's philosophy and work survived in his two disciples: the Indian, Mahatma Gandhi, to whom we will turn in Chapter 14, and the English economist, John Hobson.

JOHN A. HOBSON (1858–1940)

Hobson had studied classics at Oxford during the 1870s, where John Ruskin's influence had been extraordinarily strong and a general interest in reforming society was sweeping that university. As a student he had read and admired *Unto This Last*, though he first "regarded it rather as a passionate rebellion than as a critical and constructive work." But some years later he recognized that Ruskin's "insistence upon interpreting the terms 'wealth' and 'vitality' was not a mere freak of a literary verbalist, but a genuine scientific demand."[27] In essence, we can interpret Hobson's human welfare economics as a serious lifelong attempt to put Ruskin's artistic thought into a vigorous and scientific framework.

In 1889 he had published, together with A. F. Mummery, his famous under-consumption heresy, to which we will return in Chapter 10. This brought about his being fired from his London University extension lectureship in political economy and literature. Embittered, he was driven into a "mixed life of lecturing, controversial politics and journalism" which, he recounts, must have in some ways been "damaging to orderly thinking" but had the valuable compensation of enhancing his understanding of economic processes by "taking them out of the textbook mold and putting them into their proper human significance."[28]

The essence of Hobson's welfare economics was first comprehensively laid out in his *Work and Welfare* (1914) but later considerably refined and eloquently represented in his *Economics and Ethics* (1929). In both of these works, as well as in his earlier books, we find Ruskin's vital standard of value as the foundation on which Hobson erected his superstructures. Not surprisingly, his stress on human needs led him to write much on the quality of work and consumption. Moreover, his "wholistic" conception of Man enabled him to perceive the direct interaction of work on consumption patterns.

> ☐ Where the existing operation of industry imposes upon large classes of workers a continuous monotony of narrow manual toil, involving a constant strain upon certain muscular functions and atrophying all other productive activities, it not only evokes this productive energy in the most vitally expensive way, but it imposes upon them a corresponding narrowness of consumption and enjoyment, thus minimizing the vital value of their wages.[29]

For Hobson, economics was still helplessly caught up in utilitarianism and needed a new psychological and philosophical basis. And it was this very challenge that he tried to address in his *Economics and Ethics*. In the introduction of that book he sets the stage by stating the problem: "Economic values in their first intent are quantities of money, while ethical or human values are qualities of life." He continues:

> ☐ Here lies the supreme problem of humanity, at once ethical, intellectual, aesthetic, how to integrate the capacities of man, as a social animal, so as to enable him to make the most of a life that consists in the progressively complex control of an environment, which by the very expression of this control, is calling forth and educating new cooperations of inborn capacities.[30]

The economist needs some criteria of value in order to prescribe, and Hobson sets out to find such a standard biological (or "organic") make-up of Man. In so doing, he anticipates to an unprecedented degree the criteria implicit in Maslow's work.

Hobson rejects as too broad the Greek definition of the good life in terms of the rarified concepts of beauty, harmony, and grace. Instead, he begins his search for values

> ☐ ... not in the high abstractions of philosophic thought but in the lower levels of human nature—the instincts, appetites, and behavior of the animal man. This method recommends itself the more in that most economic "goods," which we shall seek to correlate with human good or value, are devoted to the satisfaction of the physical needs of man.[31]

By physical needs Hobson refers to the material values of food, clothing, shelter and economic security. Having derived these "lower" values from "those activities of the body and the mind which are common to all men," Hobson brought us closer to an accepted standard of welfare.

With respect to the higher values being "more individual, more 'conscious,' more interesting—though perhaps less intrinsically important—the unique value of personality,"[32] Hobson asks, how far can we bring them all under a single concept of welfare?

In other words, if the "higher" life "is an enlargement or enrichment of 'self' involving the whole personality," how can we define a welfare criteria to evaluate a social economy in terms of a maximum quality of life? Hobson answers this question (we define it like the "lower welfare") by observing the values that the biological organism and nature dictate. "If nature makes so much (directive activity) towards the preservation and growth of a species, and if social cooperation plays the distinctive part it seems to do in human survival," then he argues that the higher values attach "to the conduct and the emotions which sustain society in the elaborate structure it has attained, and assist it to further useful needs of cooperation."[33] From this he deduces the criteria of an "ordered society" or "functional" economy in which human personality is enriched through a maximum "measure of sociality."

The "ordered economic system" is Hobson's *summmum bonum*, a fully human economy. Production is according to ability (capacity to produce) and distribution according to need (capacity to consume). It is an economy where higher liberty and justice are maximized.

A necessary, if not sufficient, ingredient of a humanized society is meaningful work. Hobson realized that "after man has made provisions for the present necessities of the body his superfluous energy naturally tends . . . to explorative, constructive and decorative work in handling such materials as present themselves."[34] It is this instinctive desire for workmanship that has to be catered to in a sound human economy. But beyond meaningful work, the worker's "growing recognition of his sense of personality" will lead to his "demand for a voice in management." Such a demand would be "an essential condition for the growth of the sense of industry as a social service." And Hobson reminds us that "So long as the thoughts of a worker do not, and cannot, go beyond the near implications of his labor-bargain, and his sense of cooperation is confined to his trade union, it is idle to suppose that the more general problems of our economic system can be rightly solved."[35]

Possibly Hobson's most remarkable insight was his early articulation of the impact of *economic security*. It is in this crucial point that he anticipates the implications of Maslow's psychology most brilliantly. Let Hobson speak for himself:

□ When moralists talk of altering human nature they are often misunderstood to mean that instincts and desires deeply implanted in our inherited animal outfit can be eradicated and others grafted on. Now no such miracles are possible or needed. But substantial changes in our environment or in our social institutions can apply different stimuli to human nature and evoke different physical responses. For example, by alterations in the organization and government of businesses and industries, so as to give security of employment and of livelihood to workers, and some increased "voice" to them in the conditions of work, it seems reasonably possible to modify the conscious stress of personal gain-seeking and to educate a clearer sense of social solidarity and service. The insecurity of livelihood has been a growing factor in the discontent of modern workers, and it increases with an education that reveals the "social" cause of that insecurity in the absence of any reliable economic government. *Security is, therefore, the first essential in any shift of the relative appeal to personal and social motives. The second essential is such alterations in the government of businesses as to give to the ordinary worker some real sense of participation in the conduct and efficiency of the business.*[36]

As Hobson saw it, basic physiological needs (food, shelter, etc.) are sufficiently identical among consumers that they could be most efficiently met by mass production in the basic industries. Moreover, the government has the function to provide for health, education, insurance and pensions, all of which "lie outside the knowledge and the capacity of their personal beneficiaries."[37] The rest of the economy would remain in private hands and cater to the growing diversity of individual wants. For this reason, Hobson anticipated that the private sector would gain in relative importance as time went on. It was the kind of economy that would be "essential to the enlargement of liberty and opportunity for ordinary men and women, and help towards a realization of the values of personality."[38]

John Hobson died in 1940, an economist who had had little recognition from his peers. Even though his influence with policy-makers has been noted, his writings have been mostly ignored in academic circles. Joseph Schumpeter, for example, in his 1200-page volume on the *History of Economic Analysis* grants Hobson a mere footnote, in which we are told that "in economics he was self-taught in a willful way that made him both able to see aspects that trained economists refused to see and unable to see others that trained economists took for granted."[39] Schumpeter also lists all his books, with the notable exceptions of *Work and Welfare* and *Economics and Ethics*. It is uncertain that he was aware of their existence and even more unlikely that he actually read either. One must wonder why Hobson's contribution in humanist economics was so totally ignored, but lack of academic recognition was, of course, also common to Sismondi and Ruskin.

UTILITARIAN ECONOMICS: THE NEOCLASSICAL REVOLUTION

A full century after Adam Smith published his *Wealth of Nations* the classical tradition of political economy came to an end. Between 1870 and 1900 modern economics was born, and whatever was left of humanistic values was essentially pushed aside by it.

Most conspicuously, the science changes its name. The leading texts from Smith to Mill had mostly been called "The Principles of *Political Economy.*" With the Austrian, Karl Menger, in 1871 it became "Principles of *Economics*" (similarly with the two other pioneers of the modern period, Stanley Jevons in England and Leon Walras in Switzerland).

The innovations of Jevons, Walras and Menger amounted to more than just changing the name of the field. It was a basic change in outlook. The centerpiece of the change was a new concept of economic *value*, or the worth of things. The new concept was *marginal utility*, the amount of pleasure that one could get from an additional portion of a commodity.

There is an irony present at the outset of utilitarian economics. The success of the concept of marginal utility was due to the appeal of the Law of Diminishing Marginal Utility, discussed in the last chapter.[40] Yet, the initial explanation of this principle was based on Karl Menger's intuitively sensible concept of a *hierarchy of needs*, rather than the now-standard concept of a variety of wants. Menger presented the classic example of the needs of an isolated farmer with a poor harvest. Such a farmer would satisfy the most urgent need, to keep himself and his family alive. If the harvest exceeded this level of subsistence, he would allocate the excess to filling his other needs in the order of their decreasing importance—seeds for next year's crop, food for the animals, food for the household pets, and so forth. In this way Menger showed how the same commodity could satisfy a series of needs of diminishing importance. The irony is that this explanation was lost in the ensuing development of neoclassicism. How did this happen?

The problem was that Menger's concept of the value of commodities based on needs was not mathematical, since one could not go beyond a listing of needs or commodities in their order of importance. Meanwhile in England, Stanley Jevons was claiming that economics was as capable of being mathematized as physics:

□ Most persons appear to hold that the physical sciences form the proper sphere of mathematical method, and that the moral sciences (economics) demand some other method, I know not what. My theory of Economy, however, is purely mathematical in character.[41]

Jevons' enthusiasm for mathematizing the moral science, heartily endorsed by his fellow Englishman, Edgeworth, became an irresistible tide in economics. Edgeworth announced that utility could be measured just as soon as a "hedonimeter" could be developed, and that it was essential for the science that utility be seen as a measurable quantity.

Under this influence, Menger's own Austrian disciples, Böhm-Bawerk and Weiser, equated Menger's term *Greznutzen* with Jevons' marginal utility and the quantifiability that it implied. In this mathematical flood, Menger's concept of a hierarchy of needs was swept away.

There were other reasons as well for the establishment of the English version of marginal utility, and these had political overtones. Menger's ideas had the clear implication of value judgements being applied to economic behavior and policy, which in fact had already been elaborated by the German Historical School of economists led by Schmoller, Weber and others. As Menger said, "men may, as a result of their defective knowledge, sometimes estimate the importance of various satisfactions in a manner contrary to their real importance. Even individuals whose economic activity is conducted rationally, and who therefore certainly endeavor to recognize the true importance of satisfactions in order to gain accurate foundation of their economic activity, are subject to error."[42] But the British neoclassicists, brought up in the blinding light of Adam Smith's laissez-faire, did not see validity in such an idea. Nor did those who benefited from the economic boom in Victorian England.

Finally, there was the discomfort of these same Victorian neoclassicists with Karl Marx's use of their own Adam Smith's Labor Theory of Value. This theory held that the "just price" of a good was the labor put into it, and nothing else. Any additional profit margin added on to the selling price was only "surplus value." In a mathematically quantifiable marginal utility, the neoclassicists found the answer to Marx's classical theory of value and its disturbing implications for booming capitalism.

So, for a variety of reasons, each of which by itself was questionable, but which fit together to meet the dominant interests of the time, the British version of marginal utility came to rule the economic roost.[43]

The Rise of Economic Man

With all human needs now reduced to the common denominator of pleasure or utility, all economic behavior conforms to what Jevons called "the mechanics of utility and self-interest." This conception sees all human behavior as following the principle of rational, calculating utility maximization. As Jevons stated it, "To satisfy our wants to the utmost with the least effort—to procure the greatest amount of what is desirable at the expense of the least that is undesirable—in other words, to *maximize* pleasure, is the problem of economics."[44] Again, by making use of a term introduced by Menger, such a being came to be called Rational Economic Man. Jevons assures us that the principles of behavior of Rational Economic Man are "so simple in their foundation that they would apply more or less completely to all human beings of whom we have any knowledge."[45] So Rational Economic Man, a fragment of what a whole person really is, has been raised by the neoclassicists to the level of universal existence. A large part of the next chapter will demonstrate that modern economics has done little to change these foundations upon which the neoclassicists placed economics.

The Distribution of Income and Wealth   The issue of how income and wealth are distributed in a society was covered by what became known as the Theory of Marginal Productivity. The respective shares of income in an economy that went to wages, rent and interest were seen to be determined by the contribution that each of these "factors of production" (labor, land and capital) made to satisfying the consumer at the end of the line. People, like commodities, had market valuation (in the form of the income they received). Mill's point that the distribution of wealth is determined by the form and nature of social institutions was quickly forgotten. Instead, the function of government was seen to be merely that of upholding and enforcing the rules of the game—the game being the conceptual framework of "perfect competition" and "equilibrium."

Alfred Marshall's Rational
Economic Man

Jevons' and Menger's concept of Economic Man was crude ore that was worked and refined in the hands of the foremost British neoclassical economist, Alfred Marshall. Marshall's work still forms the basis of much of contemporary economic thinking. Marshall came out of a strict Evangelical Protestant background, and he entered college as a theology student with the goal of becoming a minister. He soon concluded that he could better serve humanity if he went into the more worldly field of economics.

In economics, Marshall was introduced by his British elders, Jevons and Edgeworth, to the utilitarian and hedonistic tradition that was bequeathed to British economics by Jeremy Bentham. In this doctrine the good and pleasurable became synonymous. As Bentham persuasively explained it, what is good is also pleasurable.

Here is a long-standing economic principle with strong ethical implications that in a fundamental way is ethically deficient. This was the problem to which Mill was sensitive. For it is the case that the "good" action so often involves a restraint of impulse, or a resistance to temptation, these being efforts that are anything but pleasant. In fact, the good often means the *resistance* to pleasure. In the same way, growth or maturity means the restraint of previously indulged desires. The hedonism that had become established doctrine in economics eliminated this distinction. Good and pleasure were now one. How well this belief fit the demands of an increasingly affluent and consumption-oriented British economy!

Into this milieu came Marshall, the ex-theology student. Inevitably it became his task to resolve the various ethical conflicts that both economics and industrial British society faced.

In the first edition of his *Principles of Economics* (1890) he freely uses the hedonic terms *pleasure* and *pain*. But in the later editions he deleted pain and pleasure and changed to the more temperate *satisfaction*, or *benefit*, and *cost*. Marshall attempts to make a similar distinction to Mill's higher and lower needs, by taking "wants" as a separate entity from "efforts and activities." Activities are on a higher plane than wants: "while wants are the rulers of life among the lower animals, it is to changes in the forms of efforts and activities, that we must turn when in search for the keynotes of the history of mankind."[46]

This distinction would appear to dovetail in some rough fashion with a need hierarchy, and it would appear that Marshall recognized the higher nature of the person. However, he made the fateful decision that economics was not yet ready to include this aspect of the person in its framework.*

The "Spice of Life" Enters Economics Instead of a distinction between lower and higher human behaviors, a different kind of concept came to the fore in Marshall's analysis. This was the variety theme, Marshall's creation. In Marshall's thinking it was a general need for variety, rather than the principle of economic growth, that was the propelling force behind most changes in individual economic activity. As he stated in one place:

> ☐ Thus though the brute and the savage alike have their preferences for choice morsels, neither of them cares much for variety for its own sake. As, however, man rises in civilization, as his mind becomes developed, and even his animal passions begin to associate themselves with mental activities, his wants become rapidly more subtle and more various; and in the minor details of life he begins to desire *change for the sake of change*, long before he has consciously escaped from the yoke of custom.[48]

In this statement we see how Marshall tried to cope with hedonism and bend it to a more enobling frame of reference. "Variety," far from suggesting mere sensation-seeking, is now seen as the distinguishing mark between the civilized person and the brute.

Marshall talks about "change for the sake of change," rather than recognizing that we change to meet the change and development of

---

*"From this it follows that such a discussion of demand, as is possible at this stage of our work, must be confined to an elementary analysis of an almost purely formal kind. The higher study of consumption must come after, and not before, the main body of economic analysis; and, though, it may have its beginning within the proper domain of economics, it cannot find its conclusion there, but must extend far beyond."[47]

our needs. His concept of the marginal utility of all needs being balanced in equilibrium gives us a perfectly static picture of the person, despite the "variety" theme. There is no growth here, no evolution, only a constant attending to the same components, making sure that one doesn't get out of line with the other.

Prudent Maximizers: The Utilitarian and the Businessman The image of the utilitarian Man seeking satisfaction in consumption is certainly a central element in Marshall's work. But the puritan in Marshall brings in another element to make the hedonism of the utilitarian morally acceptable. This is *rationality*. The pleasure seeking of his Economic Man is offset by this same Man's meticulously careful balancing of his efforts and expenditures in order to gain this maximum pleasure. It is as if the hedonist is also a prudent auditor or a careful businessman as he goes about his maximizing:

> □ And in a money economy, good management is shown by so adjusting the margins of suspense on each line of expenditure that the marginal utility of a shilling's worth of goods on each line shall be the same. And this result each one will attain by constantly watching to see whether there is anything on which he is spending so much that he would gain by taking a little away from that line of expenditure and putting it on some other line.[49]

But the comparison between the careful business person seeking his or her maximum profit and the individual seeking maximum fulfillment is fundamentally incorrect. And the problem, once again, lies in the fact that the concept of utility assumes comparability between what really are separate and different needs.

All of the business person's activities can be seen as directed towards a single end, profit. In the same way all of an individual's activity was seen by Marshall to be directed towards utility. Whether someone was eating a meal, reading a book, being with friends, or working for social change, it was all the same thing, utility.

When we recognize that growth (or self-actualization) is the essence of human behavior, then the analogy between profit maximization and need satisfaction breaks down. A person has material needs and a person has social needs, for example, and *both* of these have to be satisfied in order for the person to be healthy and to grow. If people satisfy material needs, say, by ruthlessness, then they are ultimately preventing their own growth because the way in which they satisfy one need blocks the satisfaction of the other. This is a classic teaching which is embodied in the Midas myth and other similar parables. It is in the light of these traditional and universal observations and teachings that Marshall's concept of rational utility maximization reveals its shortcomings.

People have to meet their physiological needs or they don't survive, and they must do so in a way that doesn't prevent them from meeting other needs. The same goes for a society. Utility theory did not allow for the possibility of this kind of problem, incompatible and mutually contradictory need satisfaction. Materialism, or hedonism, can be seen as being fixated at the physiological level to the exclusion of further levels and further growth. These were not qualities that Marshall instinctively liked, yet by building economics on the foundation he chose, he unwittingly led it down the materialistic path—a path not known for its heart, nor its spirit. It is not surprising that this economics was easily accepted by the materialistic society that was developing pell-mell outside of Marshall's academic door, a society that took increasing wealth to mean increasing growth.

The beauty of the "variety is the spice of life" doctrine for a high-growth consumer economy is now clear. Variety seeks continual change. Under this impetus, needs and wants are unlimited, since new ones will always pop up. Fortunately, the problem of scarcity is never solved. The system keeps growing, and all because there is an Economic Man in each of us who is also rational.

The American Protest:
Thorstein Veblen

Much of the critical fire of Ruskin and Hobson was directed towards the concept of Rational Economic Man, but this criticism made relatively little impact within the neoclassical stronghold of England. It took someone more removed, and with a special flair for satiric verbal expression, to rattle the bars of orthodoxy, and that person was the American economist, Thorstein Veblen (1857–1929).

Rational Economic Man can be faulted from two directions—from above and below so to speak—and Veblen attacked both.

From above, he tried to show that the hedonic pleasure maximization stance of Rational Economic Man did serious injury to the true, dignified status and potential of the human being:

> ☐ The hedonistic calculator of man is that of a lightening calculator of pleasures and pains, who oscillates like a homogeneous globule of desire of happiness under the impulse of stimuli that shift him about the area, but leave him intact. He has neither antecedent nor consequence. He is an isolated, definitive human datum in stable equilibrium except for the buffets of the impinging forces that displace him in one direction or another. Self-imposed in elemental space, he spins symmetrically about his own spiritual axis until the parallelogram of forces bears down upon him, whereupon he follows the line of the resultant. When the force of the impact is spent, he comes to rest, a self-contained globule of desire as before.[50]

Instead, Veblen believed that the person "is not simply a bundle of desires that are to be saturated by being placed in the path of forces of the environment, but rather a coherent structure of propensities and habits which seek realization and expression in an unfolding activity."

For Veblen, economics was an "evolutionary science" which pertained to growing and developing organisms, not the static science of physical equilibrium.

But what made Veblen famous was his criticism of Rational Economic Man from below, which was pointedly expounded in his book *The Theory of the Leisure Class*. In this work Veblen made it quite clear that the wealthy, those whom neoclassical theorists, via the concept of marginal productivity, claimed were reaping deserved rewards from their contribution to economic output, were often predatory economic actors driven by the motive of socially displaying their wealth. The consumption behavior of the wealthy and even the not-so-wealthy, said Veblen, was often a far cry from the deliberate, calculated, farsighted allocation of expenditures that Marshall had described.

When wealthy individuals burned hundred-dollar bills as cigar wrappings, as happened during the heyday before income tax, or bought an item *only* if it was costly, they were hardly behaving according to the concept of Marshallian Rational Economic Man. It was clear from Veblen's pungent examples that much economic behavior is governed by social motives, and some strange or "irrational" social motives at that. This was a considerable blow to the neat, mathematically oriented postulates of neoclassical theory. Planets in their well-ordered orbits certainly did not display this kind of caprice.

Marshall had set up his Rational Economic Man as someone who, independent of the social system, knew what he or she wanted and needed. Utility maximization was intrinsic to his or her nature, and was the "given" brought into the economic arena or the marketplace. He was a Robinson Crusoe (a widely used economic image) who existed in the world of exchange as an untouchable, isolated atom.

But Veblen tried to show that, instead of engaging in pleasure maximization as an isolated, static individual, the consumer acts and reacts in regard to the attitudes and behavior of others. He or she is part of a social network. Armed with this recognition he assaulted the widely accepted doctrine of "consumer sovereignty," which claimed that the consumer is king and dictates what is produced in an economy. On the contrary, Veblen showed that social trends, fashions, and the persuasion of advertising exerted massive influence on the consumer. Veblen shows the consumer as more a creature in thrall than a rational and prudent economic agent, and that the forces of supply may have large effects on the presumably independent, self-contained, force of demand.

The Survival of Economic Man

Though Veblen rattled the bars of orthodoxy, he was not able to pry them open. Rational Economic Man was able to survive his attack, and continued as the concept of the person upon which most contemporary economic theory is based.

This ability of mainstream economics to remain impervious to the pointed revelations of its weaknesses has been described by economist Joan Robinson as its "self-sealing" capacity. Why it is self-sealing may be due in part to its nature as a "moral" science, to use Jevons' own term. A moral science always arouses passions by discussing vital issues and needs of men and women in society. These passions do not blend easily with a detached and objective search for the truth, in particular when the scientist is part of a community with its own academic interests and social privileges. The fathers of neoclassical economics were certainly no exception. Whatever can be said against Economic Man, he has never been an inconvenience for most prominent economists.

But the self-sealing capacity may be getting weaker, as Economic Man grows older, and the new image of the more complete Humanistic Person may increasingly arise as an attractive alternative.

CONCLUSION: THE NATURE OF HUMANISTIC ECONOMICS

In this chapter we have attempted to trace humanistic economics historically. We have discussed some of its most important proponents during the nineteenth century as well as the early decades of the twentieth century. Our survey ended with the contribution of John Hobson but we don't mean to suggest that there have not been many subsequent eloquent proponents of the humanistic vision. There have been, and they prominently include Mahatma Gandhi, E. F. Schumacher and Nicholas Georgescu-Roegen, all of whom will be encountered in later chapters. Some other significant names we should mention are Richard Tawney, as well as the pioneering thought of Walter Weisskopf, the latter also having been a co-founder of the Association of Humanistic Psychology. We won't have an opportunity to discuss these prominent people, despite the fact that their work had a profound effect on articulating and refining the vision.

In summarizing the history of humanistic economics sketched in this chapter, it may be helpful to visualize the evolution of humanistic economic thought from Sismondi to Schumacher by means of a simple chart which juxtaposes this history in the context of mainstream economists as well as the Marxist development. The chart lists several names which we will not discuss in this book, although economic students may be familiar with them.

As we suggested in Chapter 1, the defining characteristic of all the economists shown as representatives of the humanistic vision is their focus on human needs. Furthermore, there are some additional

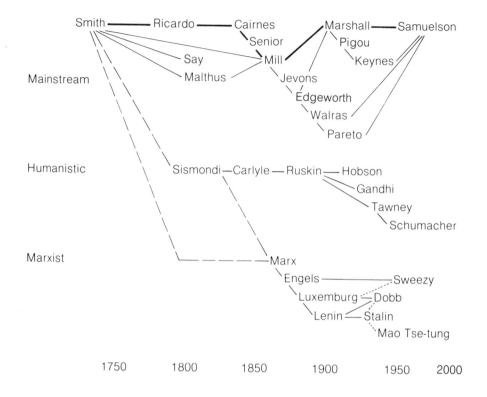

ingredients that all humanistic economists share which unite the writings of Sismondi, Ruskin and Hobson into a more coherent vision. Let us take notice of three.

All humanistic economists refused to abide by the scientific scope and method of the mainstream which is epitomized in the focus of Economic Man. Mainstream economists always have had a tendency to be inherently mechanistic, deductive, atomistic and abstractly descriptive in their analysis of economic phenomena. The humanistic economists, on the other hand, have favored a mode of analysis which can be described as organic, historical, social, and institutionally prescriptive. The economic actor is not just an individual maximizing utility, divorced of the social context, but a person with definite social needs which economics as a science cannot afford to ignore if it is to play a role in solving social problems and enhancing the quality of life. This preoccupation with the social context immediately involves the humanistic economists with ethical considerations, and an analysis of how observed social values are institutionally and philosophically derived and formulated. Once social and economic institutions were no longer taken as "given," but seen as variable and subject to change, the question immediately arose as to how to make these institutions "better" or more in accord with human welfare. This brings us to the second major ingredient.

All economists of the humanistic orientation never believed that advocacy of social reform was in conflict with their scientific credentials. Quite the contrary, it was the very task of the economist qua economist to recommend ameliorative action, especially to improve the lot of the poor and socially disadvantaged. Such was to be accomplished by means of democratic social legislation, a stance that clearly separates them from both the Marxists and the anarchistic socialists. Abolishment of child labor and Sunday work, as well as a guaranteed subsistence minimum, were seen as major priorities on the social agenda. But beyond this, the quest for social security clearly emerges already in Sismondi's writings and even more so in John Hobson's work.

Finally, the ever present concern with human welfare never allowed humanistic economists to lose sight of the importance of work as a prime vehicle to satisfy most directly the higher human needs. It is for this reason that Sismondi wanted to slow down (not reverse) the speedy industrialization of France, and why Ruskin and Hobson devoted so much of their writings to the humanization of the work place.

In writing this book we will continue this tradition. The reader will encounter all these major themes: emphasis on human needs, criticism of nonsocial Economic Man, advocacy of institutional reform, and a deep concern with the quality of work. They will be used in both a critical way, to highlight the inadequacies of modern mainstream economics, and in a constructive way, to point out the new directions that a humanistic economy needs to take.

References

1. Sichel, W., and Eckstein, P. *Basic Economic Concepts.* Chicago: Rand McNally, 1974, p. 1.

2. Plato, quoted in N. Georgescu-Roegen. "Choice, Expectation and Measurability." In *Quarterly Journal of Economics.* 68, #4, (November, 1954), p. 513.

3. Quoted in Oser, Jacob. *The Evolution of Economic Thought,* 2nd ed. New York: Harcourt, Brace and World, 1970, p. 16.

4. Smith, Adam. *Theory of Moral Sentiments.* (1753) Reprint. New York: A. M. Kelly, 1966, pp. 124–25.

5. Heilbroner, Robert. *The Worldly Philosophers.* New York: Simon and Schuster, 1967, p. 97.

6. Simonde de Sismondi, J. L. *Political Economy and the Philosophy of Government.* (1847) Reprint. New York: A. M. Kelly, 1965, p. 115.

7. Simonde de Sismondi, J. L. *Political Economy and the Philosophy of Government.* (1847) Reprint. New York: A. M. Kelly, 1965, p. 121.

8. Simonde de Sismondi, J. L. *New Principles of Political Economy.* Translated from German edition. Berlin: Akademia Verlag, 1971, p. 336.

9. Simonde de Sismondi, J. L. *Political Economy and the Philosophy of Government*. (1847) Reprint. New York: A. M. Kelly, 1965, p. 123.

10. Simonde de Sismondi, J. L. *Political Economy and the Philosophy of Government*. (1847) Reprint. New York: A. M. Kelly, 1965, p. 455.

11. Mill, John Stuart. *Principles of Political Economy*. New York: Colonial Press, 1899, v. II, p. 261.

12. Harris, A. L. *Economics and Social Reform*. New York: Harper and Row, 1958, pp. 104–06.

13. Harris, A. L. *Economics and Social Reform*. New York: Harper and Row, 1958, pp. 104–06.

14. Quoted in Tucker, Robert C. *Philosophy and Myth in Karl Marx*. 2nd ed. London and New York: Cambridge University Press, 1972, p. 173.

15. Quoted in Tucker, Robert C. *Philosophy and Myth in Karl Marx*. 2nd ed. London and New York: Cambridge University Press, 1972, Ch. 11.

16. Marx, Karl. *Economic and Philosophical Manuscripts of 1844*. Reprinted in Tucker, Robert C. ed. *The Marx-Engels Reader*. New York: W. W. Norton, 1972, p. 60.

17. Marx, Karl. *Economic and Philosophical Manuscripts of 1844*. Reprinted in Tucker, Robert C. ed. *The Marx-Engels Reader*. New York: W. W. Norton, 1972, p. 77.

18. Meek, Ronald. *Economics and Ideology*. London: Chapman and Hall, 1967, p. 109.

19. Marx, K. and Engels, F. *Selected Works*. Moscow: Foreign Language Publishing House, 1958, p. 58.

20. Fisher, Ernest, ed. *The Essential Marx*. New York: Seabury Press, 1971, p. 82.

21. Karl Marx. "Circular Letter to Bebel, Liebknecht, Bradie, and Others." London, September, 1879, in Tucker, R. C. ed. *The Marx-Engels Reader*. New York: W. W. Norton, 1972, p. 404.

22. Polanyi, Karl. *The Great Transformation*. Boston: Beacon Press, 1944, p. 152.

23. Ruskin, John. *Unto This Last*. New York: John Wiley, 1888, pp. 17–18.

24. Ruskin, John. *Unto This Last*. New York: John Wiley, 1888, pp. 18–19.

25. Ruskin, John. *Unto This Last*. New York: John Wiley, 1888, p. 19.

26. Ruskin, John. *Munera Pulveris*. New York: John Wiley, 1890, p. 9.

27. Hobson, John A. *Confessions of an Economic Heretic*. London: Allen and Unwin, 1938, p. 39.

28. Hobson, John A. *Confessions of an Economic Heretic*. London: Allen and Unwin, 1938, p. 84.

29. Hobson, John A. *The Industrial System*. (1909) Reprint. New York: A. M. Kelley, 1969, p. 329.

30. Hobson, John A. *Economics and Ethics*. London: D. C. Heath, 1929, pp. 338–9.

31. Hobson, John A. *Economics and Ethics*. London: D. C. Heath, 1929, p. 13.

32. Hobson, John A. *Economics and Ethics*. London: D. C. Heath, 1929, p. 58.

33. Hobson, John A. *Economics and Ethics*. London: D. C. Heath, 1929, p. 73.

34. Hobson, John A. *Work and Welfare*. (1914) Reprint. New York: Peter Smith, 1948, p. 24.

35. Hobson, John A. *Economics and Ethics*. London: D. C. Heath, 1929, p. 264.

36. Hobson, John A. *Economics and Ethics*. London: D. C. Heath, 1929, p. 234. (Emphasis added).

37. Hobson, John A. *Confessions of an Economic Heretic*. London: Allen and Unwin, 1938, p. 174.

38. Hobson, John A. *Confessions of an Economic Heretic*. London: Allen and Unwin, 1938, p. 174.

39. Schumpeter, J. *History of Economic Analysis*. New York: Oxford University Press, 1954, p. 832.

40. See N. Georgescu-Roegen. "Utility and Value in Economic Thought." In *Dictionary of the History of Ideas*, 1973, vol. 4, p. 454.

41. Quoted in Robinson, J. *Economic Philosophy*. London: Watts, 1962, p. 68.

42. Menger, Karl. *Principles of Economics*. Glencoe, Ill.: The Free Press, 1950, p. 148.

43. See N. Georgescu-Roegen. "Utility" In *International Encyclopedia of Social Science*, vol. 16, David L. Sills, ed. Macmillan and The Free Press, 1968, p. 25.

44. Jevons, quoted in E. K. Hunt. "The Normative Foundations of Social Theory." In *Review of Social Economy*, forthcoming.

45. Jevons, W. S. *The Theory of Political Economy* (1871) Reprint. New York: A. M. Kelly, 1965.

46. Marshall, A. *Principles of Economics*. 8th ed. London: Macmillan, 1920, p. 85.

47. Marshall, A. *Principles of Economics*. 8th ed. London: Macmillan, 1920, p. 90–91.

48. Marshall, A. *Principles of Economics*. 8th ed. London: Macmillan, 1920, p. 86.

49. Marshall, A. *Principles of Economics*. 8th ed. London: Macmillan, 1920, p. 118.

50. Veblen, T. *The Place of Science in Modern Civilization and Other Essays*. (1915) Reprint. New York: Caprice Books, 1969, pp. 73–74.

PART TWO

A HUMANISTIC CRITIQUE OF MODERN ECONOMICS

Chapter Three

THE IRRATIONALITIES OF RATIONAL ECONOMIC MAN

INTRODUCTION

An economics based on human needs is neither new nor original. Ever since Sismondi sounded the trumpet it has occupied some of the best minds and, as we showed in the last chapter, had achieved a high degree of sophistication under the restless pen of John Hobson. None of these earlier writers could have been familiar with Maslowian psychology; they simply worked with their own conception as to what constituted "higher" and "lower" needs. Nor is the specific ordering that Maslow and his followers claimed to have discovered crucially important when dealing with some of the most basic issues in economic theory. What *does* matter is the distinction between wants and needs referred to in Chapter 1. Indeed, the theoretical implications of this dichotomy are rather far-reaching and can best be illustrated in terms of the Economic Man concept.

As suggested towards the end of the last chapter, the history of Economic Man is intricately interwoven with the history of neoclassical economics. Such an interlock is not surprising, since Economic Man has been the very kingpin of modern economics. It is for this reason that we have no other choice than to aim our guns first at *homo oeconomicus*, the primary stumbling block towards a rehumanization of economic science. Our attack will be twofold: First, we want to show with more conventional means that Economic Man is scientifically quite vulnerable. The issue here is one of methodology. Next we will proceed to elaborate the need-want dichotomy, showing the relevance of an argument developed in the work of Georgescu-Roegen. We believe that the importance of his analysis has yet to be sufficiently appreciated.

During the early 1930s the scientific method changed in economics. The previous emphasis of nineteenth-century positivism was abandoned in favor of a new, updated positivism. Science, it was now stated, progresses by the formulation of axioms, equivalent to basic assumptions, from which hypotheses and laws can be derived which can be tested statistically with data from the real world. For a theory to have any scientific meaning it must generate quantitatively testable implications. An event must be predicted, e.g., when the price of sugar falls, more sugar will be bought by the consumers. If the event actually occurs, the theory is confirmed, quite apart from whether the theory appears to be realistic or not. Only if predicted events don't occur should one question the underlying assumptions of the theory. This scientific method is known by the name of *logical positivism*. Its greatest champion is the well-known economist, Milton Friedman, of the University of Chicago.

With respect to Economic Man, the implication of this new philosophy was that we should not worry about whether the psychological assumptions are correct or sufficiently realistic. Instead, all that counts is that the data show he is acting according to predictions. All the quarrelling about whether his selfish character does actually represent human nature is now seen as a waste of time. As long as he buys more sugar at lower prices he simply *is* true and real. The new stress on observable behavior in the marketplace led economists to rely more and more on behaviorism. Economic Man *is* how he behaves, and nothing more. He merely responds to the stimuli of a changing price or a changing salary in altering the composition of his shopping basket; no need to worry about what motivates him or what his nature is. It is for this reason that J. M. Clark wrote in wry language (1936):

> □ Our old friend, the "economic man," is becoming very self-conscious and bafflingly non-committal. Instead of introducing himself to his readers with his old-time freedom, he says: "I may behave one way and I may behave another, but what is that to you? You must take my choices as you find them: I choose as I choose and that is all you really need to know." The poor thing has been told that his psychology is all wrong, and he is gamely trying to get on without any and still perform as many as possible of his accustomed tasks.[1]

This transformation of Economic Man from the utility maximizer of Marshall to his modern, fully behaviorist counterpart took more than fifty years. At first sight it may appear that this change has made the economic science less vulnerable to criticism. But closer inspection suggests that this is not so. Quite the contrary. In order to see the flaws of modern Economic Man, let us take a closer look at him.

Lionel Robbins' Consistent Economic Man

We start with the Economic Man as rebuilt by the British economist Lionel Robbins, who devoted almost an entire book to the subject: *An Essay on the Nature and Significance of Economic Science* (1935). Robbins defined economics as "the science which studies human behavior as a relationship between ends and scarce means which have alternative uses." Therefore man must choose the proper means to secure the desired ends. If such choice is consistent with the ends, then he is rational. It follows that, with Robbins, rational Economic Man turns into consistent Economic Man. The underlying basic assumption is that: "The different things that the individual wants to do have a different importance to him and can be arranged therefore in a certain order."[2] In other words, if different goods have different uses in a given situation one good will be preferred over another. In the language of economics this means that consumers have *"orders of preference."** That's all. All this sounds rather like a simplifying claim.

Robbins claims that his postulate is so self-evident that it needs no statistical testing. It is "so much the stuff of our everyday experience that (it has) only to be stated to be recognized as obvious."[3] And it is this postulate that becomes one of the two pillars on which rest the laws of supply and demand and, with it then, most of economics. With Robbins we have left the Marshallian grounds of utilitarianism and hedonism. He refused to discuss "why the human animal attaches particular values . . . to particular things."[4] That he leaves to the psychologist, just as modern economists make postulates about costs while leaving the technological explanations to the engineer. Having postulated his "given" preference orders, Robbins then gets busy building his demand curves with them.

The Underlying Assumption of Consistent Economic Man

Besides the basic assumption of stipulating orders of preference, there are three other kinds of behavior Robbins takes for granted. They are:

1. *Transitivity.* This means that if I prefer A to B and B to C then I must also prefer A to C in order to be consistent.

2. *Maximizing behavior.* Robbins assumes that individuals are in "equilibrium," which means, as with Marshall, that "the possibility of advantage from further 'internal arbitrage operations' is excluded."[5] No reshuffling or switching of consumption expenditures will lead to a higher satisfaction. In other words, for Robbins

---

*In a sense we have here a behaviorist restatement of Menger's hierarchy of human needs.

this means maximizing behavior. Of course we are not told what the Economic Man is now maximizing but we do know that he is maximizing. The ends are open-ended: money, love, virtue, hate, are all potential candidates. Robbins explains, "so far as we are concerned, our economic subjects can be egotists, pure altruists, pure ascetics, pure sensualists, or—what is more likely—mixed bundles of all these impulses. The scales of relative variation (i.e., order of preferences) are merely a convenient way of exhibiting permanent characteristics of man as he actually is."[6]

3. *Separation of ends and means.* What is implied in consistency and maximizing behavior is the following: Economic Man will act as an economic man or woman in choosing the *means*. As a laborer in search of a job he or she will always dash for the highest wage, holding as given the non-economic considerations such as the type of job wanted, the locality preferred or the kind of people with whom he or she will be working. Also, as Robbins put it so nicely, "if it is assumed that I sell my labor always in the dearest market, it is not assumed that money and self-interest are my ultimate objectives—I may be working entirely to support some philanthropic institutions."[7]

Human beings behave like Economic Man, *ceteris paribus* ("other things equal"). The other things include "non-economic" considerations such as desire for social prestige, love or security, or a strong feeling of loyalty. So by holding constant all of these "non-economic" attributes, man will sell at the highest possible price and buy at the lowest possible price.

Consistent Economic Man Evaluated

What are some of the problems with this new vision of rational Economic Man?* We will discuss these assumptions in reverse order.

1. It is by no means certain that ends and means are always as distinct as Robbins assumes. Means often affect ends, the latter only becoming clear in retrospect. Also, ends may affect means. If somebody, being a total altruist, works in order to give all his earnings away, it is likely that he won't maximize ruthlessly in competing for the highest paying job. An altruist may also behave altruistically in striving to reach his goals.

More fatal from the viewpoint of scientific method, the Robbins-type Economic Man is impossible to prove wrong. From a logical positivist viewpoint he is a "non-truth." Consider this: if

---

*Much of the material in the following section summarizes some of the highlights of a brilliant analysis recently published by Martin Hollis and Edward Nell under the title *The Rational Economic Man*, University of Cambridge Press, (1975).

we test whether a housewife buys more sugar at lower prices, *ceteris paribus*, and she doesn't, then we simply blame the change on non-economic circumstances. Other things apparently did not stay equal, *ceteris* was not *paribus*. Possibly a visit to the dentist had changed the housewife's taste for sugar, perhaps she expected the price to become lower still. Who knows? The *ceteris paribus* clause is an escape hatch for the Economic Man to slip through. So Economic Man, the cornerstone of economics, is by the accepted positivistic canons quite *unscientific*. The whole science may hang in the air as a result.

2. Next, we have the assumption of maximizing behavior. On a priori grounds this is not an unreasonable assumption but its application to economic choice turns out to be more restricted than it appears at first. We will consider this issue in the section titled Resilient Economic Man.

3. The third point involves problems with the assumption of transitivity, which means that orders of choices will be consistent. That is, if I choose item A over item B, and if I choose item B over item C, I should choose item A over item C. Several controlled experiments have thrown this assumption into question. It appears that when we choose a commodity we are choosing something that has numerous aspects (dimensions), not just one.

   Let us take automobiles as an example. There are three cars, all of similar size, but among them brand A is the smallest, brand B the medium, brand C the largest. Let us say we start by choosing solely according to size, i.e., we are only comparing the single dimension, or *unidimension*. Now transitivity requires that if I prefer A to B and B to C, then I will have to prefer A to C as well.

   However, as the research of Tversky has shown, transitivity is much less likely when we choose a product that does not have just one, but many, attributes.[8] Now we have the problem of *multidimensional* choice. This can be illustrated by adding to our automobile example the dimension of color. Car A is red (my favorite color), car B is green and car C is pale blue (my least favorite color). Let us assume that, disregarding color, I would prefer the larger size to the smaller. Given all this information about my values, how will I choose between any pair of two cars? Confronted with model A and model B, both *almost* the identical size, I am likely to choose the slightly smaller red car. I prefer A to B, because I like the color, and the size differential is relatively insignificant. Now having to choose between B and C, both *almost* the identical size, I am again likely to be swayed by color considerations. As a result I pick the slightly smaller green car leaving the pale blue one on the dealer's lot. So I prefer B to C. Now what can we expect to happen when I have to choose between the red car A and the pale blue car C? Transitivity, requiring the preference of A to C, may be violated. The reason is that now (when comparing the extremes of the three sizes) A and C are *not almost* of identical size. Model C is sufficiently larger than A so that I will now choose by my primary concern for size, and will sacrifice color preferences. I drive off with the pale blue model. I have chosen C over A and behaved in an apparently inconsistent manner, even though my choice was perfectly rational.

If multidimensional choice is the general case, then the implications for transitivity are serious. Only recently the newest version of consumer choice theory has stated that we do not really buy products as such but rather their various characteristics and functions. We don't buy cars, but "transportation," involving status, comfort, gas mileage, road handling, aesthetics, etc. Some of the attributes we value more and others less.[9] Accordingly, it appears the ground is set for intransitivity to occur on a massive scale.

The Critique of Orders of Preference   Last, let us focus on Robbins' basic assumption of individual "orders of preference" as a sufficient building block for constructing demand curves.

To begin with, the orders of preference cannot be expected to be stable as the individual chooses over time. The ordinal ranking changes as the person grows, implying that the individual values of today are not necessarily the same as those of tomorrow when dealing with a dynamic personality. In fact, inner growth can be defined by a *change* in preference orderings, the (ordinal) structure of values.[10]

The orders of preference postulated by Robbins are meant to serve as the very foundation of the law of demand and the law of labor supply. To Robbins, preference orderings create demand curves just as physical factors create cost curves. It is up to psychology to explain why people have preferences, just as it is up to the engineer to explain why a production process works the way it does. This being so, the economist would like to leave these details to the engineers and the psychologists, and simply take data as given in building the superstructure of economic theory. But such a solution runs into a major difficulty. What may be proper in the case of production and costs, the engineering question, is not so proper in the case of satisfaction and demand, the psychological question. Engineering principles behave according to their own rules, the rules of physics, with no regard to the costs they generate. Psychological forces, on the other hand, are *not* independent of the economic variables that they are supposed to explain. Here we have the chicken and the egg problem. *Economics may underlie psychology as much as psychology is supposed to underlie economics.* Beer shoppers on the East Coast not only buy a six-pack of expensive Coors Beer in spite of its high cost, but also *because* of its high cost. "If it costs more it must be better," the consumer may say. Here we have the type of economic psychology that Veblen revealed to us. Similarly, there is a close interrelation between consumption patterns and the kinds of jobs people have. The commodities that one chooses are not independent of what one does for a living. Since the structure and nature of jobs is definitely an economic question, the psychological makeup that is affected by those jobs is also related to economics. Consumer preferences are not born into the economy independent of the experience of employment.

These close interconnections between economics and psychology go on and on. To try to say that psychology alone is the basis of individual preferences, and that economics is built on these preferences, is to try to separate the chicken and the egg. To do this is to drive a false wedge into the seamless unity that is nature.

Revealed Preference Theory
to the Rescue?

If it is true that a sound psychology cannot be fitted into the skull of Economic Man, it is tempting to deny the relevance of psychology. Would it not be much easier to dispense with the questions of psychology altogether? Such an attempt to rebuild Economic Man without assigning him any particular psychology is called *Revealed Preference Theory*. This refers to a new technique that allows economists to construct preference orderings on the basis of economic data alone. The consumer reveals his or her preferences in the way he or she shops. Armed with revealed preference theory the economist can, by mere observation of shopping behavior, draw the preference orderings, and can do this without any reference to utility, inner satisfactions, or willful intentions. Here we have extreme behaviorism making a forceful entry into the science of economics. To paraphrase J. M. Clark, "Economic Man chooses as he chooses and that is all we need to know."

The question we have to answer is whether such drastic brain surgery (if you don't want to call it removal) really cures the patient. Clearly, we have done nothing to avoid the transitivity problem outlined by Tversky; when choices in shopping behavior are multidimensional, as they are likely to be, how can we expect our reborn Economic Man to behave rationally?

But to get to the core of the issue, what about our two major concerns: is the New Economic Man more scientific, and is he able to give us a hand in supporting the heavy structure of the *law of demand*, the very foundation of a large part of the science?

Let us begin by examining his scientific credentials. Can we predict behavior without having to tangle with his inner being, by denying the relevance of "states of mind?" The answer is no, and the reason is as follows. The consuming Economic Man reveals his *actual* behavior, not his ideal behavior. How do we know if and by how much the actual behavior deviates from optimal behavior? In other words, if behavior does not correspond to prediction, can we blame the assumption of the theory or the irrationality of the choosing agent? A moment's thought will show that revealed preference theory does not allow human fallibility to be revealed, because it doesn't show us what human optimality is. As Hollis and Nell put it: "Making a mistake is not simply not doing."[11] The only way we can determine a mistake is in reference to a goal or an intent. But revealed preference theory was designed to operate without having to do that. It is for these reasons that Nell and Hollis concluded that "Behaviorism has to be ruled out on two counts, first that failures and mistakes are not observable distinct from simple nonoccurrences and secondly, that even if they were they would need 'mentalistic' explanations."[12] Economic Man may choose as he chooses but that is *not* all we need to know, at least in terms of being able to scientifically test his existence. If elusiveness was the main problem of the utilitarian Economic Man, the problem is even compounded with his behaviorist cousin.

But even if we ignore the issue of non-testability, revealed preference theory is by no means home free. There are other problems, the most crucial one undermining its very purpose: It cannot liberate itself from implicitly assuming maximizing behavior and thereby getting entangled once again with the thorny questions of individual goals and intentions. In short, revealed preference theory only works with economic decision-makers that have an "inner being."

As if these methodological and psychological problems were not already enough, revealed preference theory was also beset with prohibitive, logical problems.

Ironically, these problems were all scholarly demonstrated by a young mathematical economist at Harvard, Nicholas Georgescu-Roegen, two years *before* the revealed preference theory came onto the scene in 1938. In a pioneering article, he showed that it would be logically impossible to build up orders of preference by merely "spying" on the consumer while shopping.[13a]

Subsequently, some of these problems were corrected by a more refined version, the so-called Strong Axiom of Revealed Preference. Yet some crucial problems remained and continued to mar the entire idea of basing the law of demand on a rigorous, positivistic approach free of the "vestigal traces of the utility concept."

The student may wonder why and how scientific economics can continue to peddle defective merchandise and get away with it. In puzzles such as this, one is tempted to seek an explanation by quoting the eminent economist Joan Robinson: "He who is convinced against his will is of the same opinion still." For those who are interested in finding out more about the analytical crux of the revealed preference theory, we have added a "Guide to the Perplexed" in the appendix of this book.

The Resilient Economic Man

The history of Economic Man, as outlined at the end of the previous chapter, is a history of a sudden rise and a sharp fall. (It was especially the merciless pen of Thorstein Veblen that dealt him a fatal blow. Or so it seemed. . . .) But in this chapter we discussed his resurrection by two prominent contemporary economists. Robbins pulled him from under the debris by showing that he need not be the "lightening calculator of pleasure and pain" everybody thought he was. Instead Economic Man was portrayed as anyone endowed with a certain order of preference, enabling hereby the entire construct of consumer demand theory to rest on less objectionable ground. As if this were not enough, Milton Friedman imbued new life into Economic Man by insisting that all the talk of his outmoded psychology and inhuman, overly mechanistic and unreal character has been "largely beside the point."[13 b] The issue of whether rational Economic Man is real can only be settled according to the methodology of logical positivism. If he behaves according to predictions, he exists, whether we like him or not.

No doubt it is because of this strong coalition of prominent theorists that Economic Man can still perform his traditional function as bearer of so much economic theory. Yet we have shown that on closer inspection neither defense is convincing. Robbins' minimal set of assumptions is unlikely to hold; it is, in any case, psychologically inadequate to support Economic Man in the key position he has occupied. Friedman's rescue attempts have been undermined by the elusiveness of *homo oeconomicus* whenever we want to drag him to the empirical testing grounds; thus he is defeated on the very grounds that Friedman uses for his support, testability.

Rational Economic Man celebrated his hundredth birthday a few years ago, and he is still with us. For most of his life his rationality has been questioned, but never his resilience. Whatever his faults, he deserves respect for his ability to hold on to his scientific function even after many experts claim that he has now been stripped of his academic credentials.

But we cannot rest matters here, since Economic Man's stubborn resilience is the major stumbling block in vitalizing economics. As long as he occupies the stage there is no room for a need-based humanistic understudy. Why does he continue to spoil the show by pretending to be completely oblivious to the angry shouts of an increasingly disenchanted audience? What explains this apparent immunity to protest and the unwillingness to step aside for a more realistic actor? More specifically, why does he exhibit such a strong resistance to experiencing his wants as hierarchically structured?

To answer questions like these would soon move us into the field of the sociology of knowledge, an area which is beyond the scope of this book. At the same time, the present impasse is so important that we cannot resist the temptation to seek at least a partial answer. In our search, we will find ourselves moving on a trail that was blazed a long time ago by the economic theorist Nicholas Georgescu-Roegen, in a pioneering article that was published in 1954.[14] Oddly enough the trail seems little used, if not forgotten, and certainly few students have been acquainted with its existence.

We start our expedition by reexamining, this time more rigorously than in the first chapter, the implications of focusing on the basic distinction between needs and wants.

CHOOSING BY WANTS OR GROWING THROUGH NEEDS

As we saw in Chapter 1, wants imply *one* purpose, a single goal in life, the maximization of a unique desire to which all others could be reduced. As Georgescu-Roegen puts it clearly: "This is in fact what utility represents: the common essence of all wants into which all wants can be merged."[15]

The utilitarian recognized (implicity) *one single need*, the need for maximum utility. As a direct consequence, all wants are seen to be "intra" need, all different means to a common end. Now it is possible to rank such means by the criterion of efficiency, i.e., according to their ability to create utility. Moreover, since wants are all in the same (value) scale, one can be substituted for another, one can replace another in the scramble for utility. The trick is to find the best mix, the optimal variety.

Finally, wants are not only comparable but, being of the same essence, they also appear to lend themselves readily to *quantitative calculation*. It is of course this very property that enables the Economic Man to choose by rational cost-benefit calculation, acting just like a mini-computer. If he happens to be in a state of indifference, a change in the price of anything (changing his opportunity costs) is likely to affect the mathematics of his equations and to induce a certain preference.* Any preference structure such as Robbins' order of preferences is not expected to change. The need for utility always remains the same, whether he chooses water for drinking or for watering the lawn.

Turning to *needs*, a quite different scenario appears. Needs, or necessary wants, imply specific goals. Human life implies the satisfaction of a minimum amount of water, food, shelter, security, as well as

---

*In fact, individuals in theory could be made to switch back and forth between two goods: wants are reversible.

the higher social and moral needs. Unsatisifed needs compel the organism to seek gratification of those needs. Once a level of satiation is reached, new (and higher) needs dominate the organism, as Maslow has shown. Furthermore, needs—unlike wants—are not sensitive to price manipulations, unless price becomes simply prohibitive.

Comparison between different needs involves different ends, i.e., different values. As a result, *inter*-need comparisons cannot be undertaken quantitatively, but only *qualitatively*. What, under the utilitarian perspective, appeared as substitutes to satisfy the one and only goal of utility, now can be seen as *alternatives* which are not necessarily substitutes. The preference of using water for drinking or the lawn, to stick with the previous example, can be qualitatively evaluated but not quantitatively calculated. In evaluating alternative needs, people will *feel* which one is of higher priority. Rational Economic Man is here better off by relying on intuition rather than solely on the facilities of pure calculation.

All this boils down to the following problem: In comparing two goods that are likely to fulfill two separate and hierarchically ordered needs, we cannot, strictly speaking, compare them geometrically or mathematically as if they were on the same plane.[16] Overlooking this warning may lead to unpredicted, if not perverse, consequences.

So, for instance, there is the recent research with rats in which they were confronted with different goods obtainable at different efforts (i.e., prices).[17] As long as it was a question of choosing the root beer spout versus the Tom Collins spout, there was no problem, and behavior under changing relative efforts (prices) was just as the economist claimed it would be. But the same rats failed miserably to live up to the expectations of economic theory when confronted with water versus food pellets. The experimenters were puzzled to find that even after boosting the "price" of food by a whopping 400% the rats stubbornly refused to drink more and eat less. If something is good, such as water, more is not always better. What holds for substitutes does not necessarily hold for alternatives. Whatever such tests with rats may be good for, they certainly suggest caution in analyzing the choice of alternatives on the basis of utility maximization models.

One final distinction between want-based utility and need-based self-actualization ought to be made. Some economists may be led to see self-actualization as utility by another name: a want-based economics has utility as its mono-need; likewise, a need-based economics has self-actualization as *its* mono-need. But the comparison is false— self-actualization is *one* of the needs of the hierarchy of needs, and is not equivalent to each of the other needs; finding security is not self-actualization. The process of growth through needs *culminates* in self-actualization, whereas utility is completely present in every act of want satisfaction. It is the difference between a serial process and static maximization.

The General Case: Commodities
Embodying Different Needs

We have just analyzed the implications of hierarchical preferences in cases involving two alternatives, each representing a different need: food and water, food and clothing, water for drinking versus water for sprinkling lawns (the latter boosting social needs).

But in the real world most commodities can be assumed to embody different needs *in some mix*, as we have previously mentioned. We order a meal in a restaurant that not only embodies physiological satisfaction, but also provides the potential for satisfying some of our social needs, possibly even the moral needs (aesthetics, etc.). A meal at a restaurant can be evaluated against the alternative ways of spending money, such as taking a brown-bag lunch to a Sunday football game, buying a new shirt, buying five pounds of bananas, etc. Since most alternatives of choice embody a certain proportion of alternative goods, we stipulate that the embodiment of different needs constitutes the *general case*. Commodities by their very essence are not the same, they are multidimensional; they not only have utility, but different *kinds* of utilities.

Our Maslowian framework allows us to be somewhat more specific at this point. In the general case we assume each commodity to embody the following three non-equivalent types of utility: (1) material, (2) social, and (3) moral. Of course, we can always think of commodities which have only an insignificant social and moral dimension, for instance, salt. Yet from the perspective of the general case, commodities like that are seen as the exception, not the rule. Economics, on the other hand, has been operating on the assumption that all commodities are one-dimensional.

The *general case* has three intriguing features which we would like to briefly indicate, even though they bear no direct responsibility for the riddle of Economic Man's resilience.

First, the concept of substitutability is no longer absolute but relative. Two commodities may be substitutes at one need level but mere alternatives on other levels. A Toyota and a Lincoln Continental are substitutes only as long as the need for private transportation dominates. But if the prospective buyer is in the market for esteem, a mink coat, expensive jewelry, or even writing a bestselling book are possible substitutes for the Continental, while the Toyota may be a non-equivalent alternative. Obviously this raises havoc with the economist's attempt to define markets along industrial or commodity demarcations, and as a result all the quantitative measurements of the degree of competition in particular markets, or overall in the economy, lose their meaningfulness.

Second, the new social (as well as moral) dimension of all commodities requires that we take much more seriously the Veblen-type effects on individual demand for commodities. Social and ethical considerations, which tend to involve institutions, are immediately raised to an equal footing with the more traditional concept of individually based tastes and preferences. We now can witness how such concepts as scarcity and price re-emerge as a hopelessly scrambled hash of individual and institutional variables. We are back to the earlier political economy, or to what has been more recently called "social economics" or "institutional economics."

Third, the reader will recall our discussion of transitivity. There we saw how Tversky demonstrated that the problem of intransitivity arises if we engage in multidimensional choice. This is exactly what our general case assumes as the very starting point in an analysis of choice.

The Evaporation of Indifference

Going back to our main line of argument, it is important to realize that abstract Economic Man can no longer juggle his choices in a rigorous manner. Typically we expect commodities to contain a different mix of basic need gratifiers. The different qualities are no longer commensurable, and any attempt to treat them as if they were of the same essence by subjecting them to quantitative calculation and reasonable thought is bound to failure. Instead we need a new juggler that has some intuitive touch, an ability to sense the relative weight of the different needs. When choosing a car we have to qualitatively estimate whether personal safety is more or less important than gas mileage or social prestige. There is no satisfactory way to conceive of this complex choice problem as different means to some particular end.

At this juncture some economists may feel a little uneasy, but not terribly shaken. They may be expected to defend the science in the following manner: "Much of this talk stressing the qualitative element entering choice amounts to little more than beating a dead horse. There is no reason why economic analysis cannot handle non-monetary aspects, such as the social benefit one car conveys vis-à-vis another. All that is required is to assume that individuals can order their alternatives, nothing more and nothing less." And back we are with Robbins' assumption of an order of preferences.

For the sake of argument, let us grant this and see where the path will lead us. In doing this we arrive at the famous concept of the "indifference curve" which permits us to visualize the ordinal relationship between two goods, let us say beer and milk. Such a curve is shown in Figure 3-1. The consumer is here pictured as having certain preferences (tastes, if you like) regarding milk and beer. He or she may like one of the two much better than the other, just as the rats preferred root beer over Tom Collins. But one's likes are rarely absolute. Remember, the rats did choose the Tom Collins if its price was sufficiently reduced. And so it is with milk and beer. We are willing to trade one for the other if the terms are right. It is this trade-off that is pictured by the indifference curve. More specifically, it is the locus of combinations of beer and milk that make our consumer equally happy—that is, that leave him or her indifferent. In Figure 3-1, our consumer is indifferent towards consuming a lot of beer and little milk (point B) or a lot of milk and little beer (point A), or any other combination marked by the line.[18]

FIGURE 3-1 AN INDIFFERENCE CURVE

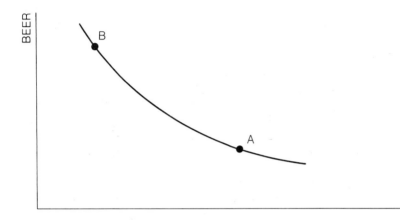

For our present purpose there is no need to elaborate further on the concept of the indifference curve, although it is of central importance in microeconomics, as a glance through such a textbook will readily confirm. Rather, we are aiming at something more basic: the very notion of *indifference* in choice.

Remember, in our general case of choosing alternatives, certain aspects in the choice are more important than others. And it is precisely this hierarchy of embodied aspects that rules out indifference, and with it the indifference curve. To repeat more formally, *indifference evaporates as soon as (1) we see a good satisfying more than one need, and (2) one need is more basic than the other(s).*

Take the beer and milk example. Let us assume we are primarily interested in quenching our thirst, secondarily in calories (the hunger need), and lastly in taste. If thirst is *all* we are interested in, no problem. The indifference curve can be easily drawn, and would indicate the different combinations (say, during a day) of the two liquids equally satisfying a given level of thirst. But now add a secondary interest in food value. Let us assume that milk contains more food value per fluid ounce. Obviously the hungry person would no longer be indifferent between point A and B; point A would be clearly preferred because of the food value. Once different points on the indifference curve are no longer on the same level of satisfaction it ceases to be an indifference curve.*

We have now reached the end of the trail and have gained more knowledge about the resiliency of Economic Man. Economics cannot dump Economic Man and still hang on to beautiful geometry and elegant mathematics, the very bread and butter of modern economics. The stubborn resilience that Economic Man has demonstrated in the face of devastating criticism need no longer surprise us; indeed, it is perfectly understandable. His scientific credentials may be lacking, his acting may be distasteful, but if we were to fire him much of the elaborately built stage show would collapse, endangering many dedicated and hard-working members of the crew.

Humanistic Man with his or her various needs will never be able to perform on the same stage. The superstructure of Euclidian economics precludes Humanistic Man's appearance. Twenty-five years ago Georgescu-Roegen pointed to this dilemma and was quick to add that on the basis of common sense and introspection the concept of hierarchical wants seems more preferable, regardless of its far-reaching theoretical consequences.

> ☐ In support of the Irreducibility of Wants, one may refer to many every-day facts: that bread cannot save someone dying from thirst, that living in a luxurious palace does not constitute a substitute for food, etc. But there is another important argument in favour of the irreducibility. If all wants were reducible we could not explain why in any American household water is consumed to the satiety of thirst—and therefore should have zero "intensity" of utility at that point—while since water is not used to satiety in sprinkling the lawn, it must have a positive "final degree of utility." Yet, no household would go thirsty—no matter how little—in order to water a flower pot. In other words if a commodity satisfies several wants, it may very well happen that its "marginal utility" with respect to some wants may be zero; (because these wants are completely satisfied) and yet the "utility" of the last unit be not null.[19]

In the meantime, we have witnessed the growth of humanistic psychology, confirming this common sense with scientific data. But all this may not be enough. Economic Man will go on with his show as long as the theater can manage to stay in business.

CONCLUSION

Economic Man, under the skillful coordination of Milton Friedman and Lionel Robbins, has been "born again." But his life in economics

---

*Technically speaking, we are now dealing with lexicographic orderings and behavior curves. (We devote more attention to them in appendix 1)

cannot be expected to extend beyond the neoclassical textbooks. And even there his appearance must strike us as unwarranted, and predicated on the following three assumptions: First, as logical positivists we must look the other way in regard to his testability; second, he is never confronted with multidimensional choice; third, he does not need water or food, only utility, which instead he may squeeze out of jewelry or motorcycles. In the vast catalog of ways in which humanity has been dehumanized and mechanized, the theoretical conception of modern Economic Man deserves special mention.

References

1. Clark, J. M. *Preface to Social Economics*. New York: Kelly, 1967, pp. 9–10.

2. Robbins, Lionel. *An Essay on the Nature and Significance of Economic Science*. London: Macmillan, 1935, pp. 16, 75.

3. Robbins, Lionel. *An Essay on the Nature and Significance of Economic Science*. London: Macmillan, 1935, p. 79.

4. Robbins, Lionel. *An Essay on the Nature and Significance of Economic Science*. London: Macmillan, 1935, p. 86.

5. Robbins, Lionel. *An Essay on the Nature and Significance of Economic Science*. London: Macmillan, 1935, p. 86.

6. Robbins, Lionel. *An Essay on the Nature and Significance of Economic Science*. London: Macmillan, 1935, p. 95.

7. Robbins, Lionel. *An Essay on the Nature and Significance of Economic Science*. London: Macmillan, 1935, p. 97.

8. Tversky, A. "Intransitivity of Preferences" in *Psychological Review*, 1969, vol. 76, pp. 31–48.

9. Lancaster, Kelvin. *Consumer Demand: A New Approach*. New York: Columbia University Press, 1971.

10. More technically speaking, the contours of the utility mountain start shifting or switching as we are in the process of climbing it. See the appendix for a simplified description of the switching process.

11. Hollis, M., and Nell, E. *The Rational Economic Man (A Philosophical Critique of Neo-Classical Economics)*. New York: Cambridge University Press, 1975, p. 125.

12. Hollis, M., and Nell, E. *The Rational Economic Man (A Philosophical Critique of Neo-Classical Economics)*. New York: Cambridge University Press, 1975, p. 125.

13a. The pioneering article is Nicholas Georgescu-Roegen, "The Pure Theory of Consumer's Behavior" in *Quarterly Journal of Economics*, 1936, pp. 545–93. A detailed though technical summary of the entire development can be found in the later paper "Vilfredo Pareto and His Theory of

Ophelimity" reprinted in N. Georgescu-Roegen's *Energy and Economic Myths*, New York: Pergammon Press, 1976, Ch. 13.

13b. Friedman, Milton. *Essays in Positive Economics*. Chicago: University of Chicago Press, 1953, p. 31.

14. Georgescu-Roegen, Nicholas. "Choice, Expectations and Measurability" in *Quarterly Journal of Economics*, 68, 4 (November 1954), pp. 503–534.

15. Georgescu-Roegen, Nicholas. "Choice, Expectations and Measurability" in *Quarterly Journal of Economics*, 68, 4, (November 1954), p. 515.

16. So, for instance, we often find "food" and "clothing" in an analysis of choice put into the same diagram. See Lancaster, *Introduction to Modern Micro Economics*. Chicago, 1969, Ch. 7.

17. Kagel, J. K., et al. "Experimental Studies of Consumer Demand Behavior Using Laboratory Animals" in *Economic Inquiry*, 1975, 13, pp. 22–38.

18. If the answer is initially at the combination A, the opportunity cost of getting more beer (Δb) is what has to be given up in milk (Δm). This is the analytical basis of the opportunity cost concept. If the move from A to B is infinitely small, the slope of the indifference curve is given by the ratio $\Delta m / \Delta b$.

19. Georgescu-Roegen, Nicholas. "Choice, Expectations and Measurability" in *Quarterly Journal of Economics*, 68, 4, (November 1954), p. 516.

Chapter Four

THE NEGATIVE VALUES OF POSITIVE ECONOMICS

INTRODUCTION

The most effective way to transmit values in a society, say, from one generation to the next, is to do so without letting on that it is *values* being transmitted; they must be disguised as objective truths. In recent times science has been the medium through which this was done, and economics has shared heavily in the process. The claim made that economics is a value-free or positive* science has been the perfect cover for the set of values which does in fact exist in economic theory. The previous chapters have indicated the considerable role that value premises play in the discipline. It is our position that social science cannot get away from value judgements, so that the danger comes, not from making value premises, but from being unaware of the values that already exist in the field.

What the theory of humanistic economics shows us is that values correlate with needs and grow out of needs, so that when we are talking about one we are also talking about the other. Therefore the sphere of values that mainstream economics promotes is essentially synonymous with the needs it is centered upon: constant material expansion, or, "when something is good, more is better"; self-interest; pleasure; and so forth. A number of these values have already been

---

*Remember that the term *positive* refers to the attempt of nineteenth-century science to find positive or definite truth. In economics it means the construction of theories that supposedly describe rather than prescribe, and avoid value judgements. For present purposes there is no substantive difference between this type of positivism and the more modern *logical positivism* briefly discussed in Chapter 3.

stated or implied in previous chapters. This chapter will elaborate on three specific areas.

ONE-DIMENSIONAL ECONOMIC MAN: LIFE AS A PLEASURE HUNT

Economic Man is a one-dimensional creature operating in a static framework. His values are constant regardless of his experiences or what he consumes. And it is this stability that allows him to calculate mechanically (just like a computer) the best means to fulfill his life goal, utility.

This picture is in stark contrast to the dynamic, growth-oriented theory of human behavior and personality which underlies humanistic economics. We have defined psychological growth precisely as change in basic values and goals. But the contrast could easily be misunderstood to imply that Economic Man and Humanistic Person are two mutually exclusive concepts. Instead, we see Economic Man as a Humanistic Person that for some reason has never been able to grow, or to put it differently: Economic Man is an individual who is fixated at the lowest need level in the Maslowian system. Metaphorically he dwells in the dark basement of the human economy, apparently not able to find the stairs that lead to the sunny upper quarters. It is in this basement that he is hunting for pleasure and utility, the common denominator of all things within his reach. Within this framework we can assume that the more he *has*, the happier he is. Life for him consists in appropriating as many *things* as possible. The ultimate value of things (as well as persons and interpersonal relationships) is determined by how much utility they yield. It is a joyless world where everything is a means, and carries its price, while values play a subordinate role at best. Economic Man gets born, educated and married on the basis of rational opportunity cost calculations. To convey a flavor of his behavior, we quote from a recent article by Becker and Landes on the "Economics of Marital Instability."[1] Here is how Economic Man is assumed to act in choosing his spouse(s):

> ☐ By assumption, each marital "strategy" produces a known amount of full wealth (i.e., money wealth and value of nonmarket time), and the opportunity set equals the set of full wealths produced by all conceivable marital strategies. The individual ranks all strategies by their full wealth and chooses the highest. Even with certainty, a strategy with marriage, then dissolution, and eventually remarriage might be preferred to all other strategies and would be anticipated at the time of first marriage. Dissolution would be a response perhaps to the growing up of children, or to the diminishing marginal utility from living with the same person, and would be a fully anticipated part of the variation in marital status over the life cycle.[2]

Economic Man also calculates the ideal number of children, decides whether or not crime "pays" for him, when to commit suicide or how to die optimally (i.e., with a zero savings account). For an enthusiastic summary of this kind of lifestyle we suggest McKenzie and Tullock's text *The New World of Economics*, a book we do not want to discuss here but instead refer the reader to two recent reviews.[3]

The outline of the consumption-oriented basic nature of Economic Man should already be sufficiently clear. With consumption on the throne, there is never enough; the wants of Economic Man are unlimited, enabling the observing economist to focus analysis on the scarcity of all things. The psychoanalyst, Eric Fromm, summarizes the picture as follows:

☐ In contrast to physiological needs, such as hunger, that have definite satisfaction points due to the physiology of the body, mental greed—and all greed is mental, even if it is satisfied via the body—has no satiation point, since its consumption does not fill the inner emptiness, boredom, loneliness, and depression it is meant to overcome. In addition, since what one has can be taken away in one form or another, one must have more, in order to fortify one's existence against such danger. If everyone wants to have more, everyone must fear one's neighbor's aggressive intention to take away what one has. To prevent such attack one m st become more and more powerful and preventively aggressive ones lf. Besides, since production, great as it may be, can never keep pace with unlimited desires, there must be competition for antagonism among individuals in the struggle for getting most. And the strife would continue even if a state of absolute abundance could be reached; those who have less in physical health and in attractiveness, in gifts, in talents would bitterly envy those who have "more."[4]

We have to wonder what is it that compels Economic Man to strive for quantity rather than quality in life. It is here that Maslow's theory of hierarchical needs sheds useful light. A person who is fixated in his or her development at the lowest level of purely material needs must be blocked in some way from further development to the next higher level. More specifically, we can point our finger at the needs of security and belongingness. No matter what he does, Economic Man does not seem able to gratify either need in a truly relevant way—and remember, Maslow maintains that higher needs cannot be "bribed" or bought. All the money in the world spent on fancy burglar alarm systems, insurance policies, or an arsenal of weapons, will not cure basic anxiety, any more than the purchase of sexual love or membership in an exclusive club can give a feeling of being accepted and loved. What Economic Man seems to lack is the proper institutional environment that would allow him to have security or belongingness. Let him have a secure and decent job and all this business about wanting more and more things will soon be outgrown in favor of an increasing desire for more quality and meaning.

With such a transformation of character, the old *having-oriented* rationality of the materialist Economic Man gives way to a new *being-oriented* rationality of the social and moral person. We now can recognize that what constitutes rationality is relative to one's position in the hierarchy of needs. At the lower levels, calculating seems like the essence of rational behavior, yet at the higher levels we would expect feeling and intuition to be at least as important in choosing wisely.

From a humanistic point of view, the most relevant concept of rational behavior is that which enables self-actualization. The striving for more material goods is only rational as long as they are *needed*, but the continued wanting of goods is irrational behavior. It is here that we see the tragic irony of Rational Economic Man. The more he strives to conform to his own concept of rationality, by calculating the best way to increase his goods, the more he risks acting irrationally.

Moreover, he may not be the only one who unwittingly wastes a lot of his time and his life. We fear that the professional economist who spends his or her time in advocacy of optimal (or rational) resource allocation is also running the risk of building a castle on sand. Take competition as the supposed optimal means of allocating resources. If it allows more wants to be satisfied, but at the same time interferes with the gratification of the higher needs of security and belongingness, then it ultimately winds up being self-defeating and irrational. More on this in Chapter 6.

ALL ALTRUISM IS ONLY SELF-INTEREST IN DISGUISE

As we have seen, an economics in which every behavior is a means to the same end, personal pleasure or utility, leads quite naturally into the view that people can only be egoistic. Thus, it is only consistent that behavior which ordinarily would be seen as generous or giving is taken by this economics to be a disguised form of self-serving behavior.

In examining this issue from the standpoint of a need-based and humanistic economics, there are a couple of logical shortcomings with the self-interest point of view that we need to mention at the outset. The first of these is one of the classical philosophical fallacies, a *tautology*. A tautology is a statement that is true by definition, so that it has no possible way of being false. The concept that all behavior serves one's self-interest is a tautology. If someone appears to be doing something for the good of another, this is only seen as self-interest in another form: "They are only doing it because they themselves get something out of it."

The same kind of definitional circularity can be used to show that all behavior is altruistic. People may at times appear to behave selfishly but their real purpose is altruistic. When presented with a choice of two apples, let us say, I will choose the larger one so that my beloved brother can have the joy of seeing me with more. Or, the real reason people seek wealth is in order to become philanthropic, etc. The point is that when a statement is set up as being true by definition it has no real content; all other possibilities have been logically ruled out.

The second logical problem has a more direct bearing on economics. It relates to the self-interest explanation of the phenomenon of gifts, or any behavior of giving. The self-interest economist sees gifts as just another form of exchange. I give a gift to you knowing that I will get one back from you, so it is all *quid pro quo*.

Extensive sharing and gift-giving has been observed among so-called primitive peoples. This has sometimes been taken as an indication of the natural altruism that forms the basis of social relationships in non-market (or pre-market) societies. However, the economist in the neoclassical tradition analyzes this giving and sharing as just another example of exchange, since gifts are both given and received.[5] But here is the same kind of catch we pointed out above: the behavior of two altruists in interaction with one another can look like exchange. A gives to B, and B gives to A. Conversely, what we ordinarily take to be exchange may really be a form of reciprocal giving. There is no logical way to distinguish between the two.

Self-Interest, Altruism and Humanism

When we deal with the question of egotism and altruism vis-à-vis Rational Economic Man, we are playing with a stacked deck. The problem is that in order to examine the issue meaningfully, as well as scientifically, we need to have what is called a *contrast class;* i.e., we need to have a way in theory to contrast self-interest behavior with altruism, just as we need to have black in order to perceive white. Utilitarian economics does not allow us to do this because it admits of only one need, self-oriented utility, and thus cannot meaningfully approach the question of altruism. We can, however, do so from the standpoint of humanism, because it presents us with the possibility of a variety of needs, and we can contrast these needs and the behavior that serves them. Thus we are able to see that people can be ego-oriented *or* altruistic, depending upon which of their needs are dominant.

The lower needs in the hierarchy, when they dominate, either naturally or through fixation, tend to generate self-interest behavior. Since this person is dealing with scarce material goods, what he gets, his neighbor loses. There is a German saying, *Selber fressen macht feiss,* which translates as "only by eating yourself do you get full." It does not help your hunger to see somebody else eat. Similarly it does not help your need for shelter if a friend or a stranger moves into a nice house. Physiological needs, by their very nature, are only gratifiable by the individual. There is a "pie" that has to be divided up; the more someone else gets the less I will be able to get. At this level, without a strong competitive drive one will tend to come out on the short end; "nice guys finish last."

But if an individual is secure about satisfying his or her physiological needs, and instead is engaged in satisfying social needs, there is much less reason for conflict and competition. If I succeed in meeting my needs of belongingness and affection nobody else need lose as a result. Quite the contrary. Higher needs by their very nature tend to be satisfied through sharing. Consequently I don't have to worry about other people's interfering with my attempts at gratification. Self-interest not only fades at this point in getting what one needs, but actually tends to interfere. In contrast to material goods there is an unlimited supply of good interpersonal feelings. I don't have to race for this kind of reward in a selfish way to beat my co-worker to it. The reward can exist by our joining hands and reaching the goal simultaneously. Thus the adequate meeting of the social needs actually requires some degree of altruism. It is at this level that we would expect to find the simultaneous existence of egotism and altruism, since insecure lower needs may exist side by side with active higher needs. Perhaps this state is the most common human condition.

With fulfillment on the two lower levels, the physiological and the social, the growth urge reaches its maturity in the need for self-actualization. Here the conflict that may have been observed previously between self-interest and altruism has the opportunity to be resolved. As Maslow writes,

□ The dichotomy between selfishness and unselfishness disappears altogether in healthy people because in principle every act is both selfish and unselfish. . . . Duty cannot be contrasted with pleasure nor work with play when duty *is* pleasure, when work *is* play, and when the person doing his duty and being virtuous is simultaneously seeking his pleasure and being happy. If the most socially identified people are themselves also the most individualistic people, of what use is it to retain the polarity?[6]

As we might expect, when we look at the question of self-interest and altruism from the standpoint of humanistic economics we find a progression. We may even express it that rationality itself goes through this progression. When only the most basic material needs are considered and everything else is excluded, it might be most rational to behave in a self-seeking way. Here, personal maximization is the name of the game. But as soon as other needs are brought into the picture, rationality must change its focus. Now sharing and reciprocation begin to make sense, for without these practices the social needs would go begging. It turns out that the way of meeting one's higher needs (i.e., altruistic behavior) can also satisfy one's lower needs, but the reverse is not the case. By sharing, we both can eat and also have good feelings towards each other. By grabbing, I may be able to eat, but you don't want to have anything to do with me.

Similarly, when we move up the ladder a further step, self-interest and altruism are no longer competing alternatives, as Maslow's statement just indicated. At this level self-interest becomes absorbed, as it were, into altruism. In terms of seeking satisfaction, it is now realized that the greatest satisfaction is to be found in what has previously been seen as self-denial, that is in giving, in helping, in appreciating, in love at the highest level. From this vantage point we can see that rationality lies precisely in the opposite direction from where the neoclassical economists placed it, not in self-seeking but in self-giving. Thus it can be said, in quite a literal way, that the job of humanistic economics is to turn the mainstream completely around.

PRESERVING THE STATUS QUO: THE DENIAL
OF INTERPERSONAL COMPARISONS

This section could have been headed "Some people are more people than others." We have described the values associated with the concept of Economic Man and the allied concept of marginal utility, and have shown some of the negative consequences of these values. Well, the case for marginal utility was not all that bleak. There was one area where marginal utility theory had implications that led to a different kind of conclusion. As the early neoclassicists recognized, marginal utility theory implied that there was a social gain in equalizing the distribution of wealth, that a society's total utility would be increased as its income distribution evened out.

The reasoning behind this conclusion derives from a basic principle of marginal utility theory, the principle of the diminishing marginal utility *of income.* This principle stated that the marginal utility of income would decline the wealthier one was, which was a perfectly reasonable idea. Here is how Marshall phrased it, "A stronger incentive will be required to induce a person to pay a given price for anything if he is poor than if he is rich. A shilling is the measure of less pleasure, or satisfaction, of any kind, to a rich man than to a poor one."[7]

When this idea was coupled with the obvious recognition that the state of poverty deprived the poor of happiness, or utility, a rather clear-cut conclusion followed: If, somehow, the distribution of income were changed so that the poor would gain some of the income of the rich, there would be a net gain in utility, since the poor would gain more utility from the transferred money than the rich would lose. Indeed, the rationale for the progressive income tax is based upon parallel, if not identical, reasoning.

There was one obstacle, but not an insurmountable one, to this reasoning. There was no way to tell exactly what utility an individual derived from a penny or a shilling, regardless of whether that person was rich or poor. Even if there were income redistribution we could not really tell the actual gain in utility. We could tell that dollars changed hands, but we could not tell if utility changed in exact proportion.

But, as we said, this problem could be overcome. In the absence of any way to measure utility directly, the most reasonable thing to do is to assume equal utility scales across people, which in effect means equal capacity for satisfaction. In fact, it is hard to see how any other assumption makes sense. And this assumption is precisely what economics adopted in order to be able to add up different individuals' incomes, and assume it was adding up utility or value. Within the confines of marginal utility theory, this is the assumption that allows us to use aggregate statistics, such as GNP. Without the assumption of additivity or utility, by adding income, there would be no basis for comparing GNP figures from one country to another, or even within the same country from year to year. This is the kind of assumption neoclassicists had to invoke whenever they made a case for the social benefits of any kind of economic policy, such as free trade or laissez-faire. Proceeding from the same basis, the conclusion that equalizing the distribution of income and wealth was beneficial appeared to be inescapable.

The "Capacity for Happiness"   Many economists objected to the conclusion that it was beneficial to equalize the distribution of income and wealth. One of the first was Edgeworth:

> ☐ This deduction (Edgeworth's) is of a very abstract, perhaps only negative, character; negativing the assumption that *Equality* is necessarily implied in Utilitarianism. For, if sentients differ in *Capacity for Happiness*—under similar circumstances some classes of sentients experiencing on an average more pleasure (e.g., of imagination and sympathy) and less pain (e.g., of fatigue) than others—there is no presumption that equality of circumstances is the most felicific arrangement; especially when account is taken of the interests of posterity.[8]

By *sentients*, Edgeworth is referring in Victorian language to people. He is saying, what if capacity for happiness is different in different people? He felt that, until there was a purely objective way to measure happiness (his hedonimeter), "The principle 'every man, and every woman, to count for one,' should be very cautiously applied," as he elsewhere put it.[9] In a sense, Edgeworth's conclusion should be exactly the reverse. Until the perfect pleasure-meter could be derived we really had no basis to assume that people differed in terms of their capacity to experience happiness; therefore, we had better be cautious about *not* "counting every man and woman as one." Of course, what the enthusiastic positivists of the late 1800s may not have quite appreciated was that an objective measure of a subjective state, utility, was, in principle, impossible.

Whatever its lack of merits, arguments like Edgeworth's that people differed in their *capacity* for happiness appeared to satisfy a substantial portion of his contemporaries in the economic field, and this has been the mainstream position ever since.* The most famous

---

*As an example see our quote from a current textbook in Chapter 5, p. 96.

debate on the issue followed in the wake of Pigou's publication in 1920 of *The Economics of Welfare*. In that book Pigou went against the neoclassical mainstream and advocated welfare principles that were based on the assumption of equality in capacity for happiness.

The most prominent critic of Pigou's egalitarian welfare economics was Lionel Robbins. Coming to the defense of the egalitarian assumption was Roy Harrod, who was then president of the British Economics Association. (This shows that not all members of the Establishment were comfortable with rejecting equal capacity for happiness.) In his 1953 presidential address, Harrod reminded his colleague, Robbins, that the whole basis of any economic recommendations depended upon assuming comparability between individuals:

> ☐ If the incomparability of utility to different individuals is strictly pressed, not only are the prescriptions of the welfare school ruled out, but all prescriptions whatsoever. The economist as an advisor is completely stultified, and, unless his speculations be regarded as of paramount aesthetic value, he had better be suppressed completely. No; some sort of postulate of equality has to be assumed. But it should be carefully framed and used with great caution, always subject to the proviso "unless the contrary can be shown."[10]

Like Edgeworth previously, Harrod is advising caution, but his conclusions are now in the opposite direction—equal capacity for happiness should be assumed, unless the contrary can be shown. And this of course would mean that application of the concept of diminishing marginal utility recommended the equalization of wealth.

Lionel Robbins' Response Robbins immediately responded to Harrod in an article that appeared in the next issue of the *Economic Journal*, and his answer is revealing.[11] The crux of the problem of modern economics, the fact that it is committed to a certain set of values, whether consciously or unconsciously, is laid bare in Robbins' reply. There, in 1938, in one crystalline moment of clarity, the issue was defined as perhaps never before or since. Let us look carefully at Robbins' argument in his article.

He begins by admitting that originally he had found Pigou's welfare proposition appealing, and felt that the approach of counting each person as one is "less likely to lead one astray." But then he came across an incident in a story he was reading that began to stir his doubts. The story involved a British official in India who was trying to explain the egalitarian meaning of Benthamism (utilitarianism) to a high-caste Brahmin. The Brahmin replied, "But that cannot possibly be right. I am ten times as capable of happiness as that untouchable* over there."[12] Robbins had "no sympathy" for the Brahmin's position, but

---

*The lowest caste in India.

he was disturbed that there was no scientific way to prove the Brahmin wrong. This disturbing thought led him to conclude that the assumption of equal capacity for happiness was strictly a moral, or value, judgement, and was separate from the other propositions of economics. But this separation did not leave him content. "For it meant, as Mr. Harrod has rightly insisted, that economics as a science could say nothing by way of prescription."[13] Therefore, Robbins accepts the necessity for economics to make this value judgement: "I was bound to admit that what I was doing was simply to carry one stage further a very common and almost universally accepted practice. All economists recognized that their prescriptions regarding policy were conditional upon the acceptance of norms lying outside economics."[14] Robbins recognized that in order for economics to be useful it had to take a stand one way or the other—it had to decide either with "Bentham" and "Saint Paul" that all people are to be considered equal, or with the "Brahmin" and "Hitler" that they are not. Robbins is quite clear where he stands with his choice: "I think that the assumption of equality comes from outside (of economics), and that its justification is more ethical than scientific. But we all agree that it is fitting that such assumptions should be made and their implications explored with the aid of the economist's technique."[15]

In coming to terms with Harrod and Pigou, Robbins almost seems apologetic for his previous criticism: "I confess I was very surprised . . . , All that I had intended. . . ." And in his conclusion he winds up on a note that is nothing less than humanistic:

> ☐ In the realm of action, at any rate, the real difference of opinion is not between those who dispute concerning the exact area to be designated by the adjective scientific, but between those who hold that human beings should be treated as if they were equal and those who hold that they should not.[16]

And Robbins, of course, now admits that he sides with those who hold that human beings should be treated as if they were equal. No caste-laden Brahmin, he, and certainly no Hitler.

While it is good to see Robbins move away from his earlier position, we cannot let the matter go at that. To do so would be to let a crucial issue for the science slip away. We quoted Robbins as saying something that many economists still believe, namely that the "assumption of equality comes from outside (of economics), and that its justification is more ethical than scientific." Put plainly, we think that this belief is wrong; the assumption of equal capacity of happiness *is* the scientific assumption. The other is the less justifiable, and the less scientific. The reason is as follows.

A capacity for happiness, or capacity for sentience or feeling, to use Edgeworth's original concept, comes from a mistaken analogy. With this idea Edgeworth is drawing on the concept of human capacities and applying it to the area of feeling. Now the notion of capacity is certainly meaningful and relevant in numerous areas of human activity and ability. These can include such things as intelligence, artistic ability, strength, and so forth. We certainly differ from each other in a multitude of ways, and we can look at these differences as variations in capacity. But—and here is the crucial point—*feeling* does not represent a capacity; rather, it is the essence of what being a person is. A person feels, and a person can be happy or sad. There is no issue of how much. Such a concept would reduce the capacity for humanness.

This is very clear in the area of mental retardation. A retarded person, by definition, certainly has less mental capacity than a normal person. But no one who has any experience with retarded people would say that they are less feeling than anyone else. They show the same joy, the same pain as anyone else, although they may express it in a less intellectual and articulate way. It is for this reason that retarded people can easily be recognized as fully human, even though they have certain diminished mental "capacities."[17]

So to say that people differ in this regard, capacity for feeling, is to say that all persons are not equal *as* persons. Certainly this is a self-contradictory proposition, as well as being foolish. No science that is about people could be built upon this ground, and it is wise that Robbins backed off. Unfortunately, he did not recognize that it was necessary for him to do this if there ever was to be a science of economics.

The Mainstream Rushes On: Equality Ignored One reason we have sketched out Robbins' argument in detail is to hold it up against the prevailing and persistent belief in economics that Robbins, or "someone," had staunchly and rather successfully refuted Pigou's egalitarian proposition regarding the welfare of society. Joseph Schumpeter, the distinguished economic historian, seems to reach this conclusion. He says in his monumental historical survey that the "idea that satisfactions of different people can be compared and, in particular, summed up into the General Welfare of society as a whole" is one that "few economists will care to defend nowadays,"[18] and at this point he refers to Robbins' 1938 article as an instance of this rejection. A little while later Schumpeter remarks that the attempt of the welfare economist to prescribe is "a long-exploded methodological error."[19]

Finally, as far as the egalitarian position is concerned, the icing on the cake would seem to have been applied by Abba Lerner when he showed in his book, *The Economics of Control* (1944) that even if we assume people differ in their capacity for happiness, as long as we are not able to measure or determine that capacity, the best social policy would *still* be one that led to a more equal distribution of income and wealth.[20]

But too much is apparently at stake for a concession ever to be made in this matter. This time the defender of the faith (or lack of it) is Friedman: "An essential step in Lerner's analysis is the introduction of ignorance. Granted, says Lerner, that individuals differ in their capacity to enjoy satisfaction, that they are not equally efficient pleasure machines, there is no method of determining how efficient they are as pleasure machines and therefore no hope of adjusting the amount of income to the individual's efficiency."[21]

Even though it is beside our point, we as humanists must point out that the term *pleasure machine* is Friedman's, not Lerner's. Our more pertinent comments follow Friedman's next statement.

> ☐ Eliminate the assumption of ignorance, and the same analysis immediately yields a justification of inequality if individuals do differ in capacity to enjoy satisfaction. And we must clearly be prepared to eliminate the assumption of ignorance. The talk about capacity to enjoy satisfaction is just empty talk unless there is at least a conceptual possibility of determining the relative efficiency of individuals as pleasure machines.[22]

We have now absolutely gone full circle. Edgeworth's original point was based on the "assumption of ignorance" in regard to different individuals' capacity for happiness (their "efficiency as pleasure machines"). Edgeworth was saying that since we cannot measure happiness directly, we have no way of knowing that people are equal in their capacity for happiness. This is how the whole disagreement began. This is not Lerner's own assumption. He is merely taking up the argument in the very terms that the critics of egalitarianism have proposed. Now refer to Friedman's last sentence, just quoted. The talk about capacity to enjoy satisfaction *is* empty talk. So Friedman, despite his intentions, is in fact refuting Edgeworth.

CONCLUSION

We are done with the argument. It is a critical one, we believe, in showing how economics will avoid the implications of its own logic when these implications go against other interests, such as not wanting to ruffle the feathers of those geese that sit on the golden eggs. So the preservation of the income status quo can be seen as one of the values of positive economics.

Even though we reject the validity of the concept of utility, we do think it is meaningful to talk about the diminishing marginal utility of *income*. This simply means that money is more useful in satisfying material needs than social and moral needs, which is implied in the concept of the hierarchy of needs. The higher needs depend less on money than the lower needs. Therefore, it is *humanly efficient* for an economy to move towards greater income equality, because the money goes where the need is the greatest. Such an economy promotes the highest human welfare and well-being. We have seen that even marginal utility theory was led to this conclusion when it did not resort to the notion that "some people are more people than others," a supremely elitist concept which has sometimes carried even a racist aura.

Of course, it is not from utility theory that we ultimately want to derive the principle of equality (or "optimum equality"); it rests on firmer humanistic grounds than the quicksand provided by neoclassical economics. We saw in Chapter 2 that Adam Smith implied it in his concept of the invisible hand, and that it was present in humanistic thought all the way back to Plato.

Even though it is revealing to see the theoretical gymnastics that mainstream economics has to go through to legitimize inequality, there is a danger of getting lost in the artificial maze of neoclassical concepts. Remember, we have shown in Chapter 3 that utility is not a "thing," an object that can be measured and calculated. So the entire debate about interpersonal comparability of utility is largely beside the point. What *does* matter for policy is the alternative conception of hierarchically structured *needs*. And as Georgescu-Roegen has long recognized, "such a scheme provides an *objective* basis for many welfare issues which otherwise would require the assumption of interpersonal comparisons."[23]

Let us also not forget this basic point when observing the next act of theoretical gymnastics; the magic of the Pareto Criterion.

References

1. Becker, Gary; Landes, Elizabeth; and Michael, Robert. "An Economic Analysis of Marital Instability" in *Journal of Political Economy*, 1977, 85, 6, pp. 1141–87.

2. Becker, Gary; Landes, Elizabeth; and Michael, Robert. "An Economic Analysis of Marital Instability" in *Journal of Political Economy*, 1977, 85, 6, p. 1143.

3. Officier, Lawrence H. and Stiefel, Leanna. "The New World of Economics: Review Article" in *Journal of Economic Issues* X, 1, March 1976, pp. 149–58. Also Rohrlich, George F. "Beyond Self-Interest: Paradigmatic Aspects of Social Economics" in *Review of Social Economy*. XXXV, December 1977, particularly pp. 335–36.

4. Fromm, Erich. *To Have or To Be*. New York: Harper and Row, 1976, pp. 112–13.

5. For diverging viewpoints among anthropologists, compare:
    Schneider, H. K. *Economic Man*. New York: Free Press, 1974.
    Bohannon, P. *Africa and Africans*. Garden City, New York: Natural History Press, 1964.
    Polanyi, Karl. *Primitive, Archaic, and Modern Economics*. Garden City, New York: Doubleday, 1965.

6. Maslow, Abraham. *Motivation and Personality*. 2nd ed. New York: Harper and Row, 1970, p. 179.

7. Quoted in Robinson, Joan. *Economic Philosophy*. Garden City, New York: Doubleday, 1962, p. 53.

8. Quoted in Robinson, Joan. *Economic Philosophy*. Garden City, New York: Doubleday, 1962, p. 69.

9. Quoted in Robinson, Joan. *Economic Philosophy*. Garden City, New York: Doubleday, 1962, p. 81.

10. Harrod, Roy F. "Scope and Methods of Economics" in *The Economic Journal*, September 1938, p. 397.

11. Robbins, Lionel. "Interpersonal Comparisons of Utility: A Comment" in *The Economic Journal*. December 1938, pp. 635–41.

12. Robbins, Lionel. "Interpersonal Comparisons of Utility: A Comment" in *The Economic Journal*. December 1938, p. 636.

13. Robbins, Lionel. "Interpersonal Comparisons of Utility: A Comment" in *The Economic Journal*. December 1938, p. 637.

14. Robbins, Lionel. "Interpersonal Comparisons of Utility: A Comment" in *The Economic Journal*. December 1938, pp. 637–38.

15. Robbins, Lionel. "Interpersonal Comparisons of Utility: A Comment" in *The Economic Journal*. December 1938, p. 641.

16. Robbins, Lionel. "Interpersonal Comparisons of Utility: A Comment" in *The Economic Journal*. December 1938, p. 641.

17. Wolfenzberger, W. *The Principle of Normalization in Human Services*. Toronto: National Institute of Mental Retardation, York University, 1972.

18. Schumpeter, Joseph. *History of Economic Analysis*. New York: Oxford University Press, 1954, p. 1071.

19. Schumpeter, Joseph. *History of Economic Analysis*. New York: Oxford University Press, 1954, p. 1073.

20. Lerner, Abba. *Economics of Control*. New York: Macmillan, 1944, Ch.3.

21. Friedman, Milton. *Essays on Positive Economics*. Chicago: University of Chicago Press, 1953, p. 310.

22. Friedman, Milton. *Essays on Positive Economics*. Chicago: University of Chicago Press, 1953, p. 310.

23. Georgescu-Roegen. N. *"Pareto"* in *Energy and Economic Myths*, p. 318.

Chapter Five

THE NEW WELFARE ECONOMICS: VALUE-FREE OR VALUE-LESS?

INTRODUCTION

As we have seen, modern economics would be fairly ineffectual in dealing with the real problems of welfare* and the formation of social policy if it had to practice strictly its (supposed) abstinence from value judgements. This is what Harrod had pointed out, and what Robbins was essentially forced to admit. In order to have something at all to say about welfare, modern economics came up with its own unique solution to the value judgement problem. This apparent solution was termed the *New Welfare Economics*, to contrast it with earlier welfare economics that Pigou had tried to introduce.

The New Welfare Economics has been considered an unusually successful innovation which now occupies a central position in the science, as browsing through textbooks and journal articles will readily confirm. But by now the reader should be prepared to regard such a "triumph" with the greatest scepticism. What fits the vision of the practitioner of neoclassical "truths" so well more often than not makes little sense from a humanistic perspective. We have already encountered the hidden problems of the neoclassical core concept, Economic Man, with its crude psychology and questionable logic. The situation of the New Welfare Economics will be found to be similar: the attempt to discuss well-being more "scientifically" reduces the entire endeavor to a contradictory and meaningless exercise.

Even though the issue at hand is generally considered to be among the more difficult ones, we will attempt to explain the essential

---

*The term *welfare* as used by economists refers to well-being and not welfare, as in public assistance.

problems in a way that is comprehensible to the general reader. The student should keep in mind that every fault of the New Welfare Economics constitutes a plus for our alternative perspective. In fact, we see humanistic economics as eventually occupying its very place within an enlarged framework of the scientific edifice. A relevant welfare economics has to outgrow the constraints imposed by the ghost of nineteenth century utility analysis and align itself with the essence of human nature.

The Pareto Optimum

The guiding principle behind the New Welfare Economics was formulated by the Italian economist, Vilfredo Pareto (1848–1923), who succeeded Leon Walras at the University of Lausanne. It was ushered into the mainstream of economics after the Second World War. The principle is known as the *Pareto Optimum* and can be stated, *a social optimum exists whenever it is not possible to make somebody better off without making somebody worse off.* Conversely, whenever it is possible to make somebody better off without making anybody worse off, it is considered a *good* move, and should be undertaken in the interest of maximum social welfare.

Why was it that the Pareto Optimum caught on in economics as a welfare principle, when other propositions such as Pigou's were bound to fall by the wayside? We believe the answer is that the Pareto Criterion accepts two of the implicit value judgements previously discussed: (1) Economic Man and (2) denial of interpersonal comparisons.

Let us restate the Pareto Optimum to see clearly what it says. Let us say that we are considering two states of society, state alpha and state beta, and we want to determine which one is preferable (our value judgement). Here is how we use the Pareto Optimum to do this: State alpha is preferable to state beta if at least one person would prefer being in alpha, and no one would prefer being in beta. To put it slightly differently, at least one person is better off in alpha and no one is worse off. It is the situation where at least one person wins and no one loses.

We can easily see why the Pareto Optimum is appealing as a basis of making value judgements about social policy. How could anyone object to the desirability of a social change where no one would be worse off, and at least one person would be better off, or, to put it in monetary terms, where no one would be poorer, and at least one person richer? Perhaps only curious misanthropic humanists like ourselves could object to such a boon. We shall see.

First let us look at how the Pareto Optimum supports free trade: As long as trade (or exchange) is mutually advantageous and voluntary, it will make some people better off and nobody worse off. If free exchange is blocked or prohibited, Pareto optimality is violated. Consider the case of government *rationing* in allocating consumer goods such as natural gas, water, gasoline or whatever is in too short supply to satisfy everybody's need. Any such rationing, whether by coupons, empty shelves, queueing or favoritism still directly violates Pareto optimality, at least as long as people differ in their tastes and needs. Take, for example, a vegetarian family who has been given a meat ration. They would clearly benefit if they could get together with another family and swap the meat for something they prefer, let us say, brown rice. No doubt, many families would like to enter a trade with the vegetarians. Everybody would be better off, and nobody worse off, but the law forbids such "black-market" trade. Free markets for consumer goods, on the other hand, would enable a Pareto efficient distribution of consumer goods. Similarly, take the example of government price setting in the labor market, the federal minimum wage. How many unemployed teenagers would be willing to work for less than the minimum, how many employers would not object to hiring them for less? Both sides could be made better off. But the government says no. The same principle applies to government freezes on prices of natural gas, meat, or bananas, as well as government rent control. Moreover, it is possible to demonstrate that any deviation from pure competition, such as government tariffs on foreign goods, excessive pricing by monopolists, government sales taxes, etc., all distort free market prices and thus violate the Pareto Criterion. From this it did not take economists very long to deduce, usually in mathematical and rigorous form, that a competitive economic system based on private-property rights, free exchange and markets would be the best (i.e., the Pareto optimal) way of organizing society. And all this could be said without having to make explicit, strong value judgements. That was the whole beauty of it! But two of our values discussed in the last chapter did enter and form an integral part of the Pareto Criterion. Let us look at them in turn.

The Implicit Value of Economic Man First we consider the value of Economic Man, the market person who is always rationally maximizing his utility. According to this concept, whatever he or she does in the market is deemed the rational and preferable thing to do. Pareto was certainly aware of the more glaring problems with this, and went to great pains trying to avoid using the word *utility*. He coined his own word *ophelimity* and used it to mean only *economic* utility. He put the matter this way: "In the ordinary sense of the word, morphine does not have utility because it is hurtful to the one addicted to it; yet, on the other hand, economically speaking it has utility for him because it satisfied one of his needs, even though it is injurious to him."[1] So morphine would be said to have ophelimity, but not utility as ordinarily defined. Pareto seems to imply that social welfare is a function of utility, but not necessarily of ophelimity. How one is able to distinguish between these two without making a value judgement is a good question. But we can forget this petty quibble, as the rest of economics soon did.

The isolated nature of Economic Man, his inability to relate in any way to society at large, leads to a major problem with the Pareto Criterion; it assumes that wealth and satisfaction are absolute and not relative. That is, as if each person were a Robinson Crusoe on an island, rather than a family head trying to "keep up with the Joneses," the consumption principle which Veblen so pointedly demonstrated.

A poor tenant farmer, if he is aware that his wealthy landlord has just had another huge leap in income while he and his family remain just where they are, is not very likely to feel unaffected by this new state of affairs. As a matter of fact, without any unusual degree of malice on his part, he may well feel embittered by what has come to pass. Using Pareto's own term, his "ophelimity" may be less than what it used to be, thus contradicting the assertion of Pareto's Criterion that we here have a case of increasing the social welfare. Pareto's Criterion allows us this: We can all agree that if the rich get richer and the poor get poorer, *that* is a bad state of affairs. But if the rich get richer and the poor stay the same, that is a good state of affairs. Convenient, isn't it?

The point that one's sense of economic well-being is *relative* to others in a social context, and not *absolute*, is nothing more than elementary psychology. Certainly the major thrust of advertising copy, with its emphasis on status—on being the handsomest, the prettiest, the best, the most—shows a well-developed appreciation that this is the way it is. And yet theoretical economics acts as if things were not this way, that we all are Robinson Crusoes, gauging our own worth, both literally and figuratively, in the complete absence of anyone else's existence. Again the value preferences of economics reveal themselves in this stance. Certainly there is sufficient data to indicate that our judgements about self, or ego, are social, because in fact the ego is a social phenomenon.

One interesting study[2] that presents data on this point was done by Easterlin. A number of opinion surveys which asked U.S. citizens whether they were "happy" show that a positive answer to this question tends to be more prevalent the higher the income of the respondent, although the relationship is a complex one. Then a different set of data was gathered showing what percentage of the people in *other* countries said they were happy. When these data are related to the GNP per capita in each of these countries there is found to be little or no correlation between reported happiness and GNP across countries. For instance, the study, based on 1961 data, showed Great Britain had the highest percentage of "very happy" people (53%), and a $1777 GNP per capita, while West Germany, with a $1860 GNP per capita, had only 20% of the respondents reporting that they were "very happy." Thailand with a $202 GNP per capita had 13% of the respondents reporting to be "very happy," while Italy with a $1077 GNP per capita had only 11% indicating "very happy." If we can accept these data as reasonably valid, they seem to show that *within* a country (at least in the U.S.) happiness tends to be a function of one's income standing, but *between* countries, where there is certainly much less basis for people making comparisons with others, happiness is largely unrelated to income.

But as we said, the social relativity of welfare judgements is an elementary fact, and does not need fancy research to prove it. Any parent will be keenly aware of it. Just think of the situation where there are two siblings of roughly the same age. Now imagine giving just one of them a present, and not the other. According to Pareto optimality you have increased the welfare of the situation, because one child is better off, and the other child is not worse off. The total welfare of the situation is increased. But what happens in reality? It is more likely that the probability of *warfare*, not welfare, has increased. To dispense presents in this fashion would clearly be a socially foolish thing to do. These children, as well as most other people, cannot and will not act as they are supposed to according to the socially insulated principles of the Pareto Criterion.

This error in basic economic theory, that wealth is absolute rather than relative, has a long history that precedes Pareto. Its roots, in fact, may lie in Adam Smith.

In the index to Smith's book *The Wealth of Nations* under the letter A, we find the following curious entry, "Africa, powerful king much worse off than European peasant."[3] In the text Smith relates how the division of labor of the European economy contributed to the "accommodations" of the commoner:

> ☐ Compared indeed with the more extravagant luxury of the great, his accommodation must no doubt appear extremely simple and easy; and yet it may be true, perhaps, that the accommodation of a European prince does not always so much exceed that of an industrious and frugal peasant, as the accommodation of the latter exceeds that of many an African king, the absolute master of the lives and liberties of ten thousand naked savages.[4]

As Smith saw it, the peasant was ipso facto better off than the African king. This certainly was one way for a moral philosopher to justify the overwhelming gap that admittedly existed between the princes and peasants of his world.

The Pareto Optimum was an attempt by economists to make the transition from an analysis based on people as isolated units, as if they were atoms in a physicist's laboratory, to one based on people in the social setting. This is what welfare economics aims to do. But the effort based on the Pareto Optimum approach is doomed to failure, because it attempts to talk about society without acknowledging the specifically interpersonal or relational nature of social phenomena. If we attempt to begin our analysis by treating a person as an isolated unit we are already off on the wrong foot. It does not matter if we then try to graft on a social judgement principle like the Pareto Criterion. We must *begin* by looking at the individual as he or she is related to others.

The Implicit Value of Preserving Inequality Much of what has been said about Economic Man, especially about relative income, could have been discussed in connection with the other covert value, namely the implicit bias toward maintaining income inequality. Let us look more deeply into the relationship of this value and the Pareto Criterion.

Acceptance of the income/wealth status quo is the real essence of the *Pareto Criterion.* The whole idea of Pareto's "new" welfare economics was to be able to say something about efficiency in terms of satisfying consumer wants without having to talk about equality and the income distribution. The Pareto Criterion was seen as a way for economists to make value judgements, in other words to talk about better or worse, without having to make interpersonal comparisons in satisfaction. Here is how it worked: We have seen the Pareto Criterion only applies if both (i.e., all) sides of a bargain are made better off, or at least if nobody suffers as a result of it. Yet most economic activity will tend to hurt somebody somewhere in society, especially in such questions of public policy as environmental cleanup, bans on sales of non-returnable beverage containers, raising or lowering import tariffs, taxation, zoning, etc. But the case of redistributing income or wealth poses the greatest problem, since here there are always bound to be losers. Consider the following example taken from a current textbook as an illustration of Paretian thinking in action:

> □ If $200 is taken away from an industrial tycoon and given to a poor sharecropper, the tycoon may decide not to paint his yacht a new color this year, while the sharecropper may decide he can afford to add meat to his diet for one meal a day. If we looked at these alternatives from the perspective of a single individual, we would say that the additional utility, or satisfaction, from gaining the meat would be far greater than the loss of utility from doing without the paint job, so the total utility would be higher. However, we cannot prove that the sharecropper increases his utility by more than the tycoon increases his, because these are two distinct individuals with differing capacities for deriving pleasure from worldly goods. (A hedonistic tycoon may get more satisfaction from the paint job than an ascetic sharecropper would get from the meat.)[5]

According to the Pareto Optimum the transfer that is described above *would not be* a desirable state of affairs, because the tycoon would be worse off.*

---

*Note also how the refusal to make the egalitarian assumption of equal capacity for happiness operates here.

In general it should be clear that any move towards greater equality is by definition prohibited by the Pareto Criterion. Democracy is irrelevant; the rich or currently privileged, no matter how small in number, have a veto.

The Complementarity of Equity and Efficiency

The problems of the new welfare economics don't stop here. As it turns out, *nothing* can be said without bringing in the question of income distribution. This important point may be best illustrated by a simple example. Imagine two traders, Mr. A and Mr. B, with identical tastes regarding left shoes and right shoes. Mr. A has twenty left shoes, Mr. B has twenty right shoes. What is a Pareto Optimum allocation of shoes in this two-person economy? It is when voluntary trading stops and, given our assumption about tastes, this will be when both Mr. A and Mr. B have an equal number of shoes, i.e., ten pairs. But now consider the Pareto Optimum with a different initial endowment of shoes. Let us say Mr. A has twenty left shoes and ten right shoes, while Mr. B has only ten right shoes. Both start swapping shoes and we can predict that as voluntary exchange comes to an end Mr. A will be in possession of fifteen pairs, Mr. B only five pairs. Remember, tastes have not changed.

We are told that the 15/5 distribution is Pareto optimal, yet before we had just found out that a 10/10 distribution was Pareto optimal. Evidently, there is more than just one Pareto optimal point. In fact any particular Pareto Optimum is directly related to the initial endowment of the trading partners, or to a particular distribution of wealth and income.

In general, there are as many Pareto optimal situations in an economy as there are possible distributions of income, so for all practical purposes there are infinite Pareto Optimums. What it all boils down to is that free markets are merely *one* condition for defining an ideal output in the economy. A *necessary* condition for the definition of a Pareto Optimum is to start with ideal initial endowments, that is with a perfect income distribution, however defined or derived. Economists have long recognized this particular difficulty. On an abstract level it has been dealt with by the following trick. In talking about the Pareto efficiency of a competitive market economy the *prevailing* income distribution was simply taken as *given*, i.e., as determined outside the sphere of economics proper. It was then the economist's task to accept this distribution, regardless of its quality, and show under what conditions consumer satisfaction would be maximized. Convenient as this assumption may be, it does affect the meaningfulness of the "maximum consumer welfare" proposition of a competitive economy. Take, for instance, the extreme case where income distribution is particularly lopsided. The richest two individuals in a society receive *all* the income. Taking the income distribution as given, and defining maximum social welfare as the position where neither of the two could be made any better off, while all the rest of society is heading for mass starvation, amounts to playing dangerous intellectual games.

In any event, the assumption of a *given* income distribution does not really allow one to take apart maximum consumer satisfaction without having to relate to questions of distribution. Rather, by assuming the prevailing distribution, we are implicitly making the value judgement that it is adequate. Once again we find a bias towards the status quo in matters of inequality. Consumer welfare is confounded with the welfare of the rich; consumer sovereignty is conveniently approximated by dollar sovereignty. Most textbooks work on this premise, taking the "solution" of the income distribution dilemma for granted. Students are then proudly introduced into the wonder world of curves, tangency points and elegant mathematical formulations and manipulations, to establish the doctrine that a competitive market economy will tend to secure economic bliss.

But there is a further problem which is generally "solved" by being ignored. If a certain state of the economy is Pareto optimal, then moving towards this state should be an improvement; otherwise, the Pareto definition of economic welfare would be of little use in guiding economic policy. If minimum wages are bad, we would expect the removal of minimum wages to be good; similarly with tariffs, price controls, rent controls and monopoly. But this is not so. Any change in these restrictions to free trade automatically involves changes in prices. Some labor will be made cheaper, some import goods cheaper, some rents more expensive, etc. Yet any *change* in prices will lead to a *change* in the distribution of income. Some laborers will get lower salaries, some consumers of imported coffee will be made poorer, some landlords richer, etc. The income distribution changes, even though salaries don't necessarily have to change. The money distribution of income may not be altered by removal of a tariff, but the *real* income distribution will always change as soon as we change one price.

The new "real" distribution of income will immediately define a new (and different) Pareto Optimum, and the new optimum is neither better nor worse than the old one; it is simply incomparable *unless* we want to compare the two alternative income distributions, something that the new welfare economics was set up to avoid in the first place. As an alternative argument look at it this way: the freeing of markets will tend to generate losers or victims! Abolishing of monopoly will hurt the monopolist, abolishing of tariffs on wheat, the domestic wheat producers, abolishing of rent controls, some low-income apartment dwellers. We help some members in society, but we *hurt* others in the process and Pareto would have to object. The problem, already discussed, is that we are not allowed to make personal comparisons of utility. In other words, we cannot tell if a losing monopolist loses more than the consumers benefiting from the lower price of his product. Monopolists and consumers are people, and we are not supposed to compare their respective pleasure or pain. This leads us into the last topic relating to the inapplicability and sterility of the Pareto Criterion.

The Compensation Principle

As we said earlier, one of the severe limitations of the Pareto Criterion is that it only recommends a move if such a change is in the interest of all parties. Yet in the real world, any change, no matter how beneficial to society at large, will generally have some victims. In order to deal with such situations, economists have advanced the compensation principle. It works as follows.

Take the example of a monopoly in the production of coal. Some mine owners have managed to corner the market and effectively kill competition for coal. As a result they fix prices according to what the market will bear, and coal prices climb sky high. Many poor people can't afford to heat their houses anymore. The repercussions for society are grave. Price fixing has replaced the free interplay of supply and demand. The economist will be quick to point out that this situation herewith violates the Pareto Criterion. On the other hand, restoration of competition through some anti-price-fixing legislation will hurt the mine owners. So what does the economist recommend?

Kaldor, back in 1939, proposed the following rule: If it were possible to restore competition and *compensate* the victims of the change (i.e., the mine owners) adequately, so that they are indifferent, and society, after making the compensation, is still better off, then competition ought to be restored.[6] Society gains while the mine owners don't lose. We have been able to move in accordance with the Pareto Criterion. Of course, compensation will actually have to be paid, otherwise the mine owners would be worse off in the competitive situation—and trampling their interests implies that their dissatisfaction is less important than society's gain in being able to purchase coal at a cheaper price. If we didn't compensate the victims, we would implicitly be comparing interpersonal utilities, something the new welfare economics attempts to avoid.

At first economists rejoiced at the new idea. Regardless of its practical problems* (i.e., how to locate all the victims and determine the appropriate compensation) it did at least seem to rescue the applicability of the Pareto Criterion in terms of pure theory. The economist's joy was shortlived, however. Only two years after Kaldor had published his refinement, another economist, Tibor Scitovsky, spoiled the show.[7] He asked, what if the prospective victims of a contemplated move, in

---

*Even George Stigler, an early proponent of the new welfare economics wrote, "Until the principle of recompensation becomes capable of realistic application it must necessarily appear to be little more than an analytical trick."[8]

our example the coal monopolists, find it in their interest to compensate (call it "bribe") the public just enough so as to induce them *not* to make the move? In such a situation, i.e., under maintenance of price-fixing, the mine owners would be better off, while society would be indifferent to restoration of competition. Now, price-fixing would be Pareto optimal.

It is perfectly conceivable to reach the following dilemma: Restoration of competition would improve the general welfare after monopolists have been bribed or compensated to accept the change voluntarily, while at the same time rich monopolists could bribe consumers to leave them alone, because for them the required compensation is less than what they expect to lose with the repeal of the price-fixing scheme. What we have in such a case is a contradiction. Competition is good and monopolist price-fixing is good, too. How could this happen? In the first case we have been able to establish the potentials for successful compensation with the income distribution (and income flows) under conditions of competition, relatively poor mine owners and enriched consumers. In the second change we have the prosperous mine monopolists successfully able to bribe the relatively poor consumers. It is always easier (i.e., cheaper) to bribe a person with little income than one with a high income.

To repeat, before we can say that restoration of competition increases general welfare, we must not only know that (through competition) income can be redistributed after prohibition of price-fixing, so as to make everybody better off, but also that it is not possible to improve welfare before restoration of competition simply by redistributing income. Hence, the potential of successful compensation hinges on income distribution. We can only separate maximum consumer satisfaction from the question of income distribution by defining an improvement in social welfare as one in which, for *every possible distribution of income* the change and necessary compensation make nobody worse off and at least one person better off. Situations with different income distributions are incomparable. Each distribution weighs (or adds up) individual utilities differently.

In our description of Pareto welfare economics, once again we have come full circle. The new welfare economics attempted to say something about maximum consumer welfare without value judgement or reference to income distribution or reliance on interpersonal comparisons of utility. Mark Blaug, otherwise known as an eloquent defender of mainstream economics, concludes that in terms of substantive content of the new welfare economics "very little survives once the taboo on interpersonal comparisons is imposed." Any quest for an ideal pricing criterion under such conditions "is doomed to failure." He concludes that Paretian welfare economics does succeed in "a stringent and completely positive definition of the social optimum;" the "practical relevance of this achievement for policy," on the other hand, he considers "nil."[9]

The upshot of all this is that the economist can't say very much about the desirability of tariffs, monopoly, minimum wage, or pollution control, without making interpersonal comparisons. For anybody familiar with the Harrod-Robbins debate this is nothing new, yet inspection of any textbook suggests that economists do prefer competition, free trade and free market prices. But sadly, they don't make a similar case for equality. It appears to us that as a prerequisite for any rehumanization of the science, we have to drop the fascination with the criterion advanced—more than 70 years ago—by Vilfredo Pareto. His idea has been overused and deserves a final resting place.

Human Dignity, at Last

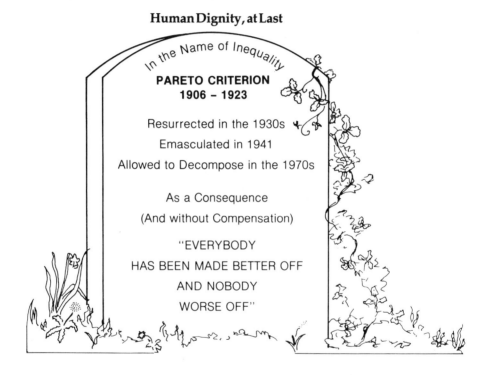

In the Name of Inequality

PARETO CRITERION
1906 – 1923

Resurrected in the 1930s

Emasculated in 1941

Allowed to Decompose in the 1970s

As a Consequence

(And without Compensation)

"EVERYBODY

HAS BEEN MADE BETTER OFF

AND NOBODY

WORSE OFF"

References

1. Pareto, Vilfredo. "Manual of Political Economy." 1906. In *Source Readings in Economic Thought*, edited by P. C. Newman, et al. New York: W. W. Norton, 1954, p. 481.

2. Easterlin, R. A. "Does Economic Growth Improve the Human Lot? Some Empirical Evidence." In *Nations and Households in Economic Growth: Essays in Honour of Moses Abramovitz*, edited by David Paul and Reder Melvin. New York: Academic Press, 1974, pp. 89–125.

3. Heilbroner, R. *Worldly Philosophers*. New York: Simon and Schuster, 1967, p. 47.

4. Heilbroner, R. *Worldly Philosophers*. New York: Simon and Schuster, 1967, p. 57.

5. Sichel, Werner, and Eckstein, Peter. *Basic Economic Concepts*. Chicago: Rand McNally, 1974, p. 403.

6. Kaldor, N. "Welfare Propositions and Inter-personal Comparisons of Utility." *The Economic Journal*. September 1939, pp. 549–52.

7. Scitovsky, T. "A Note on Welfare Propositions in Economics." *Review of Economic Studies*. November 1941.

8. Stigler, George. "The New Welfare Economics" in *American Economic Review*. January 1943, p. 357.

9. Blaug, Mark. *Economic Theory in Retrospect*. Homewood, Illinois: Irwin, 1962, p. 552.

Chapter Six

COMPETITION: DREAM OR NIGHTMARE?

We live in a society that is highly competitive. Our educational system is to a large degree based on competition as a motivating force. We prepare our children to go to school to meet that competition. In school we teach that one of the basic principles of evolution is survival of the fittest. On television we are fascinated by the drama of competitive sports. We compete for jobs, even for a mate, and we know that one of the mainstays of our economic system is competition. So it is all around us.

Being so steeped in competition, we are aware of some of its pitfalls—the fostering of aggression and insecurity, and the exacting of a certain toll in human well-being. But most of us believe that, in principle, competition is a good thing, and probably necessary.

Asked to justify the principle of the virtue of competition, we would probably turn to the science of economics. We know that for a long time economic theorists have developed the concept of competition, pointing out why it is essential for a healthy economy and, in turn, a healthy society. But, when we look closer at the development of the concept in economic theory, our belief that competition is a sound principle begins to be shaken.

This does not happen right away. Looking at Adam Smith and the other classical economists, we feel on reasonably comfortable ground. For one thing, the competition they talk about is familiar to most of us and seems to make sense, even if we have some slight moral misgivings. For the classicists, competition is a social ordering force, or at least an economic ordering force, very similar to Newtonian gravity in physics or astronomy. It consists of businessmen underselling each other, bringing down costs of production through innovations and organizational improvements, outbidding rivals in acquiring raw materials and labor, and so forth. A market consisting of two sellers was assumed to be as competitive as one with a hundred or a thousand sellers. In classical theory competition was to a large degree dynamic. Economic agents interacted and affected each other. Through this process the system developed and perfected itself over time.

But then comes the neoclassical revolution and the economics of Edgeworth, Jevons, Walras and Marshall. The dynamics of capital accumulation was replaced by the statics of resource allocation. The image of competition in economic theory underwent a corresponding change. Perhaps the neoclassicists were also responding to some of the observed consequences of economic competition, which were found to be less than desirable or ideal.

Now economists began talking about the condition called *perfect competition*, which would exist under the circumstances of a competitive equilibrium, something yet to occur. Under *these* conditions the consumer would be king. This ideal state of affairs did not necessarily apply to business behavior, as the classicists had described it. Competition was now seen as the existence of a large number of firms, or the absence of monopoly. It was an instance of market *structure*, not market behavior. Now the numbers of sellers counted.

Neoclassical economics erected a theoretical structure that described the beneficial effects of competition, if the present undesirable effects were just let alone to run their course. By allowing and not taking steps to eliminate the undesirable, you would come to the desirable—natural law, of course—letting economic nature work itself out. And since this ideal of competitive equilibrium was so close to the surface, the present economy might as well be described as if that were already the case.

THE MODEL OF PERFECT COMPETITION AND CONSUMER SOVEREIGNTY

Every economics textbook takes considerable space in describing and elaborating this model; it is the core of modern microeconomics' explaining the determination of relative prices (e.g., why cars cost more than motorcycles). What can explain the changing price difference? Faced with such puzzles, the economist draws conventional demand and supply diagrams, and in doing so implicitly assumes the existence of perfect competition.

We are talking about a world with so many small competitors that no one is capable of influencing the market price. Because of this, each firm is called a *price taker*. Each firm is faced with an unlimited demand for its product at the going price. As soon as it would charge more than the market price, it could not sell a single unit. It is the world of the small-scale farmer selling potatoes. If the price is above cost, there would be profits, but the profits are a fair return to the entrepreneur. If price would be above that fair return, other profit seekers would enter and this additional supply would force price down again to costs plus fair profits. If too many other firms enter, price will go down too much, wiping out the fair profit and so inducing entrepreneurs to leave that particular industry. If price does not even cover the costs of production, losses will *force* a more limited supply through bankruptcies. Bankruptcies and the diminished supply will cause prices to rise again until they just cover costs plus a fair profit margin. That is the competitive equilibrium. Everybody is struggling to make it, cutting costs wherever possible in order to survive, but nobody is a winner except the consumer, who gets what he or she wants at the lowest possible cost. Here is the basis for the concept of *consumer sovereignty*. It means the consumer is king. He dictates production. If consumers happen to like apples but dislike pears, the economy will produce apples but there will be no demand for pears and no profits for pear growers. The consumers may suddenly switch preferences and prefer pears. The economic system will adjust. Profit-maximizing farmers will not graft their apple trees with pears. The consumer gets what he wants and gets it at the lowest possible cost.

The economist's dream world of perfect competition is a world of profit maximizers struggling to satisfy the royal consumer. Competition is the big stick that enforces order and fair play. It is a self-policing world; no government intervention is necessary. It is a world of desirable laissez-faire, laissez aller which is ruled by Adam Smith's invisible hand. It is a world where mass-production economies are assumed away. It is a world where there can never be excessive profits, or unearned income. Everybody gets what he or she is worth in the marketplace. Profit-seeking employers will not be able to pay somebody less than what he or she is worth since the worker would—like any Economic Man—immediately seek out another employer, offering a higher net advantage. Competition may not produce an equal distribution but it will certainly produce a fair one. Everybody gets as much as he or she produces. Too bad for the blind, the elderly, the handicapped, but they are a small minority and could be taken care of separately by some charitable arrangements or some humanitarian government institution. It is a world of no economic power, nobody can extort the other; alternative opportunities always exist for escaping the power play. It is a world of no inflation, prices are flexible, always in line with costs. Some prices may rise temporarily, others fall. But there is no reason to suppose that all prices will persistently rise. What about unemployment? Not possible. Unemployment means simply that at the going wage there are more workers seeking a job than jobs are available. The wage is too high. Employers, in order to maximize profits, will rather hire the unemployed at a lower wage. Wages will drop until the labor market has restored equilibrium.

Even at this stage of the game consumer sovereignty has a big flaw. *What really counts is not the consumer's needs but his or her needs backed up by purchasing power.* Imagine an economy where only one single individual has all the money and all others have none. This is the case of the ultimate unequal income distribution. Who is king? Here it is our rich individual. The economy will produce what he or she desires. It would be producing different kinds of cars, fancy wines, swimming pools, airplanes, speed boats, private space ships, etc., while the rest of society is starving. Obviously, we should object that such an output mix is not optimal and not in the social interest, but it is what competition would produce given that particular income distribution. Therefore, the concept of consumer sovereignty should be renamed *dollar sovereignty* to be more correct.

What comes out of all this is that perfect competition is the modern economist's utopia. We have a smoothly functioning economy constantly geared to meet consumer wants at minimum costs; no unemployment, no inflation, no unfair distribution of income.

But there are some blemishes nevertheless, to which the economist refers as "market failures": Here we have some instances where the invisible hand breaks down. As a consequence, there is a rationale for a "visible hand" of government. Let us look at these "exceptions" to the general rule. They are pollution, public goods, and "natural" monopoly.

Enviromental Pollution as a
Market Failure

As we saw, competition forces firms to maximize profits in order to survive. Each entrepreneur will attempt to minimize his costs in the process. He will buy labor and raw materials as cheaply as possible; he will install the most profitable machinery and run the factory in the most efficient manner. What does he do with the waste products of his plants? The market will leave him little choice in this matter. Dispose of them as cheaply as possible. As a result, unabated gas and vapors will climb his smoke stacks and pollute the air. Solid or liquid waste products will most cheaply be disposed of by dumping them in the nearby river. Air and water pollution will result. The products will be cheaper for the consumer, but does he really gain? Not necessarily. The consumer ends up paying indirectly. The river in which he used to swim is declared unfit for such purposes. The water he used to drink has to be treated now and will cost more. The factories downstream will have to clean water if it is needed in pure form for production purposes. Fish and clams will become more scarce and expensive. Houses will have to be painted more often. Lung cancer and other respiratory diseases will have to be treated at an extra cost to the victims. It is conceivable that all these costs outweigh the gains from the cheaper product upstream. As a result the consumer is not necessarily well-served by the competition. He is no more the total king. He might have liked more swimming and more fish than he actually gets. With pollution we have the classic example of a *market externality*. Significant costs that eventually occur as a result of pollution do not enter a firm's cost account, so that market-type decision making ignores them. Now prices don't reflect actual costs, so how can the consumer choose intelligently? Corrective action must be taken.

A simple way to eliminate the problem is to legislate pollution away. Require industry to abate its effluents, and require car manufacturers to install emission control systems. If the laws are tough enough, the pollution problems will be solved. The visible hand of governmental law has corrected the deficiency. The ball game can now go on with the new set of rules. Competition regains its beauty. The invisible hand can operate again within the political restraints.

Economists do not like such a political solution. Instead, they advocate a different kind: *internalization* of the externalities, some sort of scheme whereby enterprises are charged a price by the public for the dumping of the waste and the price should reflect the cost to the environment that their waste inflicts.* It can be shown that such a procedure will *internalize* the previously "external costs" to the polluting enterprise. Consumers will be paying the real cost of products. Such a scheme will give the enterpreneurs an incentive voluntarily to avoid pollution, where feasible, in order to avoid the pollution charge. On the other hand, a polluter who cannot easily stop the effluence of polluting wastes will rather pay the (cheaper) cost of the damage. The very essence of the economics of pollution control is to show that, under this type of effluent charge approach, the environment can be cleaned up to the extent that the consumer wants it. More important, the job will be done in the cheapest possible way. In contrast, by political across-the-board treatment of all polluters, the same cleanup will be accomplished at a much higher cost.

Alternatively, the externality could also be internalized by a redefinition of property rights. If the polluting firm also *owned* the river and all its fish, or conversely, if the fisherman, etc., owned the firm, then the potential damage to the river would not be ignored. Here again the costs of pollution would be internalized.

But what matters for our purpose is that the problem of pollution can be corrected, one way or another; the consumer will regain sovereignty and the dream world of competition can persist undisturbed thereafter.

---

*It should be recalled that this "modern" approach to a social "vice" such as pollution was already outlined more than 450 years ago by Thomas More. Perhaps economists, given sufficient time, will "discover" some of the more essential points of his book.

Public Goods as a Market Failure

Imagine a neighborhood in a suburb. The question is whether or not to have street lamps on a 500-foot-long section of a residential road. Ten families would benefit. Let us assume that the electric company is willing to install and operate the necessary three lamp posts for $500. But each benefiting household would only be willing to spend $100 for the lights. Even if there are one hundred such households that would be benefited, nobody will order a street lamp. So, in a pure laissez-faire market, the consumers will be walking their street in the dark. But is this really what they want? Are they really king? The answer is no, because provision of street lighting would clearly make them better off. Each lantern will serve a large number of households. As long as more than five households gain, it is clearly in the interest of the households to have street lights installed. But there will only be demand for such lights if there is *collective action.* The households will have to get together and vote on whether or not street lights are in their interest. It will be necessary to order lights in a political decision, by legislation of some sort, and to finance the venture by pooling individual tax money. The moral of the story is that many goods are public, not private, by which we mean that they can be consumed simultaneously by many consumers; they can be shared. In a laissez-faire market system with no government, public goods will either not be produced at all or produced in insufficient amounts. It is here that we need government to provide us with defense systems, police protection, fire departments, preventive health services, education facilities, courts, roads, airports, public transportation, and the like.

But, as in the case of pollution, the problem can still be solved. We can democratically decide on the provision of these goods. After that we leave matters once more to the invisible hand. Instead of consumer sovereignty, we simply speak of citizen's sovereignty.

"Natural" Monopoly as a Market Failure

This is the case of ever-decreasing costs due to mass production. Economists realize that it may happen, but it is treated as an exception rather than the general rule. In some sectors of the economy technology is seen to operate in such a way that there can only be one seller. The prime example is the field of electrical utilities and the phone business. The more customers that can be plugged into an already existing system with all its overhead outlays, the more lucrative operations become. One company pulls ahead in this race, increases its lead, and before long takes over its former rivals. Leaving these matters to competition will inevitably (i.e., "naturally") produce monopoly and kill competition.

Traditionally, we have treated these public utilities separately. Legislative commissions, both at federal and state levels, have been set up to regulate such "natural" monopolists. The rates are so fixed that companies can recover their legitimate business costs and receive a fair profit. In the rate-fixing process, the key issues are: (1) what are the legitimate costs, (2) what is the fair assessment of a company's assets, and (3) what is a fair return on those assets? Traditionally the regulators, lacking inside information and expertise, have avoided the first question and concentrated on the other two. But there is a widespread sentiment that the company with highly paid, specialized lawyers and rate experts tends to win favorable settlements, for various reasons. As one result, utility rates keep going up. It is for this reason that few economists are happy with the functioning of public regulation. At the same time they recognize that the alternatives of unregulated private monopoly or outright nationalization are even less desirable. Regulating natural monopoly by special legislative commissions is hence tolerated as a necessary evil.

ALLOWING FOR MARKET POWER: FROM PERFECT COMPETITION TO "IMPERFECT COMPETITION"

We have just discussed three particular instances where mainstream economics and the model of perfect competition acknowledge that the market system may fail. These instances are seen as exceptions to the generally successful functioning of a system based on the model. The following development, however, is quite another matter, because it strikes the first blow at the *general* validity of the model.

The model of perfect competition was more and more strained by the increasing levels of concentration in most sectors of the country. Already in the early part of the twentieth century most markets in manufacturing and mining were dominated by a handful of giant firms doing most of the selling. For instance, U.S. Steel was born in 1901 by merging together nearly five hundred formerly independent steel manufacturers. Similarly, International Harvester, American Can, Standard Oil, International Business Machines, and virtually all of the companies now quoted on the New York Stock Exchange as "blue chip" stocks were created by merging many independents under one new name. In two or three decades following 1895 the economic structure changed from something resembling perfect competition to something resembling one dominant seller (monopoly) or a few large sellers (oligopoly). In the meantime, economists continued to preach the gospel of the small, perfectly competitive firm struggling for survival, similar to the economics of a small family farm.

It was only in the early 1930s that an alternative model of *imperfect competition* was developed simultaneously by the English economist, Joan Robinson, and the American, Edward Chamberlin.[1] No doubt these theoretical revisions recognizing the brute fact of market power constituted an important step towards a more realistic description of our modern industry. Yet the reader is warned not to take this revised model as a completely satisfactory description of reality. As we will show, there are too many flaws remaining to warrant such a status.

In essence, the Robinson–Chamberlin "revolution" amounted to allowing for "price-making" power of the monopolistic firm. Rather than having to "take" the prevailing market price and adjust output to it, the "less than perfectly competitive" firm could, within a range, choose the price at which it wanted to sell. In the extreme case of monopoly where only one firm was selling in a particular market, it was faced with the downward sloping demand curve of the entire market. It had the *choice* of either selling few goods at a high price or more goods at a lower price. For the first time, real choice could enter the price decision of the firm. (In perfect competition the entrepreneur is forced to sell at a given price; he is the prisoner of the market.)

For the sake of mathematical determinacy, Robinson and Chamberlin both continued to assume that the monopolist will maximize his short-run profits, just as the small competitor—for the sake of survival—was forced to do so. Since profits are maximized when there is the greatest difference between sales and costs, there is only one profit-maximizing price and output in the "given" demand curve facing the monopolist.

The essential flaws in the theory become apparent when we realize that it ignores the monopolist's ability to increase demand. The means to do this include successful advertising of a product, as well as designing a product with a shortened life expectancy. Also, economic theory does not appreciate the possibilities open to a monopolist who reduces cost by way of innovations. Innovations generally require large expenditures on research and development, money that the monopolist may obtain by overcharging the consumer. The struggling small competitor does not have this research capital. Granting such an argument, monopoly would suddenly seem to have certain desirable properties that are not found when there are many small competitors. But, as we have repeatedly stressed, the economist has shown little interest in innovations and other business decisions oriented towards the future (dynamic behavior). Instead, he is interested in the allocative (static) efficiency of competition. For the sake of mathematical determinacy it is convenient to assume given demands and given costs. The difference between sales and costs is profits. This is what the monopolist is after. No questions are asked by the economist about the effect of plans for the future, for growth, for market dominance—in fact, the ways in which real human beings operate in corporations, for better or worse.

Oligopoly as "Shared Monopoly"

What about oligopoly? What are the economics when we have a few important sellers in the market? The question is not merely academic, since statistics support that oligopoly is indeed the typical structure in U.S. industry. Research has shown that the average manufacturing industry is dominated by four to eight sellers. It was Chamberlin's prime contribution to demonstrate that a tight oligopoly will tend to behave as if it were a monopoly. In other words, the oligopolists simply share their monopoly. To illustrate, imagine light bulbs being produced by two firms, General Electric and Westinghouse. For simplicity we assume that each is of equal size and supplying one-half of the U.S. market. Each has production costs of five cents per light bulb. Will they price at five cents a bulb? Not if they could get more, and they can. If, according to GE, ten cents per light bulb seems in the (profit) interest of the industry, it will act as the *leader* and increase the price to the more profitable ten cents, expecting Westinghouse to follow. Westinghouse knows that if it doesn't follow suit its GE "price leader" will rescind the increase and go back to the original five-cent price. If Westinghouse agrees that both firms are better off selling at ten cents, it will follow suit and raise its price. What about fifteen cents a bulb? If the people of Westinghouse agree, the fifteen-cent price will be uniform, otherwise the price will hold at ten cents. Through such price searching, firms will attempt to find a mutually agreeable industry price. All members of the industry will be most satisfied with the price at that level; in other words, industry profits are maximized. Such an outcome is identical to that of monopoly. For the consumer there is no difference between the outcome of tight oligopoly and monopoly. In both situations the goods are seen to be overpriced and not produced in sufficient quantities. Moreover, in both cases will there be excessive profits.

A little reflection will suggest that the oligopoly theory outlined above suffers some of the same drawbacks as the theory of monopoly. It flatly assumes that the oligopolist is out to maximize profits, and that demands and costs are *given* or dictated by consumer preferences and the state of technology. Not surprisingly, modern economics' new child (the model of imperfect competition) has in the meantime been essentially repudiated by its own mother, Joan Robinson. In an article reviewing her contribution twenty years after its publication, she writes: "In my opinion, the greatest weakness of the *Economics of Imperfect Competition* is one which it shares with the class of economic theory to which it belongs—the failure to deal with time." And she concludes, "I have the impression that in the twenty years since the Chamberlin–Robinson duopoly first set up imperfectly monopolistic competition, a great deal of mental energy has been devoted to a theological discussion in whether an existing state of imperfect (or impure) competition is (a) beneficial, (b) harmless, (c) a necessary evil, or (d) an unnecessary evil, while an analysis of the causes and the consequences of the process of survival or decline of competition has hardly begun."[2]

Despite the flaws of oligopoly theory, it does demonstrate the possibility of the implicit coordination which can take place in an industry dominated by a few large sellers. Whether the common objective is maximum profits or something else, large corporations can accomplish the goal by this kind of Chamberlin-type tacit collusion. And they do so without risking persecution by the anti-trusters in the Justice Department. Such collusion needs no meetings in smoke-filled rooms, no signatures on illegal documents. Oligopolists can accomplish their non-competitive goals under virtual immunity from criminal indictments. But what works so well and so smoothly for tight oligopoly will not work when there are numerous sellers in a market. Then there is much less interdependence between sellers, and the task of successful coordination becomes considerably more arduous. Meetings or memos to establish the "conspiracy in restraint of trade" are typically unavoidable. Some kind of illegal contact is also necessary to discourage participants from breaking the rules of the game by seeking their own individual self-interest in the competitive market. It is in these markets that evidence of collusion can be found. To the antitrust division such conspirators are easy prey. To no one's surprise, we hear much more about price-fixing agreements being uncovered in the relatively competitive industries.

GALBRAITHIAN COMPETITION: THE CRUMBLING OF COMPETITIVE EQUILIBRIUM

The ability of oligopolistic rivals to agree on a best price through the procedure described by Chamberlin is the starting point of Galbraith's analysis of oligopolistic "competition." Yet the best price is no longer a short-run, profit-maximizing price. As a result, just about everything that neoclassical theorists have built up starts to crumble.

John Kenneth Galbraith maintains that the professional managers of our large corporations do not simply maximize short-run profits. Instead, the mature corporation will first attempt to keep stockholders from rebelling by providing them with a flow of acceptable minimum earnings. Having accomplished this "protective purpose," they will strive for growth, a goal which requires successful manipulation of consumer demand. Their primary tools are advertising and other sales-promotion techniques, or redesigning products to have a shortened life span. Large corporations participating in "shared monopoly" are not producing "too little," as the theory of monopoly would indicate, but "too much." Let Galbraith drive the point home in his own words:

> ☐ No point is better accepted by the neoclassical model than that the monopoly price is higher and the output smaller than is socially ideal. The public is the victim. Because of such exploitation, oligopoly is wicked.[3]

☐ Yet exploitation by modern oligopoly leads to no serious public outcry that production is too small or prices too high. The automobile industry, rubber industry, oil industry, soap industry, processed food industry, tobacco industry, and toxicants industry all fit precisely the pattern of oligopoly. All are held by neoclassical theory to maximize profits as would a monopoly. In all, comparative overdevelopment—as compared, for example, with housing, health care, urban transit—is regularly cited in complaint. Or the effects of their growth on air, water, countryside, health are held against them. Never—literally—is it suggested that their output is too small. Nor are their prices a major object of complaint. . . .

. . . The neoclassical model describes an ill that does not exist because it assumes a purpose that is not pursued. And proof lies in the fact that the ill it describes provokes no grave public complaint. It is inconceivable that the public could be universally exploited without being aware of it.[4]

With Galbraith, consumer sovereignty yields to the doctrine of *producers' sovereignty*. Now the large corporation is king in the economy. Whatever happens (decline of railroads, excessive pollution, lack of urban mass-transit systems, the continued use of non-returnable beverage containers) is not because the consumer wants it that way, but simply because powerful, large corporations prefer it that way: the public now serves the preferences of big business. The consumer has to be persuaded, and this is done by advertising. The government is persuaded through lobbying, campaign contributions, and the revolving-door relationship between jobs in Federal regulatory agencies and jobs in the corporations. The adoption of growth as a goal not only replaces its alternative, short-run profit maximization—and with it, consumer sovereignty—but also introduces dynamics into the competitive process, since growth is obviously a change over time.

Business decisions are made with an eye on the future. Massive advertising campaigns, labor-replacing innovations, mergers and acquisitions at home and abroad are pushed for the sake of company growth. The race is on for a share of tomorrow's market. Winners are rewarded with even more control over economic resources, i.e., more economic power. Successful managers pay themselves even more generous salaries. But for what? Have they been productive from a social point of view? It is not clear that the public benefits at all in this wild race for company growth. The consumer must choose among products that companies want to produce, all prices to include advertising and lobbying costs. The public will have to contend with more "technological unemployment" without the benefit of lower costs and prices. Small businessmen, farmers, artists, educators will increasingly lose their independence, bargaining power and economic subsistence. Growth-oriented big business prospers, the rest of society falters. And behind all this is the competitive race for maximum growth.

Competition as Warfare

Implicit in Galbraith's new perspective is the viewpoint of a competitive process leading towards the goal of market dominance rather than a static state of affairs. This leads to quite a different picture of what competition is.

From the new focus, competition changes into a race for the monopoly, and the competitive process resembles economic warfare. The market, far from its traditional function as a static allocator of resources, now takes on the function of a great contest, or battlefield. It is here where the great competitive drama is staged. Just as in a political war, there will be plenty of victims and casualties. There will be agony of defeat and simultaneous jubilation of winning. The end result of competition left to run its course will have to be monopoly for the winner, extinction for the losers. Similarly, competition, when seen dynamically rather than statically, far from ensuring the existence of a "competitive equilibrium," promotes the existence of either a permanent "dis-equilibrium," or a noncompetitive monopolistic victory.

We may well ask why, ever since Marshall, have economists been so fascinated with their stable world of "perfect competition," presumably lasting forever. The economist's model of perfect competition seems to contradict this analogy of warring armies, each seeking to gain monopoly. It is as if two armies were in a permanent deadlock, nobody loses, nobody wins—except perhaps the onlooking consumers who are supposed to gain from this stalemate. But the answer to the question has been suggested by what we hinted at earlier. Perfect competition is no competition at all, at least as the word implies interpersonal, or intercompany, awareness. In competition whatever I do will affect my competitor, either positively or negatively. But does it, in the theory of perfect competition? Clearly not. Each seller is so tiny that its influence is effectively zero on the market and on its "co-competitors." When one wheat farmer competes, he is indifferent to what his neighbor, another wheat farmer, does. He is not his competitor in the usual meaning of the word. Both are "competing" against impersonal forces, the market and the adversities of nature, etc. They can both be winners and losers in the process. There is no prize money to be distributed between the two. So perfect competition is stable because it is not real competition. Here we see again the influence of the mechanistic, Newtonian point of view. The forces that affect economic process are impersonal and "out there," as if we are talking about barometric pressure or gravity. The interpersonal nature of the real economic world is filtered out by the lenses of a still lingering nineteenth-century physics.

True economic competition occurs in a market where scale, or mass-production, economies can only accommodate up to ten or so large sellers. Therefore oligopolistic markets provide the fertile ground for the real competitive struggle. Each firm has an effect on its rivals. It will seek a strategy to maximize the likelihood of survival and eventual victory. The weaponry stored in the arsenal includes many devices, some legal and some illegal. A good summary of the multitude of various techniques can be found in the famous antitrust case against Rockefeller's Standard Oil Trust, where the defendant was convicted of monopolizing the production, transportation, refining and distribution of oil. It took a full fifty-seven pages of trial record merely to list all the various alleged offenses.[5] They included not only a host of means to gain an unfair advantage over smaller competitors, but also, more significantly, many ways to *inflict costs* on the rivals. Among the latter, the practices of exclusion, foreclosure of markets and raw materials, and predatory price cutting deserve special emphasis. In the final analysis, it was the evidence of predatory price cutting that persuaded the courts to pronounce the oil trust guilty of intent to monopolize. Predatory pricing means, literally, pricing to kill. Prices are temporarily dropped below cost in a regional market in order to get rid of a rival. The aggressive competitor seeking the monopoly will sell at a loss until the rival collapses. His own losses are financed through profits in other regional markets. As soon as the monopoly is assured, prices can be raised to lucrative levels. True, another capitalist could try to buy the bankrupt refinery and enter the race in a renewed challenge of the trust. Yet the prospect of another devastating price war will make him think twice and will, in any case, dissuade bankers from financing the risky venture. The economics of predatory pricing ultimately rest on such intimidation backed by a display of brute economic power. Through power and strategy the powerful become stronger and the less powerful become weaker. The implications are far-reaching, once we have introduced economic power (defined simply as command over economic resources) explicitly into the analysis: "competition becomes the race for the monopoly." That the consumer stands to gain from competition so defined is something that cannot be assumed. Indeed, as this chapter will attempt to demonstrate, the public can expect to be more harmed than helped by the net results of the competitive process.

The Comparison with Biological Competition What we have discussed so far is economic competition in relatively unifom (i.e., homogeneous) product markets such as steel, cement, flat glass, etc. These are the classic markets that the economists have been interested in and that provide the core of conventional (albeit static) analysis. Competition between firms is equivalent to the competition of species in biology and zoology.* And one of the first lessons we learn in those fields is that

---

*The idea of applying biological concepts of competition to economics has been elaborated in the most recent and unpublished manuscripts of Professor James Wilson. The following paragraphs are to a large extent based on his original work.

perfectly competing species (feeding on the identical source of inputs) will not co-exist for a long time. One will take over and drive the other to extinction. It is for this reason that we won't find pike and bass in the same mountain lake. Similarly, California anchovies have driven their perfect competitors, California sardines, to extinction. The fields of zoology and biology also teach the economist another lesson. There is an inherent strong propensity for perfectly competing species to avoid, wherever possible, the competitive struggle. Each species will, through inter-generational mutation, seek to find its own niche (i.e., a special protected place in the natural environment in which it will have a natural advantage and can successfully defend its survival). In biological equilibrium each species has its monopoly, and competition is relegated to the (more marginal) borderlines of overlapping territories.

Just like the various species in the animal kingdom, economic firms in the marketplace seek to avoid confrontation in the open battlefields of homogeneous product markets. Ask any businessperson how he or she competes with rivals and the answer will always stress the factors that make the product or service different, i.e., how it *does not* directly compete with the others. In order to secure survival, powerful competitors will seek their own niche by attempting to differentiate their product. This is usually accomplished successfully in marketing consumer goods. Products are "branded" and then heavily advertised as different and superior. Winston smokes fresher than any other cigarette. Only Coca Cola is the "real thing," etc. As long as skillful advertising can persuade the less-than-fully-informed consumer, each brand will have its own following of loyal buyers. American Motors has dominated in the sale of domestically built small automobiles with better-than-average fuel economy. It found a niche in which it could, at least for the moment, avoid the competition of its larger rivals.

In contrast, product differentiation works less well in the markets for raw materials and industrial goods. Here the buyers are typically well-informed corporate purchasing agents who cannot be easily led to believe that one company's cement is superior to another's. Competition is hard to avoid; there simply are no protection niches to enable survival. The only alternative to cutthroat competition is collusion, where once again the competitors provide for stability and survival by eliminating competition. The most common form of collusion among sellers is an agreement not to compete. It usually entails the fixing of a commonly agreeable price or the sharing or allocation of markets among the rivals. In Europe, such agreements are sanctioned by law and labeled *cartels*. They can be encountered in just about every industry. In the United States we have explicitly outlawed such noncompetitive "conspiracies in restraint of trade" by the Sherman Act passed in 1890. Yet, as already mentioned in our earlier discussion of shared monopoly, the large oligopolist can collude without risking criminal prosecution. Prices can be coordinated without an explicit agreement and so the FBI will search in vain for the necessary evidence to prosecute. The same does not hold true in markets that for technological reasons preclude large firms.* The classic example is the suppliers of building materials. There are many relatively small companies marketing plumbing supplies, concrete, cement, gypsum wallboard, plywood, etc. It is here that every year dozens of elaborate price-fixing schemes are uncovered. Both *The Wall Street Journal* and *Business Week* make no secrets about the prevalence of such illegal agreements.[6] Neither are we led to expect an imminent decline in such behavior, in spite of the higher criminal fines. In a recent report by *Business Week*, one vice-president of an indicted leading vending-machine company is quoted as saying, "I don't see an end to price fixing. People are people." In the same article we are told how an indicted owner of a paper-label company insists that price fixing will continue in his industry. "The last one blew up because there were too many people in on it. I don't know if my son, when he takes over the business, will be able to avoid discussion of prices. I never thought I'd be a felon, and you don't think of your son as having to make that choice. But it's always been done in this business, and there's no real way of ever being able to stop it—not through Congress, not the Justice Department. It may slow down for a few years. But it will always be there."[7] In other words, collusion, either tacit or overt, is a necessary evil, but only because mutual cutthroat competition is seen as an even greater threat to the survival of the competitor. Competition may be a desirable feature, both in nature and industry, but survival through avoiding competition has been equally stressed, both in the animal kingdom and in the real-world economy. It is no wonder that warlike confrontation among firms has been the exception rather than the rule in the business community.[8]

The Costs of Competition

In the economist's dream world of perfect (static) competition it is the very function of competition to induce efficiency. All inputs are allocated to goods and services in such a way that no resources are wasted with respect to consumer welfare, that is, in the production of the goods and services that consumers want. There are no costs of competition, only benefits.

Once we start looking at competition from the dynamic, or process-oriented, angle all this changes. Competition becomes inherently costly, and emerges as one of the prime sources of social waste. Let us briefly consider the issue of social waste.

---

*Similarly, tacit collusion does not work easily among doctors, lawyers and psychologists. Prices are fixed according to some professional schedule and any price competition through advertising, etc., is considered unethical.

What are some of the more obvious wastes intrinsic to competition? The answer lies in the process of *duplication* and mutual *cancellation* of efforts. In the economic sphere, duplication arises primarily in the dissemination of information and in the production and distribution of goods. Information gathering is particularly inefficient. Take the example of a manufacturer who is interested in acquiring a new machine in order to expand output. The manufacturer will be visited by sales representatives of the competing firms. Each salesrep will attempt to persuade the manufacturer that his or her machine is the best. In the process the rep will attempt to bias description of the product in an opportunistic way. Good salesmanship is, by its very nature, skillful distortion of information. The good points of the product are praised and emphasized, the weak points are omitted or de-emphasized. True, after having listened to all the alternative presentations, our manufacturer will have probably acquired enough information to make an informed decision concerning the most suitable brand, but at a certain price for the salesperson's services. The price of the machine selected will not only cover its production costs, but also the cost of selling it.

Assume there are six competing brands of similar quality but differing suitability for the manufacturer's particular needs. If all companies sell a similar number of machines it follows that every salesperson must make six expeditions to secure one order. The price of that one successful order will have to reflect the losses of the remaining five unsuccessful expeditions. The markup over production costs will have to cover these expenses. The manufacturer and ultimately the consumer will have to pick up the tab. But what the public loses, the seller does not gain. Most of it has been lost in the abortive effort. Any one of the six salesreps, if equally supplied with the records of all six companies, and if impartially related to all six, could have supplied the necessary information in a fraction of the time. The deliberate misrepresentation of relevant information, which is intrinsic to the competitive process, makes for unnecessary cost and social waste. How much more efficiently would the same task have been accomplished by a speedy visit to a standing, industry-wide exhibit with a permanent staff of one professional employee equipped with sufficient engineering knowledge and a cooperative, rather than a competitive, spirit.

A similar problem is involved in the advertising of consumer goods. How many pages of newsprint, how many hours of TV prime time, are necessary to adequately inform the consumer about the relative benefits of the products he intends to buy? Again, it is the very business of the skillful advertiser to disseminate half-truths, rather than the whole truth.

But it is not only in the provision of information that competition wastes resources. Whenever the production of goods involves common property rights, that is, resources owned simultaneously by more than just one producer, competition will do the job much more wastefully than it could be done through some cooperative agreement, or even by a monopolist. Take the classic example of the fishing industry. Each fisherman is out to beat his competitor. He will attempt to catch as many fish as quickly as possible out of the common pool. Given the modern technology with which he is equipped, the combined efforts of all fishermen may lead to over-fishing, i.e., the resource will not be able to renew itself sufficiently and the catch of every fisherman declines in spite of an increased effort. Clearly all fishermen would be better off to agree on some quota that would allow more optimal harvesting. Equivalent problems are encountered in the drilling for crude oil in large oilfields and in the hunting of wild animals. Of course it is for these very reasons that we have traditionally had government regulation of oil production, fishing, hunting, etc.

Duplication also arises in competitive research and development and in the composition of inventories of competing firms. A good illustration of the latter is the proliferation of automotive parts. Every car dealer will have to have access to some complete array of parts that service his particular brand of car. How much duplication could be saved if we had fewer brands, fewer model changes, fewer dealers. Economists proudly hail the greater magnitude of choice that competition produces, but the inherent cost is rarely, if ever, mentioned. Another example of everyday duplication can be encountered in the real-estate business. The seller of a house may appreciate the possibility of marketing his property through several agents, and of course he chooses to pay the resulting fees. But the buyer of the property would clearly be better off if he could make one trip to a single agent. The list of competitive waste due to duplication could go on forever, but the lesson should be sufficiently clear by now.

"Meeting competition," i.e., imitation of an aggressive move on one competitor by another, is synonymous with cancelling the initial benefits of the move. Yet competition compels all the parties involved to continue for defensive reasons with the now-useless new strategy. Standing on your toes will put you ahead of the crowd but only as long as the others don't react. Competition will soon have everybody on his or her toes, but everybody suffers and no one is better off than before. The international arms race, a tragically vivid example of the nightmare aspects of competition in general, and the cancellation effect in particular, comes immediately to mind. Economic resources have to be wasted in the production of new weapons although we know that the enemy has already been able to match them.

Meeting competition is, of course, just as prevalent in the non-military sector of the economy. Here, however, many competitive moves, although imitated by rivals, do benefit the consumer in the form of lower prices, better quality products, etc. The important exception to this rule pertains to the area of advertising. A company, if it wants to hold its market share, will have to match the advertising expenditures of its rival. But the higher expenditures on all sides will cancel each other, benefiting neither producer nor consumer. The costs of this expensive means of waging economic warfare are of course ultimately borne by the consumer. If this is so, why do companies advertise? The answer should be evident by now. It is because of competition, and competition alone. The most vivid illustration of the social waste of advertising comes from the cigarette industry. In the late 1960s millions and millions of dollars were spent by the six or seven rival companies, mainly through TV advertising. In 1970 Congress prohibited TV advertising altogether. What has happened to the sales picture in cigarettes? Not much, sales and market shares are pretty much what they were when the companies spent all that money for promoting their brands on the tube. Yet, it needed an Act of Congress to eliminate the millions of dollars' annual waste produced by the mutually cancelling effect of competition.

The costs of competition are not limited to the wasting of economic resources. For the humanistically oriented critic, there is a far more serious indictment against competition. Economic competition inflicts heavy costs on *human* resources. Competition can be seen to degrade human nature and promote social evils such as corruption and crime, and all that follow from them.

Competition and Corruption   It is a featured characteristic of a free-market economy that people are "induced" rather than coerced into action. Yet we often don't realize that the market's "inducements" are not easy to distinguish from bribes. Most economists have no qualms about using the two terms interchangeably when discussing how the market works as an allocator of resources. Both bribes and inducements employ the means of sufficiently high monetary incentives towards the goal of individual enrichment.

The market can and will bribe unwilling employees to work in Alaska, or overtime, or on Sundays, or on night shift, or in otherwise unpleasant working conditions. Students can be induced to choose a career that they otherwise would never have considered. Business people will want to sell just about anything to anybody as long as profits are right. Similarly, the consumer can be "bribed" to buy lower-quality goods or products of which there is a momentary surplus. Such consumer bribes are the very nature of close-out sales and other low-price promotions. In short, the market assumes that everybody has his or her price. It is supposed to be the beauty of the market and free competition that nobody is directly coerced to do anything against his or her will, yet we frequently fail to mention that force is replaced by market bribes, compulsion by some sort of corruption. We expect business persons to pursue their own self-interest, to leave no stone unturned in the search for lower costs and lower prices, and we rely on competition to accomplish just that. At the same time, we become outraged when *The Wall Street Journal* reports that United Fruit bribed a high official of the government of Honduras in order to avoid paying a banana tax.[9] Coal-mining companies will seek to keep down costs by avoiding legislation on strip mining, and they seem to operate with the understandable belief that the more generous the campaign contribution the less likely such legislation will pass. Similarly, the oil companies and airlines have a strong incentive to make friends in Congress to protect themselves from adverse legislation. Regardless of whether a particular monetary inducement is successful, corruption is nothing other than an unrecorded business expenditure to buy an intangible resource, such as government goodwill, that promises to have definite productivity.

Our equating of material incentives with the immoral act of bribery may appear to be overstated. After all, there is a formal difference between a bribe and a material incentive: the former benefits only the two parties to the agreement, while the latter also benefits society at large. When workers leave their families in order to double their incomes by working for an oil corporation on the Alaskan pipeline there is also a benefit to the oil consumer. But if the same oil-company representatives bribe Alaskan officials in order to secure special drilling rights, all the gain is limited to the corrupt parties. What Exxon gains, Shell and others lose; there is no social benefit. Yet, even granting this basic distinction, there is no distinction from the standpoint of the management of the oil company. In both cases the oil company offers a monetary premium in order to gain control over a profitable resource. In both cases the invisible hand of the marketplace works through the doctrines of self-interest and competition. Can we really expect management constantly to consider the social consequences of their decisions? Whatever the answer, it should be remembered that one of the primary advantages of a market economy is precisely the lack of concern of the economic agent over the social consequences of actions. Thus the market itself does not differentiate between moral material incentives and immoral bribes.

The clearest manifestation of the interlink between competition and corruption can be observed in the foreign sales of arms. The public got a glimpse behind the curtain through the Lockheed scandal. *The Wall Street Journal* reported that the Conference Board, an independent research organization financed primarily by American companies, had made a survey on the issue of corporate bribes in competition for overseas contracts. Leading executives of seventy-three United States corporations answered, and nearly half of them felt "companies should pay bribes and kickbacks overseas if such practices were a routine method of doing business in the host country." And about 25 percent of the executives conceded that bribes and kickbacks were a problem in their own industries, which included, besides military hardware, electronics, industrial equipment and pharmaceutical companies.[10] The prime rationale for corruption is competition. Only one foreign competitor need do it and everybody will be eager to emulate them. *It is through competition that corruption becomes compulsory.*

These developments have taken us a long way from what Adam Smith believed was the effect of competition. For him competition would serve to limit the inevitable selfishness and greed that did exist in economic agents. He did not really imagine that the force of competition could lead to a competition *in* selfishness and immorality.

COMPETITION AND COMMAND

We have pointed out in Chapter 3 how competition tends to interfere with the satisfaction of the basic needs of security and belongingness. As a result, competition promotes Economic Man, the self-centered individual, always insecure, who seems to pursue unlimited material wants. Similarly competition inhibits or even destroys human relationships; instead the impersonal dealings of the commercial market set the social tone.

Since the costs of competition, both in economic and human terms, are considerable, a logical alternative is to try to build an economic system that does away with competition. But competition also performs an important function, that of coordinator and regulator of individual acts. These are primary features of Adam Smith's invisible hand.

One traditional alternative to competition as a coordinating and regulating force in the economy has long been the centralized planning of a command economy. We will examine it further in Chapter 14, but some comments are in order here as we seek a solution to the problem of competition. A command economy consists of planning and having a state bureaucracy to implement and enforce the plans. Just as in the military, there is a chain of command from top to bottom. Power resides primarily with the top: the bottom reacts, rather than acts, to the top. Implicit in a command economy is the important notion that there is only one top, which is to say that planning is centralized. In this way the entire economy works like one big army. Decisions are coordinated by conscious planning, and individual behavior is regulated by explicit commands or government orders. Motivation comes from the desire for individual advancement to the sources of power and by fear of the consequences of disobeying orders. Historically, we have had a near-perfect example of a command economy in Stalinist Russia. But even in this post-Stalin era, the Soviet-type economies are still run primarily on the command principle.

Economists have tended to regard the principle of competition, with all its costs, when evaluated against the background of the command economy, as a superior social regulator and coordinator. For one thing, central planning has serious flaws with regard to the day-to-day operation of the economy, flaws which the Soviet economists are painfully aware of, and which have induced them to introduce more and more decentralization and competition into the decision-making process. This is manifested in the attempt to "reform" the Soviet economy, a process many feel will reach its ultimate conclusion in the removal of the annual plan and a switch over to so-called market socialism, as it is practiced today in several countries in Eastern Europe.

Besides these purely economic drawbacks, there are also the ever-present, serious political problems resulting from the lopsided distribution of power. As Stalin has so vividly demonstrated, the command economy can be easily used to exploit, and even exterminate, the masses at the bottom of the pyramid. We should note that a society arranged and run in hierarchical terms need not be as cruel and inhumane as was Stalinist Russia. There have been examples of benevolent command economies, such as pre-market societies. Yet even there competition eventually became the dominant system.

Our conclusion must be that from a humanistic standpoint *both* economic principles, competition or command, are essentially unacceptable. The problem with both of them can be summarized by the words *Economic Man*. Whether we are analyzing individual competition or central planning, we find an economic system that is based on the concept of Economic Man. Factory managers in the United States and the Soviet Union are both motivated, by their respective systems, to try to secure maximum bonuses. In both societies consumers attempt to enhance their lives by seeking material fulfillment. Both in competition and in a centralized economy of the Stalinist type there is a lack of basic security which induces fixation at the lower motivational levels. Similarly, in both societies there is inequality, either in wealth or in power, with each of these systems having a different mix of these two inequalities.

As long as we are talking about Economic Man, we are talking about a being that must be regulated and coordinated by either competition or central planning. If one dislikes competition the alternative is perhaps even more unacceptable central planning. There is no "third force." Human nature is seen to be typified by Economic Man, and he needs either competition or a command-giving bureaucracy in order to harmonize his decisions with the social interest. Both systems not only serve, but also *breed*, Economic Man. In either system most of the higher needs of human beings will be left unsatisfied, at least within the framework of the system.

It is clear then that to break out of the bind that these two alternatives pose we must part company with an economics that can see no further than a humanity driven by survival needs and self-interest.

When we abandon the philosophy of Economic Man we come upon new solutions and possibilities. In the dictionary, the origin of the word *compete* is found to be the Latin *competere*, which literally means "to seek together."

The virtue of competition is that it's supposedly the best way to serve the interests of the consumer. Since the producer is driven by self-interest, it is the presence of other similarly motivated producers which keeps him or her from charging too much or paying the employees too little, etc. In other words, competition keeps the producer "honest," and the public benefits as the result.

But competition is a double-edged sword, as Galbraith and others have tried to point out. It inevitably means warfare between competitors, each of whom has the natural goal of eliminating the others by beating them or, failing that, joining them. Thus competition, in the "atomistic" or Smithian sense, as a way to regulate the selfish passions in the public interest, was at best of only short-term effectiveness, probably within the historical phase of economic development of Smith's time.

For a more permanent and contemporary solution to directing the economic process towards the public interest, we need to provide the human touch to those features of economic and social systems which breed and reinforce Economic Man in the first place. The direction for this solution will be elaborated in Part III of the book. For now let us indicate the outlines.

We need an institutional arrangement that as far as possible guarantees physiological well-being for every member of society, regardless of what one does and what one believes. Without this guarantee there can be no overcoming of the survival instincts that breed competition. When we have such a guarantee, the higher needs of people—belongingness, self-esteem, and self-actualization—come to the forefront like plants beginning to grow out of the ground once the snow has melted away.

A second step involves the increasing application of the concepts of economic democracy and self-management. Here the idea of cooperation and harmony between individual interests is raised as a principle of organization within the firm. Now, in the workplace, the division between management and worker becomes increasingly indistinct, with a corresponding decrease in the previous disparities in pay scale. The whole principle of organizational hierarchy and pyramidal management structure, resembling the chain of command of an army, becomes replaced by organizational designs that look like networks of interacting wheels. Permanency in work task and in position become replaced by rotation. New motives and qualities come to the surface—group solidarity, mutual aid, self-worth, service to others, perfection. In this climate, competitive instincts are increasingly seen as a barrier to economic growth and development, because the material sphere and the personal sphere must now be run concurrently with each other, rather than in conflict. Incentives now tend to come out of the higher values, rather than monetary ones. In many ways, we already see these changes beginning in many areas of our economy. The foregoing still presupposes competition *between* firms. But now the predatory nature of this competition will be tempered by the new values of cooperation and harmony that prevail within the individual firm. All of this will enable the further development of a society, so that the higher values can evolve into the more mature motive of service.

The Producer and Consumer are Joined The centerpiece of the humanistic answer to competition is the cooperation between the producer and the consumer, so that the interests of the customer are served because he or she takes part in directing the productive process. Competition is no longer needed to serve the function. It is now done directly by consumers. No more are the producer and consumer seen as natural antagonists, each trying to get the better of the other. In the humanistic economy they are joined, and have a common interest. As an example, the producer and consumer cooperatives are two branches of a stream that are heading towards this natural confluence.

In this economy, overall social coordination is accomplished increasingly through planning on a community basis, instead of through competition or command. The successful development of these new forms depends upon an expansion of democratic processes at all levels of decision-making, not just in form but in practice. The change from a competitive philosophy to a cooperative one is not only a change in institutional arrangements but a change in spirit.

Just as Economic Man is directly related to competition, so the Humanistic Person is closely allied with cooperation. Each reinforces the other. In an advanced humanistic society individuals and groups will seek together in a way that bypasses the intrinsic costs and wastes of competition. The goal of economic activity will be the satisfaction of the highest human needs. The economist's dream of competition, in reality, bears too much resemblance to a nightmare. If we are to dream again, let it be a dream of cooperation.

References

1. Robinson, Joan. *Economics of Imperfect Competition.* London: Macmillan, 1933. Chamberlin, E. H. *Theory of Monopolistic Competition.* Cambridge: Harvard University Press, 1933.

2. Robinson, Joan. "Imperfect Competition Revisited." *Economic Journal.* September, 1953, pp. 590, 593.

3. Galbraith, J. K. *Economics and the Public Purpose.* New York: Signet, 1973, p. 115.

4. Galbraith, J. K. *Economics and the Public Purpose*. New York: Signet, 1973, p. 116.

5. See, for instance, Einhorn, A. H. and Smith, P. *Economic Aspects of Antitrust*. New York: Random House, 1968, Ch. 3.

6. "Busting a Trust." *The Wall Street Journal*. October 3, 1975, p. 1. "Price-Fixing: Crackdown Under Way." *Business Week*. June 2, 1975, p. 43.

7. "Price-Fixing: Crackdown Under Way." *Business Week*. June 2, 1975, p. 43.

8. An intriguing alternative thesis has been advanced by James Clifton (1974) that competition has not diminished since the classical period but, rather, has increased. But now competition takes on increasingly new, more highly developed forms that cannot be recognized within the classical framework, such as the rapid development of new products and new markets, and competition *within* the different dimensions of the giant firm for the investment dollar. Clifton, James. *Cambridge Journal of Economics*, 1977, 1, pp. 137–51.

9. *The Wall Street Journal*, September 21, 1973.

10. *The Wall Street Journal*, February 13, 1976.

Chapter Seven

FREEDOM OF CHOICE AND THE CHOICE OF FREEDOMS

INTRODUCTION

Freedom, like love or justice, is a beautiful word; it has traditionally stood for both the ends and means of economic or political activity. Few people are openly *against* freedom. History shows how people have again and again risked their very lives in defense of freedom. Almost all wars have been fought, one way or another, in the name of freedom or in the name of religion, and both sides typically feel that they are the virtuous defenders. We may wonder how this is possible, but the answer is that, just as religion may mean different things to different people, so does freedom.

FREEDOM IN ECONOMICS

It is quite curious that a discipline like economics, which traditionally has gone to great lengths to keep itself "positivistic" and "scientific," seems to have had few qualms about taking on such a value-laden abstraction as the concept of freedom. The explanation for this lies in modern economics' attempt to get away from the concept of utility. We will see that economists' discomfort with utility, for many of the reasons we have just pointed out, led them to seek refuge in the concept of freedom. But the binds that economists got into by trying to talk about utility have followed them as they moved into this new territory.

After becoming aware of the weaknesses of the concept of utility, as well as some of the embarrassing conclusions that seemed to follow from its related propositions, many economists decided that it was not utility at all that was at issue in people's market behavior. Instead it was concluded that market behavior only reveals to us an individual's *preferences*. There is nothing said about whether these preferences benefit the individual (increase their utility), only that this is what they prefer.

But economists knew full well that they could not let matters remain there. To do so would be to consign economics to the realm of pure aesthetics, as was pointed out by Harrod (Chapter 4). If economics is to have any relevance it needs to point out that something is good and something else is bad. In other words, it needs to be moral. Once again, this is the difference between a physical science and a social science. So in trying to let go of the value *utility*, economists grasped on to the value *freedom*. Economic freedom was defined as non-interference with an individual's market preference. The argument for the virtues of the market, and competition, is not that they are necessarily the means of maximizing utility, but that they are the means of providing the conditions of freedom. Free trade is a positivistic value, precisely because it is *free*.

However, it can be said that the use of the term freedom in this way does not at all get us around the problem of value judgements. The value judgements that are implied when we deal with the concepts of utility are just as necessary when we phrase the matter in terms of freedom. This arises because my "freedom" may be your imposition. I want to be free to play my stereo, but you want to be free not to hear it in your apartment. I want to be free to drive my car whenever I please, but you don't want me doing it when I've had too much to drink. General Motors wants to be free to sell any kind of car it wants, but I won't exist at all, let alone my freedom, if the thing is a death trap. Likewise, I do not want the drug companies to be free to sell me or anyone else a substance that will cause harm.

Defining Freedom as the Ability to Choose Without Coercion

Like any other glittering abstraction, the term *freedom* can be a smoke screen unless we understand that it has its limits, and that the determination of those limits is a matter of social or political judgement. Nevertheless, there are economists who believe that the term freedom *is* almost equivalent to the market system itself. One of the foremost spokespersons for this position is Milton Friedman. In his book *Capitalism and Freedom* he makes the point that any society has to choose a coordinator for its economic activity; the choice is then between command and coercion or the voluntary cooperation intrinsic to the market system. Market society coordinates without coercion, anybody can either take it or leave it. Milton Friedman attempts to illustrate the point by making the following argument:

☐ In its simplest form, such a society consists of a number of independent households—a collection of Robinson Crusoes, as it were. Each household uses the resources it controls to produce goods and services that it exchanges for goods and services produced by other households on terms mutually acceptable to the two parties to the bargain. It is thereby enabled to satisfy its wants indirectly by producing goods for its own immediate use. The incentive for adopting this indirect route is, of course, the increased product made possible by division of labor and specialization of function. Since the household always has the alternative of producing directly for itself, it need not enter into any exchange unless it benefits from it. Hence, no exchange will take place unless both parties do benefit from it. Cooperation is thereby achieved without coercion.[1]

In Friedman's household model, exchange is made to appear as true voluntary action, with the individual only entering into exchange if he or she stands to benefit. If he or she does not expect to benefit, then Friedman makes it appear that the household can either rely on, or turn back to, its own productive capacities, as if households today were little self-sufficient farms just waiting to be put to use supplying most of the essential needs of the family. From this perspective the family's exchange becomes merely a trading off of its productive surplus. A nice mythology.

Friedman realizes the artificiality of his simple model pitting self-sufficient traders against each other. Therefore, he goes on to introduce a more complex model in which the institutions of business firms and money are presented as intermediaries in the barter process. But, in spite of the greater complexity, Friedman proudly finds that coordination is still purely voluntary, i.e., freedom is not impaired in the world of a complex market economy. Once again, in Friedman's words:

☐ Despite the important role of enterprises and of money in our actual economy, and despite the numerous and complex problems they raise, the central characteristic of the market technique of achieving coordination is fully displayed in the simple exchange economy that contains neither enterprises nor money. As in that simple model, so in the complex enterprise and money-exchange economy, co-operation is strictly individual and voluntary *provided:* (a) that enterprises are private, so that the ultimate contracting parties are individuals and (b) that individuals are effectively free to enter or not to enter into any *particular* exchange so that every transaction is strictly voluntary.[2] (italics added)

The argument is herewith complete: the capitalist market economy of today not only produces goods and services but produces and distributes them in freedom as well. But is it really convincing? The careful reader may have noticed the basic flaw in the argument. We have italicized the word *particular* in this statement to show where Friedman gives the game away. In the simple model described by Friedman he talks about households having the option of entering or not entering into exchange *at all*, but here as he begins to discuss the modern economy he is compelled to talk about not entering into a *particular* exchange. Friedman, without warning or mention, has changed the entire logic of the argument by adding this word. It is clear that most of us are forced to enter into one particular exchange or another. My range of choice in purchasing is determined by what is available in the market, what the market allows. I have very little freedom beyond the market, and within it my choices are, of course, governed by my income.

Since, for Friedman, the operation of the competitive market is the essence of freedom, any government involvement in the market is the antithesis of freedom.

□ Viewed as a means to the end of political freedom, economic arrangements are important because of their effect on the concentration or dispersal of power. The kind of economic organization that provides economic freedom directly, namely, competitive capitalism, also promotes political freedom because it separates economic power from political power and in this way enables the one to offset the other.

Historical evidence speaks with a single voice on the relation between political freedom and a free market. I know of no example in time or place of a society that has been marked by a large measure of political freedom, and that has not also used something comparable to a free market to organize the bulk of economic activity.[3]

There are many who find plenty of problems with such a point of view. John Kenneth Galbraith, for example, writes:

□ The instinct which warns of danger in this association of economic and public power is sound. . . . But conservatives have looked in the wrong direction for the danger. They have feared that the state might reach out and destroy the vigorous, money-making entrepreneur. They have not noticed that, all the while, the successors to the entrepreneur were uniting themselves ever more closely with the state and rejoicing in the result.

The danger to liberty lies in the subordination of belief to the needs of the industrial system.[4]

Unlike Friedman, he contends that in a competitive capitalist society economic power and political power are more allied than separate and offsetting. Consider for example the news report in the mid 1970s about the huge financial contributions from corporations to political candidates. The story points up an increasingly alarming fuzziness in the traditional distinction between private business and state.

The Alliance Between Government and Economic Power: Lobbying

This alliance does not just function through illegal channels, as alluded to in Chapter 6. It is institutionally established in the Congressional lobbying system, and is revealed in the revolving-door interchange that operates between the government regulatory agencies (such as the Federal Trade Commission and the Federal Energy Association, etc.) and the industries they are supposed to regulate. In a 1976 study by Common Cause—itself a lobby—it was shown that one-half of all federal regulators shuttle between jobs in the government and in the same private sector their agencies regulate.[5] These ties between government regulators and industry show up in the sources of influence on government activity. For instance, logs kept by the Federal Energy Association for a six-month period showed that 80 to 90 percent of the top officials' contacts and communications with outside interests were with the energy industry, and "only a scant 6 percent" were with non-industry interests such as consumer and environmental groups.[6]

Common Cause, as we mentioned, is in the unusual position of being a public-interest lobby. It was created by a former cabinet member in recognition of the overwhelming influence that private-interest lobbying groups have on government. It is the largest of the public-interest lobbies. Therefore, it is enlightening to compare its size to the total Washington lobbying activity. According to a 1975 estimate, it spent in its lobbying efforts 1/10 of 1 percent of the estimated one billion dollars spent on lobbying in a year. Just one private-interest lobby alone outspent Common Cause by over 25 percent, and had over double the number of staff.[7] A recent example of the power of business lobbying was the defeat of the Consumer Protection Act in 1978. This was an act designed to offset the power of large economic interests in the various federal regulatory agencies, by having the interests of consumers also be represented before these agencies. The Act had been supported by a full array of consumer and public-interest groups for many years. For three years prior to 1978 such an act had handily passed Congress, only to be vetoed by two unsympathetic presidents. In 1978, under a president who supported the Act and said he would pass it, the Act was defeated in Congress. The reason: Large corporate interests through a massive lobbying campaign were now able to get Congress to vote against the bill. *The Christian Science Monitor* headlined this, and other related Congressional actions, under the words, "Lawmakers talk 'consumer rights,' but industry wins key vote."[8]

The standard textbook justification for lobbying is to picture it as an "informal third house of Congress," in which economic interests can be represented, in addition to the usual popular and geographical representation in the other branches of government.[9] But what happens when most of the finances for a Congressional race come, not from the citizens of the particular district, but from nationally organized economic interest groups? Recent trends in campaign funding point out that "funds from outside interests overshadow local contributions."[10] This informal third house of Congress increasingly must be seen as representing one of the most powerful elements in the total political process.

Lobbying: The Great Loophole   The existence of lobbying comes about through an interpretation of the First Amendment in the Bill of Rights which states that people have the right "to assemble, and to petition the government for a redress of grievances." When Jefferson put forth the Bill of Rights he did so to protect the rights of individuals from the powers of the federal government, which was identified with powerful commercial and financial interests. Among the Federalists (those who supported a strong federal government), "was the almost unanimous opinion," according to the historians, Charles and Mary Beard, "that democracy was a dangerous thing, to be restrained, not encouraged, by the Constitution, to be given as little voice as possible in the new system, to be hampered by checks and balances." Gerry declared that "the evil the country had experienced flowed from the 'excess of democracy' . . . Arguing in favor of a life term for Senators, Hamilton explained that 'all communities divide themselves into the few and the many. The first are rich and well-born and the other, the mass of the people who seldom judge or determine right.' "[11]

The great loophole occurred, which Jefferson certainly did not foresee, when corporations were granted the legal status of individuals, thus being able to take advantage of the Bill of Rights. The effect of this "personification of the corporation" is described by Thurman Arnold, former Attorney General under Roosevelt. "The ideal that a great corporation is endowed with the rights and prerogatives of a free individual is as essential to the acceptance of corporate rule in temporal affairs as was the ideal of the divine right of kings in an earlier day. . . . So long as men instinctively thought of these great organizations as individuals, the emotional analogies of home and freedom and all the other trappings of 'rugged individualism' became their most potent protection." As a result of this, Jefferson's intent with the Bill of Rights was undermined, ". . . the great corporation actually worked to monopolize completely the mantle of protection designed for the individual."[12]

So the Bill of Rights became an entryway for the institution of corporate lobbying, in which vested economic interests could exert a powerful influence on legislation. And it also seems to have an effect on the economic status of the people who make up our legislative bodies. The Senate has been referred to as a "Rich Man's Club." Out of the one hundred Senators in the 1976 Senate, twenty-two were millionaires, and a few others were well on their way. In the general population, whom the Senators are supposed to represent, .03 percent are millionaires, or, one person in every three thousand. We might add that in 1977 there was not one woman in the Senate. So at the top lawmaking level a very exclusive strata of the population (male millionaires) are extremely well-represented. [13]

The reason for this connection between government and economic interests is intrinsic to the nature of our economic system. As

Friedman himself has said, one of the functions of the government in a free-market system is to "foster competitive markets." In the United States the government enforces the complex body of antitrust laws for this purpose. The maintenance of a competitive market system or, in any event, the *attempt* to maintain one requires the continual and active involvement of government regulation. Left to itself, a competitive market will naturally drift towards monopoly or collusion, and there is even doubt that tough enforcement of our present antitrust laws can significantly arrest that tendency. The fact that the government must be actively involved in the modern corporate economy implies that concentrated economic interests cannot be indifferent to what the government is doing, and therefore seek to influence it as much as possible. As a matter of fact, all economic and social groups in any society try to influence the government towards their own interests.

Economic power presents us with a dilemma to which neither the absence nor presence of a strong government is the answer. To see the answer in only one or the other of these alternatives is to court disaster. Rather, we believe, the answer lies in what *kind* of government there is—what are its overall goals, purposes, and values. Another way to put this is, whose interests are most effectively represented by that government? If it is the interests of the economically powerful, then that government is suspect. If it is the interests of the economically disadvantaged, then that government is welcomed.

The question may be raised, as a result of our lobbying discussion, how can a government be anything else than the representative of the interests of the economically powerful? For the briefest answer we state the word *democracy*, and for a more extended answer we refer the reader to Chapter 9, particularly the section entitled, *The Evolution of Democracy: A Paradox*.

Freedom and Government

Friedman's second point, on the historical relation between political freedom and the competitive market system, is only one reading of history. Other writers, even those supporting mainstream capitalism, see it differently. One such is Paul Samuelson. (Here we are pitting one Nobel Prize winner against another!) Samuelson believes that the free-market system, and political or personal freedom, are two independent issues:

> □ A mixed economy in a society where people are by custom *tolerant* of differences in opinion may provide greater personal freedom and security of expression than does a purer price economy where people are less tolerant. Thus, in Scandinavia and Great Britain civil servants have, in fact, not lost their jobs when parties with a new philosophy come into power. In 1953, the Eisenhower Administration "cleaned house" in many government departments for reasons unconnected with McCarthyism. In

1951, when the Tories came to power, they deliberately recruited Fabian socialists to the civil service! Business freedoms may be fewer in those countries, but an ex-Communist probably meets with more tolerance from employers there.

This raises a larger question. Why should there be a perverse empirical relation between the degree to which public opinion is, in fact, tolerant and the degree to which it relies on free markets? In our history, the days of most rugged individualism—the Gilded Age and the 1920s—seem to have been the ages least tolerant of dissenting opinion.[14]

And then a little later he points this out: "For years libertarians have been challenged to explain what appears to most observers to be the greater political freedoms and tolerances that prevail in Scandinavia than in America. In Norway, a professor may be a communist; a communist may sit by right on the board of the Central Bank or as an alternate board member. The BBC and Scandinavian airwaves seem, if anything, more catholic in their welcome to speakers of divergent views than was true in McCarthy America or is true now. In 1939, I was told that none of this would last; active government economic policy had to result in loss of civil liberties and personal freedom. One still waits."[15]

Friedman, as spokesman of the libertarian conservatives, equates freedom with *absence of coercion*. This implies that freedom already exists in society in its complete form, and can only be limited by government. Why does an economist like Friedman appear to be so pessimistic about the possibilities of government? At one point in *Capitalism and Freedom* he says, "Underlying most arguments against the free market is a lack of belief in freedom itself."[16] This must appear to be true if one equates freedom with the free market, as Friedman does. But we would like to turn Friedman's phrase around: underlying most arguments against government is a lack of belief in democracy. In a democratic society the *government* operates democratically, if it is properly representative of the public. Does the libertarian believe that this is not possible? If so, then the libertarian point of view becomes a philosophy of cynicism.

What *is* government? We would like to put forth an extremely simple definition: Government is the means by which people in a society organize their activities. What this definition points out is that government is necessary, and always with us. The absence of government is chaos.

The absence of government is not anarchism. Anarchism refers to a society that is ordered, and has a diminished need for centralized authority. The order comes from the evolved capacities of people to regulate their affairs. It is an easy and natural order, rather than a forced or coerced order as in the German *ordnung* ("law and order"). In this sense even anarchism is not a society without government, but a society in which the regulating and organizing functions have been increasingly assumed by each individual. From this perspective, *anarchism, democracy* and *decentralization* are all words that ultimately point to the same goal. The absence of coercion that Friedman talks about either goes to *ordnung*, as in fascism, or to chaos, but not to freedom. It certainly is not anarchism in the sense of being an evolved social organization. [17]

Materialistic Freedom and the "Debt Trap"

There is another aspect of freedom that we would like to discuss that, while not part of Friedman's presentation, is implicit in the radical market economics that he espouses. Here freedom is equated with range of choices in the market; the more goods available, the more freedom. This concept of freedom underlies the wry expression that "the best answer to The Communist Manifesto is the Sears, Roebuck Catalog." While this statement is put forth with a touch of humor, it is still too literally accepted for comfort.

The problem with defining freedom in terms of available market choice is its blatant materialism. From the materialistic perspective, the more one can buy, the freer one is. Certainly many hope to accumulate enough money to be able to buy their "freedom." This freedom means being able to own a car, a snowmobile, or a quadraphonic stereo, or to take a trip to Europe, etc. From this perspective the more one has available and the more one can afford what's available the more one is considered to be free. Though there are other problems with this point of view, one of the most painful things about it at the humanistic level is that too few people have the money to taste this kind of freedom. The reason for this is economic inequality. New products are geared to those with enough excess income to afford them, but this is a minority. The new products keep spilling out of the research and development centers, and they are always some degree beyond the reach of a significant majority of the population. If we really want what is glitteringly displayed before us, we are faced with the experiences of deprivation and insufficiency. The gap of relative poverty never closes.

Thus, borrowing looms up as the great answer. A compelling, market-stimulated logic insinuates itself—if money is freedom, and money can be borrowed, then freedom can be borrowed.

This argument appeals to more and more people, since we find that consumer debt has been dramatically increasing over the years. This is shown in the data of Table 7.1

A study of the Morgan Guaranty Trust Company has found that this consumer debt is rising faster than after-tax personal income. [18] Let us see what this may mean in practical terms.

We boast that even our poorest people have the "freedom" that our affluent society brings. In the wild 1970s, in households with annual incomes of under $5000, we find the following: 82 percent have

TABLE 7.1 CONSUMER CREDIT IN THE UNITED STATES, 1929–75

Year	Consumer credit (in billion $)	Consumer expenditures (in billion $)	Consumer credit as proportion of consumption expenditures
1975	198.5	973	20.3%
1970	127.2	617.6	20.5%
1960	56.0	328.2	17.1%
1950	20.8	192.0	10.8%
1929	7.6	79.0	9.6%

Source: *Federal Reserve Bulletin*

refrigerators, 80 percent have one or more television sets, 70 percent have one or more cars, 62 percent have washing machines, 45 percent have air conditioners, and so on. One textbook refers to this as the "Paradox of Poverty."[19]

But the paradox is explained by the buildup of debt. One more set of figures will illustrate this. Surveys on consumer wealth show that the poorest 11 percent of American households owe as much as, or more than, they have; in other words they have a *negative* net worth. They owe more than they own in personal belongings and financial assets. The next poorest 5 percent have a zero net worth. Altogether one quarter of our households have an individual net worth of less than a thousand dollars.[20] It is therefore not a big exaggeration to say that the bulk of our families in poverty *own* nothing: Their TVs, cars refrigerators, etc., typically belong to some creditor. The argument that freedom can be borrowed runs into a contradiction. Certainly, being in debt cannot be freedom. In many ways it's the opposite. If we define wealth as freedom, then negative wealth is negative freedom.

The contradiction hinges on the issue of time, and once again we find this dimension is a critical one in economic matters. We borrow in the present and pay off in the future. This is the "buy now—pay later" theme that is trumpeted in our culture. If we accept for the moment that money is freedom, going into debt means that we gain some freedom in the present by giving up freedom in the future. Borrowing money will expand a person's present options at the cost of reducing future options. From a humanistic perspective, this act is decidedly a step away from freedom. Any act that provides choice in the present at the cost of limiting choice in the future is an act leading toward bondage. Here is the critical reason: An act that is free, in any meaningful sense, is an act that opens up one's future rather than forecloses it. A present act that is really an act of freedom is one that is consistent and in harmony with freedom in the future. With this principle in mind we can see why consumer debt is ultimately a limiting of freedom, rather than an expansion of it. When we take on a debt for the purpose of more present consumption we mortgage our future, and when we mortgage our future we are mortgaging our freedom.

We said that the equating of money with freedom was a trap, and that the debt issue is one way of showing why this is so. Third World countries who have gone into debt in an attempt to develop their economies have become very familiar with what they call "the debt trap." Being in a trap is, precisely, being unfree.

HUMANISTIC FREEDOM: THE ABILITY TO SATISFY ONE'S NEEDS

True growth from a humanistic perspective is not only, or even necessarily, growth in quantity or wealth, but growth in quality. From the vantage point of humanistic psychology this is growth through the hierarchy of human needs and values. Growth in this sense requires open options in the future, because it is in the future that we may actualize our potentialities. Anything we do that limits our future is something that directly limits our freedom, because it limits our ability to grow, in the humanistic sense. This also follows directly from what Herbert J. Muller says about freedom. (Muller is an historian who is writing a three-volume history of freedom). For him, "A person is free to the extent that he has the capacity, the opportunity, and the incentive to give expression to what is in him and to develop his potentialities."[21] Economic Man hardly fits this description.

Humanistic freedom is quite different from the notion that freedom is equivalent with the range of things on which you can spend your money. Humanism says that freedom is more a matter of the Self, the inner person, rather than of the ego and its possessions, more a thing of the soul than the pocketbook. It is a state of being rather than a state of having. This means that the *way* we live, rather than our standard of living, determines our freedom. Ironically, as we indicated in Chapter 4, the GNP growth of our economy has in important ways curtailed our freedom rather than expanded it. The protection of nature—of our woodlands, lakes and streams—of quiet, of peacefulness, of social harmony and equality is more important to our experience of freedom, in any real sense, than the addition of a new motorized vehicle to the GM product line, or the supersonic transport plane to our transportation "options," or some such similar new technological plaything. Paradoxically, any action to curtail the crumbling away of the quality of life tends to necessitate government action through appropriate enforcement of the relevant legislation. And with this we run headlong into the concept of freedom that Friedman advocates, which is the absence of government action. So we can see that different definitions of freedom may contradict each other. It becomes clear that humanistic freedom may constitute libertarian coercion.

The Road to Humanistic Freedom

Applying Maslow's hierarchy of basic needs, true freedom is only possible if we can assume the basic freedoms of survival and security, both of which constitute the philosophical foundation of the European welfare state to be discussed in Chapter 11. These basic freedoms should be available, regardless of whether one is employed or not. Without this fundamental guarantee there is no real freedom, as we shall soon see.

The next step is the freedom to have meaningful work. This means a full-employment policy, and democracy in the work-place, or self-management.

CONCLUSION: FREEDOM WITH GOVERNMENT

We feel that the matter is clear. Freedom is the opportunity to grow. In the economic sphere this does not translate into the right to grow rich, but into the freedom from the fear of destitution, as well as the reduction of necessary work to be replaced by creative work allowing inner growth.

Social changes in the direction of the freedoms we are now discussing cannot be accomplished without institutional change, and this means government policy. We will discuss this further in Part III. It's important to recognize that the provision of freedom in the humanistic sense involves social decisions that can only be exercised through the political process. Indeed, that is what the political process is for. Thus, standing Friedman on his head, we don't see legislative action as contradicting freedom, but as necessary for it. To a humanist the issue is not government or the absence of government, but democratic and socially just government. In the absence of democratic government sheer economic power rules the day. Feudalism may have been charming, but it was never freedom.

References

1. Friedman, Milton. *Capitalism and Freedom*. Chicago: University of Chicago Press, 1962, p. 13.

2. Friedman, Milton. *Capitalism and Freedom*. Chicago: University of Chicago Press, 1962, p. 14.

3. Friedman, Milton. *Capitalism and Freedom*. Chicago: University of Chicago Press, 1962, p. 9.

4. Galbraith, John Kenneth. *The New Industrial State*. New York: Signet, 1960, p. 404.

5. "Study Finds Financial Conflict in Bureaucracy" in *Christian Science Monitor*, October 21, 1976.

6. Lobbying. Four articles by Peter Stuart. *Christian Science Monitor,* October 8, 9, 10, and 14, 1975.

7. Lobbying. Four articles by Peter Stuart. *Christian Science Monitor,* October 8, 9, 10, and 14, 1975.

8. *Christian Science Monitor,* March 7, 1978.

9. Burns, James M. and Peltason, J. W. *Government by the People.* 4th ed. New Jersey: Prentice-Hall, p. 312.

10. *Christian Science Monitor,* November 11, 1974, Ch. 9.*

11. Beard, Charles A. and Mary R. *The Rise of American Civilization.* Vol. 1. New York: Macmillan, 1931, pp. 315-16.

12. Arnold, Thurman. *The Folklore of Capitalism.* New Haven: Yale University Press, 1937, pp. 189-91.

13. *Christian Science Monitor,* January 28, 1978.

14. Samuelson, P., "Personal Freedom and Economic Freedoms in the Mixed Economy" in *The Business Establishment,* edited by E. Cheit. New York: Wiley, 1964, p. 218.

15. Samuelson, P., "Personal Freedom and Economic Freedoms in the Mixed Economy" in *The Business Establishment,* edited by E. Cheit. New York: Wiley, 1964, p. 227.

16. Friedman, Milton. *Capitalism and Freedom.* Chicago: University of Chicago Press, 1962, p. 15.

17. Read, Herbert. *Anarchy and Order.* Boston: Beacon Press, 1971.

18. *Christian Science Monitor,* April 16, 1975.

19. Spencer, Milton H. *Contemporary Economics.* New York: Worth, 1971, p. 518.

20. *Survey of Consumer Finances.* Federal Reserve Bulletin, 1953, p. 151. As far as we know this is the most recent study.

21. Muller, H.J. *Freedom in the Western World.* New York: Harper and Row, 1963, p. viii.

---

*Also see "Harnessing the PAC Bomb." *The Wall Street Journal,* Dec. 4, 1978.

Chapter Eight

WORK: THE UTILITY OF A DISUTILITY

INTRODUCTION

We now turn to one of the most important topics in economics: work. Ironically, work occupies only a peripheral place in most economics textbooks. To the extent that it is discussed, it is referred to as "labor," and labor, in turn, is seen as a "factor of production." This is another comment on the values of contemporary economics.

An official step in this country to compensate for the lack of sufficient professional attention that the issue of work has received was a large study conducted by the Department of Health, Education, and Welfare (HEW) called *Work in America*. In a number of ways this is a positive and humanistic document. It seems that the very process of thinking about and examining work naturally brings out humanistic tendencies. In contrast to this, the usual approach of putting the issues of production and economic growth in the forefront seems to run in directions that are abstract, mechanistic, and less tied to the lives and needs of people.

In fact, it is the very humanness of work that the HEW study points out:

> ☐ To the archaeologist digging under the equatorial sun for remains of earliest man, the nearby presence of primitive tools is his surest sign that the skull fragment he finds is that of a human ancestor, and not that of an ape.[1]

Next, the study goes on to try to define work. The first and most immediate definition is that *work is employment for pay*. This is a concrete and down-to-earth definition, an obvious starting point. But it is inadequate. We do many things without pay that we would still like to consider work. Housework is perhaps the most prominent example.

And what about studying? Or planting a garden? Or fixing the car? Or painting a picture? So the study comes up with another definition: *work is an activity that produces something of value.*

THE TWO NECESSITIES

What these two different definitions say is that work meets two different necessities. The first necessity is to keep oneself alive; this is why we need to be paid. The second necessity is to grow, to self-actualize. From a humanistic standpoint work needs to fulfill both of these necessities or, to put it slightly differently, work is necessary for two reasons. When we look at these two necessities from the standpoint of Maslow's hierarchy of needs we can recognize that the first necessity for work corresponds to the lower needs, especially the physiological; we work in order to eat. The second necessity corresponds to the higher needs; we work in order to actualize our human potential.

Therefore let us state again that it is desirable to eliminate as much as possible of the first necessity, needing to work in order to survive. This is a form of freedom. But, and here is the critical distinction, it is detrimental to eliminate the second necessity, which would mean not having the means or opportunity to grow and fulfill one's potential. As a social policy we would like work to be able to meet the second necessity, and not *have to* meet the first necessity. Albert Camus, the French humanist and existentialist, catches this principle when he says, "Without work, all life goes rotten. But when work is soulless, life stifles and dies."[2]

MAINSTREAM ECONOMICS AND WORK

One of the greatest problems with economics is that when it *does* talk about work it only deals with the first necessity. It sees work only as a means to a livelihood. Work is seen as an *input* into the economic system—a factor of production, along with resources and capital—that enables people or households to consume goods and services. Work is seen strictly as a means, both towards consumption and leisure, but never as an end. It is a "necessary evil."

The necessary-evil quality of work reveals itself from several vantage points. From that of business, work, or the need for workers, it is a cost. Therefore the fewer workers needed, the better. From the vantage point of the worker, work is seen as a *disutility*. It is viewed as an unpleasant, burdensome activity that is only engaged in for the material rewards it produces. Thus it is not difficult to see why economists refer to payment for work as *compensation*. The pay compensates the worker for his or her disutility in expending effort. The assumption is that the only reason people work is to get paid. Nobody would work if they didn't have to.

The problem with unemployment, as mainstream economics views it, is the resulting lack of income, nothing else. Therefore the utopian goal of conventional economics is a completely automated and mechanized society. No work. As we have already indicated, the goal of humanistic economics is quite different. It is not to eliminate work; it is to provide work that fulfills the higher needs. While we also agree with the idea of eliminating the first necessity, we don't see this as the elimination of work itself, but the transformation of work into that which is personally fulfilling.

It is hardly necessary to point out that the conventional economic conception of work as a disutility follows quite directly from the psychology of Economic Man. He avoids pain and seeks pleasure. Work is painful, and consumption is pleasurable, so that Man puts up with the pain of work (its disutility) because he is compensated by the pleasure (the marginal utility of consumption). We return to Jeremy Bentham and his hedonistic utilitarianism to find the historical roots of this conception.

HUMANISTIC ECONOMICS AND WORK

Several extensive surveys have been conducted recently that asked people whether they would still work even if they did not need the money. Two-thirds answered that they would. This kind of finding has also been confirmed in research conducted by the reputable University of Michigan Survey Center.[3]

A finding such as this strains the Economic Man conception of work, but fits very well into the framework developed by humanistic economics. People need to work in order to grow, and most people are aware of this (among the exceptions are the neoclassical economists). From the humanistic perspective, an unemployed person is someone who is lacking the opportunity to produce something of value, to be meaningfully involved in life, to become self-actualized. Thus we find that an involuntarily unemployed person is not only someone who may be hungry (with unemployment compensation, perhaps not), but, also more significantly, is someone who feels worthless. All the higher needs in the hierarchy, beginning with belongingness, through self-esteem and beyond, are deprived by unemployment. This is a much more significant problem than merely one of income. The result of not being able to meet these higher basic needs frequently becomes visible in the form of alienation, alcoholism, drug addiction, crime, broken homes, and even suicide.

From a humanistic perspective the most valuable resource that an economy has is not raw materials, good soil, nor sources of energy. It is people. Human potential is the most important resource that an economy can develop. An economy *is* people, people developing themselves. From this we can see that unemployment is ultimately the nondevelopment and non-use of resources. When we look at the high rates of unemployment among young people, and particularly among young blacks and other minority groups, we become painfully aware of how we are wasting our most important resource. But, as we pointed out, conventional economics is generally only concerned with this problem because of the issue of poverty, income, and wasted GNP. It misses the whole matter of the other dimension of work, since it does not recognize that social and higher needs are economically relevant. And yet somehow *that* economics is supposed to have *something* to do with people.

Work, Labor, and the Social Context

There is a theme in Western economics that goes back at least to Plato, which takes physical work, or labor, to be unpleasant and undesirable. It's better to avoid it if at all possible. In Plato's time physical work was done by slaves; in our time we hope that machines will do it. This attitude is quite clearly what lies behind the concept in economics that work, or at least labor, is a disutility.

The reader may notice that in our treatment of work from the humanistic perspective we have not distinguished between work and labor. We should also point out, at this point, that when we talked about the distinction between the two necessities for work, we did not mean that physical work was what met the first necessity while mental work met the second necessity, and that therefore the goal of economic policy should be to eliminate physical work and leave only mental work. It is only the longstanding bias against physical work that would lead to this kind of interpretation. Rather, when we are talking about eliminating the necessity to work in order to be able to eat, we are talking about eliminating work that is done *only* for that reason. Referring to the survey mentioned on page 143, what we believe should be eliminated is the work of the one-third of the people who would give up their jobs if they did not need their paychecks. The distinction between these two groups of people, the one-third and the other two-thirds, is not necessarily a distinction between physical and mental workers. It is, instead, a distinction between those who are only working because it gives them a paycheck, and those who, in addition to a paycheck, are able to fulfill some of their higher needs in their jobs.

The false idea that physical work is not fulfilling and meaningful, and that mental work is, obscures the dimension of work that determines whether work meets the higher needs. This dimension can be called the *meaning* of the work which, broadly speaking, reflects the social context of work.

Let us use an instance of physical work, and show how it is the social context of work that determines its meaning and significance, and not merely the fact that it is physical. The example involves one of the most plainly physical activities there is, lifting or moving a large rock. This is an activity that is almost pure labor; there is almost no brainwork involved. And yet we will see that the social context solely determines the meaning of the work.

There you are, you and the rock. You can be lifting the rock because you are a prisoner and are involved in forced labor. Lifting the rock may have no other meaning than that you do it because you are told to do it. You will be punished if you do not. So, lifting that rock is not pleasant—you are doing it under the worst of conditions and you hate it.

Let us now take this same act of lifting a rock, the same rock, and place the act in a somewhat different context. You are a member of a work crew that is being paid to clear a field for a prosperous farmer. You may not be crazy about lifting this rock, but you know that you have *agreed* to do it. You will get something out of it, some money. You will not hate this work as much as you would if you were a prisoner performing the same task.

And now let us place this act in another context. You are clearing a commonly owned field to make a garden and grow organic vegetables for yourself and some friends. The same muscles and the same effort are involved in lifting this rock as in each of the other contexts, but now it has a completely different meaning, and feels different as a result. You do not hate what you are doing, you may even enjoy it. You see desired results, have a feeling of real achievement, and enjoy the exercise.

Moving the rock could be regarded merely as an act of brute strength, but the relationship between the persons involved in the work is what determines its meaning. In the first context there was a master-slave relationship and the work was dreaded. In the second, there is an employer-employee relationship and the work is tolerated. In the third, there is a peer relationship, or you are doing it for yourself, and the same act is enjoyed. In the latter case you might no longer want to associate this ·work with the word *brute*. It may even be noble; you are moving the earth, making it useable, preparing to grow food that you and those you love will eat. And you do not have to break your back doing it. If the rock is too heavy, you gather the others together to help. When you need a rest you take it. The work exercises you, strengthens you; it does not destroy you.

This enables us to understand the basic humanistic revelation: unpleasant toil is a result of *the meaning of the work*, rather than the task itself. Technology will never eliminate toil, but the right social relationships will.

Another example will further illustrate these points. It is the case of the math professor who, when he comes home from the university, loves to go out in his field, get on his tractor, and proceed with his avocation of farming. "I am a farmer at heart," he says. He also admits that he really would rather not teach but he needs to do it "to make a living." How paradoxical this is in terms of the conventional economic conceptions! Here is someone who teaches in order to feed his family, and does the work of a farmer in order to engage in something that he finds meaningful. Everything is reversed.

While we don't present this anecdote in a very serious way, it is nonetheless instructive in terms of our theme. What our math teacher demonstrates is that the significance of work cannot be determined by just examining the work itself, but is only determined by understanding the worker's frame of reference.

We see even more clearly now how inadequate and distorted are the usual categories in which economics analyzes work. Not only do we see that work need not be disutility, but also that the social context or meaning can change a disutility into a utility. Work becomes enjoyable for its own sake, its intrinsic values, its ability to fulfill the higher needs. Also, the technological dream of eliminating all physical work, indeed all work, is quite misguided. Instead, we need to aim for a restructuring of the social conditions of work, so that all people are engaged in work they find meaningful, work that fulfills their higher needs. From this perspective, less work is not necessarily better than more work. The humanistic dream is consistent with plentiful work, as long as it is meaningful.

Alienation

The term commonly used for work that is not meaningful is *alienating* work. As we mentioned in the last chapter, the concept was introduced into economics by Marx, who adapted the term from Hegel's original usage. Since that time, one hundred and thirty years ago, alienation has been used to explain all manner of social problems, from the spread of pornography to the Warfare State.

We would like to restrict the use of this term to refer to work that does not meet the second necessity. Even more specifically, *alienation refers to those technological and institutional features of work that interfere with the satisfaction of social and higher needs.*

What are some of these features?

Unstable Work Groups The need referred to in the hierarchy of needs as belongingness also covers such experiences as esprit de corps, morale, and social cohesion. It is clear that in order for this need to be fulfilled, a minimum requirement is that a group of people stay together for some substantial period of time. Anything that serves to break up the group will prevent the formation of those relationships that can adequately fulfill the social needs. Also, the expectation on the part of the worker that he or she may not be working with this same group of people for any length of time will probably prevent that person from fully investing his or her total self in the work relationships, even when there is the opportunity. To indicate the extent of this problem of work group instability the Bureau of Labor Statistics shows that out of every one hundred jobs occupied there will be fifty separations each year.[4] These separations consist of two categories, layoffs and resignations, about evenly divided.

The practice of employees being laid off, which is so usual and accepted a part of our system, constitutes a clear violation of humanistic principles, in particular, the basic needs of security and belongingness. The reasons for layoffs usually come under two headings, (1) economic downturns, meaning that less work is available, and (2) technological developments, meaning that fewer people are needed to do a given amount of work. Let's look at each of these reasons.

When there is an economic downturn, and less work is needed or called for, the usual practice, often supported by both business management and labor unions, is to lay some workers off, in most cases those with least seniority (frequently women and minority groups) while the rest continue to work at the same level as before.

What a travesty this is in human terms. Any group of people who have a sense of belongingness and some degree of closeness will naturally share whatever work is available. If there were an increase in work they would all take on the extra load—or opportunity. It would certainly be unfair, and rather ridiculous, for some people to increase their work while others continued as before. Likewise if there were a decrease, it would be nothing less than absurd, in a human sense, for some to have to stop working and lose all benefits, while the others continued as usual. This just naturally violates human sensibility. All these adjectives that we have used—*unfair, ridiculous, absurd*—should be applied to the current practice of laying some people off while others continue to receive the benefits of working the standard eight-hour day. How destructive this is of the fabric of social relations on the job. How much more humane it would be if a decrease in available work meant that all workers would have a proportionate reduction in their work day.

A similar argument follows for the matter of layoffs due to technological development, what is called *technological unemployment*. The promise of technology has been that it will lighten the load of routine work and free people for more creative work. This promise is clearly violated when the result of technology is to increase the amount of repetitive work for *some*, and to eliminate the possibility of any work for others. Again, how much more humane it would be, how much saner, if technology were used to reduce the routine and repetitive work for all, but what *remained* of that work was shared by all. For some to gain while others lose is always a violation of humanistic principles. We will shortly return to the issue of technology.

At the managerial level, a problem related to layoffs is the practice of some companies to have their managers move to a new location every few years in order to avoid their forming close work relationships. It is the belief of these companies that close relationships will interfere with the manager's toughness towards his subordinates, and lessen his attachment to his own career. This is another case where the values of Economic Man explicitly prevail over human considerations.

Competitive Pay Systems   This is the situation where pay depends upon how much better than other workers one performs. An example of this is merit pay increases for public employees. This is the system where the allotted money available for raises has to be given out so that some employees get a large amount while other employees get less, or even no raise at all (even worse when we take inflation into account). On the surface it may appear that such a system is socially beneficial because it serves as an incentive for employees to work harder to try to get the raise. In practice it does little but generate competitive *attitudes*, such as envy, and a system of building favoritism with the boss. The employee's feeling of belongingness gets trampled in the process.

A better known instance of this is *piece work*, where workers are paid according to how many units of work product they turn out. It is estimated that fully one-third of industrial workers are on a piece work system, including a majority of workers in the textile, footwear and clothing industries.[5] It is not surprising that these particular industries have the highest employee turnover rates. It may appear that piece work has little to do with generating rivalry between workers, since what one worker turns out should have no effect on another worker's rate of activity and pay. In practice, however, the piece work rate (of expectation) is developed out of group averages, so that a fast worker or a slow worker has effects on the overall rate. Nobody knows this better than the piece worker; and with this worker awareness, group pressures begin to manifest, with the resulting breakdown in social cohesion.

Fragmented and Isolated Jobs   Here the villain is the very pride of the early industrial system about which the classical and neoclassical economists spoke so glowingly—the division of labor, and specialization. The worker works on only a small part of the total process and has no relationship to the whole, or to the equally fragmented work of the other workers. In essence the worker has become a cog in a machine, and is often controlled by the operations of a machine.

The effects of this kind of work on the social and higher needs of workers, and on their ability to self-actualize, are devastating. Karl Marx believed that the "discipline" of industrial work would form the industrial workers into an organized and unified group that would develop "class consciousness," and rise up to overthrow the conditions of alienating work. The sad truth seems to be that involvement in fragmented and repetitious work probably dulls and crushes out consciousness, be it class or otherwise. According to John Hobson:

> ☐ The (modern) "conditions of labor" . . . are realized as an invasion and a degradation of their humanity, offering neither stimulus nor opportunity for a man to throw himself into his work. For the work only calls for a fragment of that "self" and always the same fragment. So it is true that not only is labor divided but the laborer. And it is manifest that, so far as his organic human nature is concerned, its unused portions are destined to idleness, atrophy, and decay.[6]

Since machines are generally involved in the kind of work that is dehumanizing and alienating, observers are often led to conclude that technology is the cause of the problem. Some even go so far as to say that the problem is a result of science, or progress, implying that we must pay some penalty for what otherwise are advancements. But this is a false conclusion, or at least a premature assessment. The problem is not technology, but how technology is chosen. To assign the problem to technology itself, or to science, is to impute causation to an abstraction. Instead, we must realize that if technology is used in a dehumanizing way it is because certain *people* have made the decision to use it that way. We will take up the implications of this later in the chapter, when we discuss solutions to the alienation problem.

Alienation and Externality   In Chapter 6 we discussed the concept of externality. These are effects of production that do not show up in a company's profit-and-loss sheets, and yet may have considerable social and economic costs. Pollution is the prime area where economics has recognized externalities. A company that pollutes a river has no reason to enter the costs of this pollution into its business, or internal, accounts, and thus these costs remain external to the company's reckoning of its profit or loss. And yet a polluted river has many costs that somebody, eventually, will have to pay for—such as the cost of increasingly scarce fish, the necessity to build artificial swimming areas, the loss of property values, and so forth.

What many economists have not yet recognized is that alienation as a result of working conditions is another externality. E. F. Schumacher is an exception. He has pointed out that most people ignore the most important pollution of all, the degrading effect of alienating work.[7] Commenting on a British Government report on ecological problems, which was titled *Natural Resources: Sinews for Survival*, Schumacher explains the following:

> ☐ The most important of all resources is obviously the initiative, imagination and brainpower of man himself. We all know this and are ready to devote very substantial funds to what we call education. So, if the problem is "survival," one might fairly expect to find some discussion relating to the preservation and, if possible, the development of the most precious

of all natural resources, human brains. However, such expectations are not fulfilled. "Sinews for Survival" deals with all the natural factors—minerals, energy, water, wildlife and so forth—but not at all with such immaterial resources as initiative, intelligence and brainpower.[8]

Once economics recognizes that alienation is another, and the most important, instance of pollution, it will then be able to apply the concepts of externality to seek a solution. Let us take a closer look at this comparison.

It is relatively easy *now* to see that "bads" have been produced along with goods as a result of our industrial system, although seeing this has taken a long time. These bads are what we call pollution. Like the goods, the bads are also *tangible*. You can see the chemical froth on the river, you can smell it, and you know that the fish are dying. But the bads of alienation, the pollution of the human resources, are intangible and not as easy to recognize. But they take the same economic form as tangible pollution, since they are undesirable by-products of the productive process.

Perhaps the best way to understand the pollution of alienation is also suggested by Schumacher. As a society we invest a large amount of our money in education, and rightly believe that it is one of our prime resources. What this present analysis points out is that alienation is the negative of education; it is *minus education*. Whereas education builds up intelligence, creativity, and so forth, alienation tears these resources down. Hobson's statement on p. 149 indicates how this happens.

Although alienation appears to us to be an externality of production just like environmental pollution, some economists may feel more comfortable if it is viewed separately. Taking this approach, we might categorize alienation as falling between a production externality and an externality of consumption like alcoholism. Let us look at alcoholism for a moment, in order to examine this comparison.

Alcoholic beverages are a good like any other, but their consumption can produce certain obvious bads—absenteeism, family disruption, hospitalization, auto accidents, and so forth. All these bads are social costs, which are not only external to the account sheets of the alcohol industry, but to the inclusion of the industry's sales into a national wealth index like the GNP.

Alienation has similar effects to alcoholism in that a lot of its effects are social. And yet alienation is not a spillover of consumption, but of the work experience.* Therefore, it is possible to see alienation as an externality that occupies a middle ground between production and consumption externalities.

---

*To quote John Hobson, "A man who is not interested in his work and does not recognize in it either beauty or utility, is degraded by that work, whether he knows it or not."[9]

Once we see that alienation is an externality, we know where to look for solutions. What we need to do is to review how other kinds of externalities, such as environmental pollution, are dealt with, and then see to what extent this applies to alienation.

The basic approach to the externality problem follows logically: Enact a policy that will internalize the externality. We will discuss the ramifications of doing this.

The Levying of an Alienation Tax

When we turn to the area of alienation, we should first recognize that presumably the normal labor market in a market economy takes this into account in the form of wages. This is what is implied, in part, by the idea that wages reflect a compensation to the worker for the disutility of work. If we assume that alienation is a part of the disutility, then we can see that wages are an attempt to offset this. It would follow that the more alienating a particular job is, the higher would be its turnover rate, and thus the costlier it would be to the company, in terms of retraining and so forth. So, in some sense, excessive wage rates represent a charge or a "tax" to the company for the extent of alienation of its jobs.

Following this line of reasoning, any improvement in working conditions, such as instituting work breaks, providing for recreation, lessening of noise, etc., will be implemented in order to avoid the "tax" as much as possible.

Empirical Refutation of Competitive Wage Theory   The validity of the above argument depends upon one very important premise—that we have a full-employment economy. In a full-employment economy workers have the opportunity of "voting with their feet" by leaving a job with high alienation and going to another, so that in order to keep workers a company will have to pay the penalty for relatively excessive alienation. In the situation where there is unemployment, or other related restrictions to worker mobility, the worker has little choice but to stay with an alienating job. Therefore, in practice, with full employment not the general case, employers do not have to incur extra costs to keep workers on alienating jobs, such as mill work, assembly lines, dull office work, and other similar jobs.*

Even if there were full employment, we do not think that this natural-tax argument would work to reduce alienation significantly. There have been periods of relatively full employment in the past, and

---

*A recent study by one of the co-authors provides evidence that the labor market does not operate in the smooth fashion pictured by theory. Some jobs are clearly better than others in spite of actual potential labor mobility between them. [10]

alienation has not been significantly reduced during those times. Since alienation is an experience of the worker on the job, only the worker is really able to determine what conditions or job features are alienating. This means that, in order for the alienation of a particular job to be overcome, the worker himself or herself has to be able to direct the changes. Since few work situations allow the worker this kind of control, it is not likely that by changing jobs a worker will be able to find a truly non-alienating work situation. A worker may find a job that offers more pay, thus higher compensation for alienation, or a company that has put some money into job improvements, but not one in which alienation can be significantly eliminated.

Job Evaluation Programs An approach which is based on a "tax" method of reducing alienation is job evaluation and rating programs, which are often bargained for and instituted by trade unions. This is the system where each job is rated according to criteria such as: What skills are required? How unpleasant is the job? Does it require night work? Is it outdoors or indoors? What are the noise levels? And so forth. The ratings on these criteria will determine the pay rate for a particular job. It is interesting to note that Holland has, on a nation-wide basis, instituted a job rating scheme for most jobs, so that a criterion that we would call alienation enters to some extent into the pay schedule of a job.

     Whether programs like the Dutch have are an adequate answer to alienation is an open question. It is quite possible that such a nation-wide system, while meeting some humanistic goals, contradicts others by the creation of a large bureaucratic system that develops a rigid "book" on each of its jobs. Revelant human factors of the person on the spot are necessarily glossed over.

The "Forgiven Tax" Another approach is put forth in the proposal of what is called a "forgiven tax" by Harman.[11] It is equivalent to an effluent tax in controlling environmental pollution. This is a tax that is destined to provide an increased incentive for corporations to reduce work alienation. It is a tax that is levied on some appropriate measure of business activity, such as total payroll or gross income, that is *forgiven* or dropped if the corporation meets certain standards for restructuring work to increase job satisfaction. In other words, the business firm can either abate alienation or simply pay the tax and continue with business as usual. Of course, Harman's scheme comes very close to Thomas More's proposal of a royal tax on social vices, in this case alienating jobs. Harman sees this scheme as having the advantage of avoiding the wastage of collecting taxes and then dispersing them again, and also being less coercive than a direct legislative approach. The obvious shortcoming of such a "forgiven tax" is that it is rather difficult to establish practical criteria for when the tax should be forgiven.

The Redefinition of Property Rights:
Towards Industrial Democracy

Another, and perhaps most humanistic, approach to externalities lies in the re-examination of property rights. Contrary to what habit and custom lead us to assume, the rights that go with ownership of property are not absolute and all-encompassing. They change with changing times, and are themselves based on law and changes in the law. A striking historical example is that of slavery. At one point, not that far in the past, one group of people, the owners, had the right of commanding the lives and work of another group, the slaves (or chattel). *Chattel* is a word that is not widely used anymore, but it means property. At one time people were chattel; they were the property of other people. But society has changed, and so have the laws, and now people can no longer be considered the property of other people.

On a more ordinary level we find that all of our property has both rights and restrictions attached to it, and these are subject to change. We may own a car, but we can't drive above a certain speed in it. We may own a house, but building codes only allow for it to be of a certain size and design. The list goes on and on. This recognition about property can be applied quite effectively to the problem of externalities in environmental pollution. One such use is to define the public as having certain property rights, say, in regard to a river. Therefore, before a plant decides to get rid of its wastes by letting them go into the river it must first obtain permission and necessary abatements from a duly constituted body that represents the public's ownership of the river. Another kind of use of property rights, still staying with the example of the river, is to give every citizen the right to bring a damage claim or suit against a company for polluting the river. The settlement of such a suit in favor of the citizen would clearly internalize the pollution costs for the company.

The question is, can the property-rights approach to environmental externalities be applied to the problem of alienation? The answer, which we believe is yes, appears to us to be important enough within the sphere of humanistic economics to devote a separate heading to this solution.

Industrial Democracy At least twice previously in this chapter we hinted at a basic solution to the problem of alienation. Discussing the role of technology in alienation, we pointed out that it is not technology itself that is the villain, but how technology is chosen and applied to the work situation. Looking at the conventional approach to alienation, we asserted that if a worker cannot control his or her work conditions the worker will not be able to change those features that are found to be alienating, regardless of whether the economy is at full employment.

These instances point in the direction of a real and substantive solution to alienation, which can be simply stated as control by workers over their work environment. This is the only direct solution, because there is a direct relationship between control and alienation: the more control over the work environment, the less alienation; the less control, the more alienation.

Workers who control their work can decide when they take breaks, how the work should be divided, how the work can be made maximally creative, and so forth. Since the workers experience the alienation they are the ones who are most motivated and know best *how* to change it, and also *how much* to change it. All other attempts to get at alienation are at best secondary, and do not reach the heart of the problem. The heart of the problem is input, direction, and control over one's own work. The situation of controlling one's work is the one that most closely corresponds to the third instance of moving the rock in the earlier example.

The concept of control over one's work also goes by several other names: one is self-management, and another is industrial democracy, the heading of this section. Self-management refers to the situation where the workers and the managers do not constitute two separate groups of economic agents, but are one single body. Sometimes it is not so apparent that self-management implies an extension of democracy.

Democracy exists when people have control over their own affairs, and are not controlled by the decisions of a few, or an outside party. We are used to and expect the operation of democracy in political matters. One person, one vote, as we say. Whether we have it or not is another matter, as we will further discuss in Chapter 9. But we are not so used to the operation of democracy on the job.

We accept, through long habit, as natural that the owner(s) of a company make decisions affecting the working lives of the employees. We also accept as natural that the owners will make these decisions in accord with what is most profitable to the company. However, we know by now that what is maximally profitable does not necessarily accord with maximum human well-being, and certainly does not accord with meaningful and satisfying work experiences. It often turns out that what is maximally profitable is a work procedure that increases alienation. This results from the fact that maximum profits go with greater productivity, and greater productivity is largely a function of increased mechanization; increased mechanization, in turn, usually demands increasingly machine-like work from the worker. Therefore, when owners choose the technology, they will generally tend to choose alienating technology. Putting decisions like these in the hands of the workers provides a greater chance that less alienating technological methods will be used, or even technology that leads to increased fulfillment on the job.

The opportunity for workers to make these decisions has been seen as an expansion of democracy into the work setting. Thus there is the concept of *industrial democracy*. Now when workers make these decisions they might not necessarily choose the technology that is least alienating. They might prefer to accept some degree of alienation in return for a higher level of output, profit, and ultimately material goods. But now the optimal degree of alienation, or mix of alienation and material output, is up to them.

The concept of industrial democracy, or worker self-management, raises many questions and has many implications, even beyond the issue of alienation. In Chapter 13 we will devote more attention to these matters. For now we would like to point out that worker self-management is an instance of the redefinition of property rights. Through custom we accept the current rights of owners to decide how their property, the company, is to be run in regard to matters like working conditions and choice of technology. But these rights have been different in the past, and can change again in the future. If workers gain the right to have certain control, or "ownership," over their work situation, this will be one more change in the continual redefinition of who owns what, and what that ownership implies.

CONCLUSION

We began this chapter by talking about work and we have ended by talking about ownership. In the course of this discussion we have shown the close connection that lies between these social institutions.

The word *institutions* brings us to think once again of Thorstein Veblen, who thought this word was so important in matters of economics. And when Veblen talked about ownership he harked back to the classical notion that when a thing was mixed with one's work, only then was one legitimately entitled to think of that thing as "mine." But he knew that legitimacy is granted to economic activities only by institutional arrangement. He also knew that these institutional arrangements evolve. Ownership evolves. And so does work.

References

1. O'Toole, James, ed. *Work in America*. Boston: MIT Press, 1973, p. 1.

2. O'Toole, James, ed. *Work in America*. Boston: MIT Press, 1973, p. 186.

3. Strumpel, Burkhard. "Economic Life-Styles, Values and Subjective Welfare." In *Economic Means for Human Needs (Social Indications of Well-Being and Discontent)*, edited by B. Strumpel. Ann Arbor: University of Michigan Press, 1976, pp. 19–65, 293–4.

4. Organization for Economic Co-operation and Development (OECD). *Wage and Labor Mobility*. Paris, 1965, p. 50.

5. Stellato, George E. "Incentive Pay in Manufacturing Industries." In *Monthly Labor Review*, July 1969, pp. 49–53.

6. Hobson, J. A. *Work and Wealth: A Human Valuation*. 1914. Reprint. New York: Allen and Unwin, 1949, p. 00.

7. Schumacher, E. F. "Philosophy of Work." In *The Catholic Worker*, February, 1977, p. 1.

8. Schumacher, E. F. "Philosophy of Work." In *The Catholic Worker*, February, 1977, p. 1.

9. Hobson, J. A. *Work and Wealth: A Human Valuation*. 1914. Reprint. New York: Allen and Unwin, 1949, p. 88.

10. Lutz, Mark A. "Quit Rates and the Quality of the Industrial Earnings Structure." In *Industrial Relations*, 16, 1, February 1977, pp. 61–70*

11. Willis, W. Harman. "Humanistic Capitalism: Another Alternative." In *Journal of Humanistic Psychology*, 14, 1, Winter 1974, p. 19.

*See also the subsequent "Note" *Industrial Relations*, 18, 1, February, 1979.

PART THREE

TOWARDS A HUMANISTIC ECONOMIC SYSTEM

Chapter Nine

THE POSITIVE VALUES OF HUMANISTIC ECONOMICS: TOWARDS POLICY

INTRODUCTION

This chapter serves as a bridge between the first section of the book, which is essentially theoretically oriented, and the third, which sets forth concrete examples and issues in the application of humanistic economics. It is the applications of economic theory that are ultimately important to a humanist, because that is where words and ideas become translated into lives—and since each of us is one of those lives, touching other lives, it is truly rational that this should be our ultimate concern.

In order to make this transition from theory to practice we will summarize the argument of the first section, which compared mainstream economics with humanistic economics, and then develop the policy implications that flow from the humanistic alternative.

The basic concepts of each system are conveniently highlighted in Table 9.1, which compares their basic aspects.

TABLE 9.1

	Basic concept	Psychological goal	Social principle	Freedom	Work
Economic Man	Wants	Utility (Pleasure)	Competition	To consume	Disutility a bad
Humanistic Person	Needs	Self-actualization	Cooperation	To grow	A potential good

COMPARISON AND SUMMARY

Encountered in his full array, Economic Man looks like quite an unappealing creature. As an economist friend of ours humorously put it, "The pure Economic Man is a bore and a clod. I would not want my child to marry one." But, to an observation such as this, a mainstreamer may cry "Unfair!" and try to assert that this is not an accurate picture of Economic Man. He or she would point out that such a being no longer exists in economics, but has been transformed into the pure, value-free axioms of choice theory, such as indifference analysis or revealed preference. Our previous chapters have shown why this protest does not carry the day, and that mainstream economics has either to sink or swim with a rational Economic Man out to maximize his utility. Thus, it is not surprising that these concepts continue to be presented in the textbooks as fundamental, and presumably valid, economic concepts.

The same friend just quoted has also said that "Reality probably lies somewhere in the middle between Economic Man and Humanistic Man (sic). That is, the selfish but careful counting of the costs and benefits, the desire to maximize one's utility and profits, and the concern for friendship, brotherhood, love—which cannot be based on personal loss or gain—are both part of human and social reality." To this friend we have pointed out that the humanistic image embodies the Economic Man image as well, but sees it as only a fragment of the complete human being. Real people are capable of evolving from being Economic Men to healthy and whole human beings. The Economic-Man aspects of people dominate the scene under institutional conditions that promote what we have called the negative values: competition for basic life-supporting commodities, concern for oneself rather than others, and a materialistic orientation. (These are really not separate, as we have listed them, but part of a total value complex.) Economics has tended to deny that these are its values, and instead has seen them as scientific descriptions of the way people really are. The work of economists such as Becker, McKenzie and Tullock, referred to in Chapter 3, shows this quite clearly.

Under different institutional conditions, those that support what we can call the positive values, a different kind of person emerges, one whose values relate to the upper levels of the growth hierarchy. This person displays those characteristics that are closer to what Maslow found in his study of self-actualized people.

From a humanistic perspective the complete picture of the person must involve a broader range of motives and values—all the way from the materialistic and the competitive to the social, moral and altruistic. The function of economics should be to explain how people evolve from the lower end of this range to the higher, and to recommend policies that facilitate this evolution. Such policies can be said to be humanistically efficient.

Pareto Efficiency

Mainstream economics takes a different view of efficiency, and this view has generally gone under the heading of Pareto Efficiency, or Pareto Optimality. In a strong sense, the essence of what economics has come to is represented in Pareto Efficiency. Once again, this is the concept that economic policy is optimal if some people are made better off while nobody is made worse off. As we showed in previous chapters, this criterion goes hand-in-hand with high GNP growth and affluence. The only time Pareto Efficiency can possibly apply is when the economy keeps growing. Then a surplus is produced which is received by some, while nothing has to be lost or given up by anyone else.

This has been the mainstream's answer to the problems of poverty, lopsided income distribution, and justice. No need to concern ourselves with these issues because, when we all get richer, then even the poor will benefit. We saw in Chapter 5 the limitation and lack of relevance of the Pareto Criterion for meeting these problems adequately.

At its most successful, an economy that follows the dictates of mainstream thinking still rests on the values of materialism. At its least successful, it becomes a clutching after a rapidly receding affluence. If older, moral values have diminished, then a new value system, well represented by conventional economics, has almost come to take its place. E. F. Schumacher has gone so far as to label conventional economics as a "Religion of Materialism." And as a religion,

> ☐ It is a poverty stricken, unsatisfactory religion, for after all, success, total economic success leaves behind a taste of total unfulfillment, the taste of ashes. So economics is not concerned with reality, it takes us away from reality. . . . You can't say it's bad science—it's logical, it's systematic, a lot of hard work and hard thinking have gone into it—but its starting point is wrong, its moral and metaphysical basis is wrong. And it follows that once you start wrongly you can never get right again. It starts not from any picture of the real purpose of human life on earth. In simplified terms, the homo economicus is a person who is interested in nothing but consumption, accumulation . . . (He) has no sense of beauty. . . . And this reductionism may be tolerable for awhile—it can work out in its full glory and be applied, but in the end, it has no connection with reality. It is self-destructive."[1]

Humanistic Economics as Positive Science

It may not be bad science, as Schumacher says, but which is better science? In other words, let us compare the two concepts of human nature as to which is a better description of reality. Which is more accurate, the wants of Economic Man or the needs of the Humanistic Person? Modern economists have been led to believe that the issue

here is between rigorous, positivistic science and philosophical, normative metaphysics. Economic Man may seem ugly, perhaps ridiculous,
but at least scientific. Generally it can be expected that the more
scientific an observer considers himself or herself to be, the less would
be the inclination to accept the dichotomy of higher and lower needs.
Who is to tell what the higher needs are? Or what amounts in their
view to the same thing, who is to tell what the higher needs ought to
be? Whose values count?

Maslow himself saw the need to defend his value hierarchy
against such criticism "because so many still consider that values can
never be more than the arbitrary imposition on data of the writer's own
tastes, prejudices, intuitions, or often unproved and unprovable assumptions."[2] But he replies that, "if it could be demonstrated that *the
organism itself* chooses between a stronger and a weaker, a higher and
a lower, then surely it would be impossible to maintain that one good
has the same value as any other good, or that it is impossible to choose
between them, or that no one has a natural criterion for differentiating
good from evil."[3] (emphasis added)

How do we know that it is the human organism who does the
ranking? Maslow gives us a long list containing sixteen distinct reasons, some of which we have—albeit implicitly—discussed earlier. We
mention only the first two:

1. The higher need is an evolutionary development. We share the
    need for food with all living things, the need for love with the
    higher apes, the need for self-actualization with nobody. In other
    words, the higher the need, the more specifically human it is.

2. Higher needs are later ontogenetic developments. By this we mean
    that they assert themselves later in the development of the infant.
    The newborn will strive first for gratification of the lower needs
    relating to hunger, warmth and security. Only after months will
    infants show the first signs of interpersonal ties and selective
    affection. Still later comes the urge for independence, achievement
    and praise. And as Maslow puts it, "As for self-actualization, even
    a Mozart had to wait until he was three or four."[4]

Moreover, Maslow found a "gold mine" of support for this theory
in his own clinical practice and that of hundreds of other therapists.
Such data is hard to qualify and therefore tends to be ignored by the
more scientifically inclined.

During the last ten years several psychologists have subjected the
humanistic image of man to experimental testing. Four out of five
studies strongly support the notion of a hierarchy of needs in confor-
mance with Maslow's thesis.[5] True, the evidence is still coming in and
it would be premature to claim unconditional empirical support at this
stage. But remembering what we found earlier concerning the scientific

status of Economic Man, it now appears that Humanistic Person need not shy away from meeting his rival on the (positivistic) grounds of modern science. The humanistic vision lends itself to empirical verification, along lines stipulated by logical positivist methodology, and it has been quite successfully tested.

It is for this reason that we have chosen to use the adjective *positive* in the title to this chapter. Humanistic economics has, like the conventional economics, its own fundamental values. But in contrast to its utilitarian rival, the humanistic values are not only life affirmative, but they are observable and have been observed.

POLICY IMPLICATIONS: EQUALITY AND THE HISTORY OF ECONOMICS

There is some truth in the view that the development of mainstream economics has resulted from attempts to avoid the implication of equality. Certainly we have seen that some notion of economic quality goes back to Plato, and was expressed by Smith, Sismondi, and so on throughout all the writings of the humanists. At the end of the classical era in economics this theme is expressed in the humanistic side of Karl Marx. It is embodied in his adaptation of Smith's Labor Theory of Value. If everyone is paid according to his or her labor, then there is little to explain the hugely disproportionate shares of wealth accumulated under nineteenth-century, laissez-faire capitalism. To counteract these ideas, the marginal-utility theory of value was put forth to replace the labor theory. As we all know, it became a huge success.

But there was an embarrassment—the diminishing marginal utility of income and its implication that the overall utility of society would be advanced if the excess wealth of the rich could be distributed to the poor. In other words, the closer to equality a society moved, the greater its overall utility or happiness.

As we saw in our examination of the Harrod-Robbins debate, economists tried to avoid these implications by claiming that individuals differ in their capacity for happiness. That this argument was spurious did not bother them. Moreover, even if equal capacity for happiness were strictly a value judgement, Robbins admitted that it had to be made, or else economics could say nothing on any other policy matter. In their enthusiasm for not having to touch inequality, economists failed to hear Robbins' general point about policy.

Sporadically, some economists have stood up in protest, recalling as Nicholas Georgescu-Roegen did, that the fact of urgent needs of the poor is a priori more important than a scientific theory which overlooks such a fact.[6] The mainstream economists did not heed this advice. Instead they sought to abandon all welfare concepts based on utility, and in doing so they turned to Vilfredo Pareto for assistance. Yet, as we pointed out in Chapter 5, many of the old problems remained.

Humanistic economics makes a fundamental departure from the Pareto Criterion and all that it represents: its inapplicability, its materialism, its support of the status quo, and its failure to promote a just society. Instead, humanism arrives at a criterion for social and economic well-being that affirms the opposite of each of these qualities: it has practical application, it promotes human potential, it does not kowtow to the status quo, and it is fundamentally grounded on the principle of justice. We refer to this criterion as *optimum equality*.

Social Justice is Optimum Equality   There has always been much debate and disagreement as to what constitutes a just society. Economists have tended to throw up their hands in the face of this controversy, and claim that any position in the matter is merely a value judgement.

The work of Harvard philosopher John Rawls, in his book *A Theory of Justice*, makes the stance of mainstream economics increasingly difficult to uphold.[7] Rawls believes that society has not been able to agree on what constitutes a just allocation of income, wealth and power because everyone approaches this question from his or her current social position. In the textbook example quoted on page 96, clearly the millionaire with his yacht and the penniless sharecropper would not agree on a just division of income.

Rawls' insight, which has been arrived at independently by Sidney Alexander, is that true principles of justice are those that individuals would choose if they did not know what social position they would occupy in a society. He calls this social position "the original position." Alexander says that the most just (or desirable) society would be the one where a person would least mind being *anyone at random* in that society.[8]

Rawls has argued that, from this original (or random) position, no one would want to chance being at the low end of a steep disparity of income or power (especially with the majority of the people being at the bottom rather than at the top). Therefore, it follows that from the original position an individual would choose to be anyone at random in a society in which the degree of disparity was acceptable, if the person was at the low end. Some may even argue that from such a position a perfect society is one in which there is no disparity at all. In either case, the practical outcome of this conception points in the direction of equality. This is for Rawls the principle of justice: The social welfare of a society is increased when the welfare of the worst off in a society is increased or maximized. Rawls' careful arguments accord well with the intuitive conclusions reached by humanists over the ages, that the most socially just society is one that raises the level of the most disadvantaged.

A case can be made that there is an optimum level of inequality (or equality) according to Rawls' principle. By way of example, let us consider income tax as a way of distributing from the wealthy to the poor. Let us assume that all the wealthy give up through taxes is given to the poor. One issue that needs to be taken into account is incentive and disincentive. As an individual is taxed he or she may lose incentive to work, cut down on the amount of work, and thus on overall income (pre-tax). If overall income drops below a certain point (the optimum point), then the poor could actually lose out because there would be that much less income to go around. To take the extreme instance, just for illustration because it doesn't make sense, if a wealthy person (pre-tax) were taxed 100 percent, he or she probably would stop working altogether, and that original income would no longer exist for anyone's use. So, the optimum taxation level from the standpoint of Rawls' principle is that point where the poor would no longer gain from the tax since the total to be distributed would have dropped too low. This can be shown in Figure 9-1.

FIGURE 9-1. REDISTRIBUTION BY AN OPTIMAL INCOME TAX

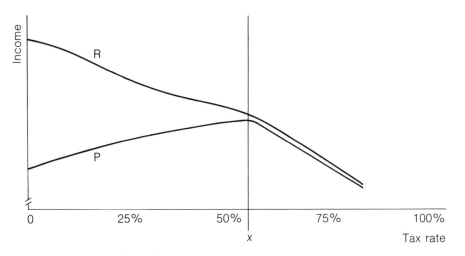

Individual R (rich) before any taxes earns twice as much as individual P (poor). The figure shows the effects of redistribution from R to P as the tax rate varies from 0 percent to 100 percent. Point X, which for the sake of realism we will call 58 percent, is the maximum point, because taxation past this point leaves too little to distribute to both individuals. Such calculations have actually been done according to Rawls' principle, and optimal tax rates have been arrived at (it is from one of these that we got our 58 percent figure).[9]

The principle of optimum equality is quite at odds with the Pareto Criterion. In the example of the sharecropper and the millionaire, Pareto argues that social well-being is not advanced by a redistribution from the latter to the former. Optimum equality argues for quite the opposite, that justice and human fulfillment would be considerably advanced if we did not have a sharecropper and a millionaire, and instead had two individuals roughly equal in worldly goods. Policies that move society in that direction are, *ceteris paribus,* the desirable ones. We say *ceteris paribus* somewhat tongue-in-cheek, but we are referring to the sticky question of the appropriate means to accomplish this, which we will return to shortly.

Equality, unfortunately, has sometimes been thought to imply sameness, which is quite inaccurate. When we use the term *equality,* or *optimum equality,* we are referring to the condition of economic equivalence (and perhaps power equality) in which people relate to each other as peers. It is, in fact, in this condition that true individuality and uniqueness are able to emerge. In this condition of equality, no longer are people bound to pre-set roles defined by their position in a socio-economic hierarchy. Without this limitation they are truly able to be themselves, as one always is with equals.

Optimum Equality and
Humanistic Efficiency

A society at optimum equality in income is the most efficient from the point of view of humanistic economics, because such a society promotes the most human growth. It does this because it meets the most important growth needs first, the physiological and the security needs, before it expends resources on less vital needs. In other words, it is a society that allocates resources to priority needs. This allocation is assured by the principle of optimum equality. It is a society where economic help is given to those most in need, not those least in need.

From the standpoint of human growth, another desirable feature of the optimum-equality principle is that it takes advantage of the fact that material resources are most pertinent to meeting the lowest needs on the hierarchy of needs, which are needs for material things, and least pertinent to the social and self-actualization needs. Therefore, a humanistically efficient society does not waste resources by applying them where they are least relevant (e.g., the millionaire refinishing a yacht while others are starving). In fact, when additional income is lavished on those who already have their material needs met, this can actually inhibit their growth, by promoting materialism—again, the millionaire and his or her yacht. From the standpoint of the growth hierarchy, our millionaire might be much better off if he or she diverted personal energy from keeping up a yacht to pursuing truth, love, beauty, and the service of others. As it has been told from ancient times, in the West's moral and ethical tradition, "It is easier for a camel to pass through the eye of a needle . . ."

A final point which flows from the above is that a society moving in the direction of optimum equality is one that is most efficient, because there is a *synergy,* rather than antagonism, of the higher and the lower needs. We just hinted at this in reference to the millionaire. What this means is that, when those at the higher end of the need hierarchy help those at the lower, they are in fact promoting their own growth. This follows because service and help to others is one of the needs at the top of the hierarchy. The highly evolved person is one who increasingly moves in this direction. Therefore, there is a perfect synergy of needs when the higher help the lower. Both gain, and in this mutual benefit it can actually be said that each group gives the other what they need; the rich give the poor enough to take them out of their poverty, and the poor give the rich the opportunity to serve. Of course, under conditions of optimum equality we no longer can speak of poor and rich. How beautiful is the humanistic economy!

The Way Towards the Humanistic Economy: Institutional Change

One of the most important levers for institutional change in a society is through legislation, or government policy, and this is the issue that we will concentrate on for the remainder of the chapter.

Let us look at the specific issue of the income tax again as a way to focus the discussion. If it is determined that a certain tax rate, say 58 percent, is socially beneficial, how is that rate put into effect? The answer is obvious: the same way that any other tax rate is put into effect, through government. Furthermore, the fact that there is an income tax at all is a result of government action. There was none before 1912, the year it was enacted into law as the Sixteenth Amendment to the Constitution amidst great controversy.

Now let us look at a more substantial change in the same general area. Income tax may not be the best means to bring about income redistribution, regardless of what tax rate is adopted. A better system may be through an adjustment of wage rates, or what we will call an "income redistribution policy." It works by changing the rate of pay so that the poor earn more for what they do, and the rich earn less. One way to accomplish this is by holding the highest wages at their current level, and allowing the lower wages to rise so that they gradually approach the higher wages. The great advantage of such a system is that the work disincentive to the rich would be balanced out by the added incentive to the poor, as a result of the higher wage (and probably more than balanced out). Therefore in this method of redistribution nothing would be lost in total productivity, and there might be an overall gain. Furthermore, this system has the added advantage that no one gets something for nothing, all income is received through work and is earned. The increase that goes to the poor is a result of the increase in productivity. Nothing is being taken away from the rich. They are just not gaining from additional productivity until a just level of equity is attained between high and low wages. What this implies is that the present position of the rich is due to an unjust appropriation of past productivity, and this is being corrected by putting a freeze on their current ability to gain from additional increase in the product. This, of course, is one general example of such a system. There are numerous other related possibilities.

What would it take for such a system to be put into effect? Let us begin to answer this question by recognizing that the concept of a minimum wage is already a step in the above direction.* The minimum wage was established by an Act of Congress, and it is constantly adjusted, as are taxes, by Congressional action. And the very currency in which we receive our wages, its regulation, the interest rates on it, and so forth, are all matters of government policy.

The Matter of "Big Government"   We mention the above about tax policy to get across the point that a society has the power to institute whatever economic policy it chooses. This is what we referred to in Chapter 7 as "the choice of freedoms." Government is nothing other than the name given to that power of a society to fashion and regulate itself. This point of view runs counter to a laissez-faire current in mainstream economic thinking that we should try to avoid big government.

To us, the concept of *big government* obscures the essentials of the issue. For it is not a question of whether government is big or not, but what values that government puts into practice. More specifically, does it move society towards meeting its basic needs and self-actualization, or towards inequality and all that implies? That is, or should be, the question. If "small" government is what is needed to put these values into practice, then that government should be small; if "big" government is needed, then that government should be big. As history shows us, whether one supports or opposes government action depends upon what interests and values are promoted by that action. It is all a question of whose interests we are talking about. For humanists the interests of the socially disadvantaged are the ones they opt for, because that promotes the *humanistically* efficient society.

Optimum Equality and Liberty   We can gain further understanding of the issues involved in instituting our incomes policy by looking at an additional aspect of Rawls' concept of justice. Rawls argues that optimum equality is the most just social goal, given that the implementation of this goal does not violate the basic civil liberties as provided for in the first ten amendments to the Constitution, the Bill of Rights.

What we need to keep in mind is that these civil liberties, or democratic rights, are essential to the fulfillment of the higher needs—belongingness, esteem, and self-actualization. If a society were to try to meet its material needs through methods that violated civil

---

*For a discussion of wage policies, and their ramifications, see Chapter 10.

liberties, then in meeting these lower needs it would be blocking its progress towards the higher needs. Such a society, if one were truly possible, would become increasingly materialistic, since progress past the material level was blocked by the curtailment of democratic rights. So it is humanistically inefficient for a society to meet material needs in a way that prevents passage to the higher needs.

EVOLUTIONARY STEPS TOWARDS HUMAN WELFARE

The Evolution of Democracy:
A Paradox

Humanistic economic goals, which are in essence democratic, only become enacted into law when a political system has sufficiently evolved to allow that degree of democratic expression. The more far-ranging the humanistic policy goal, the deeper the democratic process will have to be. In other words, economic justice requires democracy.

The enacting of an income redistribution policy, for example, depends on the extent to which democratic interests are able to overcome special interests in the political process. Since humanistic reforms generally run against the status quo, or the existing power structure, they always have to run against the active opposition of this structure in order to become enacted into law. This struggle has occurred along every step of the way in building a humanistic economy and a humanistic society. This has included the passage of the labor laws protecting children, the referendum system, the minimum wage, the Federal Reserve Banking System, the income tax, as we mentioned, and even the federal assurance of a secret ballot. All of these in their time were labeled as un-American, or some such similar denigration, by the groups wanting to maintain the status quo.

The accomplishment of political reform always presents us with a study in paradox. Certain vested interests have undue control of the political process. We want to change that process so that these influences are diminished. But it is precisely because of the control of those vested interests that the political process is not open to democratic change. This is a chicken and egg problem: a paradox. Can it be solved?

We know that the problem has been solved, because we have witnessed continual change in the direction of increasing the democratic process. If the paradox of democratic political change were unsolveable, there would never have been any change in the first place, and we would never have witnessed the evolution of democracy.

The basis for this change, or its explanation, lies in the tenets of humanistic psychology. It is that in each of us, whether politically powerful or politically weak, lies the force of self-actualization, the drive towards higher needs and higher values. If democracy is one of the higher truths, and the evidence is that it is, then the continuing evolution of each of us brings us ever closer to that realization and understanding. It is this evolutionary force that allows the paradox of political control to be broken. Both the controllers and the controlled (to set up a cut-and-dried distinction) are in the process of evolution. For the controlled, it is the recognition that they have been treated unfairly, and the greater political cohesion that this recognition brings. For the controller, it is the loss of the will to control and even the recognition that control should be given up. That is how democracy evolves, and thus we find a gradual development of economic structures that meet human ends. In addition, each new structure, or humanistic advance, in the sense that it reduces inequality and expands the democratic process, sets the stage for the next advance. We can expect that the broad institutional advances would roughly follow the order of the hierarchy of human needs.

Combining Maslow's hierarchy with political democracy can be expected to propel societies on an evolutionary path that will ultimately make possible the highest quality of life for everybody. The next series of chapters will take a closer look at each of the major stages one would expect a democratic society to go through. Let us briefly summarize the steps towards increasing human welfare.

(a) First and foremost, as a necessary condition of social welfare, *the basic physiological needs will have to be satisfied for every citizen*. Persistent hunger, starvation, or malnutrition of any member(s) in a society denies the existence of social welfare. It is inefficient (or wasteful) to have a system satisfy higher (and less urgent) needs without satisfying all the basic (and more urgent) physiological needs in the economy. The poor, hungry, ill-housed will not have the same chance for happiness as the wealthy. Chapter 10 will take a closer look at poverty and ways to end it.

(b) After the basic physiological needs of society are satisfied, it is the function of the state to provide a *basic institutional framework enabling freedom from fear of potential future adversity*. In other words, while principle (a) demands a basic minimum standard of living, principle (b) guarantees this standard for the future—security. To further illustrate the distinction: a booming laissez-faire economy may very well satisfy condition (a) but there is always the possibility (and fear) of recession, precluding the satisfaction of principle (b), security.

Principles (a) and (b) constitute the basic philosophy of the contemporary European welfare states that we will examine in greater detail in Chapter 11. But to a humanist economist there is more to welfare, something beyond the welfare state. This leads us to the third principle.

(c) Provided the physiological and safety needs are both universally met, *every citizen should have the right and opportunity to satisfy his or her social needs of belonging, being esteemed, and having self-respect.* Equal opportunity on this level is directly related to the socio-economic activity of the individual: buying, selling, and—above all—working. The right to work is fundamental here; any prolonged unemployment, regardless of how well the unemployed person is compensated, will preclude "advanced" humanistic status.

Next we focus on the quality of work and the nature of the jobs. The need for employee participation in decision-making, and for less alienating jobs, must be widely respected. Failure of an economic system to deliver here is indicated by a high degree of rank-and-file labor unrest manifesting itself in excessive absenteeism and a tendency towards spontaneous wildcat strikes. Chapter 12 will discuss the basic issues. Moreover, the highest stage under principle (c) would be reached where full employment and meaningful jobs are supplemented by industrial democracy in the form of worker self-management. As Chapter 13 will show, self-management is a delicate issue and will have to be instituted properly, if it is to hold up its promise.

The advanced humanist economic system as described under principle (c) is the necessary and sufficient condition for maximum human welfare, or well-being, on a society-wide scale. Self-actualization cannot be legislated, but the economic institutions can be organized or reorganized so as to enable it. The recognition of this, and its practical implementation, is an exciting and soul-stirring journey. That is why we see humanistic economics in the same terms.

References

1. Schumacher, E. F. "An Interview with E. F. Schumacher." In *Catholic Worker*, May 1977, p. 4.

2. Maslow, Abraham. *Motivation and Personality*. 2nd ed. New York: Harper and Row, 1970, p. 97.

3. Maslow, Abraham. *Motivation and Personality*. 2nd ed. New York: Harper and Row, 1970, p. 97.

4. Maslow, Abraham. *Motivation and Personality*. 2nd ed. New York: Harper and Row, 1970, p. 98.

5. Graham, William K. and Balloun, Joe. "An Empirical Test of Maslow's Need Hierarchy Theory." In *Journal of Humanistic Psychology*, 13, 1, Winter 1973.
   Also Alderfer, C. P. "An Empirical Test of a New Theory of Human Needs." In *Organizational Behavior and Human Performance*, 1969, 4, pp. 141–75.

6. Georgescu-Roegen, Nicholas. "Choice, Expectations and Measurability." In *Quarterly Journal of Economics*, 68, 4, November 1954, p. 518.

7. Rawls, John. *A Theory of Justice*. Cambridge (Mass.): Harvard University Press, 1971.

8. Alexander, Sidney. "Human Values and Economists' Values." In *Human Values and Economic Policy*, edited by Sidney Hook. New York: New York University Press, 1967, pp. 112–13.

9. Grout, Paul. "Rawlsian Justice and Economic Theory." In *Economics and Equality*, edited by Rt. Hon. Aubrey Jones. Oxford: Phillip Allan, 1976, p. 138.

Chapter Ten

AN END TO POVERTY: THE TOP PRIORITY

INTRODUCTION

It happens every time. Take a professional like an economist, a sociologist, a lawyer, a psychologist, a doctor, or even a politician, and have him or her visit homes of people living in poverty. This professional might well have been aware that there are substantial numbers of poor families in industrialized and affluent countries like America. He or she would probably have been sympathetic to the problems of poverty, and have hoped that modern society would eventually eradicate such a condition. But, nevertheless, the person is shocked and moved after having made the visit to the poor family. Something has happened.

A doctor has been persuaded to make a rare home visit. "My God, that's awful. They don't even have running water in that trailer."

"But I told you," says the social service worker, "that the children couldn't be bathed as often as you asked because they don't have water."

"But when you said no water, I just thought you meant no good water. I never imagined they didn't have any water, and had to carry it inside in big plastic containers."

"But that's what I told you."

"I never imagined. What do they do for a bathroom?"

"An outhouse."

"In the winter?"

"They also have a chamber pot inside."

"A chamber pot! I thought those went out with gaslight. Haven't they tried to get any water and plumbing?"

"Oh, they'd love to have it, but they're nowhere near affording it. They owe around $500 now on back bills, utility, medical, and so forth, and they are going further into debt."

The doctor shakes his head and answers his own question when he immediately realizes that they could never get a loan for the plumbing. "How are people allowed to live like that?" he wonders. "All of them, the four kids and all, cramped into that tiny space. And that reeking oil stove they use for heat is a total health hazard. The place ought to be condemned." And the doctor also realizes that if it were condemned they would be out on the street. "It's hard to believe," he says quietly to himself.

Few of us of the professional class, college students, the middle class, really know. We may know the statistics, and we *may* be sympathetic. But few of us have really been there, have seen it and felt it, and we don't really know.

Knowing about poverty abstractly is not adequate. What's more, having mere intellectual knowledge is often deceptive. When we "know" statistical facts we think that we know and understand the problem, but we don't. That doctor in our illustration is just beginning to know and understand the problem. He had, for one of the first times in his life, gut-level contact with what it means to be poor. He might even begin to understand how the abstract facts can lull a person into thinking that he or she understands.

Economics is greatly plagued by this problem. Like any other academic field, it is dominated by abstract and analytical thinking. As a social science it ought to be concerned about the lives of people, but as a positivistic science it often has the barest contact with the feeling level of reality. The head is fortified and reinforced, and the heart is choked off. Then economics becomes an ivory-tower exercise that mentally manipulates this variable and that variable, and theorizes about factors of production and general equilibrium, while people literally go hungry in the streets below.

A particular sociologist who, by rare good fortune, was able to raise himself to that profession out of a childhood of severe poverty, has a feeling for the realities of poverty that few of his colleagues have. He has these memories:

- Mother putting hot cloths on her children's bellies to calm hunger pangs.

- Mother putting hot pepper in the flour so the children wouldn't eat up all of the cake. Birthday cake made without sugar or shortening.

- Going to bed early on Christmas because there are no presents.

- His brother being "laughed out of school" in the third grade because he wore funny clothes.

For him this kind of poverty meant, 'The slow death of our spirit that is not just a memory, but remains with us like a scar—a scar easily opened by a reminder of what having nothing is all about.''[1]

In the early 1900s when the social-work field was beginning, many of the first social workers were upper-class women who, out of a combination of sympathy for the poor and zeal to reform the poor's alcoholic and morally deficient ways, marched into the slums to bring Judeo-Christian self-betterment to these woeful souls. These social workers were also shocked, not only at the extent of the dire poverty, but also at the fact that the majority of the poor were not drunken and lazy, as these crusading members of the upper crust had been led to believe. Despite the preset expectations of these slum visitors, many of them were forced to recognize that the plight of the poor was to a large degree a result of the crushing weight of social and economic circumstances.

The attitudes of these early social workers were not confined just to the wealthy, and just to that period of time. It is quite evident that even today there are widespread attitudes *against* the poor. The poor are seen as somehow deficient, and believed to be poor because they are unworthy of anything better. The popular image is that of the welfare cheat who lives the soft life at the expense of the working person.

In the experience of those who have been poor, or others who have had actual contact with the poor, such as our doctor friend, the reality is quite different. They are quite convinced of the genuine difficulties and deprivation that loom in the lives of the poor as all but insurmountable barriers to changing their own condition. In the face of this experience the attitude we just referred to appears as a set of cruel myths that damage both the poor and society at large.

As we have seen in other instances, myths such as these have a historical origin and development, and fulfill a particular social purpose. When we turn to what we can call the history of poverty, we may be able to discern what these are.

For now the question is, who are the poor?

The Poor: Figures and Facts

It was only in 1964 that the United States government tried rigorously to estimate the number of poor in this country. They went about it in the following way. The Department of Agriculture devised a "minimal food plan (budget)" for "emergency and temporary use when funds are low." The cost of this food budget, say, for a family of four, was calculated on a year's basis. The Department then turned to the findings of a study that was done in 1955 which showed that the average poor family spent about one-third of its total income on food. Therefore, by multiplying the calculated minimum food budget by 3, the government arrived at the minimum overall budget that a family of four needed to live on. This amount of income defined the poverty line. The number of families who had a lower income than this were called the *poor*. By adjusting for changes in the cost of the minimum food budget in different years, the number of poor could then be calculated for years previous to 1964, as well as the years since.

By this method, for example, the poverty line for an urban family of four in 1960 was roughly $3000. The number of people who fell below this level was approximately 40 million, which amounted to 22.2 percent of the population. Table 10.1 shows trends in absolute poverty compiled by the Bureau of the Census for the years 1959 to 1975. A number of comments about this table are in order.

First of all, as noted in footnotes of Table 10.1, in 1966 a change in the way of collecting data *statistically* reduced the number of poor.

TABLE 10.1 TRENDS IN POVERTY, 1959–75

Years	Number of poor (in thousands)	Percentage of population
1959	39,490	22.4
1960	39,851	22.2
1961	39,628	21.9
1962	38,625	21.0
1963	36,436	19.5
1964	36,055	19.0
1965	33,185	17.3
1966*	28,510	14.7
1967	27,769	14.2
1968	25,389	12.8
1969**	24,147	12.1
1970	25,420	12.6
1971	25,559	12.5
1972	24,460	11.3
1973	22,973	11.1
1974	24,260	11.6
1975	25,900	12.0

*After 1966, the data rely on a different procedure for processing income data. The new procedures reduced the estimate of poor people in 1966 by about 6.2 percent. In other words, the 1974 estimate of the poor as a percentage of the population might be about 12.6 percent, rather than 11.6 percent, if based on the earlier methods.

**After 1969, the data rely on new procedures for collecting income data. It is not clear what effect these changes have had on the estimates of the poverty population.

This correction was not introduced into the previous years of the table, so that the decline from 17.3 to 14.7 percent from 1965 to 1966 represents, at least in large measure, a change in statistical method, not a change in the number of poor.

Second, the method of calculating a minimal food budget, developed in 1964, is based on careful and precise, essentially computerized budgeting—so that *just* the right amount of potatoes are bought (say, 5.7 pounds) and just the right amount of milk, and so forth. It is easily recognized that this is not the way people really buy their food, rich or poor, and thus the minimum food budget is not realistic, and is set too low. A poor family lacks the necessary information and knowledge to live on this minimal amount of food. However, even with this method of estimating the food budget, the poverty-line level of food expenditure according to 1973 figures was a meager 33 cents a meal per person.

Third, and most important, the estimation that a poor family spends one-third of its income on food depends upon the assumption that increases (or any changes) in food prices over the years since 1955 are in proportion to price increases in other commodities, such as housing. If these other costs have increased at a faster rate than the cost of food then the multiplication by 3 becomes an underestimate. This, in fact, has been the case. Professor David Gordon has estimated that to take this differential cost increase into account we would need to update the 1973 figures, for example, by multiplying the food budget by a factor of 4 rather than 3. (He estimates that food costs as of 1973 amounted to only one-fourth of a poor family's budget.) Using this estimate, the poverty line moves upward, and roughly 18 percent of the population falls below it, not the 11.1 percent the table shows.[2]

In summary, if we use Gordon's adjustment and note that the number of poor have increased since 1973 we arrive at the observation that there has been relatively little decline since 1960. With all these considerations we conclude that the official estimates of poverty are underestimates, and the decline in percentages in the table may be largely exaggerated.

This is not to say that there has not been some real decline over the years in the number of poor. Certainly, since the Depression years of the 1930s this has been the case. In President Franklin Roosevelt's famous 1937 Inaugural Address he said, "I see one-third of a nation ill-housed, ill-clad, ill-nourished," a figure which economic studies have supported. By today's statistics we can make the broad estimate that roughly 20 percent of our population are living in poverty, which is a decline from the 1930s. But the impression of a continuing and constant elimination of poverty that some analysts suggest does not seem to be supported by a careful look at the data.

Profile of the Poor   Now that we have discussed the issue of overall numbers we need to see who makes up this group of absolute poverty.

What people find themselves in this unfortunate position? It might be expected that a large majority of the poor do not work. But this is not the case. As Table 10.2 indicates, over 50 percent of the poor work either full- or part-time. If people work full-time how could they be poor, it might be asked? The answer is that a full-time job at the minimum wage by the wage earner in a family of four would not earn that family enough income to put it above the poverty level.

TABLE 10.2 WORK EXPERIENCE OF POOR FAMILIES, 1973

	% of poor families
All families	100%
Worked full year	26%
Worked part year	30%
due to unemployment	10%
other reason (sickness, injury, etc.)	20%
Did not work at all	44%

Source: U.S. Bureau of the Census.

Being black or a member of another minority group greatly increases one's chances of being poor. About one-half of all the poor are in this category. To look at this racial factor from a different statistical perspective, more than one-half of *all* non-white children are growing up in poverty. A very large percentage of the poor come from families with a single woman as head of the household. As of the middle 1970s, approximately 40 percent of all poor families were in this situation, and the percentages appear to be getting larger.

Other large groups of the poor are the aged, the sick, and the disabled. It is interesting to note that not counted in the estimates of the poor are the residents of mental hospitals. A sizeable number of this group are in the hospital because they lack adequate employment. Many social scientists recognize that to a considerable extent our state mental hospitals function as large poorhouses.

Conclusion

Once again we need to point out that a presentation of data on poverty, and the attempt to arrive at exact figures, may obscure the *experiential* reality. This is that one person's economic deprivation and suffering is equal to the suffering of an infinity of persons. If a million people suffer, each is suffering as an individual. The arithmetic of suffering, therefore, does not respect the adding machine. For a humanist, if one person is ill-housed, ill-clad, and ill-nourished, that is one too many.

It generally comes as a surprise to people to discover that, in a very important sense, poverty did not exist four hundred years ago. Poverty as we know it is a relatively recent phenomenon.

How can this be, it is asked? Haven't we actually begun to eliminate poverty over these last several hundred years, the years of the growth of the modern industrial economy? Not entirely true. Part of the effect of the rise of the industrial era has actually been the *creation* of the kind of poverty we know today.

In many respects poverty is relative. For example, before the invention of the washing machine and clothes dryer, washing your clothes in a tub or a brook and hanging them out to dry was not a sign of poverty. Today the sight of clothes hung out to dry across a porch or a fire escape is a mark of a slum. Of course, being hungry is absolute. Either you are or you are not. But many other aspects of poverty—such as what are the means by which you live, what is your style of life—are relative. The concept of what is necessary for a minimally decent life is not absolute, but changes with the times.

Surprising as it may sound, the modern phenomenon of poverty had its beginning with the Enclosure Movement in England (Once common land was enclosed for commercial purpose). Previous to that, under the stable social order of traditional society, poverty pockets as we know them now were almost nonexistent. In such a society people's needs were met by extended kinship and family ties. For those relatively few people who did not have family support, in particular the migrating unemployed and immigrants, their needs were fairly adequately met by the churches and monasteries.

Certainly there was a great disparity in wealth, which largely meant land, between the feudal nobility and the commoners. But this wasn't crucial. The commoners made up the overwhelming percentage of the population, probably at least 80 to 90 percent. Those who made up the aristocracy had that position by birth. What we call social mobility was practically non-existent then. If you were a commoner you accepted that status, the status of most other people, and there wasn't the slightest expectation of changing. In that vast multitude there was little social differentiation or inequality. Everyone had about the same and, what's more, everyone had about enough. In this kind of situation the concept of poverty as we know it does not have much meaning.

With the breakup of the feudal order, and the increasing practice of enclosing the heretofore common lands, an overflow of uprooted and migratory persons was created, and suddenly the practice of begging appeared on the scene on a scale not previously imagined. The churches could no longer cope with this; their capacity for charity was stretched past the limit. Thus we find that in 1531 Poor Laws enter

English history for the first time (and English history at that point is also American history). The Poor Laws were originally passed to regulate begging. They required that a license was needed in order to beg. People considered able-bodied were denied such a license.

In 1536 the Laws were amended to allow all children under fourteen who were then roaming around the countryside to be turned over to an "employer" and be "taught" a trade. Some forty years later, work projects were instituted for adults as well. The able-bodied poor were assigned to the processing of wool, hemp, flax, etc., in order to receive relief-level wages.

The Attitude Towards Poverty

In the sixteenth century we observe an increasing number of poor laws, which indicate that society was confronted with a new and growing problem. Perhaps the term *social problem* becomes appropriate here for the first time. Of course, there were problems before then that we could describe as social problems, but the society of that time saw all such problems as falling within the province of the Church, and it was up to the Church to solve them. The monasteries had provided shelter and relief for the indigent before this time. This social function was quite acceptable to the Church, and to the society of which that Church was an integral part. Wasn't the Savior himself poor? "Blessed are the poor," it is taught, and the lesson formed a central part of church philosophy. Likewise, the masses of common folk took contentment in the words of the Bible, "It is easier for a camel to pass through the eye of a needle than for a rich man to enter the Kingdom of Heaven." As for the nobility, it was widely recognized and accepted that they had their wealth through birth, and not through covetousness. Any anxieties in this matter were allayed by their support of the Church's charitable work.

This attitude of respect, and even reverence, for the poor was to undergo a change. By the middle 1600s, a century before Adam Smith, we find almost its opposite. A transformation had taken place, and the poor were now looked down upon, and even despised. The spirit, and the duty, of charity of the Middle Ages was replaced by a new point of view. Those who were suffering the misfortune of poverty were now seen to be paying for sin. Religious chastisement, which had previously been reserved for greed and avarice, was instead turned toward idleness. A typical expression of this was by Milton's friend, Samuel Hartlib, "the law of God saith, 'he that will not work, let him not eat.' This would be a sore scourge and smart whip for idle persons if . . . none should be suffered to eat till they had wrought (worked) for it."[3] A stance of severity towards the poor, which was once considered sinful, was now considered a duty.

The new Puritan attitudes towards work and the poor were expressed in the 1669 passage of an act under which a company was to be established with power to apprehend vagrants, offering them the choice between work and whipping, and to set to compulsory labor all other poor persons, including children, who were without means of maintaining themselves.

The concept of putting the poor to work continued to develop in England for the next two hundred years. In 1722 the law created the institution of the *workhouse*, which often meant that the poor were farmed out to a private entrepreneur who built the facilities to employ large numbers of workers. Later on the workhouses were found to be inadequate to absorb the number of poor, and the government took the step in 1795 of providing *wage supplements* for minimum subsistence. This was one of the earliest instances of the principle of direct work relief. It should be kept in mind, however, that this was not a departure from the new Puritan morality, for the levels of support were indeed minimal; the principle was that relief should be set not merely to relieve, but also to deter. David Ricardo saw in welfare allowances, since they were adjusted for family size, an encouragement for large families, and argued that the allowances should be abolished.

The laws relating welfare to work were continually tinkered with and adjusted depending on matters like economic conditions, the number of indigent, and the current philosophical fashion. A writer in 1771, arguing for a reduction in wages, expressed a common point of view, "Everyone but an idiot knows that the lower classes must be kept poor, or they will never be industrious."[4] In 1834 workhouses were further enlarged to accommodate every able-bodied person. Only in cases of "sudden and urgent necessity" could direct relief be given to people in their homes. But whatever modifications the original Poor Laws went through, and despite the negative and inhumane attitudes that formed them, they did firmly establish the principle of work relief or public assistance.

In the next chapter we will discuss the recent development of public assistance, and particularly in modern Europe, where we find the most thorough implementation of the concept. It is in Europe that the rather revolutionary idea has taken hold that part of a citizen's human *rights* is the guarantee of a decent life on a physical level. On the other hand, this concept is still frowned on in the United States and Canada, where it tends to be seen as a failure or limitation of a free-market economic system. We will try to show in that chapter the fallacies of this North American attitude, and the unfortunate consequences for society.

FULL EMPLOYMENT AND THE DECLINE OF POVERTY

For now we turn to other ways to end poverty that are based on the concepts of full employment and adequate wages. These approaches are not alternatives to the idea of welfare guarantees, since the two areas are blended together in the European welfare concept, but they can be seen as a separate approach to the problem of poverty and human fulfillment. Looking at Table 10.2 (see p. 178) should give us a clear idea what kind of action is needed. Almost half of our families are poor because of unemployment, and it is for this reason that providing them with suitable jobs is priority number one. The government has to be committed to this end.

Traditionally, economists had objected to any such government policy, and they did so on the basis of scientific reasoning. A case was made using an old doctrine of Jean-Baptiste Say, enunciated in the early 1800s, that unemployment could not be anything more than a temporary disequilibrium problem in the labor market. As such it would cure itself if the market was allowed to adjust itself. All that was necessary would be flexible wage rates, flexible enough to decline as much as required by the law of supply and demand. Everybody could get a job, if he or she really tried, or if there were no rigidities in the system due to trade unions. As a result, unemployment was seen as essentially a voluntary phenomenon, a self-imposed misery by the workers. Economics had little else to say about it and certainly did not worry about the problem. The only policy they saw government fit to perform was that of resisting the unions, or at least restraining their wage-fixing powers.

The Protest of Humanistic Economists: A Brief Digression It was always one of the distinguishing characteristics of humanistic economists to take poverty and unemployment very seriously. As we saw in our historical survey, it was Simonde de Sismondi who first studied the recurrent economic crises of early industrialization and attributed them to a lack of purchasing power of the increasingly impoverished new working class. Unemployment he saw as the result of an industrial system that channels too much of revenue into profits and too little into wages. Only through periodical slumps in which prices and profits, as well as employment, tumbled could the necessary balance between production and consumer purchasing power be reestablished.

The same idea was advanced in a much more elaborate and refined form by John Hobson around the turn of this century.[5] In fact, as we saw in Chapter 2, it was this very idea that caused him to be fired from the London School of Economics. To blame underconsumption (or overproduction) as the main cause of unemployment and to advocate government spending as its cure was considered ample proof of total incompetency in economic matters.

In retrospect, an interesting thesis could be maintained that it was this cardinal "error" of going against Say that stripped humanistic economics of its credentials in academic matters. Challenging J. B. Say and the orthodox wisdom of the times implied that whatever else they had to say could not be taken seriously and was not worth entertaining by their more scientific colleagues.

It took the Great Depression of the 1930s and the reputability of leading economist John Maynard Keynes to recognize as entirely valid what up to then was mere heresy. Hobson was rehabilitated and given due credit for his pioneering thought several years before he died. But by that time nobody bothered to reexamine the rest of his economic thought, which had been so prematurely dismissed. The same, of course, pertains to Sismondi's economics.

Keynesian Full Employment Policies

It took the outstanding contribution of Keynes to convince the scientific community that much, if not all, unemployment results from a lack of total demand for goods and services. As a result, any government policy that would increase total spending in the economy was apt to mop up unemployment. This could be achieved indirectly by reducing taxes so as to replenish purchasing power of workers and businessmen or by making credit more available to the private sector through the monetary authorities—in the United States, the Federal Reserve System. More directly, government could increase its own spending on public goods, such as highway construction, military expenditures or other employment-creating measures. Any modern textbook will devote multiple chapters to expounding and comparing those alternative approaches to full employment. What used to be humanistic heresy is now mainstream orthodoxy.

Thanks to these developments there is much less public opposition to the notion of enlisting government for the cause of full employment. Most recently the older Full Employment Act of 1945 has been strengthened by the Humphrey-Hawkins Full Employment Act, which commits the Federal Government to make full employment one of its foremost concerns.

In spite of all these positive developments over the last two or three decades, there are still millions of unproductive citizens unable to find jobs, and because of it, forced to raise their families in an environment of poverty, if not despair. Typically, 6 to 8 percent of the civilian labor force has been unemployed, the only exceptions having been the years of the Korean and Vietnam Wars when unemployment temporarily dropped below 5 percent.

Apparently the Federal Government has been unwilling to make the necessary effort to stimulate the peacetime economy. The Keynesian medicines have not been administered in sufficient doses and the question *why* needs to be asked.

There appear to be two main, and related, reasons. First, the contemporary economist has chosen to define 4 or even 5 percent unemployment as full employment, and he or she defends this redefinition by the presence of what is called *structural* and *frictional unemployment*, neither of which (according to theory) can be greatly reduced by pumping more purchasing power into the economy. Structural unemployment refers to a mismatch between job vacancies and job seekers, brought about by unwanted or inadequate skills or geographical shifts in industrial jobs. The frictional component of unemployment consists of people that happen to be caught between two jobs when the monthly unemployment survey is conducted. It is for these reasons that economists have been advocating a 5 percent unemployment target as a reasonable goal of a full-employment policy. But the great majority of economists never bother to ask the question why the economies in Continental Europe, as well as in Australia, have been able to run on something like 2 or 3 percent unemployment, and this for decade after decade. Until we can explain why the U.S. should have more structural and frictional unemployment than most of the rest of the developed world, declaring 5 percent unemployment as full employment, then these theories of unemployment lack credibility.

Second, economists have been making it one of their most cherished functions to remind the public constantly that too strong a commitment to full employment is likely to be inflationary. We hear and see everywhere elaborate commentaries about the costs of inflation, ranging from disruptions in the market to the ailing dollar abroad. Rarely does the economist address the human costs arising from being unemployed, the feeling of being useless to society and the disturbance of family life.

We do not quarrel with the basic conception that in a market economy the move towards full employment is not costless. The costs of heavy inflation are painful and real. However, the humanist value of full employment is prepotent, meaning that in a humanistic economy there is no so-called *trade-off* between inflation and unemployment. As long as there are unemployed poor, considerations of humanistic economic efficiency and Rawlsian justice require that we address this issue first. True, there may be poor families and individuals that are further impoverished through rampant inflation, but that is a different question, and can be solved differently. This brings us to the second elementary policy tool in the arsenal of a society's all-out war on poverty: an effective minimum wage policy.

Combatting Poverty with Minimum Wage Legislation

According to the data in Table 10.2, a quarter of all families living in poverty have a head of household who has a full-time job. Thus, these are people who can be referred to as the working poor. What can be done for them? Common sense would say that if working a job at inadequate wages is the problem, then making the wages adequate would solve the problem. All that is needed is the legislation of a minimum wage high enough to ensure that the income from work takes one above the level of poverty. But this common-sense approach has been constantly challenged by a small but influential group of economists ever since 1938 when the Federal minimum wage was set at 25 cents an hour.

Let us illustrate this problem by referring to a recent interview with William Winpisinger, the president of a large AFL-CIO industrial union, when he was asked about labor's political clout in Congress:

WINPISINGER: Take the minimum wage just as a starting point. We had to fight hammer and tongs, and down the gutter, to get it passed. We had to call chits that we could have left uncalled on that one. Who benefited from it?

EDITOR: You know the reactions of many economists to this one? It increases the unemployment rate of black youngsters.

WINPISINGER: Bull. Those economists don't happen to live on $3.30 an hour. They ought to try it some time. Why should we hold down the living standard of huge numbers of people on the phony altar that it creates unemployment, when there isn't a single statistic anywhere that will support that argument. As a matter of fact, the minimum wage is up now and unemployment is dropping, isn't it?[6]

Here we have it in a nut shell: Whenever there is talk about the minimum wage, immediately there is the economist's mention of unemployment. By associating one with the other as if there were a natural link, willingly or unwillingly a case is made against minimum wages. Now the unionist boldly claims that all this talk about unemployment is false, and even denies any statistical basis for this association. Who is right? The issue appears sufficiently important to warrant a closer look.

Economic Theory and Minimum Wages   In answering the previous question, we first have to understand on what kind of assumptions the phony altar of unemployment has been built; is it built on rock or is it built on sand? The economist will approach the question of minimum wages from the standpoint of theory; more specifically, from a conception of how the labor market works for teenagers. Immediately, he or she sees two curves, one demand, the other supply, and the intersection yielding the equilibrium price of labor, which is the wage rate. In the process the economist makes the following assumptions that are relevant for our purposes.

1. The least efficient workers in each factory or business establishment are paid poorly because they are contributing only marginally to the firm's output. Workers are paid according to their productivity.

2. Firms are operating in (almost) perfectly competitive product markets, making it impossible for them to pass legislated higher wages on in the form of higher prices.

3. Firms are all working at all times with the most efficiently designed business organization. The harsh winds of competition don't allow for survival of the enterprise, unless there is no slack (or call it waste) in the production scheduling, job assignments, etc.

If any of these three assumptions are violated, the alleged adverse employment effects are much more uncertain. Let us see why this is so.

First, if a company has hired a janitor and pays him or her $2.50 an hour, could it not be that the employee is really "worth" $3.00, but that $2.50 is the going rate, let us say the minimum wage? The answer is likely to be in the affirmative, unless the labor market is "perfect" with respect to the information that the janitor possesses about alternative job opportunities, "perfect" with respect to job mobility (i.e., instant no-cost switching of jobs all around the country is necessary) and "perfect" with respect to competition among employers for janitorial services (i.e., a very large number of potentially interested bosses). These are the most important assumptions, but there are more. Clearly, in the real world there is very little that is "perfect," let alone the labor market for janitors. But any evaluation of the altar hinges on *how* perfectly the labor market works. The basic problem is that we cannot know; it is a question that cannot be tested empirically. If the economists' assumptions seem intuitively true, then you better believe in the soundness of the altar. But if you don't, it certainly does not follow that boosting the minimum wage from $2.50 to $2.90 would in any way endanger the job of our janitor. He or she is still worth the cost, only now a little less underpaid.

Second, if product markets are oligopolistic or monopolistic we would expect employers to be able to pass any higher minimum wage cost on to the consumer in form of higher product prices.* As a result, the productivity of all workers will rise in proportion to the product prices as well as to the minimum wage increase. Everybody is still "worth" their wage and nobody will be laid off.

Third, it is not uncommon to observe small firms like restaurants, sawmills, etc., operating at less than full efficiency because wages are so low that the entrepreneur can afford to tolerate inefficient production processes and a relatively undisciplined work force. Once the minimum pay is drastically raised, however, management gets shocked

---

*In order to be perfectly rigorous we have to assume, as Galbraith does, that large corporations maximize growth rather than short-run profits and for this reason employ a cost-plus-pricing formula.[7]

into tightening labor discipline and exploring more carefully ways to cut production costs. Through such greater efficiency, the average productivity of the workers rises, making massive layoffs less than certain.

To conclude, even though simplistic supply-and-demand economics would strongly suggest that the altar is anything but phony, one walks away with a different impression after having studied the underlying issues more carefully.

Statistical Evidence of Minimum Wages Causing Teenage Unemployment
What about the union leader's claim that there isn't a "single statistic" anywhere that can be used in support of the phony economic relationship between teenage unemployment and hikes in the minimum wage rate? Quick checking of most standard economics textbooks will not confirm Mr. Winpisinger on this point. Rather, it readily appears that most economists would take for granted some adverse employment effects of minimum wages, if not for the work force at large, at least for the teenager. But if discussions in earlier chapters have demonstrated anything, it is that we cannot always take textbook wisdom as the ultimate truth. Let us give Mr. Winpisinger a fair hearing and examine the data more carefully.

During the early Seventies, when the Nixon administration was seriously considering creating a separate and lower minimum wage for teenagers, economists showed an unusual interest in this topic. The literature was suddenly full of articles dealing with the question of minimum wages and teenage unemployment. By sifting the literature one student found a dozen studies, all published between 1966 and 1973, dealing with this question.[8] These studies appeared quite comparable, since all of them analyzed similar variables, employed similar statistical techniques, and researched roughly the same time periods running from 1955 to 1970. But, significantly enough, the results were much less similar than an empiricist would tend to expect. Of the twelve studies, seven attributed rising teenage unemployment to various degrees to increases in the minimum wage; five, on the other hand, found no such evidence.[9] Among the latter we have a careful study done by the Bureau of Labor Statistics which found that:

□ In general, the most important factor explaining changes in teenage employment and unemployment has been general business conditions.[10]

And the study then concluded that:

□ Apparently, any measure of the effects of minimum wage laws upon teenage employment and unemployment is highly sensitive to the variables included in the analysis, the measure of the minimum wage used, and the specification of the equation. When all variables that have a legitimate claim to consideration are included, the measures of the minimum wage not infrequently have the wrong sign and/or are not statistically significant at conventional levels. This is generally true whether one looks at quarterly or annual data, at data for the entire postwar period or more limited time segments, or at data for teenagers as a whole, or teenagers compartmentalized into various sex-color-age groups.[11]

Finally, in an interesting attempt to reconcile the contradictory evidence, it could be demonstrated that of the seven studies,* two suddenly showed quite different results by being slightly recast. So, for example, the study by Adie, published in 1973 and so often referred to by the opponents of minimum wages, would have come up with opposite conclusions if the author had extended his analysis to cover the years 1966 to 1972. Similarly, the findings by Burns seemed to no longer hold if an omitted variable were inserted.[12] The final score of the evidence would be drastically reversed if one takes such a recount seriously.

But, whatever the true picture, it is by no means as clear as the Chicago economists make one believe, and so many textbooks imply. On this basis it would not seem all that improper to give minimum wages, as well as Mr. Winpisinger, the benefit of the doubt.

Minimum Wages and the Policy of Full Employment

For the sake of argument, let us assume the worst, namely that minimum wages do cause some layoffs among teenagers and even (as a far greater concession) among some adult low-wage workers. But, and here comes our basic point, this is only regrettable if we passively accept the evil. As we have argued earlier, there is no reason why a true commitment to full employment, carried out selectively or across the board, will not be able to take care of the problem and provide employment in new jobs that can afford to pay a decent wage.

As a result we have to conclude that the scientific case against minimum wages, whatever its merits may be, implicitly assumes that government cannot (or should not) provide the necessary remedial action. Without this assumption—call it value judgement if you will—the case against minimum wages as an effective tool in diminishing poverty is nothing more than purely academic.

Minimum Wages and Inflation We have tried to show that a *combined* policy of full employment and minimum wages is a most effective and direct way to tackle the problem of the working poor. There is one

---

*As an interesting side note, we should add that most of the research in which unemployment effect had been attributed to minimum wages was reported by economists who have had a direct relationship with the University of Chicago or else published their respective findings in its journal, *The Journal of Political Economy*. This may be a pure coincidence, but it does remind us of the old Bible saying: "He who seeketh shall find."

remaining snag. What happens if our combined policy instruments have a serious impact on inflation? Would this not erode the purchasing power of the working man and woman and so in effect erode whatever gains had been made by legislating an adequate level of pay? It most likely would, if we didn't move towards protecting the minimum wage from inflation. This can be directly accomplished by linking it to the increases in the cost-of-living. Economists refer to this type of policy as "indexing," and have at times advocated that we so protect Social Security benefits. There is no reason why it cannot be done for both Social Security benefits and minimum wages. Nor will this necessarily lead to an ever accelerating inflation, as the experience of so many Western European countries clearly demonstrates.*

CONCLUSION

As long as there is poverty amidst plenty in an economy, any attempt to picture it as a humanistic economy misses the point; such an economic system is fundamentally wasteful and unjust.

Moreover, there is no compelling argument to allow us to treat poverty as a necessary evil. It may be necessary in terms of maximum want satisfaction for the few, but it is detrimental in an economy that aims at satisfying the basic needs of all of its constituents. We have outlined how, with just two policy measures—one full employment, the other "indexed" minimum wages—a society can take a big first step towards eliminating poverty.

These two policies would make major inroads in the battle against poverty, but the creation of a humanistic economy does not stop there, or with these policies. Other steps along the path are described in the next four chapters.

References

1. *All Things Considered.* National Public Radio. January 28, 1977.

2. Gordon, David, ed. *Problems in Political Economy: An Urban Perspective.* 2nd ed. Lexington (Mass.). D.C. Heath and Company, 1977, p. 297.

3. Tawney, R. H. *Religion and the Rise of Capitalism.* 1926. Reprint. New York: Mentor Books, 1954, p. 220.

4. Tawney, R. H. *Religion and the Rise of Capitalism.* 1926. Reprint. New York: Mentor Books, 1954, p. 224.

5. Hobson, J. A., and Mumery, A. F. *Physiology of Industry.* 1889. Reprints of Economic Classics. New York: A. M. Kelly, 1933.

---

*Most countries in Europe negotiate the minimum wage in the bargaining process between employers and unions. Inflation is one of the key variables that is considered in the bargain for higher wage rates. Moreover, just about all countries have, during the last five years, moved to fully "index" social security benefits.

6.   *Challenge*. March/April 1978, p. 52.

7.   Galbraith, J. K. *Economics and the Public Purpose*. Boston: Houghton Mifflin Company, 1973, p. 118.

8.   Colvin, John J. "The Effect of Federal Minimum Wages on Teenage Unemployment." Unpublished MA dissertation. University of Maine at Orono, August 1974.

9.   The seven studies finding an adverse effect are:

      Adie, D. K. "Teenage Unemployment and Real Federal Minimum Wages." In *Journal of Political Economy*, March/April 1973, pp. 435–41.

      Brozen, Yale. "The Effect of Statutory Minimum Wage Increases on Teenage Unemployment." *Journal of Law and Economics*, April 1969, pp. 109–122.

      Burns, Arthur F. *Management of Prosperity*. New York, 1966.

      Easley, J. E. and Fearn, R. M. "Minimum Wages and Unemployment of Teenagers." Unpublished paper, North Carolina State University, 1969.

      Kosters, M. and Welch, F. "The Effects of Minimum Wages on the Distribution of Changes in Aggregate Employment." *American Economic Review*, June 1972, pp. 323–32.

      Moore, Thomas G. "The Effect of Minimum Wages on Teenage Unemployment Rates." *Journal of Political Economy*, July/August 1971, pp. 897–902.

      Scully, G. W. "The Impact of Minimum Wages on the Unemployment Rates of Minority Group Labor." Unpublished Paper, Ohio University.

      The five studies *not* finding any such effect are:
      Barth, P. S. "The Minimum Wage and Teenage Unemployment." *Proceedings of the Industrial Relations Research Association*, 1969, pp. 296–310.

      Folk, H. "The Problem of Youth Unemployment." In *The Transition From School to Work*. A report based on the Princeton Manpower Symposium, May 9–10, 1968, pp. 76–107.

      Lovell, Michael C. "The Minimum Wage, Teenage Unemployment, and the Business Cycle." In *Western Economic Journal*, December 1972, pp. 414–27.

      Thurow, L. C. *Poverty and Discrimination*. Washington, 1969.

      U.S. Department of Labor, Bureau of Labor Statistics. *Youth Unemployment and Minimum Wages*. Bulletin 1657, Washington, 1970.

10.   Bureau of Labor Statistics. *Youth Unemployment and Minimum Wages*. Bulletin 1657, Washington, 1970, p. 45.

11.   Bureau of Labor Statistics. *Youth Unemployment and Minimum Wages*. Bulletin 1657, Washington, 1970, p. 45.

12.   Colvin, John J. "The Effects of Federal Minimum Wages on Teenage Unemployment." Unpublished MA dissertation. University of Maine at

Orono, August 1974. Chapter 4 and more specifically in Chapter 5, the author concludes:

"1. The conclusions of Burns' analysis, using 1954–1965 as the applicable time period, are essentially correct; however, if one adds a measure of either the increased percentage of adult women or teenagers in the labor force, concepts which Burns mentions but does not include, then no adverse effects are found for minimum wages on teenage unemployment; also, if one extends the time period used for Burns' analysis, and leaves his two-explanatory variable model intact, then no adverse effects are found for minimum wages.

2. Similar comments apply to Adie's conclusions—his findings are critically sensitive to the time period analyzed—1954 to 1965—for if he investigated a longer time period, such as 1954–1968 or 1954–1970, as demonstrated in Chapter 4, he would have more than likely found no significant adverse effects of minimum wages on teenage unemployment.

3. Neither Burns or Adie elected to publish R^2 and Durbin-Watson statistics obtained as a result of their regression analyses, and my attempt to "do so for them" yielded evidence that strongly indicates that additional explanatory variables should have been included in their equations."

Chapter Eleven

THE MODERN WELFARE STATE FROM A HUMANISTIC PERSPECTIVE

INTRODUCTION

Poverty amidst plenty is an explicit denial of humanistic values of any kind. In the present chapter we will focus on the problem of economic insecurity which, after poverty, is the second most important target in our stage theory of rehumanizing the economy. *Insecurity* amidst plenty may sound less offensive, but it turns out to be the major stumbling block for satisfying the higher social and growth needs of a society.

The Development of Welfare in the United States

The New World was the land of opportunity because it had an abundance of good land. Those in England who were looking for a new life, a fresh start, could look towards the Colonies as a place where this was possible. For most of the early history of the U.S., poverty was therefore not a large problem. Private relief agencies could do the job, and these were mostly needed by the newest immigrants.

But by the early 1800s private relief and charity began to prove inadequate and conditions for the poor deteriorated. A report to the New York State legislature in 1824 is reminiscent of conditions that we have observed in England. It noted that the poor were farmed out, with little distinction in treatment between them and criminals. As a result the state created a control agency that was a forerunner of today's welfare agency. Other states followed New York, and by 1929 only Mississippi, Nevada and Utah did not have such an agency.

We mentioned 1929 specifically because that was the year of the stock-market crash, which was soon followed by the Great Depression. The bread lines of the 1930s marked the breakdown of the then-existing U.S. social welfare system.

The establishment of a new welfare system in the U.S. echoed what President Roosevelt had called the "Four Freedoms": freedom from want, freedom from fear, freedom of speech, and freedom of religion. The Roosevelt reforms included the Federal Emergency Relief Act, which provided grants to states; and the Civil Works Administration, which became the Works Project Administration (WPA) and the Civilian Conservation Corps (CCC), creating public works jobs through federal funding. Both of these were passed in 1933. Finally, in 1935 there was the passage of the Social Security Act, which became the basis of our present welfare system. The main programs of this Act were the establishment of pensions (old age and survivors' benefits) and unemployment benefits.

Many Americans react to the terms *welfare* and *welfare state* in a negative way. They see it as a system that is synonymous with hand-outs to the poor, high taxes, and little else. They would hardly think it desirable that a nation move in the direction of becoming a welfare state, and they regret that their own country has supposedly become one.

In the next section we will try to show that the welfare state has a different meaning and that it is in fact a first step in humanistic economic and social development. We will also explain why, by these criteria, the U.S. is not really a welfare state.

THE MODERN WELFARE STATE

The term *welfare state* derives from the concept of welfare economics as used and developed by Pigou and Hobson, among others. It has its fullest realization in the various nations of Europe. The philosophy of the welfare state is that the government should modify the play of market forces so that the nation moves in more socially desirable directions. This is a conception that sees the state, in Sleeman's words, "as a positive agent for the promotion of social welfare. In this it can be contrasted with the laissez-faire ideal of the state acting rather as a policeman or arbiter." He continues, "Not only should the government provide social services, such as social security, medical treatment, welfare facilities, and subsidized housing, but these should go beyond the provision of a bare minimum towards ensuring that all have equal opportunity, so far as the country's resources allow."[1]

The welfare state takes active policies to promote full employment, and sees the right to a job as one of the basic rights of citizenship. This goal contrasts sharply with the American image of the welfare state as encouraging idleness.

The philosophy of the modern welfare state is echoed in Franklin D. Roosevelt's 1937 Inaugural Address, despite the fact that the U.S. has not really become a welfare state in these terms:

☐ . . . we knew that we must find practical controls over blind economic forces and blindly selfish men.

We of the Republic sensed the truth that democratic government has innate capacity to protect its people against disasters once considered inevitable—to solve problems once considered unsolvable. We could not admit that we could not find a way to master economic epidemics just as, after centuries of fatalistic suffering, we had found a way to master epidemics of disease. We refused to leave the problems of our common welfare to be solved by the winds of chance and the hurricanes of disaster . . . .

In that purpose we have been helped by achievements of mind and spirit. Old truths have been relearned, untruths have been unlearned. We have always known that heedless self-interest was bad morals; we now know that it is bad economics. Out of the collapse of a prosperity where builders boasted their practicality has come the conviction that in the long run economic morality pays.[2]

We should note that in most European countries the basic rights of citizenship that are part of the welfare state are incorporated explicitly into their constitutions.

Private and Public Goods

The welfare state recognizes and fully acknowledges the distinction between private and public goods. The private market economy is very good at providing certain goods and services but quite deficient at providing others. Those that it can't provide include public goods. We used the example of street lights when we discussed this previously in Chapter 6. It is up to the state to provide these goods and services, or they don't get provided at all.

The most obvious example of a public good is defense, although the term *bad* may be more appropriate in this case. But in principle any other public good falls within the same format. The welfare state recognized that private charity doesn't work well, just as private defense doesn't. The pursuit of self-interest that governs private expenditures does not accord well with the class of needs that have public ramifications. The attitude is, "Why should I pay for something that somebody else uses? Let the others pay." But, it may be asked, what about *enlightened* self-interest? Shouldn't such a motive operate to meet public needs? The answer: That is precisely what the welfare state is, the organization and implementation of enlightened self-interest. We should also add that what is called enlightened self-interest is nothing other than a developing form of altruism. It is ego being transformed into self. The welfare state is a manifestation of this. By the same token, the recent moves to cut taxes and expenditures initiated by California's (in)famous Proposition 13 is clearly a move to dismantle the welfare state. It is "disenlightened" self-interest.

An important instance where the private market system just doesn't meet the social needs is in the area of health care. Again, the private system does certain things very well. It provides highly trained specialists, and highly developed medical technology. What it doesn't do is adequately *deliver* the services of general practitioners and address the issues of preventive health care. There is a serious deficiency of medical services for the urban poor, in rural areas, and anywhere high income is not common. There is also little incentive for the private system to deal with the impact on health of environmental pollution.

The Evolution of the Welfare State

Figure 11-1 shows what is termed the diffusion of welfare programs.[3] It presents an interesting story. Each of the lines shows a particular type of welfare program: work injury compensation, old age security, sickness, maternity insurance, unemployment compensation, and family allowances. The line shows how many countries have adopted the program, and roughly in what year. For example, let us take unemployment compensation. The first countries adopted such a program around 1905. By 1920 about seven countries had it, and by 1960 about seventeen countries.

What the figure reveals is that an increasing number of countries adopt each of these social programs, and that it takes between fifty and eighty years for any such program to be adopted by most of these countries. Very rarely do we see a program's disappearance once it has been adopted. What we seem to have here is an evolutionary development across national and, to a great extent, cultural lines. There seems to be some intrinsic developmental force in operation which leads to the steady and continuing adoption of social welfare programs.

For some American observers, this is taken as evidence of a deplorable trend toward totalitarianism that is destroying the economies and cultures of these countries. At several points in this chapter we will try to show why we don't believe this is the case.

Comparative Welfare Spending

The Soviet Union is a country founded on the theoretical principle of the State as fully responsible for all social needs. A bill to this effect was prepared by the Bolsheviks in 1917, just five days after their coming to power. It might then be expected that the Soviet Union would be one of the leading countries in the world in social welfare spending (as a percentage of GNP). When we compare the Soviet Union to the United States this seems to be the case. According to one study, the Soviet Union in 1963 spent 10.2 percent of its GNP on social security, while the United States spent 6.2 percent. We would also

FIGURE 11-1   THE DIFFUSION OF WELFARE PROGRAMS

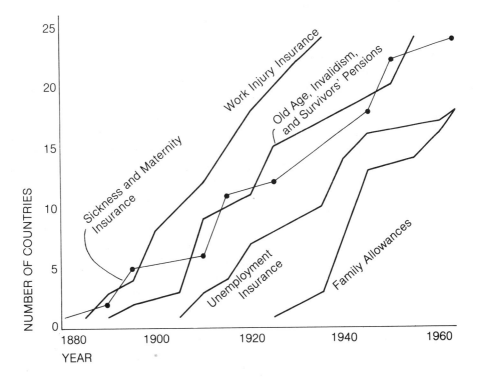

expect that the Soviet Union would outspend all other Western (capitalistic) countries in social security. This, however, is not the case. In Table 11.1 we present the data for a number of countries that were part of this 1963 study.

Surprisingly, the Soviet Union and the U.S. share the distinction of being on the bottom of the list, being the two countries in the study

TABLE 11.1   SOCIAL WELFARE EXPENDITURES (1963)

Country	% of GNP
West Germany	15.3
France	14.6
Sweden	13.5
United Kingdom	11.2
Soviet Union	10.2
United States	6.2

Source: International Labor Office. From Rimlinger "Social Security & Society" in *Social Science Quarterly* Vol 50, 1969, p. 506.

that pay the least in social welfare benefits. It is also surprising to find that West Germany heads the list—not Sweden or Britain, as many Americans might expect. Therefore, we cannot conclude from this data that welfare expenditures are a measure of something like "creeping" communism, since that would mean that these European countries are more communistic than the Soviet Union! The trend toward the adoption of increased social welfare spending does not seem to be a trend in the direction of the Soviet Union, but if anything a trend *away* from the Soviet Union.

If the U.S. sees itself as at the opposite end of the political spectrum from the Soviet Union that belief is not supported by the issue of social welfare spending. According to this criterion the U.S. is at the same end of the spectrum, and as a matter of fact defines an extreme to which the closest country is the Soviet Union. The data thus indicate that the European welfare state is developing in a direction that is quite independent of the ideological conflict between capitalism and communism. We are suggesting that this direction can better be described as humanism, and may relate to the issue of how much security each of these countries is providing its citizenry.

We presented this study because it provides us with a rare comparison between the Soviet Union and a number of Western countries. The data of Table 11.2 are more recent but now only Western countries are compared. Here the data include education and housing expenditures, as well as the usual social security expenditures. The data show us again that Britain is not the only welfare state. Other European countries have much higher expenditures, with Austria spending three times as much as the U.S. (%GNP) on social programs.

Welfare and the Life Cycle

The critics of the welfare state cynically refer to its provisions of welfare programs as cradle-to-grave security. If the truth is, as we contend, that the welfare state is a step forward in meeting the hierarchy of human needs, then the provision of the full range of human services is something to be fostered and supported. From this perspective we present a picture of the ideal modern welfare system as it meets the needs at each point of the human life cycle. There is no one country that meets each and every one of these needs, but an increasing number of them, as the diffusion figure showed us, come fairly close.

1. **Maternity and Prenatal Benefits.** In sharp contrast to the United States most countries have programs to offset loss of wages by working mothers during pregnancy. In Sweden there are cash grants and free baby equipment for low-income families. In Switzerland the mother can leave work six weeks before the expected birth at full pay. In the European Economic Community countries there is the right of taking a pregnancy vacation for anywhere from three to six months at 50 to 100 percent of salary, depending on the particular country. Just

TABLE 11.2 PUBLIC EXPENDITURE ON SOCIAL SERVICES AS A PERCENTAGE OF GNP (1965–1966)

	Austria	France	Nether-lands	Norway	Sweden	Switzer-land	United Kingdom	USA
Social Security	14.1	11.2	—	12.1	9.2	7.0	7.1	4.8
Health	4.1	4.4	—	2.0	4.3	1.7	3.5	1.2
	18.2	15.6	13.3	14.1	13.5	8.7	12.6	7.0
Education	3.9	5.4	6.2	6.0	6.0	3.5	4.4	4.3
Housing and community amenities	2.2	.8	.6	.1	2.7	.1	3.5	.3
Total	24.3	21.8	20.1	20.2	22.2	12.3	18.5	11.6

Source: OECD Economic Outlook, Occasional Studies, (July 1970)

about everywhere there is also the guaranteed right of returning to one's old job. It can be seen from these programs that the European welfare state recognizes the specific rights of women to work without being penalized for childbearing. The rights are embodied in these economic programs.

In terms of medical care during pregnancy and childbirth, the following services are in most cases provided free of charge: weekly prenatal checkups, hospitalization, drugs, doctor's services. In addition several countries provide an outright maternity grant upon the birth of a child. In Great Britain it is $25, in Sweden $230, and in West Germany $40. More significant than these grants are the *child allowances*. This is a certain sum paid monthly for each child, usually until that child is 18. These sums, for each country, are shown in Table 11.3

TABLE 11.3* TYPICAL CHILD ALLOWANCES (1975) (EXPRESSED AS % OF AVERAGE AFTER-TAX BLUE-COLLAR WORKER'S INCOME)

USA	—
Canada	3.6
United Kingdom	4.4
Belgium	11.0
Germany	3.9
Netherlands	5.5
Austria	11.7
Sweden	7.9
Switzerland	3.5

Source: Union Bank of Switzerland and Institute of Insurance Economics, St. Gall Graduate School of Economics, Business and Public Administration

*All the data in Tables 11.3 through 11.9 refer to a blue-collar worker with an average production worker income. Unless otherwise specified, the data pertain to the year 1975.

Maternity benefits after birth. If the mother wants her old job back, she can receive 100 percent of pay before returning to work for a period of six weeks to three months, depending on the country. In Sweden, as a result of that country's increasing recognition of the rights of women, *either* parent can take off from work at full pay to be with the child. In most countries, mothers who are nursing get a special nursing allowance for a period of twelve weeks. There are also free weekly visits by a pediatric nurse, and free visits to a clinic if necessary.

2. **Education.** All countries, including the United States, have free public school education. In Europe there are substantial allowances for college studies. In addition, higher education is generally sub-

sidized so that education costs are considerably cheaper for the citizen than they are in the United States. In Great Britain most college students receive a grant for full or partial support.

3. **Housing.** Government housing programs are especially strong in countries that had much of their housing destroyed during World War II, and where there were extreme shortages. In all countries that have a welfare-state orientation the provision of adequate housing is an important social objective. These programs are expressed in strong rent-control laws and in substantial government subsidization of housing costs. Again, Americans may react to this as a threat to the free-enterprise system. Yet, if we look at West Germany, which we happily recognize as having undergone an "economic miracle" of the free-enterprise system following World War II, we see a country with strong government investment in the housing program. In 1960 the average German had to spend only 10.3 percent of his or her income on housing, compared to the 20 to 25 percent of income that the average American spent on housing in the same year, or twice as much.

The combination of public housing programs, subsidies, and rent allowances that exist in most of the European countries lead to a housing environment that stands in definite visible contrast to housing in the United States. In the words of Swedish economist Gunnar Myrdal, "The United States is that country among the rich countries that has the most and worst slums."[4]

4. **Health Care.** Comprehensive medical coverage and health care is seen as a basic right of every citizen. The systems are most extensively developed in Great Britain, Australia, New Zealand, and Sweden, where the entire population is covered and entitled to virtual free health care, including hospitalization, outpatient care, dental care and prescription drugs. Table 11.4 indicates how the various countries compare with respect to these four basic categories of health services.

To illustrate how the system works, let us briefly mention the case of Switzerland, it being quite representative of public health care on the European continent.

For a monthly contribution of roughly $17 (representing about 2 percent of a typical blue-collar wage income), the Swiss buys comprehensive health insurance. Health insurance is voluntary except for the lower income groups, yet coverage exceeds 90 percent of the population. What does the $17 a month buy? Table 11.4 outlines the answer. Except for dental care, all things are either free or almost free. But let us look a little deeper into this matter. We said hospitalization is free, and of course that is so even in cases of prolonged and expensive treatment. Also, every man, rich or poor, will qualify for the most up-to-date and refined health treatment. Ability to pay has no bearing on the question of who is next in line for life-saving heart surgery. Yet

TABLE 11.4 DEGREE OF INDIVIDUAL EXPENSE SHARING BY NATIONAL INSURANCE
SCHEMES (1976)

	Hospitalization	Out-patient care	Dental services	Prescription drugs
USA*	—	—	—	—
Canada	100	100	—	—
United Kingdom	100	100	100	100
Belgium	100	75–100	75–100	75–100
Germany	100	100	100	—
Netherlands	100	100	100	100
Austria	100	100	100	100
Sweden	100	82	50–75	50–100
Switzerland	100	90	—	90

*The USA as of now has no national health plan or insurance scheme for people below 65 years of age.
Source: E. Moenig and H. Frei, Social Security in Ten Industrial Countries, Zurich, 1977.

our average medical-plan hospital patient is only enjoying third-class status in such things as hospital rooms and choice of doctor or surgeon. As a third-class patient, you can expect to be accommodated in a large ward, together with a half a dozen or more other patients. As a result, visiting hours and privileges will be held to an absolute minimum. Moreover, third-class hospital food is rather simple, although nutritionally sound.

If you prefer, hospital stays can be made a lot more comfortable by insuring oneself as a second-class patient. The monthly insurance premium is now more like $30 a month, but now you are entitled to a smaller room, usually a double room, better food and, perhaps more important, you can choose your own doctor from the hospital staff. Such second-class treatment is what one comes to expect in most American hospitals. In contrast, third-class status may seem unattractive to the average reader, yet millions of Americans who cannot afford *any* hospitalization would hardly turn it down.

In addition to providing health services, the typical welfare state will also make sure that a sick worker's dependents will be able to maintain their family income and expenditures. Table 11.5 illustrates the extent and length of sickness cash benefits to an average blue-collar worker's family with two children in the nine surveyed countries.

5. **Unemployment Compensation.** Table 11.6 shows the percentage of previous wages that are paid out during periods of unemployment. Not shown in the table is Sweden's innovative manpower program where the government finances the expenses involved in travelling and searching for a new job, as well as the necessary retraining

TABLE 11.5 SICKNESS CASH BENEFITS OF A FAMILY WITH 2 CHILDREN

	Indemnity in % of last earnings	Beginning of payments	Length of payments
USA*	50–67	After 8th day	Max. 28 weeks
Canada	66⅔	After 2nd week	15 weeks
United Kingdom	$60 per week	After 4th day	Max. 52 weeks
Belgium	100 60	Immediately After 31st day	1 year
Germany	100 80	Immediately After 7th week	Max. 78 weeks
Netherlands	80	After 3rd day	1 year
Austria	70 75	After 4th day After 7th week	78 weeks
Sweden	90	After 2nd day	Unlimited
Switzerland	100	Immediately	1–3 months

Source: "Winterthur" Swiss Insurance Company

Only in some states

TABLE 11.6 UNEMPLOYMENT COMPENSATION OF A FAMILY WITH THREE CHILDREN

	Unemployment compensation as a percentage of gross earnings	Waiting period	Duration of benefits
USA	62.6	1 week	65 weeks
Canada	70.1	1 week minimum	51 weeks
United Kingdom	84.4	3 days	Max. 312 days
Belgium	74.2	None	Unlimited
Germany	72.5	None	13–52 weeks
Netherlands	82.5	None	26 weeks
Austria	61.2	1 week	Max. 30 weeks
Sweden	91.3	5 days	300 days per year
Switzerland	83.2	1 day	150 days per year

Source: Union Bank of Switzerland and the Institute of Insurance Economics, St. Gall Graduate School of Economics, Business and Public Administration

expenses for that job. Similarly, layoffs in Sweden, as in most European countries, are usually accompanied by generous severance payments averaging several thousand dollars per laid-off employee.

6. **Invalidity Insurance.** The most serious financial burdens are placed on a family when the breadwinner has been disabled due to accident or sickness. In most cases the payments are greater when the disability is the result of an occupation-related injury or illness. If it is occupation-related, more compensation is paid for accidents than for sickness. The Invalidity Income for a family of three if the husband is fully disabled is shown in Table 11.7

TABLE 11.7 INVALIDITY INCOME OF A FAMILY WITH THREE CHILDREN IF THE HUSBAND IS FULLY DISABLED

	Invalidity due to sickness or disease	Invalidity due to accident
	Invalidity income in % of final gross earnings	Invalidity income in % of final gross earnings
USA	82.8	82.8
Canada	64.9	96.5
United Kingdom	92.0	133.0
Belgium	80.5	107.6
Germany	74.6	103.0
Netherlands	82.2	82.2
Austria	71.0	154.9
Sweden	116.1	127.4
Switzerland	96.5	96.5

Source: Union Bank of Switzerland and Institute of Insurance Economics, St. Gall Graduate School of Economics, Business and Public Administration

7. **Survivor's Benefits.** This program secures the living costs of the closest family members if the breadwinner dies before retirement age. The example of a thirty-year-old widow with two children is used in Table 11.8.

8. **Old Age Benefits (Pensions).** This is everywhere the dominant program in social security schemes; more money is spent here than in any other program. For many years the aim of these programs was to provide a minimum subsistence. Now this is changing so that the aim is to try to provide benefits that maintain the former income level. (Note Table 11.9)

9. **Old Age Assistance.** In the United States we are familiar with the use of nursing homes for the elderly. We are also aware of the tendency for institutionalization to occur in these homes, and the resultant dehumanization of the aged residents. The European welfare states have also recognized these problems and are fairly advanced in

TABLE 11.8 SURVIVORS' INCOME OF A FAMILY WITH TWO CHILDREN AFTER THE HUS-
BAND'S DEATH DUE TO AN ACCIDENT

	Survivors' income in % of final gross earnings
USA	97.5
Canada	48.5
United Kingdom	98.6
Belgium	60.3
Germany	62.8
Netherlands	58.6
Austria	65.2
Sweden	89.7
Switzerland	95.3

Source: Union Bank of Switzerland and the Institute of Insurance Economics, St. Gall Graduate School of Economics, Business and Public Administration

TABLE 11.9 RETIREMENT INCOME OF A MARRIED COUPLE

	Retirement income in % of final gross earnings before retirement
USA	60.4
Canada	53.1
United Kingdom	59.1
Belgium	46.8
Germany	62.6
Netherlands	55.5
Austria	79.9
Sweden	104.1
Switzerland	82.6

Source: Union Bank of Switzerland and the Institute of Insurance Economics St. Gall Graduate School of Economics, Business and Public Administration

implementing new programs. The major thrust of these new programs is to keep old people at home, and provide whatever support services are needed to make this possible. This includes food catering, social workers making home visits, and related activities.

In Sweden the program aims at housing developments where old people can live and where young children can go to play in playgrounds. This follows from the recognition that old people and young children are natural companions. These housing developments are designed so that several small, non-institutional residences face a central playground area. The old people can come out of their houses and be with the children if they choose.

It has been said that the quality of a civilization is most clearly shown in how it treats its elderly persons (as well as its children). The fact that the European welfare states are distinctly trying to avoid the fragmented and mass care of the elderly that we observe so often in our nursing homes is another sign that human values are a prime consideration in the formation of the welfare state.

10. **Death Benefits.** In addition to the survivor's benefits that all Western countries grant to some degree, several European countries provide an additional outright grant at the death of a wage earner. In France it is three-months' salary to the surviving family; in West Germany it is three-months' pension, and Great Britain provides a standard cash grant. Generally, in all European welfare states each citizen has the right to a free funeral. The latter includes everything from casket and sermon to the disposal of the body or the ashes.

11. **Red Roses for the Grave.** Finally, the government often provides free of charge a minimum maintenance of the grave. In Switzerland, for instance, the local government will plant a rosebush on the grave of every dead person whose relatives or friends are either incapable or unwilling to do so.

The Financing of the Welfare State

The last section surveyed the various elements of the modern welfare state. No doubt, the level of benefits available to the entire population is impressive, but two questions immediately come to mind: what is the *total cost* of such an accomplishment and, more importantly, *who will foot the bill?*

To answer the first question: As Table 11.2 indicated, European countries spent nearly 20 percent of their GNP on social security and social services of all kinds. In addition, modern governments have to budget money for defense, police, postal services, public transportation, roads, environmental projects, public administration, public enterprises, etc. So it is not surprising that the total financial needs of government amount to one-third to one-half of gross national product. Table 11.10 lists the combined total of all taxes and social security contributions as a percentage of GNP.

In answering the second question, it must first be pointed out that the average blue-collar worker carries his share of the burden. According to a recent study, income taxes and social security contributions claim almost 30 percent of the Swedish and Dutch blue-collar worker's earnings, and 25 percent for their German counterparts, but only a modest 12 percent in the USA and Canada.[5] Of course, the European worker also pays an additional share as consumer of the various prod-

TABLE 11.10 TAXES AND SOCIAL SECURITY CONTRIBUTIONS AS % OF GNP, 1973

USA	28.0
Canada	33.9
United Kingdom	32.8
Denmark	44.1
Belgium	36.6
Netherlands	43.8
Germany	37.3
France	36.9
Australia	36.6
Sweden	43.5
Switzerland*	22.6

excludes health insurance contributions

Source: OECD

ucts, most of which are heavily taxed with so-called 'indirect' taxes, such as gasoline tax, tobacco tax, and other excise and sales taxes.

Yet, all European governments do make a determined effort to take a more than proportionate share from the rich. So we find that the incidence of the income tax in Europe is typically much more progressive than that of the United States. In this country, for instance, even the very rich do not pay more than 33 percent of their income to the IRS.[6] This is because the various exemptions and loopholes allow the rich to avoid the higher rates. In Germany, on the other hand, the top income recipients end up paying more than 50 percent in income tax; and in Sweden the corresponding figure is 76 percent.

It is not surprising that we find greater equality after taxes in Europe than in the United States. For example, after taxes of all kinds, the richest 20 percent still retain ten times as much money as the poorest 20 percent in this country, while the corresponding ratio in Germany and England is 7 to 1 and in Sweden and Norway the ratio is 5 to 1.[7]

Finally, because government benefits in the form of transfer and expenditures find their way more readily to the poor, the most striking gains in equality of the welfare states become even more manifest when we consider the income distribution after all taxes as well as all social services. Most recently the well-known British economist Peter Wiles compared the United States, Canada, the United Kingdom and Sweden.[8] The results of his study can best be understood in the following way: Imagine taking a random sample of 100 households and ranking them by income after taxes and social services. Now take the income of the fifth richest and the fifth poorest and divide one by the other. The resulting percentile ratio is shown in Table 11.11. It gives us a picture of the ratio of income disparity between the richest and the poorest in each country. The data warrant the conclusion that inequality is greater in the United States than in Germany and the United Kingdom, and twice as great as in the Scandinavian countries.

TABLE 11.11 INCOME DISTRIBUTION AFTER GOVERNMENT REDISTRIBUTION (95th PERCENTILE DIVIDED BY 5th PERCENTILE)

USA (1968)	12.7
Canada (1971)	12.0
United Kingdom (1969)	5.0
Sweden (1971)	5.5

Source: Peter Wiles, Economic Institutions Compared, Oxford, 1977.

THE UNITED STATES AND THE EUROPEAN WELFARE STATES

In the last two sections we presented a host of tables comparing the benefits and costs of the modern welfare states. Using the data contained in those tables one can attempt to rank each country in terms of its welfare-state status. Of course the rankings given depend on the relative weights a person decides to assign to the various kinds of benefits. But it could be anticipated that to a large majority the following general assessment would seem fair: Sweden, the United Kingdom and perhaps The Netherlands can be considered the purest representatives of the modern welfare state. Austria, Germany, Belgium and Switzerland may exhibit small gaps here and there, such as the lack of a dental program in Switzerland, but all of these countries have successfully managed to satisfy the major objectives of providing some minimum level of income and economic security for everybody. Much the same could be said of Norway, Denmark and Finland. Northern Europe has essentially brought about two of Roosevelt's freedoms, the freedom from want and the freedom from fear. Poverty has ceased to be a social issue. No doubt, the successful maintenance of virtual full employment and a high degree of solidarity exhibited by the trade unions both share major credit for such an accomplishment.

What about the United States and Canada? Clearly, according to the data presented, both countries score relatively low by most indicators characterizing the welfare state. Not only does the United States allocate less money to social services (Table 11.2) but the benefits discussed in Table 11.3 to 11.9 tend to compare quite unfavorably with the European countries. The only exception is old age protection (Tables 11.8 and 11.9), but even here—as the next pages will show, the United States would look bad if we had examined the low-, rather than middle-, income worker. Finally, the data on taxes (11.10) and redistribution (11.11) further underline the difference between the USA and the modern welfare state.

Just about all experts agree that in the United States there are too many "casualties of the welfare state." Why does the United States fall short of the essential objective of the welfare state? Let us summarize some of the most important reasons.

1. Our Social Security System Is Deficient

In 1975, 90 percent of all American workers carried Social Security, but the benefits have been traditionally geared to those workers who have adequate pay in reasonably steady jobs. Those employees have few worries. On the other hand, a worker whose job history is replete with layoffs and temporary and low-wage work, will tend to qualify for only minimum benefits. For example, a couple can expect a monthly retirement check of $152 a month, providing an annual income of $1820, which is well below the poverty line. We may also add that in 1975 the average benefits per retiree was $207.18 per month, which amounts to roughly a third of what the average Swede can expect.

The story concerning unemployment benefits is much the same. Most workers drawing $40 to $100 a week cannot escape poverty. And of course there are millions who have lost eligibility in any benefits because they gave up looking for work or have simply exhausted their benefits. In some states, a pregnant woman quitting her job because of impending childbirth will also forfeit her benefits. The reader is reminded of the generous treatment an expectant mother is accorded in Europe.

Public assistance, the third pillar of the Social Security Act, suffers the same basic shortcoming. Payments are inadequate and often fail to reach the most needy. Myrdal, in a 1976 speech at Columbia University, summarized the problem in the following words:

> ☐ the major aid schemes within the U.S. system exclude the whole underclass of the more permanently unemployed and the "subemployed"—indeed all those not in the mainstream of economic life: Since Roosevelt there have been further social reforms in America, but from the beginning they showed a tendency to stop above the reach of the poorest and the most needy. Even with the gradual increase of those who benefit, the reforms, for the most part, fail to reach down to the underclass.[9]

A study by the (University of Wisconsin) Institute for Research on Poverty, statistically documents the inadequacy of our welfare system to alleviate poverty. In 1970, 68 percent of all poor Social Security recipients remained poor *after* obtaining the benefits. For a family with a non-retired head the respective proportion was 80 percent. If we also allow for public-assistance payments and food stamps, the picture brightens somewhat, but 57 percent of all such recipients still remained poor. Similarly, 61 percent of the nation's welfare mothers remained among the casualties of the welfare state.

Even worse, many of the poor never receive help. McConnell, in his well-known text, writes: "It is established that about one-half of all those families and individuals now classified as poor receive no transfer payments at all."[10]

2. There Exist Vast Disparities in Benefits Among States

Unlike Europe, the bulk of our assistance programs are administered by state and local governments. Here we meet our old foe, competition, once again. The stingy treatment of one's poor constituency will keep down the tax burden on the local business community, while at the same time providing employers with a vast pool of cheap and docile labor. At first sight this appears to boost the local output of goods and services although it is at the expense of human well-being. The problem is that if all communities are after the same game, among the participants there can be no winners. There are only losers, and the losers in this case are the poor of the so-called parsimony states. Mississippi, Alabama and Oklahoma have opted to keep their benefit package to the poor to an absolute minimum. The very desperate, we are told, can always emigrate to the more generous Northern states. The financial plight of the city of New York makes more sense when we take into account the many poor Southern immigrants the city also has to take care of.

Let us look at some examples of the existing disparities between the states. First, a welfare mother of three children obtains in Mississippi $2400 per year; the same family would get $3800 in New York. When it comes to old-age assistance, the average benefits by states varied in 1970 from $48.70 in South Carolina to $166.50 in New Hampshire. With respect to medicaid a study by the Brookings Institution found that in 1972 the average poor received $85 in services in the South, while their counterparts in the Northeast collected $526 worth of health services. In unemployment benefits the range was from 28 percent of weekly earnings in Oklahoma to 43 percent in Colorado and North Dakota. The average aid to the blind and permanently disabled tends to be twice as high in New York as in Mississippi. Compensation for work injuries also varies a great deal from state to state. Claire Wilcox writes that in the Sixties the loss of an eye entitled the victim to an $18,000 lump sum payment in Hawaii, while the equivalent payment in Alabama is only $3100. The loss of a foot is "compensated" in Arizona by $22,000, while across the border in New Mexico one would get a mere $3800. Why is it that a part of the body is worth more in one state than another?

3. The United States Is the Only Modern Industrialized Country Without a National Health Program

Most Americans have some kind of private health insurance. But in 1970, 15 percent under 65 were without any protection, and it is these people that tend to need it the most. Statistics for 1971 tell us that while virtually everybody with an income over $7000 had insurance, only half of the people with incomes of $4000 and less carried some sort of health-care protection. But even for the insured the protection is typically limited to the payment of hospital costs, and perhaps the costs of doctor's services in the hospital. Most Americans visiting a doctor have to pay for the medical services out of their own pockets. Similarly, dental care and the costs of prescription drugs are typically not insured at all. Medicare for the retired was introduced in the middle sixties as an amendment to the Social Security Act, but most experts agree that the protection is highly inadequate in cases of prolonged illness. Hospital benefits, for example, only cover the first 150 days. Similarly, the patient has to pay 20 percent of the costs of physicians from the very beginning. Greenberg concludes in his book, *The Quality of Mercy* (1971), "Medicare falls short of need. The biggest gaps are those of out-of-hospital drugs and dental care, which are not covered at all. On the average Medicare meets only 45 percent of the total health care expenditures of the aged."[11]

4. There Is Not Full Employment

As we discussed earlier, the goal of full employment is an important objective of the welfare state. The United States and Canada both flunk this test of a modern welfare state. Table 11.12 speaks clearly for itself. (It could be added that Switzerland, which is not represented in the table, has the best unemployment record of all. Never since 1959 has the unemployment rate exceeded 1 percent of the labor force and, typically, joblessness was less than 1/10 of a percent.) We included Australia in the table, since some American economists attribute the poor record of Canada and the United States to the relatively large size of those countries.

It may also be worthwhile to point out that the proportion of teenage job seekers is about the same in Europe as it is in the United States. By the same token, there are as many or more women in the labor force of Europe, so that attributing the greater unemployment in the U.S. to these categories does not hold up.

5. There Are Too Many "Working Poor" in the United States

In the early 1970s, 10 million workers worked for less than $2 per hour, usually in non-union jobs in the service sector (such as laundries,

TABLE 11.12 UNEMPLOYMENT IN SEVEN COUNTRIES, 1959–76 (AVERAGE ANNUAL RATE ACCORDING TO U.S. DEFINITIONS)

Item and Year	United States	Australia	Canada	France	West Germany	Great Britain	Sweden
Unemployment Rate							
1959	5.5	n.a.	6.0	2.4	1.7	3.1	n.a.
1960	5.5	n.a.	7.0	2.2	0.8	2.3	n.a.
1961	6.7	n.a.	7.1	1.9	0.5	2.1	1.5
1962	5.5	n.a.	5.9	1.9	0.4	3.0	1.5
1963	5.7	n.a.	5.5	1.9	0.5	3.8	1.7
1964	5.2	1.4	4.7	1.6	0.3	2.6	1.5
1965	4.5	1.3	3.9	1.8	0.3	2.3	1.2
1966	3.8	1.5	3.6	1.8	0.3	2.4	1.6
1967	3.8	1.6	4.1	2.3	1.0	3.8	2.1
1968	3.6	1.5	4.8	2.7	1.2	3.7	2.2
1969	3.5	1.5	4.7	2.1	0.8	3.7	1.9
1970	4.9	1.4	5.7	2.8	0.8	3.1	1.5
1971	5.9	1.6	6.2	3.0	0.8	3.9	2.6
1972	5.6	2.2	6.2	3.0	0.8	4.2	2.7
1973	4.9	1.9	5.6	2.9	0.8	3.2	2.5
1974	5.6	2.3	5.4	3.1	1.7	3.2	2.0
1975	8.5	4.4	6.9	4.3	3.8	4.7	1.6
1976	7.7	4.4	7.1	4.6	3.8	6.4	1.6

Source: Bureau of Labor Statistics

filling stations, restaurants, motels, etc.). To spell out how this occurs, assume a 40-hour week and 50 working weeks a year and you obtain 2000 fulltime hours. The annual wage for such low-paid workers is as a result not much more than $4000, which places them deep in poverty where there is a family to support. The essence of the problem here is the lack of an adequate minimum wage and the great disparity of wages among workers. A skilled worker in •the United States gets about 100 percent more than an unskilled worker, while the skill premium in Europe is more like 20 to 50 percent.

To take a European example: In 1975 a Swiss unskilled woman worker in a laundry received approximately $3.25 an hour, just about the lowest pay in the country, while the average hourly pay for all skilled workers was not much more than $5 an hour.

One cause of the working poor is the lack of homogeneity of the American working class. As a result, trade union protection in this country is rather limited as soon as we leave the high-wage sector. In Europe, on the other hand, every worker tends to belong to a union.

The absence of the working poor, combined with 100 percent full employment, explains why people in Switzerland know poverty only from the reading of history books, or from their travels to the Third World and North America.

6. There Are Too Many American "Working Insecure"

The working poor are not only haunted by low wages but by a heavy dose of job insecurity as well. A recent dissertation by Roger Kaufman at M.I.T. analyzes this problem from an international perspective, and finds that it is quite peculiar to the American economy.[12] Not only are the working poor in the United States typically non-unionized and therefore lacking some protection against unwarranted firing or arbitrary layoff procedures, but they also work in an environment where there are few, if any, public constraints on layoffs.

In Europe, on the other hand, the low-pay worker is more often than not a union member. Moreover, he or she typically enjoys some protection against layoffs. In almost all European countries, layoffs must be preceded by consultation with worker representatives and notice must be given at least one week in advance. If work is scarce, employees will tend to press for work-sharing, i.e., shorter hours for everybody, instead of no work for some.

Moreover, if a worker is laid off after all, he or she is typically entitled by law to a substantial sum of redundancy pay or severance pay. And finally, as long as anybody is laid off, employers will find it next to impossible to schedule overtime for the remaining employees.

Statistically, these constraints have been manifested in significantly lower separation rates abroad.* The working poor in the United States appears to be several times more threatened by imminent layoffs than his counterpart in Europe.

CONCLUSION

The United States still has some way to go before it has the benefits of the modern welfare state. Until that day, we will have to confront the twin issues of poverty and economic insecurity. Not surprisingly, a recent study by the University of Michigan Survey Institute found that the dominant concern among American workers is the lack of security, in particular the fear of being laid off, or any other development that would threaten their standard of living.[13]

The lack of security that is typical in the United States economy interferes with Maslowian inner growth for most citizens. The system compels the typical worker in the United States to concern himself with

---

*"Job separation," which includes both layoffs and quits, is twice as high in the United States than in Europe. Labor market experts believe that most of Europe's separations are actually quits, while in the United States quits just about balance layoffs, especially in times of low unemployment.

satisfying the basic material and physical needs. No wonder Economic Man walks so strong on this side of the Atlantic.

From the perspective of humanistic welfare economics, the movement towards a modern welfare state has to be an item of top priority in this country. But we know such a suggestion does not sit well with traditional views. The American public has been told for many decades that government taking care of its people through Washington is economically detrimental. The abolition of poverty through governmental action and the virtual guarantee of a decent standard of living for everybody, regardless of individual effort and output is not only extremely costly and inflationary but, worse than that, it is bound to interfere with productivity and will sooner or later lead to economic crisis, if not collapse. Insecurity, we are told, is an excellent spur to hard work; security, on the other hand, leads to laziness and moral decay. If the student is not quite convinced, he is told that it has been, after all, the individualistic laissez-faire economy which had made the United States the richest country in the world. In the following section we will attempt to examine statistically the accuracy of such beliefs.

THE ECONOMIC PERFORMANCE OF THE WELFARE STATE

There are many ways to study economic performance. Some economies do well in certain areas, say, productive efficiency, while others do well in equality. Some are troubled by pollution, others by poverty. Also among the criteria we can include economic growth, a state of full employment without inflation, and of course, our own humanistic goal of maximum general well-being. No one economic system or economy performs well in all of these diverse criteria.

For our present purposes we will just concentrate on the criterion of growth, since it is growth that so many opponents of the extension of welfare and security are worried about. Economic growth can be measured in various ways, but it is generally agreed that the simplest and best way is to look at the growth of total output over time, or real GNP.

What has been the record of growth in real GNP among the advanced economies within the Western world? In order to remove any bias resulting from the postwar American aid to European reconstruction we will ignore the first ten years after World War II and observe the trend from 1955 to the present. Table 11.13 presents the data.

Looking at the annual growth rates, it does not seem that the economies of the welfare states in Europe have performed more poorly than that in the United States. Quite the contrary. Over the entire twenty-year period the growth record of the U.S. is barely better than that of Great Britain, but far behind that of Sweden, The Netherlands

TABLE 11.13 GROWTH IN REAL GNP, 1955–1975 (AVERAGE ANNUAL RATES)

	1955–1960	1960–1965	1965–1970	1970–1975	1955–1975
USA	2.2	4.8	3.3	2.2	3.1
Canada	3.4	5.5	4.5	4.2	4.4
United Kingdom	2.8	3.3	2.4	1.0	2.4
Austria	5.2	4.4	5.1	4.2	4.7
Belgium	2.5	5.1	4.8	3.8	4.1
France	4.8	5.8	5.8	3.6	5.0
Germany	6.3	5.0	4.8	1.7	4.5
Netherlands	3.2	5.0	5.6	2.7	4.1
Switzerland	4.0	5.3	3.8	2.1	3.8
Sweden	3.4	5.3	3.9	2.6	3.8
Norway	3.2	5.4	4.6	4.0	4.3
Denmark	4.7	5.2	4.5	2.7	4.3

Source: OECD

and the remaining modern welfare states. Canada's performance appears surprisingly good, but to a large extent it is explained by a rapid population growth, as we will see later.

Furthermore, comparisons of the annual rates in Table 11.13 tend to understate the differences in performance among the various countries. In order to demonstrate the impact on output after twenty years of apparently small annual differences in growth rates, we show Table 11.14. The data on real GNP is transformed into index form with the year 1955 as the base. This procedure allows all the "competing" countries to start the race together, and then we can observe who pulls ahead and by how much.

From Table 11.14 we can see that the United States economy grew 84.2 percent between 1955 and 1975. The corresponding figures for Sweden, Great Britain and The Netherlands are 107.4 percent, 67.4 percent and 138.0 percent. With the exception of England, all the European welfare states have from the very beginning moved ahead of us, and their lead has been steadily increasing. Figure 11-2 pictures this graphically.

We also need to point out that the data in Tables 11.13 and 11.14 have a bias in favor of the United States and Canada. The reason is the much higher population growth in these two countries, in part caused by continued immigration. If we look only at real GNP/capita growth statistics, as a more accurate measure representing the real growth of output during the last two decades, the relative standing of Canada and the U.S. worsens. Table 11.15 summarizes the new picture.

TABLE 11.14   GROWTH IN REAL GNP, 1955=100

	1955	1960	1965	1970	1975
USA	100	111.5	144.5	165.8	184.2
Canada	100	117.9	154.0	192.2	240.5
United Kingdom	100	114.8	135.0	151.9	167.4
Austria	100	129.0	159.8	205.3	248.2
Belgium	100	113.2	145.4	184.2	219.2
France	100	126.3	167.8	222.7	266.1
Germany	100	135.9	173.7	219.2	238.9
Netherlands	100	122.2	147.9	204.6	238.0
Norway	100	115.9	150.7	188.4	233.9
Switzerland	100	121.5	157.2	189.7	197.3
Sweden	100	117.87	153.2	185.0	207.4

Source: OECD

The statistics of Table 11.15 suggest that the European welfare states have had a tendency to grow twice as rapidly in terms of real GNP per capita. No wonder we are no longer the richest country in the world. Recent data by the OECD and the World Bank reveal that Sweden, Switzerland and Norway are now wealthier.[14] The economies of Germany, The Netherlands and France are in the process of overtaking us. If the trend of the last twenty years continues, America will be

FIGURE 11-2 GROWTH OF REAL GNP IN THE USA AND THE EUROPEAN WELFARE STATES, 1955–1975

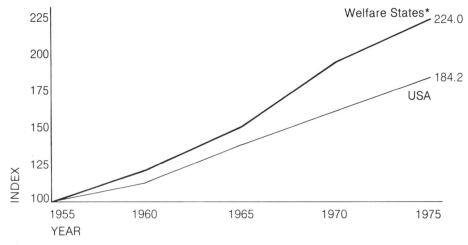

*Welfare states refers to an unweighted average of the UK, Austria, Belgium, France, Germany, Netherlands, Norway, Switzerland and Sweden.

TABLE 11.15   REAL GNP/CAPITA GROWTH, 1955–1975

USA	43.1%
Canada	65.6%
United Kingdom	53.0%
Belgium	96.8%
France	119.1%
Germany	106.4%
Netherlands	87.2%
Sweden	82.1%
Switzerland	58.8%

Source: Computed from data by OECD

by 1990 the poor relation within the family of advanced Western industrial countries.

Next, let us take a look at productivity in Table 11.16. The statistics are from a research study undertaken by the Bureau of Labor Statistics and they refer to growth of industrial output per man-hour. Once again the same story emerges. The European welfare states can be proud of their performance. For our purposes it is interesting to note that both Sweden and The Netherlands are among the front runners, and that even Great Britain manages to surpass the United States.

With these strong annual gains in the output per labor input, it is not surprising to find that wages and fringe benefits have risen very

TABLE 11.16   GROWTH IN PRODUCTIVITY, 1960–1976 (MEASURED BY OUTPUT/MAN-HOURS)

	1960–1965	1965–1970	1970–1976	1960–76
USA	4.3	2.0	3.8	3.3
Canada	4.4	4.4	3.4	3.9
United Kingdom	4.1	3.7	3.0	3.5
Belgium	5.1	7.7	7.6	6.9
Denmark	4.9	8.5	7.8	7.0
France	4.9	6.5	5.6	5.7
Germany	6.4	5.6	6.1	6.0
Netherlands	5.2	8.5	7.3	6.9
Sweden	7.6	7.5	4.2	6.2
Switzerland	2.4	6.7	4.1	4.3

Source: Bureau of Labor Statistics, Monthly Labor Review, July 1977.

fast in Europe. Between 1960 and 1976 such compensation rose in the welfare states on the average over 11 percent a year, almost twice the 5.9 percent rate observed in the United States. True, inflation was also greater in Europe during that period; average annual price rises amounted to 7 percent relative to the American 4 percent in that same period. As a result, the purchasing power of the typical European has gone up almost 5 percent per year, while the American worker only has been moving ahead at the pace of 2 percent a year.

In conclusion, the strong performance of the modern welfare state is undeniable. Somehow security does not seem to interfere with productivity. Quite the contrary. To many Americans this may seem surprising, since we are all continually reminded in the form of economic horror stories about the crisis in England, as an example of where more "welfarism" supposedly leads. Yet the perennial crisis of the British pound is much more of concern to the banker than it is to the average employee. In terms of security, wage gains and threat of unemployment, the British worker has certainly had it better than his American counterpart. We admit that the British economic performance has not been brilliant, yet we should keep in mind that England is not the only welfare state. Rather, its economic performance has been clearly shown in the accumulated data to be the exception that proves the general rule.

Going Beyond the Limitations
of the Welfare State

For all of its positive and humanistic features, the welfare state is not an end in itself. Actually it should best be seen as a beginning, rather than an ending. After the security needs are satisfied, we have to cope with the social needs. Just as people need to grow or else they will stagnate, the welfare state needs to grow and transform itself, otherwise it will stagnate.

The limitations of the welfare state are hinted at in the comments of one of its biggest champions, the Swedish economist Gunnar Myrdal, ". . . I will honestly confess that to me personally Sweden has become somewhat boring while I feel excited about America, the underdeveloped regions, and most other countries where there are staggering problems and spectacular struggles to wage."[15]

It should be noted that while Myrdal makes these comments he does not feel that boredom is a problem that is a fault of the welfare state, and he is not criticizing it for this.* Following the above remarks, Myrdal goes on to say this about Sweden, and its achievements.

---

*At this point we insert a brief note on the high Swedish suicide rate, sometimes cited as evidence of purposeless life in the modern welfare state. This alleged relationship is false on two counts: First, the suicide rate was high in Sweden long before it had its welfare state, and second, most similar ethnic groups (white Protestants) anywhere have a very high suicide rate.

□ The culture popularly appreciated is a material culture. In all things surrounding the body, textiles, glassware, furniture, houses, Swedish consumption has reached unsurpassed levels of beauty and quality. Indeed, in this field Sweden has even become an exporter of ideas.[16]

In these achievements, we feel, lie the real limitations and dangers of the welfare state. The welfare state was based on the primary aim of providing a materially secure life for its citizenry. This, we agree, is a necessary and desirable aim. But when material goals are pursued as ends in themselves, life begins to stagnate and higher values become dim and obscured. These values, which direct growth, do not consist of enhancing one's material situation, but in pursuing those things that are beyond the narrow material ego. To continue humanistic growth, having satisfied basic material needs, the welfare state must move on to what lies higher on the human hierarchy of values. According to Maslow's psychology we must now reckon with the social and particularly the moral needs.

These higher values are shown by the reaction of Gunnar Myrdal himself. He referred, in the first quote, to the challenge of meeting the problems and needs of other parts of the world. Myrdal is not alone in this kind of interest. Foreign aid figures show us that the Swedish nation as a whole feels a great commitment to helping others. Sweden is the world leader in this regard, contributing a higher percentage of its GNP for foreign developmental assistance than any other country.[17] Moreover, Sweden in 1977 decided to cancel all the debts of its poorest twenty-five creditors and to restrict development aid to grants and interest-free loans in the future.

Now let us return to the question of boredom. While Myrdal denies that this is a real issue, others still see this as a shortcoming of the welfare state. Our reaction is that, even if the welfare state has led to boredom, this is not a problem but an opportunity. This involves understanding what boredom is psychologically. In the life of an individual, and the same applies to a nation, boredom is a signal that the person is ready for a change. Boredom often occurs when all tasks have been accomplished and the person needs to become engaged in something new. If members of the advanced welfare state are bored, and again Myrdal would seriously object to this characterization, this could be a sign that they are ready for a new direction.

In discussing Sweden's interest in helping others less fortunate than herself, we have suggested one of these new directions. We will closely examine the direction of new economic forms in the following chapters. For now we would like to emphasize again that the critical issue for the welfare state may hinge on the question of materialism versus the higher values. If the citizens of the welfare state do not see beyond the materialism of a comfortable and secure life, they are destined to become stuck in the repetitive ruts of sensate living.

All civilizations have crumbled that have become fixated at this point. But if the welfare state can keep the ideals of its original humanistic conceptions alive, it can continue towards the realization of human potential.

References

1. Sleeman, J. F. *The Welfare State*. London: Unwine University Books, 1973, p. 4.

2. Reprinted in E. Will and H. Vatter, eds. *Poverty in Affluence*. 2nd ed. New York: Harcourt, Brace and World, 1970, pp. 7–8.

3. The figure is taken from:
    Helco, Hugh. *Modern Social Policies in Britain and Sweden*. New Haven: Yale University Press, 1974, p. 10.

4. Myrdal, G. *Against the Stream*. New York: Random House, 1972, p. 284.

5. Moenig, E. and Frei, H. *Social Security in Ten Industrial Countries*. Zurich, 1977.

6. See Schnitzer, Martin. *Income Distribution: A Comparative Study*. New York: Praeger, 1974.

7. OECD. *OECD Economic Outlook, Occasional Studies, Income Distribution in OECD Countries*. July 1976.

8. Wiles, Peter. *Economic Institutions Compared*. Oxford, 1977.

9. Myrdal, G. "The National Purposes Reconsidered, 1776–1976." Lecture held at Columbia University, October 29, 1976.

10. McConnell, C. R. *Economics*, 6th ed. New York: McGraw-Hill, 1975, p. 743.

11. Quoted in Murray, C. S. *Blueprint for Health*. New York: Schocken, 1974, p. 52.

12. Kaufman, Roger. "An International Comparison of Unemployment Rates: The Effect of Job Security on Job Continuity," republished PhD thesis, M.I.T., 1978.

13. Strumpel, Burkhard. "Economic Life-Styles, Values and Subjective Welfare" in his ed. *Economic Means for Human Needs*. Ann Arbor: University of Michigan, 1976, p. 56.

14. See for instance, the *OECD Observer*, March-April 1978, pp. 3–4, on the most recent *Annual Report* of the World Bank.

15. Myrdal, G. "What Is Wrong With the Welfare State?" *New York Times Sunday Magazine*, January 30, 1966, p. 18.

16. Myrdal, G. "What Is Wrong With the Welfare State?" *New York Times Sunday Magazine*, January 30, 1966, p. 18.

17. Baule, W. *World Development Report*, 1978, New York: Oxford University Press, August, 1978.

Chapter Twelve

BEYOND THE WELFARE STATE: FROM WORK COUNCILS TO CODETERMINATION

INTRODUCTION

We saw in the last chapter that the modern welfare state, particularly as it has been developed in several European countries, has been directed towards the physiological and security needs of people. According to the concept of the Maslowian hierarchy of human needs, its next step in development will be to meet the social needs—in particular the needs of belongingness and esteem. This chapter will attempt to show that this has in fact been happening, that in several important areas in the European economy there is a movement to something beyond the welfare state. Employees are not satisfied with the status quo, and are now pressing new demands aimed at a job environment with a "human face."

The union movement in Europe is generally much stronger than it is in the U.S., and this partly accounts for the more complete development of the welfare state there. For instance, roughly 25 percent of American workers belong to unions, compared with 40 percent in West Germany, almost 50 percent in England, and 90 percent in Sweden. One effect of labor's strength and influence has been changes in how work is done in industry. But an analysis of the European developments suggests that the initial pressure for action has not been coming from union leaders but rather from grass-root dissatisfaction among the rank and file and the increasing unwillingness of workers to subject themselves to dehumanizing jobs. As Joseph Mires notes in his review for the U.S. government publication, *The Monthly Labor Review*,

□ ... as standards of living advance and education levels and aspirations of workers rise, there is a corresponding disinclination to do boring and unsatisfying work. Employers in many nations find they must turn to foreign workers often to do the less desirable jobs. Western Europe today employs about 8½ million foreign workers who are doing most of the undesirable jobs. The Ford Co. in Cologne, Germany employs 14,000 foreign workers out of a labor force of 35,000. Eighty percent of workers employed in a Renault automobile plant near Paris are foreigners. One Swedish company recently was unable to recruit a single Swede below the age of 30 for its assembly line operation ... many union leaders and government officials see the demand for a more rewarding work experience and satisfaction not merely as a response to worker's discontent but also as a logical next step in a dynamic social policy, and part of a quest for a smooth functioning of the social and economic system.[1]

Observe how consistent these observations are with what would be expected by applying Maslow's theory to the social scene. Following are some of the job innovations that have been introduced into several European industries.

WORK GROUPS: THE ASSEMBLY LINE STOPS HERE

In England, programs to restructure jobs have been found in industries which have routine work and therefore serious problems in employee turnover and absenteeism. The Phillips Electronic Company, for example, has for quite a number of years used a variety of approaches to improve satisfaction with work. Its twenty plants in Great Britain employ about 65,000 people. The company has introduced teamwork in several plants. Teamwork means that employees no longer work in social isolation at their narrow portion of an assembly job, but work in small groups on a common, larger-scale task. Workers could participate in the teamwork plan if they wanted to, but they did not have to. It was found that more workers volunteered than could be accommodated. The teams that were set up did their own training, administration, maintenance, and stock control. What were the results? There were moderate increases in both productivity and pay. Even more important from the standpoint of the company were the findings that absenteeism declined and work quality improved.[2]

Teamwork was also introduced in several plants of the Imperial Chemical Company. The unions involved in these plants termed the program an outstanding success. Productivity and pay both increased, just as in the Phillips plants, and time out and work disputes were reduced. The key to the success, according to those involved, has been the participation of the workers who assisted at weekly staff meetings in identifying the jobs that workers can do. Those doing routine jobs were given additional responsibilities.[3]

In 1973 the French National Assembly passed a law creating an independent Agency for the Improvement of Working Conditions. Its major purpose is to focus on problems of job satisfaction. The Renault automobile plant, a nationalized enterprise, has been a leader in job restructuring. In the beginning the company concentrated on improving physical conditions to make industry more humane. Following this there was job enrichment and rotation, teamwork, and related changes in the assembly line. For example, in a new plant at Donde the overall assembly of cars was reorganized so that the workers could stop work if they needed or wanted to without stopping the whole assembly line. Thus the continuous pressure of the assembly line was lessened. At LeMans the assembly line was changed in two stages. The first was when workers were taught two or three operations, which allowed them to move with a piece being constructed instead of standing in one place doing one operation. In the second stage the assembly line was completely eliminated and replaced by "production islands." In these, four people work at a table surrounded by containers of the parts.[4] It is interesting to observe that in France some of the unions have generally kept aloof from such changes, seeing such things as basically within the sphere of management, and most of these changes have been initiated outside of union leadership. The unions went along when it was clear that the workers liked the changes.

The situation is different in Sweden, where the unions have played a very active part in the introduction of changes. This plus the reality that Sweden is probably the best developed welfare state has led to the fact that "Sweden has now become one of the world's foremost laboratories for the humanization of the workplace."[5]

The best-known example of the humanization of industry is the Swedish automobile industry, earlier at Saab and later at Volvo. The changes were begun in the late 1960s when it was observed that there was widespread employee dissatisfaction with the old assembly-line methods of production. Let us hear how the President of Volvo, Pehr Gyllenhammar, describes these changes in his company.

□ We broke up the (assembly) line, to put it simply, by not using conveyors going through a warehouse, which is what an assembly plant is, but by designing individual carriers for the product. These carriers can move very freely in a layout that is not determined by their technology. Because you have many individual carriers, you can move them and stop them independently of one another. The first humiliation that meets a man or woman in an assembly plant is that one has to run after the product. Imagine every working day of your life running after a product. Yet few have questioned the necessity for it. . . . Secondly, we have identified and done something about the social component. People need to have social contact. Even if it is very quiet in the conventional plant, people are physically isolated from one another. They are so busy working at "short tempos" (perhaps 30 or 60 seconds) that they cannot communicate and must have their social life outside the working environment instead of communicating on their jobs. They cannot even communicate on matters relating to their job, for they are encouraged not to talk. So we said, bring them together; in a collective effort they could do much more. Let them work as a group assembling a chassis, for example, and decide for themselves how to organize their work.[6]

The work groups that were set up generally consisted of from five to ten workers. These teams elect their own foreman, usually on a rotating basis, and they do their own training (with the costs of the training borne by the company). The group decides on job assignments and the extent and frequency of rest periods. The groups are fully responsible for quality control, processing of raw materials and tool inventories. Each group takes care of the transport of the various assembled parts from one workshop to another. Finally, the group competes as a team for productivity bonuses which are equally shared by all members.

How productive are these work groups? The groups were given a certain quota of work output based on previous levels of production; apart from that they are free to decide the pace of work, the scheduling of work, and so forth. After a transitional learning period, it was soon found that these work groups could meet the old output levels in a much shorter time. The group could then decide to work more and earn more pay, or take the extra time off, which several groups did. Turnover statistics indicate a tremendous improvement in job satisfaction. At Saab, the introduction of the work group concept has cut turnover from 70 percent to 20 percent and at the same time cut to one-third unplanned down time in the production process.[7] This is what we would expect, since under the previous plan one absent worker could stop an entire line.

The Case of Japan

Up till now we have almost solely concentrated on the humanistic directions in Western economies. But a look at Japan will show us further evidence for the actual effectiveness of humanistic concepts and practices.

Although Japan is a highly developed modern industrialized economy, it presents us with a particularly interesting case because some of the Japanese methods are quite different from those in the West. The uniqueness of the Japanese approach to business and corporate life can be defined by two Japanese words, *Nenko* and *Ringi*. *Nenko* is the system of employee relations with the company, and *Ringi* is the system of company decision-making. Both systems exist in Japan because they are adoptions by business of attitudes and practices that have a long history in traditional Japanese culture.

Nenko In the large corporation the worker, after a brief probationary period, receives tenure, like a university professor in the United States. The company gives the worker virtual life-long job security until he or she retires at the age of 55. Wages differ more according to seniority than by occupational skill or level. What is interesting here from a Maslowian perspective is the almost complete lower-need satisfaction the permanent worker is given in Japan. There is a decent income, shopping at discount prices in the company store, inexpensive company housing, ample opportunity for recreational activities at no cost, and most important, life-long economic security. These benefits are guaranteed as long as the worker chooses to stay in his or her firm. There is absolutely no fear of being laid off, and very little uncertainty and insecurity about one's future earnings. Furthermore, by filling a job in a stable work environment, one gets to know just about all the other workers. The employees feel that they all belong to the same family. These feelings are supported and reinforced by the emphasis on promotion by seniority rather than skill. The workers thus have no need to compete against each other, but instead "compete with" each other in striving for a higher and better quality output in the plant. Thus we find that the three major lower needs on the hierarchy, physiological, safety and security, and belongingness, are fulfilled by the *Nenko* system.

The next need on the hierarchy is esteem, and we find that Japanese workers are strongly motivated by this. They take great pride in the quality and attractiveness of their products.

Some Westerners have looked at this system and called it irrational. After all, how could employees be adequately motivated if they operate with little or no threat of being fired, and are automatically promoted rather than differentially rewarded according to how they perform? Another criticism leveled at the system is that it is paternalistic. That is, the owners of the company function like a parent figure, treating the workers like children who are protected and guided in an all-encompassing company environment. But so far this has been very acceptable to the Japanese worker. Westerners find it hard to resist a smile when they look at the company songs that are sung by employees. Here, for instance, is the song of the Hitachi Company,[8]

Over hill, over valley, each calls and each responds.
We are united and we have dreams,
We are Hitachi men, aroused and ready
To promote the happiness of others.
Great is our pride in our home-produced products.
Polished and refined our skills.

With a sincerity that pierces steel,
Unflaggingly we strive.
Difficulties we overcome, treading the thorny path.
The spirit of Hitachi carries us forward,
Conscious of the honor of our race.
Already we are world-famed Hitachi.

Filled with the hopes of dawn,
We make ready for the morrow.

Stretching the shining rainbow,
Over the seven great seas.
Forward to new fields with burning zeal,
The youthful blood of Hitachi courses in our veins.

Ringi   The *Ringi* system pertains to the way decisions are made in Japanese corporations. In a way, it is the opposite of the typical American system. In the United States, policies and objectives of the company, as well as work practices, are set by top management and then handed down. In the *Ringi* system, work policies and recommendations are proposed from the bottom and passed on to the next higher level for approval until they eventually reach the top. If approved at the top, the new policy is then put into practice. While it may sound cumbersome to Westerners, it is a system where ideas and initiatives are finally put into practice with agreement and cooperation at all levels of the organization.

Although the *Nenko* and *Ringi* systems may seem strange or even upside down to us, the fact is that they work well. In terms of economic productivity and growth no industrialized country can compare with Japan. Typically, Japanese productivity grows at a rate twice as high as that of the European welfare states, and four times as high as in the United States and Canada. Similarly, no country has experienced a faster rise in the general standard of living than Japan. There also has been very little unemployment. These systems deliver, and the reason might lie in the fact that they effectively meet vital human needs.

Paradoxically, both the *Nenko* and the *Ringi* systems are starting to come under attack in Japan. Even though they still command industrial relations in the large manufacturing corporations, every year more enterprises are converting to the Western system. The reasons for this development show the ultimate limitations of paternalism vis-á-vis real industrial humanism. It is the shareholders of the firm who are increasingly disenchanted with the system's lack of flexibility, primarily evident in the recession of 1975–76 when profits were sharply curtailed. As a result, Japanese management is attempting more and more to evade giving permanent employment by setting up shop abroad. International competition. in conjunction with profit-oriented stockholders appears to be slowly disintegrating the human foundation on which *Nenko*, in particular, rests.

EUPSYCHIAN MANAGEMENT

In a radio interview in 1960, Maslow made the following comments in regard to the labor movement, "If you dig below the surface . . . it appears that unions are following the hierarchy of needs that I have been talking about. First they struck for food, then for security; now I think we could say that unions are striking for self-respect—for a feeling of being masters over their fate, for power rather than power-lessness."[9] We can see in the description of the European labor movement—above all in the Northern Europe welfare states—the fulfillment of Maslow's predictions. However, Maslow was not entirely correct. He assumed that the changes he described would come into effect in the U.S. labor movement, perhaps not being aware that unions were much stronger and more secure in Europe than in the U.S. In the U.S. the union bargaining efforts are still very much directed toward the bread-and-butter issues of wages and work effort. (But it is interesting to note that the most recent trends, especially among the stronger unions, show a concern with achieving lifetime employment security).

Despite the fact that there has been relatively little thrust in the U.S. from the labor unions for more humanized work, participation in decision-making and work restructuring has still occurred. In the U.S., interestingly enough, many of the changes have been initiated by management. Not that management has been solely acting out of altruistic motives directed toward employee satisfaction, but out of the recognition that employees who are fulfilled in their work do a better job, are less apt to quit, and in general produce better for the company.

The change towards more humanistic management is generally traced to the now-classic experiments conducted by Elton Mayo of the Harvard Graduate School of Business Administration. The best-known of these studies were done between 1927 and 1932 at the Hawthorne works of Western Electric Company. They began with a puzzle.

Company engineers had tried to change the lighting in an assembly department to see if this could increase productivity. They were not too surprised that when lighting was increased productivity went up. However, they were astonished to find that when the lighting was decreased productivity also went up. What was going on? The Hawthorne experiment was continued by Elton Mayo with other work variables being changed, such as rest periods and scheduling, and again it was generally found that whatever was done, whether it appeared to be an improvement or not, work output increased. Mayo discovered the secret behind the puzzle when he noted that all these experimental changes had a common factor: the cooperation and involvement of the workers was elicited in the studies. As Mayo put it, "what actually happened was that six individuals became a team and the team gave itself wholeheartedly and spontaneously to cooperation in the experiment."[10]

Actually, Mayo had come across a similar phenomenon earlier in a study in a Philadelphia textile mill. There he found that when employees were allowed to participate in decisions usually reserved for management their morale and interest in their work increased, and so did their productivity. These findings were part of the foundation for what came later to be known as human relations theory.

Blumberg has reviewed and summarized the studies in "participation" from Mayo's work through the mid-1960s, which include at least seventeen major studies involving such diverse groups of people as sewing machine operators, office workers, manual workers, psychology students, supervisory personnel, salesmen, foremen, and medical scientists. As Blumberg states in his conclusion,

□ There is significance in this diversity. It is just this impressive diversity in the participation literature which makes the consistency of the findings, by contrast, even more profound, significant, and valid. There is hardly a study in the entire literature which fails to demonstrate that satisfaction in work is enhanced or that other generally acknowledged beneficial consequences accrue from a genuine increase in worker's decision-making power. Such consistency of findings, I submit, is rare in social research.[11]

An interesting example of the beneficial effects of employee participation is the case of the Lincoln Electric Company in Cleveland, Ohio. The system at Lincoln began with the idea of worker profit-sharing, which was put into practice in the 1930s. After deduction for taxes, other costs, and stockholder dividends (set at 6 percent), all the remaining profits are distributed to the employees. In 1969 the 1900 workers at Lincoln each received a profit-sharing bonus of approximately $8000. In addition to this overall bonus each employee is encouraged to put forth ideas that either will increase the company's productivity or efficiency. The employee is then given a bonus that is a proportion of the money that the company saved by instituting the new idea. The company also has regular meetings of all employees in small groups in which ideas for improvement both in the product and the way the company is run are discussed. Employees share in the economic rewards of all ideas that work. One amazing result of such a system is that Lincoln's welding machines and electrodes are still sold at 1934 prices, while the costs of the inputs—labor, copper and steel—have risen by 200 to 600 percent over the same period. One reason Lincoln was such an early leader in the movement to increase worker participation and involvement in industry was the attitudes of one of the founding brothers, James Finney Lincoln.

Innocent of manufacturing experience when he took over the business in 1914, James Finney Lincoln wanted the help of the workers in the plant. "I had one fundamental idea," he explains. "If I could make those men as anxious to make the business succeed as I was, I knew it would succeed . . . Great as American industry is, it leaves largely untapped its greatest resource, the productive power, initiative and intelligence latent in every person. The prophet states it—'Thou madest him (humanity) to have dominion over the works of thy hand.' That conception is a far cry from the normal evaluation of man by his contemporaries. Truly man is so made but our industrial system does not fully develop those abilities . . . The goal of the organization must be this—to make a better and better product to be sold at a lower and lower price. Profit cannot be the *goal*. Profit must be a *by-product*. That is a state of mind and a philosophy. Actually an organization doing this job as it can be done will make larger profits which must be properly divided between user, worker and stockholder. That takes ability and character."[12]

Do they make them like old J. F. Lincoln anymore? Let's hope so.

Another example of a similar development, although much later on, is Donnely Motors in Michigan. It instituted a plan in the early 1950s in which workers participate in both management and profit-sharing. Since 1952 Donnely has been able to both lower its prices and double its productivity. In a recent move, Donnely employees voted to eliminate time clocks at the company, a move which in ordinary circumstances could lead to a sharp decrease in working time, along with lower productivity and profit. The result at Donnely was that after the time clocks were removed absenteeism dropped from 5 percent to 1.5 percent, and lateness from 6 percent to 1 percent.[13]

Manager X and Manager Y

Findings such as these fitted very well with Maslow's theory of motivation, as first presented in his 1954 book. This book, and the whole body of human relations data, was carefully studied and integrated by Douglas McGregor, whc was a professor of management at the Massachusetts Institute of Technology. In 1960 McGregor published a book on management called *The Human Side of Enterprise*, which quickly became one of the most influential texts in the management field.[14] The book talked about two contrasting approaches to management, which he called Theory X and Theory Y. Theory X assumes that the average person does not like to work and has to be coerced and controlled into producing, and thus management based on this theory consists in the effective use of authoritarian methods. At least up until McGregor's time Theory X management has been the commonest form of management in the business world.

Theory Y management makes a different assumption about people and work. It assumes that work is natural and inherently satisfying, and that most people seek to use their ingenuity and creativity in their work. As a result of this belief the management methods used under Theory Y are democratic and seek to stimulate the motivation and morale of the worker.

It can be seen that Theory X pretty well corresponds to the concept of Economic Man, and Theory Y corresponds to the concept of Humanistic Person. Although the science of economics has not really come to grips with the humanistic concept of the person, in the practical world of business the realism of the humanistic image has made significant inroads in managerial thinking. A business-financed research organization, the National Industrial Conference Board, conducted a survey among a random sample of North American companies and asked who was the most significant social scientist for them; the most frequently chosen was Douglas McGregor.

Criticisms of Theory Y

Management expert Peter Drucker, as well as Maslow himself, has pointed out that Theory Y often gives the mistaken impression that it is permissive, or that it asks management to be permissive. Instead, as Drucker points out, "to manage workers and working by putting responsibility on the worker and by aiming at achievement made exceedingly high demands on both worker and manager. McGregor also saw this, though he did not stress it."[15]

Maslow has made an important point that follows from what Drucker has said. Management by Theory Y assumes that you are working with healthy people who have some fairly well-developed sense of self-actualization. Most important, Theory Y cannot work in an environment of poverty. As Maslow puts it, "obviously you cannot trust people with a key to the pantry when most people are starving, or when there is not enough food to go around.[16] And to drive home the point even more, Maslow continues:

> ☐ If there were one hundred people and there was food for ten, and ninety of those hundred had to die, then I would make mighty goddamned sure that I would not be one of those ninety, and I'm quite sure that my morals and ethics and so on would change very radically to fit the jungle situation.[17]

Even for people outside the jungle world of poverty, Theory Y is a long way from getting home free. Maslow emphasized that "we must *assume* that the people in eupsychian plants are not fixated at the safety-need level."[18] Obviously, a large proportion of the people is not anxiety-free, especially in matters of job security; even though they may appear to be fully "normal" and, economically speaking, "successful." The person who is insecure and vulnerable may not be able to take on the responsibility and self-discipline that Theory Y demands. People in this condition are used to being told what to do, having tasks narrowly defined for them, and being dependent on strong outside authority. If these people were suddenly switched from Theory X management to Theory Y management the results could be a disaster. One conclusion from this is that Theory Y does not work for Economic Man; in order for it to work there have to be adequate preconditions—a fertile ground.

A criticism from another perspective has been made more recently by Maccoby. First of all, Maccoby suggests that Theory Y has become popular in business not necessarily because management has become more enlightened or humanistic, or because Theory Y is better than Theory X, but because the new complex and technological nature of industry *requires* more flexible and adaptive employees than the older kind of industry where the structure of the company was relatively simple and there was not much change in the product or its marketing.

Following this Maccoby notes a kind of moral ambiguity that exists in McGregor's work. "The ambiguity that runs through the book is the question of whether the manager should act out of his own wish to maximize profit or out of a new and deeper understanding of what would be good for people. McGregor does not suggest that these two principles might conflict . . . In McGregor's system, there is no chance for even a top manager to change the corporate objectives, only to have some influence on how they are reached."[19] Maccoby refers to McGregor's example of finding Theory Y used in a military supply industry which developed intercontinental ballistics missiles, and how "tremendously excited they were over the challenge represented by their task." McGregor evidently does not raise the question of the moral legitimacy of such a task.*

Maccoby also finds fault in a lack of moral focus, or "heart" quality, in Maslow's own theories. "Few who read Maslow in the corporation are encouraged to be socially responsible, not to speak of compassionate."[21] And of course Maslow was no doubt more interested in showing what is than what ought to be. Maccoby criticizes Maslow for supporting attitudes of a certain kind of elitism in the corporate structure. Theory Y managers are those who are successful in the new technological corporate system, and those who aren't are seen as weak, deficient, and not self-actualized. Maccoby finds little explicit mention in Maslow of the need to change the structure of organizations; as Maccoby sees it, it is often that structure, hierarchical and bureaucratic, which causes failure, rather than that some people are functioning at too low a level of self-actualization. There is no doubt a grain of truth in such assertions. But part of the problem also lies in the fact that most businessmen read more *about* Maslow than read Maslow's writings. For instance, Maslow had been very critical of McGregor's continued talking "about the principle of authority, the chain of command, and so on." Maslow cautions that these concepts do not apply to Theory Y any more "than they would to a really well-integrated basketball team, for instance."[22]

---

*Maslow himself criticized his followers in focusing Theory Y too much on short-run profits and productivity rather than long-run human growth terms.

"Generally they feel they're being hard-headed if they use as the criteria of management success or a healthy organization the criteria of smaller labor turnovers or less absenteeism, or better morale or more profit or the like. But in doing so they neglect the whole eupsychian growth and self-actualization and personal development side of the enlightened enterprise. I suspect that they are afraid that this latter is a kind of a priori moralism, that is brought in only because some particular person has a moralistic character and would like it to be that way on an a priori basis."[20]

Still, we have to agree with Maccoby that Maslow may have put too much attention on individual change, and not enough on changing institutions. Both obviously mutually interact and reinforce each other.

Ironically, many of Maccoby's points could be interpreted as constituting a *humanistic* critique of the management ideas expressed by the two foremost humanistic theorists in this field, Maslow and McGregor. We don't want to argue the validity of Maccoby's criticism, but it will, no doubt, challenge many Theory Y enthusiasts. We will now move beyond Theory Y (and also beyond Maslow) and take a careful look at structural change in the enterprise and the concomitant institutional changes in the economy.

INDUSTRIAL DEMOCRACY

As we saw, the studies in the area of human relations and participation and the practical results achieved by several companies show that worker participation in company decision-making has successful human and economic results. When one surveys these various successful findings, the question naturally may arise as to how far worker participation should go. Is there a point where worker participation is no longer desirable, where it does not work anymore, and where the division between workers and management needs to be maintained? Or does experience point out that the logical result of worker participation should be full and complete worker self-management—or, as it is sometimes called, industrial democracy? Is that the humanistic goal?

Blumberg himself has very forthrightly addressed this kind of question when he states what the participation literature means to him. He says (using the editorial "we"), ". . . we do not see participation as a device to lower costs, to improve quality, to increase productivity, to undercut trade union or workers' demands, or to give workers the illusion of power without its actuality . . ." Instead, he says, "We are interested in the question of participation as it bears on the larger sociological and philosophical issue of the alienation of labor, and we are prepared to follow wherever this research leads."[23]

From Participation to Codetermination

Historically speaking, labor unions can be seen as the earliest major effort towards industrial democracy. In the United States, unions are generally seen as the only form in which workers can influence company policy. But some unions, particularly in the U.S., Britain, and Canada, have tended to put all their emphasis on wage bargaining and little effort into changing the way the work is done. As we will see shortly, there is even *resistance* on the part of unions to these changes. In Europe, on the other hand, things have taken a different direction.

Work Councils

According to Charles Levinson, an expert on the European labor scene, "History will record, I believe, that 1968 was the year that industrial democracy advanced to the center of the industrial relations stage." The year 1968 coincides with the preparation of a report by the Executive Council of the Common Market which would have required *work councils* in each major European enterprise selling in the Common Market. Such work councils, composed of workers only, not outside union officials, would have the rights of information and consultation over such questions as hiring, firing, security, vocational training, health and safety, social facilities, wages, hours and vacations. They would also make collective agreements with management in cases where there would be no conflict with trade union agreements. The bill met stiff resistance with some of the member countries, particularly Italy, Ireland and Belgium, who seem less ready for this than the Northern countries. Subsequently the proposal was dropped. In late 1975 the European Economic Community (EEC) executive council once more rekindled the controversy by asking all member countries to study in depth the feasibility of such legislation and debate the issue.

Work councils, however, are not new, and have been in effect in several countries. After World War II most major European countries moved toward setting up work councils in all large plants. National law created such councils in France (1945), Sweden (1946), Belgium (1948), Holland (1950), Germany (1952), Luxembourg (1962), and Italy (1966).

Work councils are groups of workers in a unit of a plant that represent the worker's voice in various decisions relating to the work. The changes from assembly-line production to setting up small work groups, discussed earlier, were in most cases proposed by work councils and then supported or adopted by the labor unions to which these workers belonged. It is interesting to note that in most situations the unions that were largely communist in orientation tended to resist and oppose the work councils, while the other unions, which were often Catholic or Protestant in orientation, more readily tended to support the idea.

In West Germany work councils have been obligatory for all enterprises with more than five employees. In 1972 an act was strengthened so that work councils now have a right to financial information, and to initiate discussion about new methods and standards in work. In cases of disputes, outside experts would resolve the impasse. Besides these primary rights of information and consultation, the work councils have a voice in determining work schedules, welfare, hiring, expansion or cutback of production, introduction of new technology, mergers, plant closings, and personnel matters. They discuss the physical work place, the bonus system, and fringe benefits. Studies have shown that employees in Germany view the work councils as representing them at least as much as the trade union. Trade unions have therefore watched these new autonomous bodies with mixed feelings. In many cases the unions have accepted the work councils as their "second arm," and vice versa.

In Sweden cooperative communities date back to 1946, but it was only in 1965 that modern work councils were formally introduced by a collective bargaining between the national confederations of unions and employees. It was agreed that the new councils had the responsibility of "working for increased production and work satisfaction." The first such council was introduced at Kockums Company, a ship building firm near Malmo. It has served as a model which was subsequently emulated in the entire country.

Let us take a closer look at this institution: The council here consists of eighteen members; seven blue-collar representatives, seven management delegates, and four white-collar unionists. The council meets every two to three months under the chairmanship of the managing director. The council must be informed about all prospective developments in all areas of industrial marketing, production planning, personnel matters and questions of shutdowns and cutbacks. Similarly, the council discusses these matters and is expected to express its point of view on any controversial question. The council's decisions were not legally binding but in practice were very difficult to ignore. Given the powerful force of the work-council organization it is not surprising that the researcher found that "all parties in Kockums have taken the work of the council and its supporting structure very seriously, so that it has played a major part in generating the collaborative atmosphere so apparent in the shipyard."[24]

More recently in Sweden a new law requires workers' concurrence on all important decisions, including the sale of the company and changes in the organization of production. If agreement cannot be reached, negotiations would go to a national panel and ultimately to a body known as a *Labor Court*. In effect, workers now have a veto right over all major corporate decisions.

The work-council movement has also been strong in Norway and Denmark. In Belgium the work council law was revised in 1963. Now firms with fifty or more employees must have a work council. It is composed of workers who have equal voting power with management. The size of the councils varies from eight to thirty-eight members. It is entitled to receive full information on the economic performance and the outlook for the company or plant. Its functions are, however, still strictly consultative and advisory. Similarly, in France, work councils have recently been revitalized and they have the formal right to have their own auditor examine the financial data of the enterprise.

Dutch work councils are highly developed, with a new law in 1971 broadening their powers. Any firm with more than one hundred employees must form a work council of up to twenty-five employees elected by their peers. Before making any important decision such as closing a plant, expanding, or changing supply agreements with other countries, management must consult with the work council. Also, companies have to establish a supervisory board which includes members of the work council as well as ownership. The work council can veto any particular shareholder appointment. The supervisory board then chooses members of the management board. An example that shows work councils have real power, and are not only consultative or advisory: In 1974 the work council of a large company succeeded in overriding management's decision to merge with another, though smaller, Dutch company, and chose instead to make a deal with a British firm. The Dutch example indicates how fluid the boundaries are between work councils and worker representation on highest company levels.

It is worth pointing out that it was initially neither management nor the trade unions who favored the work council developments over the last ten years, but it was worker grass-roots unrest. This unrest manifested itself in high absenteeism, turnover, and wildcat (non-authorized) strike activity. This left both sides, management and unions, with little choice but to promote the kind of collaboration that resulted in both a greater humanization of work and a period of remarkable labor peace.

This brings us to one of the final stages of participatory management, which is codetermination.

Codetermination

Codetermination means that workers participate with management in the company's highest decision-making level, the board of directors; thus it is said that workers now codetermine, along with the shareholders, the direction a company takes. A country pioneering in codetermination was Germany, where the idea was implemented after World War II in the mining industry.

The idea received a general boost when the European Economic Community executive council introduced legislation providing for more industrial democracy in the large European corporations. Besides the establishment of work councils, the EEC-proposed statute provided for the setting up of a new board of supervisors (supervising management) in which labor would be represented to at least 30 percent. In contrast to the unions' lack of enthusiasm for the work council, the attitude of European organized labor toward this proposal has been much more favorable. Big Labor sees in the codetermination movement a potential new tool to hinder management's practice of relying more and more on non-unionized cheap foreign labor for materials and sub-assemblies.

After several years of debate Germany passed in 1976 the first economy-wide codetermination law. Today German workers make up between one-third and one-half of the boards of directors of sizeable firms. The law covers between 600 and 650 companies, including 475 industrial and construction companies; forty-five banks, insurance companies and publishing houses; twenty-four wholesale, retail, hotel and restaurant chains; and thirty-nine firms involved in public transportation and services.

The inclusion of workers in a firm's board of directors necessarily means decision-making is more complicated, since more interests have to be taken into account. But that is the result of any change towards greater democracy, in any sphere. According to experts in Germany any disadvantages of codetermination are outweighed by the advantages. Dietrich Kurth of Germany's Economic Ministry sees the advantages as coming from the greatly increased "social peace" which codetermination brings. West Germany has had a very low incidence of strikes as compared to the U.S., and even the reduction of jobs in some industries, such as coal mining, was accomplished without major confrontations and conflicts. And, of course, codetermination has not hurt Germany's industrial development, as can be seen from the data on its economic performance in the last chapter. In describing codetermination, an editorial in *The New York Times*, made this observation, "The enormous strides made by German Industry under this system of shared responsibility suggest that worker involvement in management is no bar to efficiency. Neither is it a formula for socializing industry or co-opting labor into company unions."[25]

Many European countries—among these Sweden, Norway, Austria, and The Netherlands—have moved to imitate this new instrument of humanizing the work place, although nowhere has codetermination reached the extent it has in Germany. Most recently the French government has proposed that all large companies should make room for worker representation on their boards.

Even in England the government is now looking beyond security. In 1978 it introduced legislation to a large extent based on the so-called Bullock Report released in the summer of 1977. The bill would initially require one-third worker representation on a policy board of all large companies.

The opposition to the Bullock Report, mainly on the part of management, but also by other non-union groups, has been strong and its future is quite uncertain. The same applies to the French and other pending European proposals. But a new tide is clearly sweeping the modern welfare state. As one expert, Garson, concluded:

□ It is a mark of changing times that in the European context the moderate position on worker participation usually envisions at one-third worker representation on the boards of directors, directly combined with concessions increasing work councils power and worker-participation in capital. Only a few years ago this would have been regarded as the most that might be expected in European labor relations; today it seems the least.[26]

Finally, there is the question of worker participation in stock ownership, spearheaded in Denmark. Here the government introduced a bill to that effect in 1973. The Austrian Trade Union Federation has been pushing for some time in that direction. However, the best-known proposal along these lines has been the widely debated Meidner Plan in Sweden.

Worker Participation in Stock Ownership: The Meidner Plan This was named after its formulator, trade-union economist Rudolph Meidner, who came to Sweden as a refugee from Nazi Germany in the 1930s. Under this plan companies beyond a certain size would transfer a certain percentage of their profits each year, 20 percent being the figure currently considered, into a special issue of company stock that would be put into a collective employee fund and controlled by the labor unions. Note that the companies would not be giving their profits away, but would be paying out a portion of their profits in stock rather than salaries. As this continues year after year, the union's fund would eventually own a controlling portion of the company's stock, and elect their representatives to the board of directors accordingly.

According to Rudolph Meidner, the plan is an attempt to democratize Swedish industry, and one of its methods is to work toward a greater equalization of the worker's wage structure. Without the passage of the plan, as things currently stand, if the best-paid workers are asked to hold back on wage demands so that the poorer paid workers, such as women, restaurant and shop employees, could catch up with them, they would say, "Why should we place limits on ourselves? That would just leave more money for the stockholders." The Meidner Plan promotes worker solidarity by having the profits paid to the union fund, so that all workers can then share in those gains. Other goals of the plan are to alter the structure of wealth which labor feels is too narrowly concentrated at the top (even in Sweden), and to diffuse influence and power more equally throughout society.

As of now the Meidner Plan, or some version of it, is still not law, but it has been one of the hottest topics in Swedish politics for some time. The effect of the plan would be to eventually transfer the ownership of the bulk of Swedish industry to the labor unions acting as representatives for the workers. Yet, full industrial democracy does require that the employees of each factory have a direct voice in the management of their affairs. There is little talk of self-management in the Meidner proposal. Yet, an eventual transition to self-management may be very much facilitated by such a proposed transformation of ownership.

Management's Attitude Toward
Its Own Demise

Not surprisingly, management has often resisted the development of worker participation in decision-making and worker self-management. The obvious reason is that management sees its function and role threatened when workers begin taking on tasks that management assumed belonged to itself. If and when worker participation proceeds to the ultimate stage of complete self-management, then management will no longer exist as a separate entity from labor. An interesting case in point of this defensiveness on the part of management is what happened in the United States with the General Foods Corporation.

In the early 1970s, General Foods opened a dog food plant in Topeka, Kansas, that was to be run with a minimum of management supervision. Workers would make job assignments, schedule coffee breaks, interview prospective employees, and decide pay raises. The system at Topeka eliminates layers of management and supervisory personnel, and assigns areas of responsibility to self-managing teams of seven to fourteen employees. These teams work under the direction of a team leader described as "coach" rather than foreman, and team members rotate between dreary and meaningful jobs. Pay is geared to the number of tasks each team member masters. The company even removed some of the status symbols of management that they know workers resent. For instance, all employees use a common entrance, and there are no reserved parking places for management. According to *Business Week* the plant was widely heralded as a "model for the future," and General Foods claims that it still is.[27] The manager of organizational development at General Foods described it as "very successful." In fact, General Foods has applied a similar system at a second dog food plant in Topeka and a coffee plant in New Jersey; and it also has plans for similar operations in two plants in Mexico, and among white-collar workers at its White Plains, New York, headquarters.

Unit costs at the plant are 5 percent less than under a traditional factory system, according to company estimates. This would amount to a saving of about $1 million a year. Turnover is a low 8 percent. In the *Business Week* article, one of the plant workers is quoted as saying, "It's the best place I ever worked."

Despite the obvious accomplishments of the new system it is reported that this new development at General Foods is running into trouble. The reason is essentially resistance and negativism on the part of management. This difficulty has been so significant that there are predictions that the plant at Topeka will eventually switch back to a traditional factory system. Some functions that were originally assigned to workers have already been reassigned to managers, such as final decisions about pay raises. Richard Walton, professor of business administration at Harvard, who helped design this system, says, "Never has the climate truly soured or even become neutral and indifferent," which were attitudinal changes that had been reported. But he adds, "In my opinion this will happen unless concerted effort is made to evolve the organization."

Did worker management fail at General Foods? It's quite clear that it did not. *Business Week* puts the matter explicitly:

☐ The problem has been not so much that the workers could not manage their own affairs as that some management and staff personnel saw their own positions threatened because the workers performed almost too well. One former employee says the system—built around a team concept—came squarely up against the company's bureaucracy. Lawyers, fearing rejection from the National Labor Relations Board, opposed the idea of allowing team members to vote on pay raises. Personnel managers objected because team members made hiring decisions. Engineers resented workers doing engineering work.

Of course, having workers take on such duties was the whole idea [in the first place].[28]

Does the General Foods example mean that management will fight all evolution toward worker self-management, regardless of whether it is shown to be economically advantageous? We believe the answer is no. As we have seen in the example of the president of Volvo, in Theory Y, and even at General Foods, management as it matures and grows naturally comes to recognize the value of letting its own functions and role become absorbed by all the members of the organization.

"De-Managing America" A striking example of this happening is that of Richard Cornuelle. In his book entitled, *De-Managing America*, he begins with the following confession: "Five years ago I was a card-carrying member of the establishment. I was an executive vice-president of the National Association of Manufacturers. I lived at the University Club. I had a secretary I called my 'girl.' I had my shoes shined every day and counted my change. I voted for Goldwater in 1964 and Nixon in 1968. In 1969 I left. I quit my overpaid job, moved out of my oversized office, and began, hesitantly, to live another kind of life."[29] Cornuelle goes on to describe the kind of changes he observed in his new life. "Good things are happening every day in American society, and, with luck, great things will happen. But the authoritarian methods of the front office aren't working . . . I feel a powerful force pushing us inexorably toward a good society—the steady urgent pressure of men and women straining to be human, to discover and express all the things they can be. And although I can't prove it, I believe the things straining for fuller expression are good things—warmth, understanding, lovingkindness, creativity, laughter."[30]

Cornuelle does conclude from his experience that there will still be a need for business executives, and thus he does not advocate complete self-management. But his vision of what constitutes a healthy business is quite different from the usual conceptions held by management:

☐ If this tendency to de-manage continues, the distasteful trappings of authority—the executive men's room, pretentious titles and the rest—will in time disappear. Some people, according to ability and inclination, will have more responsibility than others. But everyone will have essentially the same *kind* of responsibility. A new kind of elemental equality will prevail. A company will become an association of equal specialists. Some will specialize in steering the company. Others will specialize in translating these decisions into quantified guidelines for the rest. But no one will boss anybody else. Authority, in the sense we now know it, will disappear.[31]

The Union's Attitudes Towards Its Own Demise We have mentioned in the past few pages instances where unions have resisted the development of worker participation in management. At first glance this is quite surprising. Don't unions exist to represent and promote the interests of the workers? The answer is *yes, but*. The surprise begins to diminish when we recognize that unions are an institution and operate the way most institutions operate. They have a leadership hierarchy with various degrees of power, privilege, and monetary reward distributed throughout. This hierarchical structure is possessive of its power and rewards, and reacts defensively when it appears to be threatened. In the development of plant democracy, as with work councils, the ordinary functions and powers of the union hierarchy are bypassed by the direct involvement of the workers in decision-making. This by-passing is threatening to the unions and therefore they don't readily support such developments.

This kind of union reaction is most pronounced in the countries where the union movement is largely local and shop-oriented, but weak nationally. These unions are more directly challenged by local work councils, which can be seen as an alternative to the locally organized union. This is particularly the case in the United States and Canada, and not so in Scandinavia, where the unions have a strong national organization that works hand-in-hand with a labor party. Thus we find considerable opposition in U.S. unions to the development of worker participation in management, whereas this has been tolerated and in some cases enthusiastically promoted by the unions in Europe. Characteristic in the United States is the statement of Leonard Woodcock, former president of the United Auto Workers (UAW), who referred to the report *Work in America* as "an elitist document . . . Anyone who does work—even if it is dull and monotonous—is doing useful work. There is a matter of pride in this."[32] Jack Barbash, an economist writing in the AFL-CIO *American Federationist* says, "We are confronted with two roads to work satisfaction—the road advocated by the humanization proponents and the trade union road."[33]

Another way to look at the ironic opposition of United States unions to plans for worker self-management is to recall that unions had their origins and growth in the effort to oppose the overwhelming power and control of employers. The attempt to organize in the face of this power was often met with violent repression. From this background unions define themselves in an adversary relationship to management, and to take on managerial functions is to identify with the enemy. A modern, and milder, expression of this view is that expressed by the current UAW president, Douglas Fraser, "(Our) approach stems from the traditional American worker's view, the company's right to manage, the union's right to criticize."[34] This is to say that unions exist, at least in their present form, because management exists. Take away management, as a separate business function, and you eliminate the need for unions.

A further irony is that union-leadership opposition to industrial democracy is strongest in the United States union movement, which is strongly anti-communist, and in the unions in Southern Europe that are most communist-oriented. Once again it is shown that the opposites meet. Both the United States labor movement and the European communist unions, for totally opposite reasons, define themselves by their antagonism to management, and thus depend on management's existence in order to exist themselves.

It is those countries where the adversary union attitude prevails that have suffered the most labor strife. In contrast, the countries that have opted for the cooperative approach have experienced rapid economic growth based on industrial peace.

This is where a humanistic perspective allows us to get a clearer view of what is involved. Although most unions originally developed in order to promote the humanistic goal of equality and to fight economic exploitation, the rigid commitment to an adversary role on the part of some unions has overridden their higher values. Now these unions have fallen into the typical Economic Man attitudes of materialism, separateness and competition. No doubt the relative lack of adequate welfare-state security provisions in the Northern U.S. plays a role in explaining this overemphasis on bread-and-butter issues.

The results of this antagonism have in many cases been economically and socially detrimental. In contrast to this are trade unions abroad that look forward to taking on management functions, and have a steady sight of the goal of ever-increasing industrial democracy.

The economic drawbacks of competitive unions are evident in several ways. While Japanese labor representatives serve with management on joint productivity councils, United States labor leaders believe that productivity is management's problem alone. They tend to see any emphasis on productivity as a company's way to get more work done without a corresponding increase in pay. While this suspicion may often be justified, it is not always so. To protect themselves, many unions have adopted a set of work rules, which very carefully specify work practices, such as insisting that highly paid technicians have to be present when certain machinery is run, even if their only real function is to flip a switch on and off. The accumulation of these work rules in various industries means that low levels of productivity have been built into the industrial structure.

Putting obstacles in the way of productivity does not seem to be the path towards a more humanistic economy. When labor attempts to get its just rewards through this channel it is demeaning both itself and the work, and it will fail to promote real human development and self-actualization, to say nothing of economic development and advancement. The answer lies, not in fighting management through stalling tactics, work rules, featherbedding, and the like, but in putting the principles of the higher values into practice. This means that workers recognize their own creativity, dignity, and worth, and take a management role in industry as fully as possible.

If it is true that we have to choose between humanization of work **or** trade unionism, we believe that the well-being of the workers would be clearly more directly enhanced by the former, assuming the economy has reached a certain level of affluence. But why do we have to choose? In the past trade unions have been responsive to workers' needs. As these needs change, so will the trade union goals. We do not believe that American labor unions will forever opt for the lowest road, or the negative approach, in trying to improve the lot of the workers. The European developments of today may foreshadow the American developments of tomorrow.

CONCLUSION

In this chapter we attempted to demonstrate that in Europe there is something beyond the welfare state. This something is generally lacking in the United States, where workers have been more concerned with bread-and-butter issues on the job. The push towards a humanized economy would indeed be surprising in an environment characterized by economic insecurity rather than security. The most recent developments in Europe, echoed by numerous news reports, give further support to this notion. Workers are suddenly more interested in the material needs of wages and job-security provisions than job quality and codetermination. Do these recent developments contradict our evolutionary thesis? No they don't. Quite the contrary.

The European economy, for the first time in decades, is caught in the whirlpool of world economic recession. Export demand for industrial products is way down and the traditionally successful attempts to keep the economies going by stimulated domestic demand can't work forever. You can build a bridge over a river, but what if the river turns out to be the ocean? Export demand from the U.S. and the Third World has been at unusually low levels. With the import slump, unemployment rates, particularly for young workers, have risen. Job security, once a "fact" for most employees is suddenly less solid. And the worker is responding as expected.

Time will tell whether the present impasse is only temporary or permanent. The issue is much more than the quality of work abroad; it has to do with the very question of a humanized industrial economy. Can the competitive pressures of world economic trade and commerce check the force of social evolution made possible by political democracy?

References

1. Mire, J. "Improving Working Life, the Role of European Unions." In *Monthly Labor Review*, September 1974, pp. 3–4.

2. Mire, J. "Improving Working Life, the Role of European Unions." In *Monthly Labor Review*, September 1974, p. 7.

3. Mire, J. "Improving Working Life, the Role of European Unions." In *Monthly Labor Review*, September 1974, p. 7.

4. Mire, J. "Improving Working Life, the Role of European Unions." In *Monthly Labor Review*, September 1974, p. 9.

5. Mire, J. "Improving Working Life, the Role of European Unions." In *Monthly Labor Review*, September 1974, p. 5.

6. Gyllenhammar, Pehr G. "Suiting the Job to the Person: The Volvo Experience." In *The Business System* edited by Friedman, et al. Hanover, New Hampshire: New England University Press, 1977, p. 35.

7. Jones, H.G. *Planning and Productivity in Sweden*. Totowa, New Jersey: Rowman and Littlefield, 1976, pp. 97–149.

8. Quoted in Dore, Ronald. *British Factory–Japanese Factory*. Berkeley and Los Angeles: University of California Press, 1973, p. 52.

9. Maslow, Abraham. "Eupsychia—The Good Society." In *Journal of Humanistic Psychology*. 2, 1961, p. 2.

10. Goble, Frank. *Excellence in Leadership*. American Management Association, 1972, p. 22.

11. Blumberg, P. "Industrial Democracy, the Sociology of Participation." In *Self-Management* edited by J. Vanek. New York: Penguin Books, 1975, p. 324.

12. O'Toole, James, ed. *Work in America*. Boston: MIT Press, 1973, pp. 107–108, 554–57.
    Glover, John D. and Hower, Ralph M. *The Administrator: Cases on Human Relations in Business*. Homewood, Ill.: Irwin, 1957, pp. 555–57.

13. *The Washington Monthly*. February 1974, p. 26.

14. McGregor, D. *The Human Side of Enterprise*. New York: McGraw-Hill, 1960.

15. Drucker, Peter F. *Management: Tasks, Responsibilities, Practices*. New York: Harper and Row, 1974, p. 265.

16. Maslow, Abraham. *Eupsychian Management*. Cambridge (Mass.): Irvin, 1965, p. 70.

17. Maslow, Abraham. *Eupsychian Management*. Cambridge (Mass.): Irvin, 1965, pp. 70–71.

18. Maslow, Abraham. *Eupsychian Management*. Cambridge (Mass.): Irvin, 1965, p. 22.

19. Maccoby, Michael. *The Gamesman, the New Corporate Leader*. New York: Simon and Schuster, 1977, p. 215.

20. Maslow, Abraham. *Eupsychian Management*. Cambridge (Mass.): Irvin, 1965, p. 40.

21. Maccoby, Michael. *The Gamesman, The New Corporate Leader*. New York: Simon and Schuster, 1977, p. 215.

22. Maslow, Abraham. *Eupsychian Management*. Cambridge (Mass.): Irvin, 1965, p. 148.

23. Blumberg, P. "Industrial Democracy, the Sociology of Participation." In *Self-Management* edited by J. Vanek. New York: Penguin Books, 1975, p. 324.

24. Jones, Aubrey. *Economics and Equality*. Oxford: Phillip Allan, 1976, p. 112.

25. Quoted in *Challenge*. March-April 1976, p. 56. From July 1975 *New York Times* editorial.

26. Garson, G. D. "Recent Developments in Workers' Participation in Europe." In *Self-Management*, edited by J. Vanek. New York: Penguin Books, 1975, p. 148.

27. *Business Week*. March 28, 1977, pp. 78–82.

28. *Business Week*. March 28, 1977, pp. 78–82.

29. Cornuelle, Richard. *De-Managing America*. New York: Vintage Books, 1976, p. 3.

30. Cornuelle, Richard. *De-Managing America*. New York: Vintage Books 1976, pp. 5–6.

31. Cornuelle, Richard. *De-Managing America*. New York: Vintage Books, 1976, p. 104.

32. Barbash, Jack. "Humanizing Work: A New Ideology." In *AFL-CIO American Federationist*, August 1977, p. 12.

33. Barbash, Jack. "Humanizing Work: A New Ideology." In *AFL-CIO American Federationist*, August 1977, p. 14.

34. *Christian Science Monitor*. May 18, 1977, p. 16.

Chapter Thirteen

TOWARD A EUPSYCHIAN ECONOMY: WORKER SELF-MANAGEMENT

INTRODUCTION

The term *eupsychian* was coined by Abraham Maslow to describe an organization or a society that is oriented toward meeting the higher human needs, specifically social needs and self-actualization. What Maslow had in mind was the word *utopian*, but he wanted to avoid the connotation of impracticality that had grown up around that word. For Maslow believed the evidence showed that not only was a social system directed towards these needs practical, but also in the final analysis the only fulfilling system was one that took these needs into account.

The most outstanding mark of the Eupsychian economy is the movement towards self-management in the workplace, or genuine industrial democracy. It is quite remarkable that the most progressive developments in both the labor movement and management, in capitalism as well as socialism, all point to this same goal—worker self-management. When the same conclusion is reached by people in such diverse and often antagonistic socio-economic positions, it can be recognized that here is a very powerful and compelling idea.

The evidence presented in the last chapter clearly suggests that increasing worker participation in economic decision-making has worked very well. Furthermore, there has been an observable drift towards the humanistic concept of full industrial democracy. Here we will concentrate on this concept, both in theory and in practice.

That self-management has great appeal in terms of handling the job alienation problem was already discussed in Chapter 8. From the perspective of humanistic psychology there can be no doubt that the level of well-being is maximized by organizing work under democratic principles.

Common sense also suggests that self-managed enterprises will be superior in terms of economic efficiency, particularly in relatively labor-intensive industries where labor productivity is of primary importance. Especially in small cooperatives, the extra effort of each member will pay off in a higher profit bonus for the entire team. Compare this to the situation where the extra effort of a wage earner in a typical corporation ends up in the pockets of somebody else. So, within the setting of full industrial democracy, we can expect many proposals from the shop floor leading to a more efficient way of organizing and carrying out production or marketing activities. Under the traditional ways of ownership and management, on the other hand, workers will have more of an incentive to obstruct paths towards greater efficiency by insisting on "work rules," featherbedding, etc. We cannot expect them to exert themselves as fully as their colleagues in a producer's co-op.

The theoretical advantages of worker self-managed cooperatives, or worker co-ops, were recognized back in the classical period of economics by John Stewart Mill.[1] Mill expected that the superiority of worker self-management would win out over conventionally run firms, and that eventually cooperatives would become the dominant institution in the economic landscape.

But here we are, over one hundred years later, and Mill's predictions hardly seem to be fulfilled. As you look around you will find very few self-managed cooperatives, neither in the West nor in the socialist world. This presents us with a very important puzzle. One of the foremost challenges to humanistic economics is to find the solution. The question is why are worker cooperatives (which, according to humanistic theory and several lines of evidence, should be superior economic forms) so few? We believe there is a very good answer to this question, which, when understood and applied, will open the way for the full flowering of the worker-managed enterprise.

A clue suggests itself if we look at the difference between a producer's cooperative and a consumer's cooperative. The first refers to a company that is engaged in manufacturing or production, like a steel mill or a furniture factory. The second refers to buyer's cooperatives such as a food-buying club, or a cooperative supermarket or department store selling at the retail level. Such consumer co-ops have proved viable and enjoyed increasing popularity. In contrast, producer's cooperatives, such as worker-owned factories, have had a rather unsuccessful history. Experiments of that kind have not only been rare but also typically short-lived. As the late philosopher Martin Buber summarized the contrasting developments:

□ The development of the consumer cooperatives follows the straight line of numerical progression; a considerable portion of civilized mankind is organized today, from the consumption side, on cooperative lines. On the other hand the development of the producer cooperative can be represented as a zig-zag line which, on the whole, shows hardly any upward trend.[2]

Why this difference? In understanding that we will have the basis for understanding why producer cooperatives have so far not flourished.

The Basic Dilemma of Self-Management

In the late 1950s, the economist Benjamin Ward constructed a theoretical model of producer cooperatives operating in a competitive market economy.[3] The model demonstrated that a producer cooperative has some unexpected built-in problems. The central one is this: *the natural desire for the members of the cooperative to keep their numbers to a minimum.* The fewer the members, the greater the profit share for each one. Therein lies the key to the puzzle, although not necessarily the solution.

In a *consumer* cooperative the larger the membership, the more business the cooperative does (because the members, the consumers, buy from the cooperative). Furthermore, since profits are usually distributed to each member of the cooperative in direct proportion to his or her buying, increasing membership will not dilute the profit share, but expand it. This is in sharp contrast to the *producer's* cooperative, where the new members tend to dilute the average profit bonus, even if the *total profits* of the cooperative are increased due to the output of new members. The inclination not to dilute membership through expansion means that the cooperative may act in a perverse way in the face of changing market conditions.

Ward showed that the immediate response of a cooperative to rising market prices of its product would be to curtail its output, rather than increase it, as a conventionally owned and managed firm would.[4,4a] This perversity is explained by the worker's assumed propensity to maximize net income per worker, rather than overall profits of the cooperative: for a conventional firm the costs of a new worker are just the salary and nothing more; for the cooperative it is his or her salary *plus* an average profit share. The more profitable a cooperative has become due to the price increase of its product, the more will an additional job applicant cost the firm. So the worker will not be hired unless he or she promises to be fully worth the increased cost. Mathematically it can be shown that typically this will not be the case. Moreover, the higher profits may even induce the worker's managed co-op to curtail employment, or—what amounts to the same thing—not replace some of the workers who have left the cooperative for whatever reason. The entire argument works symmetrically in case of a sudden decrease in profitability brought about by a decrease in the market price. Now the members of the cooperatives that are hit hard and are losing money will want to share these losses with more members, just as highly profitable plants will be most hesitant to share or dilute their profit bonus. Obviously, from a social and economic point of view, such behavior of the firm is harmful. There is no tendency, at least not in the short run, to follow the dictates of the market and the consumer.

An additional problem is that the prospect for a smooth-working labor market is not promising. Ideally, workers in less profitable industries would switch over to more profitable industries, but this does not happen easily in a labor-managed economy. Profitable plants don't want to hire, unprofitable plants don't want to lay off members. Most of the transfer of labor has to rely on the cumbersome process of creating new cooperatives.

Furthermore, when profitable cooperatives reinvest their earnings towards expansion of their facilities, they will tend to favor excessive automation, to minimize the hiring of new members. Likewise, there is the ever-present tendency not to replace existing workers when they retire, quit or die. The end result of such tendencies may be the following extreme situation, as satirically described by Vanek: "A director and a janitor, both millionaires, sitting together on the worker council of a completely automated labor-managed factory."[5] Notice that we could observe such excessive automation in the production process even if labor were abundant in the economy while capital were very scarce. Nothing would prevent such co-ops from operating amidst heavy unemployment and a severe capital shortage.

One final problem is that there is always a general tendency not to reinvest earnings unless the return from such investment is very high. The rationale for this underinvestment force is as follows: Workers could decide to receive the entire profits in form of dividends and then individually deposit the funds in a savings account which pays 5 percent a year and which they can convert into money for buying consumer goods at any time they desire. Alternatively, if the members of the co-op vote to reinvest the profits in the enterprise, employees will only benefit as individuals in the increased future profits as long as they remain members of the co-op. It can be shown that employees who do not expect to be with a particular cooperative for more than five years will prefer the distribution of profits so as to invest the funds in a savings account. It has been mathematically shown that such a rate of return is more attractive for the worker than even a 22 percent annual pay-off of a newly created facility of the factory. Similarly, even if the average employee expects to be with the firm for at least another fifteen years, he or she would prefer that the profit share be paid out in dividends instead of being reinvested by the enterprise for an expected annual rate of return of 8 percent. Once again we are faced with an economic behavior that may conflict with socially desirable rates of investment and industrial expansion. Furthermore, over time, consumer demand will tend to grow at a more rapid rate than increases in productive capacity. As a result, there will be more and more consumer dollars chasing (relatively) fewer and fewer consumer products, a process that can only lead to an increase in prices of goods, that is, inflation.

In summary, it looks as if the self-managed firm will have a built-in tendency to contribute to the social problems of unemployment, inflation and slow growth. Moreover, such a firm would appear to be severely handicapped in competing with traditional firms in an industry. What seemed so attractive, the cooperatively owned and managed firm, now looks quite hopeless as a practical economic entity. But we urge the reader not to despair; as we shall soon see, there is solid reason for belief in the cooperative ideal.

It may be worth noting that a modern corporation does not suffer any of the problems described. Its founding stockholders can keep their ownership rights exclusive by hiring wage labor as well as by "hiring" more capital through the issuance of nonvoting stock, or bonds, or by financing capital accumulation through bank loans. The workers receive a set salary, the capital lenders a fixed return on their borrowed funds. Neither dilutes the profit share claimed by the owners. As a result, the traditionally organized firms will respond efficiently to changes in prices and profitability. It will tend to expand more vigorously and in the process threaten the survival of any competing worker-managed firms. Before too long the cooperative would tend to be cornered by its more expansion-oriented and better-equipped competitors. Yet some producer cooperatives have survived for quite a long time. We immediately think of the best-known example of certain firms in the U.S. plywood industry, which have survived many decades. Does the observed longevity there contradict our pessimistic predictions derived from this theoretical reasoning? We will see that it does not.

The Case of the Cooperative Plywood Companies   There has been a *traditional* way out of the "Ward predicament" of producers' cooperatives: hire workers but do *not* give them ownership rights; instead pay them a wage. From a humanist standpoint this is not an acceptable solution because it again creates a two-tiered level of workers within the firm, the owner-workers and the salaried workers. As Vanek puts it, "we are herewith injecting the poison of alienation into the pure labor agreement of the participatory firm."[6] Nevertheless this has been the solution adopted by cooperative plywood firms which have existed for decades in the American West.

The first of such companies began in 1921 when 125 Scandinavian immigrants near Seattle each put up $1000 for the initial 125 shares, and secured a bank loan for approximately $25,000. Shortly thereafter, the first sheets of plywood came off the production line of the Olympia Veneer Company, as the owner-workers named their company.

The initial investment entitled each owner to a job in the plant and a pro rata share of the profits. Each founder agreed to work initially without additional compensation and "to do any kind of work in or about the plant in a creditable manner. Not to work for his personal interest but for the interest of all concerned."[7] Company by-laws also stipulated total equality in profit shares regardless of skills or tasks performed. New stockholders could only be admitted by a majority vote of a worker-elected managing board. An owner could always drop out by selling his stock back to the company at a fair market value. So we can see that at its outset Olympia Veneer operated with some very idealistic, eupsychian principles. But the problem of second-class workers to which we have just alluded quickly began to emerge.

A year later the company was down to 118 stockholders and 100 nonstockholder employees. The process continued, and by 1952 there were less than fifty working stockholders together with 1000 nonowners. In 1954 the last twenty-three surviving stockholders voted to sell their plant to the United States Plywood Corporation. It is estimated that the twenty-three individuals received over $625,000 each, a handsome return on the original investment of $1000, even counting inflation. Olympia's history came to an end at this point, but its status as a worker-owned producer cooperative began to erode almost from its beginning. Nevertheless, the company was a great financial success.

The economic success of the Olympia idea led to the founding of many other cooperatives of a very similar character. In 1953 it was the Anacortes Veneer, also in the State of Washington, the oldest plywood cooperative still in operation as of this writing. However, recent rumors have circulated that the stockholders, most of them near retirement age, were willing to sell their stock, so it appears that Anacortes will also eventually be absorbed by a larger, conventional corporation. In the 1950s new plywood cooperatives mushroomed in the American Northwest, but most of them were bootstrap operations, beginning with little funds, and taking over existing mills that had proved unprofitable under previous conventional ownership. This, and the fact that more suitable timber reserves were now available in the South, where some modern and highly efficient plants have been built by conventional companies, is responsible for the marginal performance of many of these more recently formed cooperatives. According to one report the ever-present lack of economic security for these plants causes them to "exhibit very little cooperative idealism but rather (to) exist to further the welfare of their owners."[8] Today there are still twenty or so plywood cooperatives remaining.

Bellas concludes from the experience of these firms that "Using the forty-year history of the plywood cooperatives as our best example of cooperative production, we must conclude that their organizational form is basically unstable." He goes on to explain that, "The owners, unwilling to dilute ownership, characteristically do not admit workers from an acquired firm to ownership. The democratic nature of the organization begins to deteriorate and it may eventually resemble a conventional corporation."[9] This, of course, is exactly what the cooperative self-management idea was supposed to leave behind—a conventional, hierarchical organization.

We are herewith faced with the uncomfortable basic dilemma of the worker-managed cooperative firm. It may remain pure by granting full membership rights to every employee in the factory; as a result the firm may suffer the problems of stagnating membership and employment and underinvestment—in short it will be relatively inefficient compared with traditionally operated enterprises. Alternatively, it will seek economic survival by imitating Olympia Veneer with the drawback of slowly regressing into a traditional firm again. The cruel choice seems to boil down to genuine industrial democracy *or* economic survival and growth, but *not* both.

The Resurrection of the Cooperative
Ideal: Vanek's Humanistic Solution

Jaroslav Vanek, an economist teaching at Cornell University, has been one of the most knowledgeable students of self-management. Recently, he claims to have solved the puzzle and shown the way out of the self-management dilemma. He exuberantly refers to his discovery in the following way: "The development of this analysis was to me personally most gratifying. It had always puzzled me how it could have been possible that a productive organization based on cooperation, harmony of interests and brotherhood of men, so appealing and desirable on moral and philosophical grounds, could have done so poorly when subjected to a practical test. It seems to me that we now have both an explanation and a way of remedy."[10]

Vanek's solution, derived from mathematics, is surprisingly consistent with humanistic philosophy. The villain lurking in the background of the industrial democracy issue is the old foe of the humanistic *being* mode; it is *having*, the desire to own the plant in addition to managing it. Vanek points out that ownership is the problem, not self-management.

The essential solution proposed by Vanek is that no one should own the firm. Instead, the members of the company (or its board of managers) should run it as a trust, or on lease given to them by society. This means that the self-managed firm should be *externally* financed, just as conventional firms are, rather than *internally* financed as cooperative firms have usually been. This is quite a surprising twist. But it is fitting that such a knotty dilemma would have its solution in the unexpected.

This recognition is very much in accord with the basic humanistic value of sharing through participation, that is, through work, rather than through having or owning productive property. What is needed for the producer cooperative to survive are appropriate institutional and socio-economic supports, what in effect is "a new environment for the firm." Vanek explains this with a biological metaphor: "The new firms (cooperatives), akin to the biological evolution of species, need their own environment, as mammals need air—and not water—to live in. If the production cooperative and other democratic forms did not flourish in the past, it was because they were, unwittingly, forcing mammal babies into water in which they were bound to drown."[11] We may mention that a few mammals, whales and dolphins, made it in the water, just as a few enterprises have made it in an ownership-oriented environment. But these have been the exceptions. To switch metaphors, let us say that one sparrow doesn't make a spring. And springtime is what we want.

How Vanek's Solution Works   In the West cooperatives have typically been internally- (or self-)financed and group-owned, that is they have been started and run through the finances of the participants (i.e., the workers), which also has meant putting back into the firm a portion of the company's earnings. (Of course, ploughing back funds into the firm is something that happens in all enterprises.) This is in contrast to the standard method of external financing where the company either procures a loan or issues bonds.

One reason that cooperatives have not been able to take this route is that private banks are more hesitant to make a loan to unorthodox economic ventures such as cooperatives. A second, and perhaps more germane, reason is that people who have begun cooperatives have preferred to stay autonomous in their financing, since this independence is a raison d'etre of a co-op. Vanek believes that this (forced) reliance on self-financing goes to the core of the problem. It is the economic consequences of group ownership and internal financing that are at the very heart of the self-inflicted wounds of worker-owned producer cooperatives.

Here are the specific terms of Vanek's proposal: Worker self-managed firms should be financed from the outside and not through the conventional means of ploughing back its own profits. To enable this, Vanek proposes a lending agency that would make the funds available through longterm loans to the co-op. The firm only pays a fixed annual interest charge on the funds. As the loan becomes due, it will be automatically paid off by taking out another loan. In essence then, the cooperative is financed through perpetually renewable longterm loans carrying a fixed interest rate. This is equivalent to a "lease agreement" for which rent has to be paid to the true owner, in Vanek's proposal, the society. Workers only *manage* the leased equipment; they can certainly share the profits of their enterprise, but are not allowed to employ non-members in the firm. Furthermore, workers entrusted with these social assets are under the obligation to maintain the value of the equipment by setting aside funds to meet the cost of depreciation. Of course, the cooperative can sell neither equipment nor the entire plant, since it never owned them in the first place. If the cooperative wants to cease operations it can do so at any time, but society will simply replace the original people with another team willing to make a go of it. Such is the essence of what Vanek calls *social ownership*.

Vanek then demonstrates mathematically that with external financing, all the evils of underemployment, excessive automation and underinvestment disappear. The cooperative will have all the incentives to behave just as dynamically as the conventional corporation. And of course, due to the greater motivation and productivity of its labor force, it would in due course be expected to drive the less productive traditional firms towards a minor role in the economy. Some would predict their extinction.

There are basically two methods by which exclusive reliance on external funds can be accomplished. First, as already mentioned, the government could set up a lending institution to provide the necessary financing. Vanek refers to this as the NLMA, the National Labor Management Agency, by necessity the heart of the entire externally financed, cooperative sector of the economy. What happens if the prevailing socio-economic institutions and political philosophy are unaccommodating, even hostile to the idea, and do not want to establish a NLMA? This brings us to the alternative scheme.

The external financing of the firm can also occur through loans made by the co-op members. Each worker, when hired, brings along a basic sum of investment capital, let us say $5000, which is loaned to the firm, and credited to the worker in a reserve account under his or her name. In a sense, new workers (who are also "capitalists") subsidize their entrance into the company, and thereby meet Ward's dilemma.

As long as that person works with the firm he or she is entitled to a fixed return on that money, let us say 6 percent. When the member leaves the firm, he or she gets the $5000 back and the firm has repaid the debt. Thus, capital has been raised but no collective ownership is involved.

Who manages the firm's capital fund, and what happens to the profits that the fund accumulates? The workers manage the fund, and they themselves decide what to do with the profits. They can vote to pay them out in handsome dividends, or they can vote to use the profits for reinvestment in the enterprise. If they make the latter decision, then the reinvested funds are credited to the reserve account of each of the members; in accordance with the formula for individual apportionment. The individual co-op member now not only gets the 6 percent return on his initial investment of $5000, but on the subsequent investments as well. Upon retirement, or when leaving the firm, he or she is entitled to receive back all the money loaned.*

The upshot of Vanek's solution is that all the cooperative's capital is held on a fully loaned basis with the concomitant obligation to pay a fair market price (interest) for its use. And, as Vanek has shown, external financing is all that is needed to escape the brutal dilemma of producer cooperatives. It is now possible even in the absence of a government-created lending institution. It is for this reason that this individual loan approach seems relevant to a transformation of modern industrial society in the West.

At this stage the reader may not be sure that there is a real difference between the past situations, as in the plywood companies where workers put up their own funds to start a co-op, and the present proposal where workers make individualized loans to the firm. We described the former method as internal financing, and the present method as external financing. But isn't this just a word play? The answer is no. The beauty of this is that while the distinction between the two appears to be slight, the significance is actually great, and has far-reaching implications with respect to economic results. Without getting involved in the highly technical nature of Vanek's explanation, let us look at the following argument.

The effect of a new member's being hired is no longer solely the dilution of the profits. It is also an additional member sharing the cost of finance capital. The more members in the co-op, the less the average capital cost (leasing cost) per member. Under these conditions, even highly profitable firms will hardly think twice about replacing retiring members or adding new ones.

The self-mutilating underinvestment behavior will no longer exist. Let us take the NLMA lease variant first. Now workers, even shortly before retirement, would want to install a new machine or build another wing to the plant. They have nothing to lose as long as the return from the reinvested funds per year exceeds the 6 percent interest paid on the external finance capital. As a result even a 6.1 percent yield would be sufficiently attractive to them. Any investment oppor-

---

*What happens to losses, the reader may wonder. Again, it's up to the workers. Either they decide to take a salary cut, or else they vote collectively to reduce the level of their reserve accounts.

tunity will be undertaken as long as it pays more than its socially necessary costs. In the process of new investment and expansion, more and more co-op members will be sought.*

With respect to the individualized worker credit scheme, the same holds true. Old workers will now always vote to reinvest as long as the project returns more to them than they could get by putting the money into a savings account. As long as the worker is assured of getting his or her money back when leaving the enterprise, there is nothing to lose. The necessary extra high return on investment, resulting under worker *ownership* is no longer needed under worker *management* to induce expansion. The producer cooperative has been rendered just as dynamic and future-oriented as its capitalist cousin, the corporation. The secret switch is borrowed money that has to be paid for when used. Collective ownership doesn't work; social ownership does.

Vanek's analysis and solution is consistent with the recognition of the "institutional" economists, Veblen, Berle and Means, and more recently, John Kenneth Galbraith, that ownership and management are effectively separated anyway in the modern large corporation. What Vanek does is just to extend this ownership function. If ownership has little to do with management, and can be sidestepped as a financial body, then it is no longer needed. We have outgrown it. It now stifles rather than promotes efficient production. And, of course, Vanek accepts the humanistic ideal that management should be democratic and participatory, rather than authoritarian and hierarchical as it tended to be in the worker-owned plywood companies and other earlier schemes.

Is there any real-world experience to suggest that the Vanek solution may be more than just wishful thinking based on abstract theoretical reasoning? We believe that there is, and will attempt to show this by examining what has happened in Yugoslavia during the last 25 years. Following that we will look at the interesting case of the cooperatives in Mondragon, Spain.

THE CASE OF YUGOSLAVIA

What makes Yugoslavia unique, and particularly interesting for us, is that it is an attempt to apply the principle of worker self-management on a nationwide scale. Yugoslavia is a country the size of West Germany, with some twenty million people, which has run its economy

---

*As long as we assume constant returns to scale, more machines and more workers will produce as much as their colleagues did before them. Average productivity and profit per worker will not be affected. Vanek demonstrates that the assumption of constant returns to scale is not necessary to obtain the same conclusion.[12]

along self-management lines since 1953. As a matter of fact, it was the introduction of this philosophy and system in the early fifties that brought down the ire of the Soviet Union on Yugoslavia, who accused them of "revisionism," which meant a departure from the Soviet model of centrally managed and directed economic enterprises.

So Yugoslavia presents us with a truly large-scale experiment in self-management from which there is a lot to be learned. It goes beyond the scope of this work to examine the Yugoslavian situation in detail. Instead we will focus on the point that is of most interest to us here, the question of ownership and how it affects the decision-making of the cooperative.

According to the conditions of the Yugoslavian constitution the workers in a company manage the plant in trust for society as a whole. The plant in theory is neither owned by the workers nor by the state. Everyone is supposed to have an equal access to production facilities. The workers in a plant have the right to use the property for personal production, and can decide how to appropriate the income that the plant generates.

How are the firms run? Every two years each enterprise elects a *workers' council* (as distinct from the European *work councils* discussed earlier). The workers' council consists of from 15 to 120 workers depending on the size of the firm. The council meets monthly and decides the basic questions of the business: product lines, hiring and firing, prices, and the distribution of wages and profit among all the members of the firm. The workers' council in turn elects a management board which meets weekly and sees to it that the decisions of the workers' council are implemented. This board consists of five to eleven members, all workers, who are elected annually. The board also hires a day-to-day administrator who is the *director*. A capable director will be sought after by other firms, and thus his or her salary can be quite high, as much as five times the income of the lowest paid member of the plant. In the past there has also been some sphere of influence over plant decisions from the outside, particularly the political community and various other interest groups.

For our purposes it is useful to divide the Yugoslav experience with workers' management into two distant periods. First we will discuss the years 1953 to 1964, that is, up to the year of major reforms, and subsequently the period 1965 to 1975.

The First Decade of Workers' Self-Management

Self-management got off to a splendid start. In fact, Yugoslavia performed by most criteria better than any other economy in the world with the exception of Japan. Its annual growth rates (in constant prices) averaged more than 9 percent annually. The annual compensation to the average worker increased by more than 9 percent a year, while inflation hovered around an average annual rate of 5 percent. True, there was some persistent unemployment, averaging 5 to 6 percent of the labor force, but that is what we expect in any underdeveloped economy that undergoes rapid structural change, with its shifts of excess labor from the agricultural sector to the expanding industrial sector. Few Yugoslavs left the country to seek employment in Northern Europe at that time. In short, Yugoslavia was being watched by the entire world, both East and West. Joel Dirlam and James Plummer, in their recent text on the Yugoslav economy, comment: "the average growth rates achieved during the 1952–1965 period were so phenomenal that it seemed the Yugoslavs had discovered a special key to expansion, a secret that no other nation possessed."[13] One reason the economy expanded so rapidly was a very high investment rate (over 30 percent of GNP). The profits of the cooperatives were heavily taxed and the money channeled into a centrally administered investment bank. Furthermore, the Yugoslav firm had to pay a 6 percent capital charge (the *kamata*) which was assessed on the net worth of the plant and equipment. Again, most of this revenue was reinvested by the centralized investment bank.* A large part of these investment funds was directed towards the poor mountain states of the Southeastern part of the country, i.e., Montenegro, Kosmet and Macedonia. As a result, the backward areas could to some extent catch up with the more industrialized states of the country, namely Croatia and Servia. Not surprisingly, the advanced regions started to exert pressure on the government to reduce these transfers of wealth by moving towards less taxes and greater decentralization of investment decisions. By 1965 their efforts were crowned with success, and much of the remaining pages discussing the Yugoslav experience will evolve around these 1965 "reforms" and their impact on the economy.

The Second Decade of Workers' Self-Management

The years 1965 to 1975 brought about a drastic change in performance, a change for the worse. The rate of growth slowed to 6 percent. Inflation started to raise its ugly head, averaging, according to OECD statistics, more than 16 percent annually. True, wages tended to rise at a pace of 20 percent a year, leaving the employed worker with an annual gain in real purchasing power of 4 percent. But, there were an increasing number of unemployed less immune to the double-digit annual increase in the cost of living. Unemployment tended to average around 8.5 percent of the labor force. To this we have to add the millions of Yugoslavs who, unable to find adequate employment at home, were forced to emigrate to Northern Europe. All in all, nearly

---

*In essence, the Yugoslav enterprise was financed similarly to Vanek's NLMA idea.

one-third of the labor force cannot be employed in the domestic economy. Similarly, the regional gap started to worsen. Today, the poorest regions earn only one-third as much as the richest, which is significantly worse than it was in 1952. Something is seriously wrong in an economic system that operates like this. There is certainly no more "equal access" to the social means of production. From a humanistic standpoint, the Yugoslav economy turned from best to something close to worst.

What had happened? Did the system lose its special key to expansion? Dirlam and Plummer argue that the country never had such a special key, it only seemed that way. According to them, Yugoslavia happened to enjoy the benefits of *extensive* growth prior to 1965, but thereafter it had to switch to *intensive* growth, which is much more difficult and slow. The distinction between extensive and intensive growth plays an important role when experts seek to explain growth trends, particularly in Soviet-type planned economies. Gregory Grossman, one of the leading scholars on Eastern Europe, defines extensive growth in industrial expansion as "fed primarily by a rapid growth in the supply of production factors," the latter concept meaning the supply of physical capital and the size of the labor force. Intensive growth, on the other hand, he defines as growth due to "more efficient ways of utilizing the combined factor."[14] Now it is generally agreed that an economy will be forced to switch to the slower, intensive kind of growth when it has exhausted the pool of available surplus labor. Implicit to the concept of intensive growth is a lack of labor reserves. And so it seems odd, and difficult to justify, that an economy would have to embark on the road of intensive growth while one-third of its labor force cannot find a job. Be that as it may, we feel there is an alternative explanation for the turnaround in the Yugoslav records of performance. The way we see it, Yugoslavia did hold a special key, but lost it in the process of the 1965 economic reforms. This brings us back to the question of ownership and external finance.

Social Property: The Lost Key

As already mentioned, the 1965 reforms aimed at leaving many more investment dollars at the direct disposition of the firms; this goal was accomplished by a major tax reduction. The reforms abolished a 15 percent tax on enterprise income and lowered the basic capital charge (*kamata*), first to 4 percent, thereafter abolishing it altogether. It is for these reasons that Milenkovic concludes that the 1965 reforms constituted "an assault on the entire concept of social ownership."[15] In effect, Yugoslavia, under pressure of the relatively advanced regions, chose to move in the direction of workers de facto *owning* their plant. The factory facilities and the equipment are no longer leased, but belong to the cooperative in the sense that they now have a claim to all the products that those productive assets generate. Only two aspects of the social property structure remain: the employees still cannot sell the plant property either outright or as ownership shares (i.e., stock), nor can any worker be employed without giving him or her membership and equal rights in the cooperative. It is for these two reasons that Yugoslavia has still not chosen to reintroduce the concept of private ownership of its productive assets. Their "collective ownership" is a halfway house between private and social property rights, and as such it may be cursed with the disadvantages of both.

Just like private ownership, collective ownership can have undesirable consequences on the distribution of income. One immediate effect of the reforms has been to make the already rich richer at the expense of the poor. This was certainly true with respect to regional differences. Society had, so to speak, entrusted the workers of the industrially advanced regions with much more and much better capital equipment. With the elimination of the capital charge (kamata) all this equipment was now given to the lucky recipients. In contrast, the same kind of "gift" amounted to considerably less in the backward regions of the Southeast. Even worse, they now have a serious handicap when it comes to competing with the much better equipped Northwest.

Humanistic economists in Yugoslavia have cried out against what is happening. These include Markovich, Tadic, Korac, Vracar and Stojanovich. They see the positive values of the earlier Yugoslavian economy being destroyed by the support of privileged interests. The student unrest of 1968, widely reported in the West, has been rooted in this very issue. The problem has not been resolved, and many experts fear that the political tensions will cause another, perhaps detrimental, eruption of violence once Tito, the very symbol of the country's self-management system, is no longer able to lead the nation.

But the regional problem is not the only one that has been getting hot after the reforms. The 1965 investment reforms have markedly altered the way firms finance new capital equipment, that is, *their* new capital equipment. As intended by the authorities, *internal* reinvestment by plants surged from 26 percent in 1964 to 40 percent in 1966. In addition, the previous main source of finance, government loans, was now replaced by loans of quasi-private banks founded and indirectly owned by the borrowing firms. The changes in financing investment that paralleled the changes in ownership were bound to push and shove the economy into the cruel dilemma of self-management discussed earlier. Now that the bottle of social ownership has been broken, the evil spirits behind the dilemma have been freed and may be haunting the Yugoslav economy. The performance record since 1965 does little to alleviate our fears. In fact, it is frightfully consistent with the worst expectations. This is shown by the expected evils of underemployment, underinvestment, immobility in the labor market, and inflation.

First, with respect to Ward's underemployment tendency, Holesovky writes in his textbook, "After the 1965 reforms, growth of employment immediately fell by two-thirds. The corollary has been twofold: in prosperous firms, wrong factor proportions (relative understaffing of existing equipment); elsewhere, unemployment and continued operation of substandard firms artificially shielded from bankruptcy."[16] The presently observed high levels of unemployment underline the seriousness of the problem.

What about the entry of new firms? Why hasn't that been a solution to the employment problem? The fact is that there have been virtually no new plants springing up in Yugoslavia since 1965. The existing profitable firms have no incentive to spin off new plants and create new capital in which they have no say and which would compete with them. And since the government has given up the right to tax profitable firms and create new firms with the funds, this major source of development has been eliminated.[17]

Coupled with this unemployment is the problem of inflation. Yugoslavia now has a very inflexible labor market. Government statistics indicate a labor turnover among enterprises of roughly 1 percent, a figure about fifty times smaller than in Europe or the United States. As a result, if demand should change in the economy with a corresponding change in the output mix of goods, labor does not flow very readily from the less profitable to the more profitable plants. This causes artificial shortages and unnecessary price increases. Furthermore, since workers can decide how much of the company's profits they want to reinvest and how much to pay themselves in salaries, they find investment relatively unattractive; many workers are already quite old and the return on the investments would only boost profits in the future, when they are even older or after they have left the firm. Instead, they tend to vote themselves high salaries so they can have the money either to put in a savings account or to buy consumer durables, such as real estate. Of the average profit dollar, 70 percent went to supplement workers' wages before 1965. After 1965 that percentage rose slowly but steadily, and reached 80 percent in 1970. We find therefore that the national investment rate since 1965 dropped from 30 percent to the low level of about 20 percent of GNP.* A result of this situation is that too much money gets poured into consumer demand and too little into expanding the output (supply) of consumer goods. In the end the country has to foot the bill with the twin evils of double-digit inflation and de facto double-digit unemployment.

Our thesis that Yugoslavia has tragically lost (or at least mislaid) its key is consistent with the bleak performance we have been observ-

---

*There is no conflict between this fact and the jump in internal investment of 1965 referred to earlier. The rich firms in the prosperous regions initially reinvested more but at the expense of the unprofitable firms' inability to keep investment up.

ing since 1965. But it would be premature to insist on such an explanation. Certainly, the time span since the reform is still too short to argue such a point of view conclusively and many other contrary events have happened simultaneously, above all the world energy crisis of the 1970s. Yet we are in good company when putting a large part of the blame on the 1965 reforms. Pejovich, for example, a reputable expert on the Yugoslav economy, writes in a recent article that the "low mobility of labor, high unemployment rate, and the firm's preference for capital-intensive production techniques have a solid rational explanation and are, at least in part, generated by the structure of the post-reform economic system in Yugoslavia."[18]

The loss of true social organization may very well be the Yugoslav tragedy. But the events do not in any way nullify or limit the substance of humanistic economics; quite the contrary. The answer lies in the complex problem of the *proper transition* to the eupsychian economy. Yugoslavia, a poor economy with a majority of its citizens barely earning a subsistence income, tried a shortcut and may ultimately fail altogether. Time will tell.

MONDRAGON, SPAIN: AN EXAMPLE OF A MODEL COOPERATIVE

The surprises that self-management has in store for us continue. Who would have thought that in Spain under Franco we would have the flowering of one of the best examples of Vanek's solution for self-management?

The explanation behind this anomoly lies in the unusual person of a Catholic priest, Fr. Jose Maria Arizmendi, who found himself going to the small town of Mondragon, in the Basque region of Spain, due to his support of the losing Republican cause in the Spanish Civil War. Shortly after arriving in Mondragon, Fr. Arizmendi set up a technical school, and in 1956 five graduates of the school formed the nucleus of the first industrial cooperative.

As of 1977 the Mondragon area had a group of linked cooperatives, including fifty-eight producer cooperatives that are involved in manufacturing and high technology activities. They are the largest producers of refrigerators in Spain, and among the largest producers of machine tools. All in all, the enterprises employ roughly 14,000 people. Their average age is thirty-five.

The finance structure of the cooperatives works as follows. Everyone who joins a cooperative on a permanent basis must make a minimum capital contribution to the enterprise. This minimum is rather high, about $2400 in 1972. But only 5 percent of this sum is required on initial downpayment. The balance can be paid out of earnings. This total individual investment is a loan, the equity of which is rewarded at a fixed rate of interest set at 6 percent. Workers can vote on reinvesting a portion of profits. In such a case workers will have to individualize this investment by crediting their individual reserve accounts with their proportion of the reinvestment. Allocation of total profits to individual workers is done by some formula based on hours worked and wage rates. The enterprise now owes them more, a process which repeats itself with each profitable year. On the additional funds, workers receive an interest rate ranging up to 13 percent in recent years.

A further feature of the system is that 80 percent of his or her total investment is paid back when the worker leaves the firm. This is done under a fair formula that takes into account changes in the retail price index and the increasing worth of the cooperative. Upon retirement, a worker receives the full balance in addition to a pension provided by the cooperative.

The Mondragon system illustrates Vanek's second approach to external financing. Mondragon operates on borrowed money—borrowed from its own employees. Its success suggests that the uncomfortable dilemma, conquered by Vanek in theory, has also been escaped in Spanish reality.

The Mondragon bank, whose name translates roughly as "savings bank of the people's labor," has played an important role in the development of the Mondragon system. It was established in 1958, and by 1976 had grown to a total of seventy-six branches. Its functions combined those of a savings and an investment bank, because it both mobilizes private savings and is involved in the planning and authorization of new Mondragon investment. The high economic growth rate in Mondragon owes a great deal to the operation of the bank.

It is in the management structure that the cooperatives really shine. First let's look at wage and salary differentials. They are laid down in the constitutions of each cooperative. For example, a professor who teaches in the Mondragon educational institution, or a top person at the co-op bank, cannot receive more than three times as much as the lowest paid workers. With taxes and wage increases this difference in practice generally does not exceed two-and-a-half to one. It hardly needs to be said that this is a lower wage differential than is found in the rest of Spain, or anywhere else. In some Western industrialized countries, comparable firms in private industry typically have a ratio of 10:1 or even 15:1.

The cooperatives are controlled by general assemblies of all their workers, which normally meet once a year to decide basic policy issues and to elect a management board which in turn selects a general manager. Although voting in these assemblies used to be weighed according to wage rates, this has been changed so that it is now one member, one vote. Furthermore, workers are represented (ideally, one for every ten) in a "social council" which advises the management board. One senior executive in Mondragon is quoted as saying, "You can't give orders in the tone of a general around here, and you can't walk around as if you own the place—anyway not if you are hoping for re-election."[19]

A demonstration of the strength of industrial democracy occurred when the evening shift workers demanded a pay raise. They took their case to the general assembly where the managers opposed the demand. Nevertheless, a majority of votes in the assembly awarded the evening shift a pay raise.

This example, however, points out that as impressive as worker democracy is at Mondragon it still has room for improvement. It is recognized there that two sides, workers and management, still continue to exist, albeit in greatly reduced form from conventional enterprise. This division continues to be demonstrated in several ways, such as a one-day strike that occurred against management in 1971. The fact that there was a management to strike against shows that self-management is not complete at Mondragon. But this should not be surprising in the face of the huge obstacles that the people of Mondragon had to overcome to build what is a democratic oasis in Spain. As a recent annual report of Mondragon put it: "Civilization is a matter not of giving machines, but of giving people a chance to improve themselves."[20]

Universal Capitalism: The Kelso and Speiser Plans

The urge to expand the sphere of participation of workers in industry and in the economy, and the inherent appeal of this democratic ideal, has also found expression in the concept of *universal capitalism*. This refers to the plan originally put forth by Louis Kelso, and later modified by Stuart Speiser: "How to Turn Eighty Million Workers into Capitalists on Borrowed Money."[21] Universal capitalism means the widespread expansion of the number of people who own stock in American corporations.

The basic idea of Kelso is known as the Employee Stock Ownership Plan (ESOP). It works as follows. A company finances its expansion through an issue of stock that is put into a pension-trust owned by the employees. The employees get the money to buy the stock by a loan that is guaranteed by the government. They repay the loan over the course of time by the dividends that the stock earns. The attractiveness of the idea is that the company is able to raise money (with an assist from tax breaks for setting up an employee trust); the workers gain stock without having to pay for it, and when the loan is paid off the employees, in proportion to their salaries, receive their stock from the trust, thus becoming capitalists (i.e., stockowners.)

Speiser's modification of Kelso's plan is an attempt to make even more progress towards universal capitalism. In his plan every family receives $100,000 of common stocks over a period of twenty years through self-liquidating bank loans. The loans are repaid from the stock dividends. Notice that in this plan it is not the workers who receive the stock, but every family. As a part of the plan, corporations would be required to finance their expansion through the issuance of new stock, and not through bonds or other financial instruments. In addition all earnings would have to be paid out to stockholders as dividends. The corporate income tax would also be gradually abolished.

The analysis we have presented based on Vanek's work, which differentiates between worker self-management and worker ownership (and the desirability of the former and not the latter), points out the fundamental weakness of ESOP and similar plans. While at first glance they are consistent with the humanistic ideal of broad-based economic participation, they go exactly in the wrong direction— towards ownership and not self-management. For ESOP does not touch the management structure of a company, and was never meant to. So all the forces of alienation are still present and not addressed by issuing stock that employees will eventually own. This can be seen in several ways. For one thing, the stock held in trust is non-voting, as of now; that is, the employee stockholder cannot vote the stock until he or she has already retired and left the company. Furthermore, even if the employee could vote the stock, it is a long way from owning shares of stock and affecting the direction and actual operation of a company. Even under ordinary, non-universal capitalism it is usually a relatively small group of stockholders that has any kind of controlling influence on a company.

The ESOP and the Speiser plan stem from some of the same sentiments that underlie this chapter but do nothing to correct the root of the problems of the conventional industrial system: the management and union hierarchy, and the absence of democratic self-management. From an Economic Man perspective, Kelso may be proposing an attractive goal, but humanistic economics had better look in a different direction. In terms of a transition perspective, the Swedish Meidner plan, despite its shortcomings, appears to be a superior rival. In Meidner, more and more corporate stock would be held by the Swedish trade unions in trust for the employees. Conceivably, a democratic trade union confederation could evolve to take on the role of a NLMA.

THE TRANSITION TO INDUSTRIAL DEMOCRACY

For a Western-style market economy to evolve in a self-management direction the country has to be ready for it, both on an economic and a political level. On the economic level this means the existence of basic economic security, which also implies a sufficient degree of material wealth. In Chapters 9 and 10 we showed why most countries in Western Europe, particularly in Scandinavia, Germany, Switzerland,

Holland, and possibly Great Britain would seem to meet this criterion. By the same token the United States, Canada, and most Southern European countries are not quite ready.

Despite the overall lack of readiness for a transition to economic democracy in the United States, we can still observe preliminary and tentative moves in that direction. The Northwest plywood cooperatives are an example. In many cases these efforts involve last-ditch attempts by workers to run the bankrupt plants of their former employers. Workers' management often is the only means to maintain jobs in a local labor market. As such, sporadic successes in these ventures may well be worth the many failures. But to support a general argument that worker self-management really can work, such individual case studies may do more harm than good. Opponents are supplied ample ammunition for the argument that producer cooperatives are an unworkable utopia held by some "elitist" ivory-tower idealists. These critics overlook that such cooperatives must run plants that have previously failed the market test of minimal economic viability, and that such businesses are forced to function in a generally hostile environment. Banks will be unwilling to provide sufficient funds at reasonable terms; suppliers will often have a tendency to discriminate against such unconventional operations; trade unions will be most reluctant to give support; and finally the workers themselves will be forced into fighting for survival and economic security by ruthless maximizing behavior, thereby worsening problems arising from the dilemma of the cooperative. Finally, in Congress there is likely to be intensive lobbying by Big Business and Big Labor to prevent this new way of economic organization from succeeding.

Before any significant legislation can be passed favoring a movement in the direction of self-management, which is fundamentally a movement in the direction of democracy, the political process itself must be made sufficiently democratic. This means counteracting the undue influence on government of powerful and concentrated economic interests. As our previous discussion in Part I of this book suggests, one of the critical steps in accomplishing this is the control and regulation of lobbying, as well as limiting or eliminating the private financing of congressional election campaigns.

The Transitional Steps

Let us now assume that the political process is sufficiently democratic to express the evolving needs of the population. There are then several legislative steps that can occur to make the self-management economy possible.

1. The first step is to set up a cooperative bank that would be funded through legislative appropriations and would provide a secure source of finance for both the new cooperative and the possible conversion of existing firms into worker management companies. Such a bank

would operate very much like Vanek's proposed National Labor Management Agency (NLMA) which he has described in detail in *The Labor Managed Market Economy*. In essence the new agency would provide longterm renewable "perpetual" loans to cooperatives, making it possible that such firms operate within the concept of social ownership. At first this social-ownership sector of the economy would be very small, but it would be viable and, more important, it could be expected to be profitable and dynamic. Like John Stewart Mill, we expect that worker-managed firms will out-compete the traditional forms of economic organizations. But we now know more about the necessary institutional preconditions for such a process. The example of the economic success of the cooperatives would most surely provide political support for further extensions of the model, including the conversion of the large corporation.

2. Economic decentralization is needed. In the USA this could be accomplished by a new anti-trust bill. Industrial self-management has very little meaning in a conglomerate economy where headquarters make the important decisions for various plants strewn all about the country. There cannot even be meaningful codetermination if the real decisions are made hundreds of miles away. Each individual plant of large multi-plant firms needs to have the right to decide its own economic policies. This means that industrial democracy necessitates economic *decentralization*. Of course there may in some cases be prohibitive economic costs associated with such divestitures. Therefore, such a new anti-trust bill would call for the dissolution of large multi-plant firms unless the firms could prove that such a move would create significant economic costs to society. A special anti-trust court or tribunal could make the final decision in each case. It may be desirable to have each subsidiary plant make its own decision (as is true in Yugoslavia) whether to stay with the parent company or become independent; they could become independent anytime they saw fit. Of course, we are assuming that such decisions be made in the context of codetermination between representatives of the stockholders and the employees.

It is relevant to note that the Industrial Reorganization Act by the late U.S. Senator Phillip Hart is aiming in this direction. Moreover, there has been accumulating evidence from research by leading economic experts that only a few industries are likely to be economically hurt by a major decentralization effort such as required by the Hart bill. The well-known economist Frederick Scherer, a former director of the Federal Trade Commission, summarizes a recent and representative study on minimum necessary (for efficiency) firm size:

□ In most instances, realizing the principle advantages of multiplant size did not necessitate high concentration at the nationwide level. Only in the refrigerator, brewing, and (less certainly) cigarette industries did scale economies compel anything approaching moderately tight oligopoly.[22]

Alternatively, in countries lacking the Anglo-Saxon anti-trust tradition, a move toward decentralization could be induced by appropriate fiscal measures. A strongly progressive corporate income tax would seem like a relatively simple and promising candidate. This gives us a tax disincentive to growth.

3. The first step in our blueprint for transformation dealt primarily with the creation of new cooperative enterprises. The second step addressed itself to the problem of how existing large corporations could move toward decentralized codetermination, involving workers and stockholders. This third step outlines how the move can be made from codetermination to pure self-management for these existing firms.

The essential feature of this step involves the exchange of bonds for stocks. The stock would then be held in trust by the National Labor Management Agency, and the former stockholders would now have bonds in their place. The bonds would be worth the current market value of the stock, so that the former owners would not lose any wealth, but they would no longer have voting rights in the corporation. Through this simple move the codetermination of the corporation becomes transferred into self-determination and employee self-management, since there are no more voting stockholders.

This plan of exchanging bonds for stock has been advocated by John Kenneth Galbraith in some of his more recent writings on the transforming of the large corporation. He writes:

☐ The case for private ownership through equity capital disappears whenever the stockholder ceases to have power—when he or she or it becomes a purely passive recipient of income. The management is a self-governing, self-perpetuating bureaucracy. It can make no claim to the traditional immunity associated with property ownership. The logical course is for the state to replace the helpless stockholder as a supervisory and policy-setting body; the forthright way to accomplish this is to have a public holding company take over the common stock. There is, of course, no case for singling out one class of property for sequestration. The appropriate course is to have the common stock valued, perhaps by reference to past stock market values, perhaps by more specific appraisal of assets, and then pay the stockholder off with fixed interest-bearing securities. Whether these should be guaranteed by the state is an interesting question. It is possible that they should be. It should be noted that no public expenditure is here involved, only an exchange of assets.[23]

Along with stockholders, the board of directors disappears. In its place, Galbraith put a new board of public auditors.

☐ The purpose of the board of public auditors, in addition to the conventional financial audit, is to maintain continuing surveillance—a continuing social audit—on this divergence. To this end it should have, of course, full access to the information available in the firm—to prices, costs, investment planning, product design, advertising and merchandising methods and plans, political initiatives, much more. On important or continuing matters it would function by committee and could request staff assistance. The board would appoint the top management, ordinarily from the ranks of management. It would ratify the investment plans and reconcile these with public planning requirements.[24]

However, as we see it, Galbraith's scheme leads to state, not social, ownership. In other words, nationalization. The issue of worker self-management is never addressed. Similarly, the giant corporation would remain at its present conglomerate size, well beyond the reach of any employee rank-and-file control. While we respect Galbraith's intentions and creativity, we fear, along with George C. Lodge of the Harvard Business School, that the nationalization approach pushes the problem of capitalism "from one inadequately controlled bureaucracy to another."[25]

It is important for us to reemphasize that our proposals aim at the direct elimination of excessive bureaucracy and hierarchy in economic decision-making. That is what self-management means. Of course, this does not rule out society's levying various profit taxes on the self-managed corporations and restricting them by law to operate within ecological and social guidelines. We saw what happened in Yugoslavia when the agency of government, entrusted with social ownership, surrendered its function of looking out for the overall economic well-being of the country. In our last chapter we will look at another way in which society may exercise this oversight function on the economy.

CONCLUSION

In conclusion, we feel quite optimistic about a peaceful transition towards the humanistic goal of a eupsychian economy. A progressive evolutionary change in the relevant institutions will occur if people are able democratically to implement the necessary legislation which corresponds to higher levels of the hierarchy of human needs. It looks as if many European countries will want to embark on such a path long before the United States and Canada are ready. A prerequisite for any movement towards self-management is a fully developed welfare state, something the New World still has to complete.

So we see that the New World still has something to learn from the Old World (i.e., Europe). What about the Third World, the world of the less developed countries? No doubt it can learn from the New World and Europe. But, it turns out that the Third World has a lot to teach us. We will be looking for these lessons in the next chapter.

References

1. Harris, A. *Economics and Social Reform*. New York: Harper, 1958, Ch. 2, pp. 27–32.

2. Buber, Martin. *Paths in Utopia*. Boston: Beacon Press, 1958, p. 71.

3. Ward, B. "The Firm in Illyria: Market Syndication." In *American Economic Review*, 48, 1958, pp. 566–89.

4. Ward, B. "The Firm in Illyria: Market Syndication." In *American Economic Review*, 48, 1958, pp. 566–89.

4a. Ward, B. *Socialist Economy*. New York: Random House, 1967, Ch. 8.

5. Vanek, J. "Some Fundamental Considerations on Financing and the Form of Ownership under Labor Management." In *Economic Structure and Development*, edited by H. C. Bos. Amsterdam: North Holland, 1973, p. 144.

6. Vanek, J. "Some Fundamental Considerations on Financing and the Form of Ownership under Labor Management." In *Economic Structure and Development*, edited by H. C. Bos. Amsterdam: North Holland, 1973, p. 144.

7. Berman, K. V. *Worker-Owned Plywood Companies: (An Economic Analysis)*. Pullman: Washington State University Press, 1967, p. 86.

8. Berman, K. V. *Worker-Owned Plywood Companies: (An Economic Analysis)*. Pullman: Washington State University Press, 1967, p. 86.

9. Bellas, C. J. *Industrial Democracy and the Worker-Owned Firm (A Study of Twenty-One Plywood Companies in the Pacific Northwest)*. New York: Praeger, 1972, p. 96.

10. Vanek, J. "The Basic Theory of Financing of Participatory Firms." In his edited *Self-Management (Economic Liberation of Man)*. Baltimore: Penguin, 1975, p. 446.

11. Vanek, J. "Some Fundamental Considerations on Financing and the Form of Ownership under Labor Management." In *Economic Structure and Development*, edited by H. C. Bos. Amsterdam: North Holland, 1973, p. 139.

12. Vanek, J. "The Basic Theory of Financing of Participatory Firms." In his edited *Self-Management (Economic Liberation of Man)*. Baltimore: Penguin, 1975, p. 102.

13. Dirlam, J. B., and Plummer, J. L. *An Introduction to the Yugoslav Economy*. Columbus, Ohio: Merrill, 1973, pp. 143–4.

14. Grossman, G. *Economic System*. 2nd ed. Englewood Cliffs, N.J.: Prentice-Hall, 1973, p. 126.

15. Milenkovitch, K. *Plan and Market in Yugoslav Economic Thought*. New Haven: Yale University Press, 1971, p. 254.

16. Holesovsky, V. *Economic Systems (Analysis and Comparison)*. New York: McGraw-Hill, 1977, p. 454.

17. Pejovich, Svetozar. "The Banking System and the Investment Behavior of the Yugoslav Firm." In *Plan and Market Reform (Economic Reform in Eastern Europe)*. edited by M. Bornstein. New Haven: Yale University Press, 1973, p. 301.

18. Pejovich, Svetozar. "The Banking System and the Investment Behavior of the Yugoslav Firm." In *Plan and Market Reform (Economic Reform in Eastern Europe)*. edited by M. Bornstein. New Haven: Yale University Press, 1973, p. 301.

19. Oakeshott, R. "Mondragon: Spain's Oasis of Democracy." In Vanek, J. *Self-Management (Economic Liberation of Man)*. Baltimore: Penguin, 1975, p. 293.

20. Quoted in Work in America Institute, ed. *World of Work Report*, 2, 11, pp. 130–1.

21. Kelso, Louis O. *The Two Factor Economy*. New York: Vintage Books, 1967. Speiser, Stuart A. *A Piece of the Action*. New York: Van Nostrand, 1977.

22. Scherer, F. "Economies of Scale and Industrial Concentration." In *Industrial Concentration: The New Learning*, edited by H. J. Schmid et. al. Boston: Little, Brown. 1974, pp. 53–54.

23. Galbraith, J. K. "Perfecting the Corporation (What Comes After General Motors?)" In *New Republic*, November 2, 1974, p. 16.

24. Galbraith, J. K. "Perfecting the Corporation (What Comes After General Motors?)" In *New Republic*, November 2, 1974, p. 16.

25. *Christian Science Monitor*, April 19, 1977, p. 20.

Chapter Fourteen

WORLD POVERTY AND HUMANISTIC ECONOMIC DEVELOPMENT

INTRODUCTION: THE PROBLEM IN BRIEF

So far we have limited our discussion to the advanced economies in Western Europe, Japan and North America. It is time to apply humanistic economics to other parts of the world, in particular to the vast majority of people in the Third World, which comprises the economies of South America, Central America, Africa and Asia. Most of these countries have been labeled "underdeveloped," in contrast to the "developed" industrial nations. Economically, the distinguishing feature of the Third World is a variety of rather sober statistics. Let us look at some of them.

First, economic output of material goods and services per citizen is very low. In 1970, for example, the World Bank estimated that GNP per capita was as follows: Africa, $180; Asia, $125; Latin America, $560. At the same time GNP per capita in North America amounted to $4660. According to these estimates, we in the advanced industrial nations are ten to forty times as rich as the average inhabitant of the Third World. However, these figures overstate the case. The International Labor Office estimates that a typical basket of consumer goods costing one dollar here and in Western Europe would be obtained for much less in the Third World. The respective costs range from 20 cents in Asia to 36 cents in Latin America. Yet, even making such adjustments, this leaves us three times richer than Latin America, and ten times better off than people in Africa and Asia.[1]

Second, most of these Third World countries still have predominantly rural economies. The urban labor force rarely exceeds 50 percent of the population, and in many cases constitutes not much more than 5 percent. Moreover, most of the economic development that has so far taken place has occurred in metropolitan areas, while the vast rural hinterland often remains relatively undeveloped. What we tend to find are islands of industrialization in a sea of backward farming carried on with the most primitive tools. It is for this reason that so many of the Third World countries are said to have "dual" economies.

Third, the distribution of income and wealth is much more lopsided than in the developed nations of the West. In most developed countries the poorest 20 percent of households typically receive 15 percent of income. For the Third World, according to a recent World Bank study, the respective proportion is usually less than 5 percent. Moreover, in 1970, in half of the underdeveloped economies the poorest 40 percent of the population averaged only 9 percent of total income.[2] Specific and reliable statistics are hard to get, but a recent study of Columbia indicates that the bottom 10 percent of the employed rural labor force received only 1.4 percent of total personal income, while the share of the richest 10 percent exceeded 50 percent of total personal income.[3]

Fourth, there tends to be considerable unemployment. For Africa, urban joblessness has been estimated to be higher than 10 percent. Moreover, in the countryside there is much seasonal unemployment as well as considerable *under*employment, i.e., working very short hours. Rough estimates of the latter range as high as 40 percent of the rural labor force, particularly in Africa and Asia.[4]

The upshot of this is that there is a formidable amount of poverty in most of these nations. The International Labor Office estimated that in 1972 the proportion of seriously poor—defined as having an adjusted per capita income of less than $75—typically ranged between 40 and 70 percent of the population.[5] The World Bank estimates that about 650 million persons have annual incomes per head of less than $50.[6] Not surprisingly, at the 1976 World Food Conference in Rome it was said that an estimated 460 million people, about half of them children, suffer from a severe degree of protein malnutrition.[7] Such is the alarming state of affairs when an already small income pie gets unevenly distributed. Most people have to make do with crumbs.

The conclusion can only be that the most basic human needs tend to go unfulfilled in the Third World. Thus, we can say that there is a shortage of food, clothing and shelter for large segments of the world population, while at the same time there is bristling affluence among the developed economies. Herman Daly summarizes the problem as follows: "Growth in GNP in poor countries means more food, clothing, shelter, basic education, and security, whereas for the rich country it means more electric toothbrushes, yet another brand of cigarettes, more tension and insecurity, and more force-feeding through more advertising."[8] In short, by satisfying our trivial wants we prevent satisfaction of the basic physiological human needs in the Third World.

Such a condition reflects poorly on the state of (humanistically) efficient resource allocation in the world economy.

Let us not forget that the world economy is increasingly the relevant economic unit. Whatever happens in some regions or countries will affect the others. So, for instance, it has been estimated that the oil exporting countries have been accumulating up to $60 billion a year. Cash of this magnitude means power, which increasingly threatens takeovers of even such Western industrial giants as General Motors, US Steel and ITT. Moreover, we can foresee a mounting interdependence on raw materials. The USA is expected to import 70 to 80 percent of all its raw material imports from the Third World by the year 2000.[9]

The increasingly complex and interdependent commercial patterns generate more and more global problems and will require an international solution. We cannot any longer afford to close our eyes and mind only our own business. The emerging world economic system increasingly precludes narrow-minded concern with national self-interest. We will have to live together or die together, and coexistence necessitates international sharing and cooperation.

The Third World economic situation has not been improving much during the last ten years, and, in terms of absolute numbers, it has even worsened. The International Labor Office estimates that in 1972 there were 119 million *more* "seriously poor" than in 1963, among a sample of seventeen Third World countries studied.[10] Similarly, UNESCO estimates that the number of illiterate adults rose from 700 million in 1960 to 760 million in 1970.[11]

Nor does the future look good. According to most recent ILO estimates, if the most basic needs* were to be satisfied for all citizens of the Third World countries within the present generation (i.e., by the year 2000), annual growth rates would have to increase from the present 2 percent to approximately 10 percent as measured by GNP per capita.[12] Most experts, including the World Bank economists, do not foresee any significant speedup in growth. Alternatively, poverty could be significantly reduced—in some cases, even eliminated—if there were substantial internal redistribution of income and wealth, and particularly land. Yet land reform has been extremely slow in the last few decades, particularly in South America. Since landed interests usually have a strong grip over government policies, one has to be pessimistic about any dramatic change in the near future.

If a 2 to 3 percent growth rate is insufficient, and significant redistribution politically improbable, how can these countries be helped? Traditionally, much hope has been placed on development

---

*Consisting of: (1) an adequate diet (approximately 2300 kilocalories per head per day); (2) housing space of at least 5.25m² per person; and (3) universal education (meaning a 98 percent enrollment of children aged 7–16).

assistance from the industrialized countries and agencies such as the World Bank. Total aid in form of investments, loans, and grants has for the last fifteen years been of the magnitude of $10 to $15 billion a year. Yet, as high as this figure may sound, it was just a drop in the bucket. According to statistics of the World Bank, it has not prevented the developed/developing country income gaps from widening.[13] The second Report to the Club of Rome estimates that any significant narrowing of this gap by the year 2025 necessitates total aid of the magnitude of $100 to $200 billion annually, or an accumulated aid package ranging from $2.5 trillion to $10 trillion.[14] The longer we wait, the more it will cost.

All these pessimistic statistics strongly suggest that a business-as-usual attitude will not work. From the perspective of seriously reducing world poverty and maintaining world peace, the conventional thinking and development models are increasingly ill-suited. We need a dramatically different approach, unlike both the traditional Western and Soviet models. Humanistic economics seems the only hopeful alternative if we want to turn the corner by the year 2000.

Before outlining the humanistic solution, let us briefly examine the major shortcomings of the conventional approaches to development.

ALTERNATIVE 1: PRIVATE ENTERPRISE MARKET ECONOMY

Up to 1917, national economic growth and development was seen as possible by relying on frugal and innovative entrepreneurs selling their wares in competitive markets. The driving force was self-interest, the engine of development. The entire Industrial Revolution was won that way in all the mature countries in Europe as well as North America. Frugal and unrestrained entrepreneurship in an environment of laissez-faire has enabled the present generation of the industrialized West to enjoy an unprecedented material abundance. Obviously, this model seems at first glance equally well-suited for the Third World, which in many respects resembles England two hundred years ago. But a little reflection cautions us against imposing our institutional arrangements as a cure-all for the poverty problems of underdeveloped areas.

First of all, our development did not occur overnight, but took several centuries of slow and socially painful growth. In Chapter 2 we briefly indicated the tremendous human costs of the Industrial Revolution resulting from the process of accumulation and material expansion. True, *after* our economies have reached maturity it is possible to bring general welfare to just about everybody, as the experience of Northern Europe suggests. Similarly, the United States and Canada have the resources to afford a modern market economy with a more human face.

Second, we often forget that much of our industrial progress has been fueled by transferring wealth and resources from the undeveloped economies in Asia, Africa, and South America. In the name of free trade we were able to transfer cheap raw materials and food from the colonies to the industrializing nations. It was the rich areas that dictated the terms of development. A colony could sell raw materials, such as copper, and with the revenue it then was made to buy investment goods, such as installing a railroad from the port city to the mine, preparing for more economic penetration of the motherland. The colonies were developed with the interests of the megalopolis, and little else, in mind. As Paul Baran has convincingly argued in his book *The Political Economy of Growth*, the underdeveloped countries have not been helped by our investments.[15] Quite the contrary. To some extent this underdevelopment has been inadvertently encouraged. Typically, the more intensive the economic commercial interaction, the greater the relative backwardness. Comparison of India and Japan bears strong witness to this uncomfortable thought.

These two simple considerations explain why the Third World today shows little fascination with our Western development model. The extent of prevailing poverty dictates that they develop *now*. Moreover, they are not willing to induce the severe human costs that our ancestors so coldbloodedly shouldered. Finally, unlike England two centuries ago, the undeveloped countries often have first to overcome the handicap of so many of their prime resources having been used up generations ago for industrial expansion abroad. Many of them are still burned out, depleted and exhausted, too weak to stand on their own feet. And, there is no Fourth World to turn to for exploitation.

All this is not really news, and academic economists in the development field around the world, as well as in the United States, would probably not contest our pessimistic analysis. Most economists have therefore been advocating some form of economic development aid to the Third World, usually through special agencies such as the World Bank, and an International Development Agency. Yet, the statistics of these very institutions indicate that money does not seem to do the trick, unless it is poured on very heavily. Even then, although there is economic development in and around the capital city of a poor country, life in the vast hinterland stagnates and is characterized by persistently heavy unemployment, underemployment, poverty, and human misery. Many leave their old homes in search of a better life in the city but end up in infamous "shantytowns," or with no shelter at all. Jobs are very hard to get in the city; urban unemployment, crime and corruption are what the uprooted tend to encounter and experience once they have migrated there. Successful industrial development in the cities often destroys the traditional economic and social fabric of the hinterland, which revenges itself by poisoning life in the cities to the extent of making it utterly unmanageable. Schumacher referred to this negative interaction as the "process of mutual poisoning."

What is the mechanism that pits the countryside against the urban areas, the wealthy against the poor, man against man? It is no doubt highly complex and not the purpose of this book to disentangle. Yet from a humanistic perspective we cannot close our eyes to the basic shortcomings of the production-for-profit orientation.

Production for profit is, after all, the distinguishing feature of a competitive free-enterprise economy. Production for profit may serve quite well an already mature industrial system, such as the United States economy, but it may do little to satisfy basic human needs in a poor Third World country. Producing for profit means producing material things using as inputs human labor, just another commodity bought in the labor market. All too often the production of things is enhanced by degrading, fragmenting, and alienating labor; in other words, by imposing tremendous human costs that don't enter the calculus of the marketplace. Additionally, production for profits has an inherent tendency to unbalance and fragment social life and development. As Stanford economist John Gurley[16] put it: the profit motive "builds on the best," meaning that in striving for economic efficiency, it is advantageous to make the already good better and neglect the already weak. Thus, efficiency promotes inequality, rather than vice versa. Moreover, what is economically efficient is often humanistically inefficient. New plants are more profitable in already-existing industrial agglomerations, so they are built in the city rather than in the country. Human labor must migrate to where capital has decided to locate. This is more profitable, since the human costs of labor mobility do not count in the firm's decision to locate a plant. Furthermore, excessive urbanization leads to urban congestion, unemployment, poverty and crime, again human costs that are ipso facto ignored when calculating profitability. The profit motive in education leads to lopsidedness as well; the profit criterion demands concentration of the education dollar on the brightest young men and women. It is the best high school students who go to college. The best college students go to the university. The bright get brighter, the students who need education most get it least. Economic efficiency, in promoting well-trained experts commanding uneducated masses, results in hierarchical and undemocratic decision-making.

Finally, production for profit encourages specialization. Whenever something is done well, efficiency demands even more of it be done to the exclusion of other activities. Regions that can produce sugar cane cheaply will, through the profit incentive, end up producing nothing but sugar cane. Economic development automatically becomes unbalanced and dependent on outside and uncontrollable forces. Economic self-determination is sacrificed in the name of maximum production of goods, just as was the cultural fabric of rural life and human equality. In such situations the profit motive certainly thwarts basic human needs. What is good for security, belongingness and esteem may be bad for profits, and vice versa.

ALTERNATIVE 2: THE SOVIET TYPE MODEL OF DEVELOPMENT

Faced with such negative ramifications of profit-oriented, private (but often foreign-owned) enterprise, it is not surprising that more and more underdeveloped countries have turned to public enterprise and planning. Most Third World nations have drifted in that direction. Yet, as much as they may be relying on some kind of planning, they still orient their production towards the world market. Often such a halfway-house compromise is not by choice but rather by necessity. Traditionally, the economies have been interlocked with the industrial countries. Political independence does not guarantee economic independence. Many, if not most, Third World countries are heavily indebted, thus forcing an evergrowing necessity to export. And things produced for customers abroad don't necessarily feed the hungry at home. Few El Salvadorians drink coffee, because they can't afford to consume what they produce. Moreover, the growing interest burden on debt significantly reduces export earnings. In Mexico, for example, one-third of export revenue is needed for debt servicing!

The only way to deemphasize world markets, in order to focus on their own needs, is to attempt a radical, and politically risky, restructuring of their previous economic organization, usually implying wholesale nationalization and a repudiation of the foreign debt. All too often, though, such newly liberated countries drift into a new dependence, this time within the Soviet empire. What are the promises in choosing this alternative route?

With the Soviet revolution in 1917, and especially after Stalin took a firm grasp on the Russian economy in 1928, the world was presented with a second model for development. This model is rooted to some extent in Marxist economic doctrines as worked out by such theorists as Feldman and Preobrazhensky, but perhaps more importantly in the particular situation prevailing in Russia at that time. Yet all the other socialist countries "liberated" by Stalin after World War II felt obliged to follow the Russian model, and with the exception of Yugoslavia and Albania—both of which subsequently revised their Stalinist methods—industrialization in Eastern Europe faithfully adhered to the growth model for their rapidly increasing industrial growth. The leaders and economists of these countries see no reason the poor countries in the Third World should not follow their example.

The key feature of the Soviet model consists in a preoccupation with rapid growth of the industrial sector, in particular heavy industry, such as steel and machinery. Furthermore, the industrial output mix is planned in detail by a central planning agency. The planners tend to opt for a highly capital-intensive technology, preferably the most modern technology available, and production carried out in plants of maximum size located typically in big cities. The necessary savings are squeezed out of the peasantry through heavy taxes of different kinds, and, in order to get a better grip over the peasant, agriculture was forcefully and often violently collectivized. The production of the farm collective, usually consisting of one to five villages, follows a central plan and the Party sees to it that the quotas are actually met whenever possible.

In general, the basic idea has been a tendency to perceive the economy as a giant army, run from the top down by a chain of commands reaching all the way to the individual manager, worker and peasant. Quite appropriately, the Soviet-type economy has been given the name *command economy*, as we have previously mentioned. The ultimate decision-makers are the top leaders of the Communist Party, who see it as their mission to administer the economy according to Marx's concept of the "revolutionary dictatorship of the proletariat."

What about the humanistic goals of equality and unalienated labor in the Soviet-type economy? Equality is secondary to the basic accumulation process. The salaries and privileges of the top-heavy bureaucracy need to be very high, the standard of living in the farm sector not much above subsistence. Similarly with alienation: the bureaucratic model of centralized decision-making rules out any worker self-management at the enterprise level. If the workers decide, the planners can't; it's either-or.

It is for these basic reasons that job satisfaction is necessarily lacking and the morale of workers is not very high. Nevertheless, the Soviety-type economy does do a good job in terms of providing for the lowest basic needs of its citizens. A great effort is made to assure that everybody has a modest standard of living and a secure job. Moreover, public health and education are of good quality, and available to the bulk of the people regardless of social status and location of residence. But in exchange for this the citizen has had to relinquish significantly traditional civil liberties, such as freedom of speech, the press, association, and movement, as well as any aspirations for economic democracy. A former editor of a leading Czech newspaper, during the short months of the Prague Spring of 1968, expresses the basic trade-off very well:

□ He (the worker) has no say whatever in the political functioning of the society, not even in deciding policies in his locality, not to mention being excluded from participation in matters of production, conditions of employment or anything else at his place of work. The outcome is a kind of unspoken agreement, which on the worker's side might run something like this: "I have handed over to you all my prerogatives and civil freedoms. In exchange I demand job security, a decent living standard, minimal expenditure of my labor power and adequate free time."[17]

Despite this, the Soviet model has looked attractive to many leaders in underdeveloped countries. It does provide a sure and relatively fast way to abolish within one generation the basic problem of poverty.

Let us take the example of Cuba. Before the socialist revolution in 1958 the country was, with a GNP per capita of $374, by no means among the poorest. But in the rural areas the same statistic averaged $91, and for many Cubans it was close to nothing. A recent World Bank study stated that "unemployment was some 16 percent in 1956/ 57, poverty was widespread, with a large fraction of the population illiterate and undernourished."[18] Inequality of wealth and income was extreme. In land, for example, 9 percent of owners held 73 percent of the land.[19] The study continues, "in the first few years after the revolution dire poverty and unemployment were virtually eliminated."[20] Assets, particularly land, were redistributed and, through public financing, virtually every Cuban can now obtain free health care and free education. Moreover, basic necessities (food, clothing, and shelter) have been made available to all Cubans through government subsidies and rationing.

If we define development as the progressive elimination of poverty, inequality and unemployment, Cuba has been able to make impressive gains by adopting the Soviet approach, even though the progress is not reflected in a rather stagnating GNP per capita growth performance.

At the same time, poverty and inequality have improved little in other Latin American countries. A recent UN study on El Salvador, for example, shows that the majority of El Salvadorians are poor and undernourished.[21] Moreover, the situation has tended to deteriorate during the last two decades. In Haiti the poverty problem may be even more miserable.

Cuba's ability to satisfy the most basic human needs of its population deserves full credit. Yet the experience of the more advanced socialist countries suggests that further economic development will only be possible at higher and higher human sacrifices. Given a choice, Third World countries are less and less considering development along the Soviet model. They are uneasy about buying the total package. The reasons are as follows.

First, instead of production for profits, we now have production for maximum output in investment goods. Everything is geared to that end. Agriculture will be neglected, jobs will cluster around the big cities. Yet the ideological choice for capital-intensive, up-to-date technology will minimize the need for excessive rural labor.

Second, the living standard of the peasantry will have to be kept to an absolute minimum in order to import the desired new steel complexes, etc. Yet it is not easy to squeeze too much from poor peasants, even under some sort of mandatory collectivization of agriculture.

Third, the low level of agricultural productivity typically prevailing in these countries necessitates a heavy reliance on the Soviet Union for long-term loans. Moreover, long-term contracts will have to be made committing exports of raw materials to the Soviet Bloc. In short, just as in the case of Cuba, an underdeveloped country immediately drifts into economic and political dependency on the Soviet Bloc.

Fourth, the concept of detailed centralized planning necessitates a large urban bureaucracy. Foreign experts will initially be necessary to run the planning machinery. Later the foreign experts are replaced by domestic experts. In either case there is very little room for mass participation in decision-making. In order to stimulate labor productivity, the regime will have to "bribe" workers with lucrative material incentives, thereby negating the human goals of equality and solidarity.

In short, the Soviet model will give the masses bread, but little more. The rural masses are left in the cold and their latent productive contribution is likely to remain dormant.

Closing the door to the second (Soviet-type) approach brings us to a third alternative: the humanistic model.

EARLY PIONEER OF A THIRD WAY: MAHATMA GANDHI

Gandhi was born in India in 1869. At eighteen years of age he was sent to England, where he completed his education as a lawyer in three years. Soon thereafter his outlook changed radically, a development apparently triggered by his reading John Ruskin, the British humanist. Gandhi, in his autobiography, tells us that Ruskin's critique of British political economy in his *Unto This Last* was "the one book that brought about an instantaneous and practical transformation in my life."[22] The new Gandhi soon emerged as one of the best-known disciples and practitioners of humanistic thinking that the world has seen. In 1952 he wrote that "self-realization" constitutes the prime goal of life, and "all that I do by way of speaking and writing, and all my ventures in the political field, are directed to this same end."[23]

Gandhi fought restlessly but non-violently for the humanization of India, and he saw the first step to be the country's independence from England. Upon his death in 1948, Mahatma Gandhi has been honored as "the father of the Indian nation." But today we know that he has been considerably more than that. He has been the father of a new idea, an idea that has worldwide application and promise, the idea of humanistic economic development.

In a sense he paralleled John Hobson's attempts to infuse economic activity with the ideals of John Ruskin. Hobson wrote about welfare in an industrialized market economy. Gandhi, on the other hand, applied the humanistic ideals to the problems of undeveloped India and implicitly to the current problems of the Third World. Like Ruskin and Hobson, he deplored the divorce of economic activity from human and ethical norms. Economic activity should be geared to the human welfare for all (*sarvodaya*). The goal of an economic system, he wrote, "is human happiness combined with full mental and moral growth."[24] Beyond the provision of the basic necessities of life (food, clothing, shelter) the economic system has to produce in accordance with the basic human needs and values of equality, nonviolence, and creative labor.

Since poverty and mass starvation were no doubt the most challenging problems for India at that time, any economic development had to be primarily oriented to raising the poorest to subsistence. But Gandhi advocated a development strategy that would not only do just that but *at the same time* also provide for the higher (social) needs of rural Indians. Only in such a way could the development effort be sustainable. As Gunnar Myrdal put it: "Gandhi clearly perceived that development is basically a human problem concerning attitudes and institutions. It must imply that people everywhere begin to act more purposefully to improve their living conditions and then also to change their community in such a way as to make these strivings more possible and effective."[25]

The Gandhian idea of development can be briefly summarized as follows: He foresaw, as soon as the British had left the country, an ongoing social and economic "revolution," a restructuring of the colonial economy that would emphasize self-reliant, egalitarian village economies in the rural areas. Revolution, in contrast to Marx and Lenin, had to be nonviolent. Its aim was to change the social relationships. Work, both agricultural and industrial, had to be brought to the unemployed rural masses. It was the function of machines to serve, not replace, people.

□ I am not fighting machinery as such but the madness of thinking that machinery saves labor. Men "save labor" unless thousands of them are without work and die of hunger on the streets. I want to secure employment and livelihood not only to part of the human race, but for all. I will not have the enrichment of a few at the expense of the community. At the present the machine is helping a small minority to live on the exploitation of the masses.[26]

To fit the decentralized, village-based economy, industry had to be small-scale and traditional, employing a nonviolent, non-alienating technology that would allow labor and laborers to acquire a maximum of human dignity and moral substance. Similarly, the nation's education system would have to be reoriented towards teaching the young the importance and dignity of all labor, in particular manual "bread labor," irrespective of class or caste.

Fate didn't permit Gandhi to see his ideas implemented. He died in 1948 by the bullet of an assassin. His successors first postponed the reform plans and then shelved them altogether. Inequality widened, the land tenure and education reforms never materialized and the bulk of the rural population has remained in poverty.

It is only today, thirty years after Gandhi's death, that his ideas are being revived. The Janata Party in India had published in 1976 a widely publicized Manifesto subtitled *Both Bread and Liberty–The Gandhian Alternative*, a program aimed at decentralization, rural and village economy, and an appropriate technology. India still has a choice. Whether it will choose the Third Way, a path advocated by its own father, only time will tell.

Gandhian Economics Reformulated:
Small Is Beautiful

Small Is Beautiful is the title of the bestselling book by the late British economist, E. F. Schumacher. It is in that book that we find for the first time a comprehensive attempt to formulate humanistic economics, an economics in which people matter.

Schumacher, a former Rhodes scholar and technocrat (as an advisor to the British National Coal Board from 1950 to 1970) traveled many times to the East where he was able to get firsthand knowledge of the tragic sterility of modern development economics. What was supposed to work so well, according to the textbooks, did not seem to function in reality. Economists tended to focus on such things as the investment ratio, foreign aid, the old doctrines of free trade, international division of labor and specialization and policy implications derived from elegant but highly abstract mathematical growth models. People only mattered in a quantitative sense; they were important because of their education, typically measured in years of schooling and designated as *human capital*. In short, the emphasis had traditionally been on the quantity of capital inputs, rather than on the quality of human output.

Third World development did not respond well to this traditional prescription. Something important seemed to be missing in the economists' models. Schumacher was one of the first to speak out. Back in 1966, at a conference on African Development in London, he posed the question: "Could it be that the relative failure of aid, or at least our disappointment with the effectiveness of aid, has something to do with our materialistic philosophy which makes us liable to overlook the most important preconditions of success, which are generally invisible?"[27] And then he proceeded to put his finger on the real factor: "development does not start with goods; it starts with people and their education, organization and discipline. Without these three, all resources remain latent, untapped, potential."[28] From this he draws the logical policy implication:

☐ Here lies the reason why development cannot be an act of creation, why it cannot be ordered, bought, comprehensively planned: why it requires a process of evolution. Education does not "jump"; it is a gradual process of great subtlety. Organization does not "jump"; it must gradually evolve step by step. And much the same goes for discipline. All three must evolve step by step, and the foremost task of development policy must be to speed the evolution. All three must become the property not merely of a tiny minority, but the whole society.[29]

He concluded that any successful development policy has to *involve the entire population.* "People are the primary and ultimate source of any wealth whatsoever. If they are left out, if they are pushed around by self-styled experts and high-handed planners, then nothing can ever yield real fruit."[30]

In the Third World, the great majority of people live in rural areas, and most of them are poor by any standard of human decency. This is the heartland of world poverty, Schumacher's "two million villages." Any development effort has to touch these rural masses, it has to help them help themselves. The task is to create millions of new workplaces in the villages and small towns. How can this be done? Fifteen years ago, at a UNESCO conference in Chile, Schumacher outlined the task in four propositions:

1. Create workplaces where people are living now and not primarily in the metropolitan areas.

2. These workplaces have to be cheap enough so that they can be created in large numbers without the need to import expensive machinery and equipment.

3. Production methods should be simple to minimize the need for highly skilled experts, elaborate financial institutions and marketing techniques.

4. Production should be mainly from local materials and mainly for local consumption.

There are two requirements for meeting these propositions; First is a stress on regional self-sufficient growth geared towards meeting the basic needs of the particular district, having its own economic administration and small school system, as well as basic health facilities. Second is the need for an "intermediary technology," something in between a $3 equipment cost per workplace on the one hand, and the $3000 job cost typically prevailing in the industrialized world. Schumacher is proposing a $300 technology. His idea of intermediate technology does not mean going back to the traditional, indigenous $3 production methods; rather it implies a suitable upgrading and transformation of such methods.

Schumacher realized, of course, that intermediate technology is not universally applicable. Many products can only be produced by the most sophisticated methods. Oil refineries are capital intensive, and it would be foolish to design and operate them otherwise. Similarly with many other industries, typically in the investment goods sector, such as steel, cement, and machinery.

Yet the Third World primarily wants products to meet their most urgent needs. As Schumacher put it:

□ What the poor need most of all is simple things—building materials, clothing, household goods, agricultural implements—and a better return for their agricultural products. They also most urgently need in many places: trees, water, and crop-storage facilities. Most agricultural populations would be helped immensely if they could themselves carry out the first stage of processing their products. All these are ideal fields for intermediate technology.[31]

It is through the mutual interaction of intermediate technology and villagization of the economy that the rural poor are able to help themselves and gain self-respect and a sense of human dignity. *Production by the masses* is the humanistic alternative to mass production. And there will be little economic development as long as the people are not involved but merely "pushed around by self-styled experts and high-handed planners." The underdeveloped countries need a new economics in which people matter, and nothing shows this more clearly than the current plight of the Third World.

Schumacher's ideas are finally gaining respectability. A recent International Labor Office conference has advocated a new basic-needs strategy against chronic poverty in the Third World. A program of action has been adopted by the 1976 World Employment Conference recommending a shift in development enterprises from industry to agriculture, from city to countryside, from large-scale to small-scale production, from exports to self-reliance. It is worthwhile to note that neither the United States nor the Soviet Union supported the resolution, although for different reasons.

The Third World cannot expect support from the superpowers, both jealously protecting their own approaches. They do need enlightened and courageous leaders willing to demonstrate to the world the power of humanistic thinking. One country in Africa has done just that. Let us now look at this pioneering experiment.

Nyerere's Tanzania: A Very Special Kind of Socialism

Tanzania, a country more than twice the size of California, in southeastern Africa, has not had it easy. Its previous colonial masters never bothered to educate the country's 14 million rural people, constituting over 90 percent of the population. Furthermore, most of the land is semi-arid and devoid of any significant amounts of natural resources. In brief, besides lots of land, the 13 million mostly illiterate people from various tribes are Tanzania's primary asset. From a material perspective the country has traditionally been ranked among the twenty-five poorest in the world. In 1976, its GNP per capita amounts to a mere $125. But despite this, life goes rather well in Tanzania, and the level of human welfare appears unrelated to that dismal dollar figure. To understand Tanzania and its economy, we have to acquaint ourselves with Julius Nyerere, the country's leader and *mwalimu*, meaning teacher.

Nyerere's Way   During the 1950s Nyerere emerged as one of the strong leaders of colonialized black Africa, fighting for the independence of his country. In a speech in 1959 he pledged that when that day arrives "we would like to light a candle and put it on top of Mount Kilimanjaro which would shine beyond our borders, giving hope where there was despair, love where there was hate and dignity where there was only humiliation."[32] And sure enough, two years later at Independence a team of climbers was dispatched to ascend Africa's highest mountain and plant a burning torch on its peak. Today, sixteen years later, the light is still shining. Perhaps more than ever, Nyerere is considered by friend and foe to be the conscience of Africa.

What sets Nyerere apart from some other African leaders, as well as from the overwhelming majority of politicians around the world, is his unqualified striving for New Man. "The purpose of (economic) development is Man. It is the creation of conditions, both material and spiritual, which enables Man, the individual, and Man the species, to become his best,"[33] he flatly proclaims. For fifteen years, and especially since 1967, Tanzania has embarked on a massive national development effort to create a New Man who avoids selfishness and works for the good of his countrymen. Nyerere readily admits that Tanzania is still far from attaining such a noble goal, but his relentless efforts towards it, coupled with some real (although small) accomplishments, have brought him admiration at home and around the world, and even the respect of the World Bank.

Nyerere's own words best convey his unique and purely humanistic viewpoint:

☐ The truth is that development means the development of *people*. Roads, buildings, the increase of crop output, and other things of this nature are not development; they are only tools of development. A new road extends a man's freedom only if he travels upon it. An increase in the number of school buildings is development only if those buildings can be, and are being, used to develop the minds and understanding of people. An increase in the output of wheat, maize, or beans, is only development if it leads to better nutrition of the people. An expansion of the cotton, coffee, or sisal crop is development only if these things can be sold and the money used for other things which improve the health, comfort, and understanding of the people. Development which is not development of people may be of interest to historians in the year 3000; it is irrelevant to the kind of future which is created.[34]

The economy is seen as a mechanism to fulfill the basic needs of its own people; if GNP can only expand by catering to the wants of affluent citizens or foreign tourists, then it better not grow at all.

Almost all Tanzanians live in the countryside. It is there where poverty has traditionally been a distinguishing feature. So we see Nyerere put rural development on the top of the list of priorities, long before similar ideas have gained currency in other countries of the Third World. And, to bring the country's top government officials closer to the peasants, a brand new capital city, Dodoma, has been built in the countryside. Within a year or two, all government offices will be moved there from Dar es Salaam. It is beyond the scope of this book to give a detailed account of the Tanzanian economy in operation. Instead, let us briefly sketch its prime institutional feature and reflect on its humanistic performance.

Ten years ago, it became clear that rural development could only occur if the scattered tribesmen could be persuaded to create cooperative villages called *ujamma*, meaning "family-hood" or "self-help." "Until we have changed our way of living in the rural areas, we have changed nothing in Tanzania," Nyerere proclaimed in a speech ten years ago, explaining: "We have a lot of land, our people are scattered and this is very difficult for development. It would be much easier for development, using the limited resources that we have, if people were living in compact communities."[35] After an all-out education campaign with the assistance of the local Catholic church and its missionaries, more and more subsistence farmers were persuaded to move to live in an *ujamma*. Today there are in excess of 10,000 such cooperative villages inhabited by more than two-thirds of the rural population.

Let us take a brief look at the model *ujamma*, Chamwino, set up in 1973. There are 664 families living today in Chamwino, each owning a little brick house and a two- to three-acre vegetable garden. We find a school, a clinic, a church, even electricity and access to telephone service. Moreover, there are several hundred acres of communal land growing cash crops. Each family works three days of the week on the common property, the tasks being assigned by the elected village council. The elected officials also decide what to grow, how much to store locally, and how to market the surplus of the crop.

The profits of the cash sales are reinvested in the cooperative. Chamwino now has a small poultry operation, a pig farm, and a small woodworking enterprise which manufactures doors and window frames.

Life is simple but comfortable and secure in Chamwino; for instance, there is running water in each house. Few other villages enjoy a comparable living standard yet, but all are striving for similar achievements. A few miles down a dusty road we find a much poorer village, Chamangali, still in the first phase of development. There is no electricity, no phones, but we do find a little schoolhouse educating the children through the third grade. As in all rural schools the children are taught the humanistic values of bread labor by spending a larger part of their time in raising food crops and other skills for village self-sufficiency. The villagers still live in the traditional mud huts but they do have access to clean water supplied by a central water supply system. Most land is privately worked with some animal herds and agricultural implements held collectively. The inhabitants of Chamangali are expected to succeed in emulating their better-off neighbors at Chamwino. The first step will be to make their own bricks for new houses. As one local official put it: "We may be socialists, but that is the competition we want. We want each village to have pride in itself and to feel it can be better, more productive than any other."[36]

But there is no rigid blueprint showing how these cooperatives should organize and function. Nyerere maintains that "different types of land, different climates, different people and different crops mean that there should not be a single model: for an *ujamma* village will only succeed when it takes all these things into account in its organization and practice."[37]

Given Tanzania's development goals and patterns, we can better understand the relative unimportance of the very low GNP/capita figure. The best way to boost GNP is to specialize where your country has a comparative advantage internationally. For Tanzania, this would mean large and mechanized farms producing cash crops for the international market, in particular in coffee, sisal and cotton. Most of these commodities are not produced for internal consumption, nor would they feed the hungry and the poor. Of course, the neoclassical economic expert will interject that the export revenue can be used for importing the things that the country needs. But even assuming that an enlightened government would want to do just that, there are things that cannot be imported easily no matter how high the foreign exchange. We not only think of such items as clean water, a balanced nutritional diet, good health and literacy for all, but also such humanistic goals as equality, human dignity, freedom from dependency and, finally, the beauty of harmonious development. It is precisely such goods that constitute the basic human needs of society and the best way to meet them is directly, by the self-reliant, decentralized type of policy advocated by Gandhi and Schumacher. Tanzania strives for the development of New Man, self-actualization, not the development of things.

The first decade of Tanzanian development was financed by a minimal reliance on foreign loans and grants. Between 1967 and 1971, 75 percent of capital accumulation expenditures have been funded from internal sources, a truly exceptional statistic in modern Africa. Emphasis on small-scale cooperative farming diminishes the need to import consumer goods, food, clothing, construction materials, etc. All these things can be produced by the farmers themselves. Ninety percent of the total imports have been in the form of investment goods, such as crude oil for fertilizer production, industrial chemicals, and vehicle parts.[38]

But another reason for the country's relative self-sufficiency has been the encouragement of an agricultural technology that could be relatively easily implemented and maintained by the rural cooperatives. Tractors are expensive; Tanzania cannot afford too many. They are being used on some of the few large state farms and on some advanced *ujammas*. "In most areas," Nyerere observed in 1967, "all that we see are people with backs bent under the hot sun, breaking the land with heavy hoes just as their ancestors have done for centuries."[39a] But rather than waiting for years and years until sufficient tractors will have arrived, the government has been advocating the use of animal-drawn implements. Ox training centers have been established all over the countryside and villagers are instructed in how to manufacture simple ox ploughs. Here, Tanzania is a case study of intermediate technology in action.

What has been the performance record of Nyerere's Tanzania? The World Bank estimates that GNP per capita grew at a rate of 2.6 percent from 1960 to 1976, in spite of an almost 3 percent annual rate of population increase.[39b] What is important from a humanistic perspective is that more and more basic human needs have been satisfied since Independence. Per capita food production has increased 13 percent between the mid-sixties and the mid-seventies. At the same time the same index declined on the average by 4 percent for the other low income countries. In neighboring Kenya the index dropped 12 percent. Similar percentages hold true for water. Almost 40 percent of the population today has access to safe water. The average figure for poor countries is 25 percent, and for somewhat higher income Kenya it is 17 percent. World Bank also indicates that the average life expectancy at birth has gone up from 37 to 45 years since 1960. The government estimates that infant mortality was reduced by a magnitude of 40 percent, and that maternity mortality rates have been cut in half. Most of the population is now inoculated against smallpox, and anti-malaria drugs and treatment are readily accessible. The provision of elementary health care in the rural population has been facilitated by the establishment of 100 rural health centers and between 1500 and 2000 dispensaries. Most pregnant women now get some kind of prenatal care, as opposed to only 30 percent before 1961.

In education, thousands of new schools have been built, mainly in rural areas. Since 1960 the proportion of primary school pupils increased from 24 percent to 57 percent of the relevant age groups. A strong effort has been made to provide for adult education. In 1971 almost one million adults were attending literacy classes. Obviously, the ambitious goals of universal primary education set for 1989, as well as general adult literacy, have not yet been attained. Yet the World Bank estimates an increase in the adult literacy rate from 17 percent in 1960 to 63 percent in 1975. Such progress is rather unique for a rural economy in Africa. Even in Kenya only 40 percent of the adults are literate.

The high degree of inequality from the colonial years has been greatly reduced. The World Bank estimates that today a Minister in the Tanzanian government, after personal and income taxes, receives about thirteen times more than a man or woman earning the minimum wage.[40] Not so long ago the difference between maximum and minimum earnings was 60 to 1. Moreover, the government taxes private consumer durables, such as automobiles and luxury goods, very heavily, and at the same time attempts to provide maximal free public services. According to a recent report by the World Bank, Nyerere's egalitarian commitment consists of more than mere preaching:

□ An important regulation is the rule forbidding leaders of the party, middle and senior civil servants, and middle and senior public productive sector employees from having second jobs, earning rental or share incomes, or running any business except a small farm without permanent (as opposed to seasonal) paid labor. Spouses of these individuals face similar restrictions. This code is enforced with relative strictness even at the rural level, although its impact there is less.[41]

More importantly, Nyerere assures us that "hundreds of thousands of people now take an active part in their own village government, their district government, and indirectly in their national government. The people are more self-confident; not only is the future theirs to determine, but they know it is theirs to determine."[42]

There are some darker areas in contemporary Tanzania which we should mention as well. First, despite all the efforts to bring power directly to the people, there still is an excessively large bureaucracy in the country. There have also been complaints that lower level bureaucrats often can be bribed. Such complaints are fairly typical in Third World economies, yet they are clearly incompatible with Nyerere's idealism.*

---

*There is a rather straightforward answer to this problem. In the early sixties, after independence, the bureaucracy had to be "africanized," and yet there was a very small pool of Tanzanians who had received any education under the colonial administration. The leadership of the country could not be selective, and many individuals gained civil servant posts and political power that they have been using for their own material benefit. Yet there is widespread confidence that as more and more young Tanzanians take over these jobs, the problems will fade away.

Another problem has been the recent economic difficulties which have forced Nyerere to resort to heavy borrowing from the World Bank, the International Development Agency, and the International Monetary Fund, to keep the economy afloat. Yet the critics rarely mention the true reasons for such a departure from self-reliance. First, the country experienced a severe two-year drought in 1974 and 1975 which decreased cotton and tobacco output by 40 percent. At the same time, the world price of sisal collapsed while oil prices tripled, pushing the country's oil bill from $20 million to $100 million. It's no wonder the country needed to borrow. Now that events have stabilized we would expect the previous brand of self-reliance to reassert itself. In any case, there is no reason to sound the alarm in Tanzania today. The interest on public debts only amounts to 4 percent of government expenditures and much of the debt is domestically held.

To many Westerners the net balance of economic achievements may look somewhat modest, yet we tend to forget that we cannot expect miracles on so wide a battlefront within ten or fifteen years. There is no doubt that the average Tanzanian enjoys today a much higher degree of well-being than under the colonial period. Similarly, the progress that the country was able to make has been spread much more evenly than in neighboring Kenya or any other East African country.

Nyerere's Ideology Julius Nyerere uses every opportunity to stress the socialist goals and character of his policies. Yet he never mentions Marx, Lenin, or even Mao. The socialism of Nyerere is non-Marxist; he himself likes to describe it as *communitarian*. In Nyerere's words, "Increased wealth in the hands of the people, used by them for their own development and their own betterment, and used in a spirit of cooperation and human equality, this is almost a definition of socialism in itself."[43] Above all it is a nonviolent type of socialism that seeks to benefit the individual without coercion and with a minimum of bureaucracy and a maximum of freedom.

Nyerere once more: "As far as we are concerned, the people's freedom to determine their own priorities, to organize themselves, and their own advance in welfare, is an important part of our objective. It cannot be postponed to some future time. The people's active and continued voluntary participation in the struggle is an important part of our objective because only through this participation will the people develop. And to us, the development of the nation means the development of the people."[44]

Gandhi could hardly have said it better. His Indian followers never dared to take the message seriously. Yet Gandhi's nonviolent socialism is not dead. A torch has been burning on the highest mountain in Africa for the last two decades. Its light gives us hope and inspiration for the future. What Gandhi and Schumacher advocated, Nyerere is courageously putting into practice! Much of the entire world's future may hinge on the continued success of his large-scale humanistic experiment.

Maoism: A Marxist Interlude
with a Human Face?

Humanism has not only entered development economics in Tanzania. Another even larger-scale experiment has been carried out in China under the leadership of the late Chairman Mao. The Chinese, after following the Soviet model for the first seven years, decided in 1957 to switch to an alternative strategy with its predominantly rural economy. In the process, Mao led his people down a path which very much resembled the Gandhian approach. Agricultural development was put in the forefront; industrialization was to come to the rural areas in the form of relatively small-scale and labor-intensive plants to produce for regional and local needs. *Self-reliance* became one of the key words. Central planning gave way to predominantly decentralized decision-making carried on the regional, town, or even neighborhood, level. Due to local self-sufficiency the task of coordinating these regional plans was minimal. Finally, a maximum stress was put on egalitarian and mass participation in decision-making at all levels.

Even more significant, from a humanistic perspective, has been Mao's stress of the human factor in development. Instead of the Soviet-type stress on rapid industrialization in order to meet human needs, the Chinese believed in prior fulfillment of the basic human needs as a necessary condition for rapid industrialization. Economic development depends not so much on machinery and investment as it does on people, on what they believe, what they do, and how they operate the equipment. Less poverty, more equality, more mass participation, more education and better health care, all these indicators promote the human factor in economic development.

Mao preached a socialist morality, a collective selfless attitude leading to an economic growth where everybody rises, not just the urban and educated people. To that extent, Maoism—in total opposition to production for profit—attempts to build on the "worst," to educate the least educated, to industrialize remote areas, etc. Such a humanistic approach is believed to create selflessness and unity of purpose, and thereby to release a huge reservoir of enthusiasm, energy and creativeness; the "socialist initiative latent in the masses will burst out with volcanic force" and allow the people to literally pull themselves up by their bootstraps. Economic growth happens almost automatically as a byproduct of human growth.

Some of the sharpest criticism of such Maoist philosophy came from Soviet economists. The Soviets deplored the overestimation of the subjective (i.e., human) factor to the neglect of the "scientifically objective laws of socialist development." Maoist "revisionism" is explained to the Russian student as follows:

□ The truly scientific Marxist-Leninist theory was supplanted by a system of views deeply hostile to Marxism-Leninism and covered up with "Leftist" ultra-revolutionary talk.

Without being a coherent theory, this system is largely eclectic and pragmatic, comprising elements of the most diverse doctrines (like Confucianism, Marxism, utopian socialism, idealism, populism, anarchism, and Trotskyism). Hence, the attempt to turn the subjective factor, politics and ideas into an absolute, to whip up socio-economic development and execute leaps and bounds, to exaggerate the potentialities of the peasantry and small-scale production, and to extol primitive universal egalitarianism and closed, subsistence level and self-sufficient complexes.[45]

The Soviets ridicule the small-scale industry "idealization" and the faith put in Mao's moralist preaching as a way of changing "the working people's spiritual make-up and (to) convert spiritual power into a great material force." Moreover, the Soviets have been sharply critical of the "perverted forms" of factory management in which "everything was handed down to the workers," instead of relying on the expertise of centralized planners.[46]

The Soviet protests notwithstanding, China has prospered under its Maoist game plan. Between 1957 and 1974, GNP/capita has been estimated to have grown at an average annual rate of 3 percent.[47] More important is the overriding fact that China "for twenty years has fed, clothed, and housed everyone, has kept them healthy, and has educated most."[48] And all this was accomplished with very little help from anybody. In fact, China has been one of the few countries with no foreign debt. It is one of the ironies of history that Gandhi's India is increasingly trailing China in this respect.

Several sympathetic Western economists visited China in the sixties and wrote firsthand accounts of this success story. Such reports were immediately discredited and had little impact initially. But, when China was visited in the early seventies by such well-known and reputable economists as Tobin, Reynolds, and Galbraith, the accomplishments could no longer be ignored. One theme runs through their individual accounts: they all found a country with no unemployment, no dire poverty and extreme equality. Literacy and health care were up to highest standards. The people seemed content, optimistic and proud of their achievements. No wonder the Chinese version of humanized communism found many admirers in the Third World.

From a humanistic perspective the Maoist experience was surprisingly successful, but it did not survive Mao's death. Since 1976, a different breed of people have taken firm command. With Hua Kuo-feng and Teng Hsaio-ping in the driver's seat, the Maoist elements of the economy are being dismantled day by day. The top Maoist ideologists have been purged from the party leadership and are now referred to as the so-called Gang of Four. We hear of a virtual manhunt on all remaining "ultra leftists" and there are even unconfirmed reports of mass executions.

China is recentralizing its economy, "labor discipline" has been restored in the factory and the prime goal is, once again, more material production and not human development. Finally, the new regime now emphasizes efficient technology and much greater reliance on foreign trade. In some ways, China is moving back towards the Soviet model. Maoism may suffer a similar fate to Gandhi's ideas in India thirty years ago. Today Maoism remains a force only in Albania, a small country in Eastern Europe that has broken its diplomatic relations with China and lives in an unprecedented "splendid isolation." As such it remains a light within the Marxist-Leninist camp, and a likely candidate for increasing world attention.

The Lesson of China

As humanists, we have to ask ourselves what is the lesson of the Chinese experiment? They had a successful, somewhat humanistic economy, and now suddenly it's going in a different direction. What is the essential difference between Tanzania and a Marxist country such as China? Both have a one-party state, and in both cases it was an inspired leader who formulated economic philosophy and policies almost single-handedly. Yet, there is a difference, and it lies in the organization of politics. The Communist Party in China is a closely knit, homogeneous and elitist organization. It is (as in the USSR) a *vanguard* party with an explicit Marxian proletarian ideology and little internal democracy. The party defines socialism and sees as its task the waging of a relentless class struggle against anybody departing from the line. With few exceptions this ideological purity has been strongly slanted towards an urban-type materialistic socialism of the Marxist and Leninist tradition.

The ruling party in Tanzania, TANU, is quite a different affair. It has been a "nationalist movement from which no section (of the population) is excluded." TANU comprises just about everybody who wants to join, regardless of occupation. The party had been heterogeneous from its very beginning, as one African scholar explains: "Because the growth of this organization was in part spontaneous, the activists in the early days were those who had both the time, education, and private means independent of government employ, to allow them to get involved in politics—often the local big farmer or small traders in a district."[49] As late as 1970 Nyerere still complained there were only a handful of socialists in the party. TANU is characterized by a high degree of internal democracy and grassroots decision-making. Party units consist of elected leaders representing ten households. Rather than acting as a guardian for class struggle and the dictatorship of the proletariat, it is seen as one instrument for mass participation, as the vanguard of humanist values seeking to bring human welfare to all Tanzanians alike. TANU's emphasis is on reconciliation of alternative ideas and philosophies by compromise as long as the policies are consistent with non-violent humanistic evolution of the economy. Nyerere has been an articulate and gifted leader, and there is little reason to believe that his successful policies will be reversed once he relinquishes his leadership role. Humanist values don't change; the humanistic "line" is inborn in all men and women, including Nyerere's eventual successors. If the democratic structure of decision-making in Tanzania that Nyerere has developed is strong enough to hold, then its humanistic future should be secure. So far there is hope for the Third World, and something to be learned for the industrialized nations as well.

References

1. International Labor Organization. *Employment, Growth and Basic Needs: A One-World Problem.* New York: Praeger, 1977.

2. Chenery, Hollis, et al. *Redistribution with Growth.* London: Oxford University Press, 1974.

3. Urrutia, Montoya and Berry, R. *Income Distribution in Colombia.* New Haven: Yale University Press, 1976.

4. International Labor Organization. *Employment, Growth and Basic Needs: A One-World Problem.* New York: Praeger, 1977, p. 18.

5. International Labor Organization. *Employment, Growth and Basic Needs: A One-World Problem.* New York: Praeger, 1977, p. 22.

6. Chenery, Hollis, et al. *Redistribution with Growth.* London: Oxford University Press, 1974, p. 12.

7. International Labor Organization. *Employment, Growth and Basic Needs: A One-World Problem.* New York: Praeger, 1977, p. 20.

8. Daly, Herman E., ed. *Toward a Steady-State Economy.* San Francisco: W. H. Freeman, 1973, p. 11.

9. Mesarovic, M. and Pestal, E. *Mankind at the Turning Point.* New York: Signal Books, 1976, Ch. 3.

10. International Labor Organization. *Employment, Growth and Basic Needs: A One-World Problem.* New York: Praeger, 1977, p. 23.

11. International Labor Organization. *Employment, Growth and Basic Needs: A One-World Problem.* New York: Praeger, 1977, p. 23.

12. International Labor Organization. *Employment, Growth and Basic Needs: A One-World Problem.* New York: Praeger, 1977, pp. 35–43.

13. World Bank. *Annual Report 1977.* June 1977, pp. 104–105.

14. Mesarovic, M. and Pestal, E. *Mankind at the Turning Point.* New York: Signal Books, 1976, Ch. 5.

15. Baran, Paul. *Political Economy of Growth.* New York: Monthly Review Press, 1957, Ch. 5.

16. Gurley, John. "Maoist Economic Development." In *America's Asia,* edited by Friedman and Seldon. New York: Random House, 1969.

17. Liehm, A. J. "The Prospects for Socialist Humanism." In *Essays on Socialist Humanism,* edited by K. Coates. Nottingham: Spokesman, 1972, p. 117.

18. Chenery, Hollis, et al. *Redistribution with Growth.* London: Oxford University Press, 1974, P. 263.

19. Chenery, Hollis, et al. *Redistribution with Growth.* London: Oxford University Press, 1974, p. 264.

20. Chenery, Hollis, et al. *Redistribution with Growth.* London: Oxford University Press, 1974, p. 263.

21. United Nations. *Macro-Analisis de las Communidades Rurales de El Salvador.* Comision Nacional de Desarollo Comunal, Projecto ELS/73/003 — PNUD/OTC, El Salvador, 1976.

22. Gandhi, Mahatma. *An Autobiography.* Ahinedabad: Navajivan, 1927, p. 22.

23. Gandhi, Mahatma. *An Autobiography.* Ahinedabad: Navajivan, 1927, p. x.

24. Huq, A. M. "Welfare Criteria in Gandhian Economics." Paper presented at *3rd Annual Convention of Eastern Economics Association,* April 1977.

25. Myrdal, G. *Against the Stream.* New York: Random House, 1972, p. 238.

26. Quoted in Madan, G. R. *Economic Thinking in India,* Delhi: Chand, 1966, p. 134.

27. Schumacher, E. R. *Small Is Beautiful (Economics as if People Mattered).* New York: Harper and Row, 1973, p. 156.

28. Schumacher, E. R. *Small Is Beautiful (Economics as if People Mattered).* New York: Harper and Row, 1973, p. 159.

29. Schumacher, E. R. *Small Is Beautiful (Economics as if People Mattered).* New York: Harper and Row, 1973, p. 159.

30. Schumacher, E. R. *Small Is Beautiful (Economics as if People Mattered).* New York: Harper and Row, 1973, p. 160.

31. Schumacher, E. R. *Small Is Beautiful (Economics as if People Mattered).* New York: Harper and Row, 1973, p. 175.

32. Nyerere quoted in *The New York Times.* September 16, 1976.

33. Nyerere, J. K. *Freedom and Development.* London: Oxford University Press, 1973, p. 215.

34. Nyerere, J. K. *Freedom and Development.* London: Oxford University Press, 1973, p. 59.

35. Quoted in *The New York Times*. January 27, 1977, p. 2.

36. Quoted in *The New York Times*. January 27, 1977, p. 2.

37. Nyerere, J. K. *Freedom and Development*. London: Oxford University Press, 1973, p. 307.

38. This and other data, unless otherwise specified, from a report on the first ten years of Tanzania's independence. Nyerere, J. K. *Freedom and Development*. London: Oxford University Press, 1973, p. 290.

39a. This and other data, unless otherwise specified, from a report on the first ten years of Tanzania's independence. Nyerere, J. K. *Freedom and Development*. London: Oxford University Press, 1973, p. 303.

39b. Unless otherwise specified, all of our data referring to recent years and trends can be found in World Bank, *World Development Report*. New York: Oxford University Press, 1978, Statistical Annex, Tables 1, 2, 17 and 18.

40. Chenery, Hollis, et al. *Redistribution with Growth*. London: Oxford University Press, 1974, p. 269.

41. Chenery, Hollis, et al. *Redistribution with Growth*. London: Oxford University Press, 1974, p. 271.

42. Nyerere, J. K. *Freedom and Development*. London: Oxford University Press, 1973, p. 330.

43. Nyerere, J. K. *Freedom and Development*. London: Oxford University Press, 1973, p. 43.

44. Nyerere, J. K. *Freedom and Development*. London: Oxford University Press, 1973, p. 333.

45. Korbash, E. *The Economic 'Theories' of Maoism*. Moscow: Progress, 1974, p. 9.

46. Korbash, E. *The Economic 'Theories' of Maoism*. Moscow: Progress, 1974. Chapters 2 and 3.

47. Ashbrook, A. "China: Economic Overview, 1975." In Joint Economic Committee, *China: A Reassessment of the Economy*, 1975, p. 23.

48. Gurley, John. "Maoist Economic Development." In *America's Asia*, edited by Friedman and Seldon. New York: Random House, 1969, p. 31.

49. Cliffe, Lionel. "Underdevelopment or Socialism? A Comparative Analysis of Kenya and Tanzania." In *The Political Economy of Africa*, edited by Richard Harris. New York: Wiley, 1975.

Chapter Fifteen

HUMANISTIC ECONOMICS AND THE CHALLENGE OF THE STEADY STATE

INTRODUCTION

There is a problem that looms large over the world economies as well as over the science of economics. It is the problem of the limits to growth. We believe that humanistic economics provides the germane solution to the problem, and in this chapter we will show how and why. We can begin to do this by recounting the following conversation that occurred between a high official in the Japanese government and a journalist:

> ☐ Whether in Japan, or America, or Britain, we've tried the orthodox solutions, and none of them have worked. Why? Because all of us lack the confidence that is required to make them work. Each of us has our individual and national selfishness, our reluctance to make the sacrifices necessary to bring the world out of recession. But that is not the fundamental point. The fundamental point is that we have accepted that we live in a world of finite resources, that we have no power to change the environment in which we live . . .
>
> That is why I say we need a new invention. It doesn't have to be a Japanese invention. It could be an American one. Or Iranian—it could come from anywhere in the world. Suppose, for instance, that someone were to invent a marketable car that didn't run on gasoline. That's just an example. Basically, what I'm looking for is an idea—to counter the idea of limited resources that's made all of us so depressed and gloomy . . . We have to take man himself, Japanese man, into a new dimension, where he has a new view of himself and his environment. That new view will create new needs, qualitatively different than the needs of today.[1]

The journalist's reaction to the official's comments was: "his fundamental prescription was not economic. Rather, it had to do with lifting man's spirits, in his country and the world."

We agree with the official's feelings about the problems of the contemporary situation; his is a sensitive perception of a social and economic malaise that underlies most countries in the developed world.

But we disagree with the kind of solution he hopes for. He gives an example of a car that doesn't run on gasoline. But, this kind of solution is the *technological fix*, the belief that our current problems can be fixed or solved by a new technology (there is also the implication of a *fix*, like a drug fix). But from the perspective of this book, the essence of the current problems is not technological; if anything, the development of new technology has the high likelihood of creating further problems.

Let us take the example of the gasoline-free car, a car which no longer depletes petroleum resources. The development of a new mode of travel, accessible to a large number of people, means that increased pressure is put on all related resources, and in the case of a transportation vehicle this fans out to an almost infinite range of items: metal, rubber, roads, restaurants, food, motels, etc. The problem is that gasoline is not the only resource that is becoming critically scarce; this is happening to a lengthening list of earth's goods. The official's prescription that what we need to do is counter the idea of limited resources is a medicine that spells disaster. What we need to do is almost the opposite—construct a sane economy that *fully accepts* the idea of limited resources, that no longer looks for the technological fix. And, likewise, the journalist's conclusion about the official's remarks also has to be corrected. The official's fundamental prescription *is* economic; it depends on a new technology. We do agree with both of them that the need of the time is to lift humanity's spirits, but this will no longer happen through spectacular technology. How will it happen? In attempting to answer this we need to take another look at the problem of economic growth.

THE PROBLEM OF GROWTH: MATERIALISM AT A DEAD END

We live in a finite world. To use Kenneth Boulding's term, it is *Spaceship Earth*, an enclosed sphere that moves through the reaches of a vast cosmos. Infinite growth, or infinite consumption, in a finite world is impossible. Sooner or later we reach the bottom of the resource barrel. And the evidence is that it will be sooner rather than later.

One way to appreciate that it will be sooner is to realize that growth is *exponential*. This means that in order to maintain a constant level of expansion, say, 5 percent per year, the economy needs to use *more* than that same increase in resources; it needs a continuously increasing quantity of resources, rather than just 5 percent per year. The reason is that each expansion of the economy enlarges the arithmetic base upon which further growth is to be measured; it's the same principle as compounding interest. In more vivid terms, it's like a snowball rolling downhill to become an avalanche. The same thing goes for the waste that the system produces. It too is exponential. An economic system that uses and expels resources in an exponential fashion cannot long endure. Eventually we will find ourselves scratching at stone, and suffocating in our own effluvia.

A few figures which have been gathered by economist Emile Benoit serve well to illustrate this point.[2] Let us begin with coal, a supposedly abundant energy resource, at least in the United States, upon which a lot of hope for the future has been placed. The currently estimated amount of recoverable coal in the earth's crust ought to be enough to maintain our current level of coal usage for over 5000 years. Sounds comforting. However, if we expand our use of coal by a rate of just over 4 percent a year, which is probably a conservative estimate given current plans for coal use, this same amount of coal would be used up in 135 years. Now let us turn to a basic metal resource, aluminum. The currently estimated supply of aluminum at current levels of usage should be enough to last for another 68,000 years. This sounds like forever. But the current *rate of expansion* in the use of aluminum is approximately 6.4 percent a year. At this rate of expansion all this aluminum will be gone in a mere 140 years. The same kind of stark results occur when we apply the exponential calculation to most of our major minerals. It is doubtful that we could sustain our present rate of growth in any of them for over two hundred years. To show the utter finality of these limits it needs to be pointed out that if, by some miracle, we would be able to continue at our present rates of growth for the next thousand years we would consume a weight of materials greater than the earth itself!

Growth Limited Economy and the Problem of Poverty   A growth-limited economy poses a tremendous problem for the orthodox economic approach to the problem of poverty. That approach relies on growth to meet the problem of the poor rather than facing the question of the distribution of wealth. As long as the economy is in continual growth, the question of distribution doesn't have to be faced. Today's poor can expect to have more tomorrow, and thus have a hope of moving out of a state of deprivation. Everyone's standard of living, rich and poor alike, is on the rise, so each can look forward to a better day ahead. This is the welfare objective related to the Pareto Criterion, as we explained in Chapter 5. However, when the economy can, or should, no longer grow, then this solution to inequality becomes closed. Orthodox economists look aghast at the prospect of a limited-growth economy because then they see no hope for the poverty problem.

The Social Limits to Growth

Another problem for orthodox economics must be brought in at this point. It is what Fred Hirsch has called "the social limits to growth."[3] *Even* when an economy is growing, Hirsch points out, there is still a definite limit placed on personal satisfaction, because many goods have a strong social or "positional" component; everyone can't have them at the same time. Everyone, for example, can't have a home by the seashore, even if no one is poor—there is just so much seashore to go around; everyone can't live in the suburbs—if everyone did there would no longer be suburbs; everyone can't get top jobs in the university—there are just so many top jobs available; and so forth. In all of these social-scarcity situations it is still the richest, or the most favored, that will get these positional goods, despite the general rise in everyone's wealth or education. Thus, despite overall growth, relative standing is still tremendously important. Congestion, for example, occurs when too many people have access to a limited space, or any other necessarily limited resource, and wealth itself may not help. Buying an expensive car cannot get you a pleasant unobstructed drive on the highway. As a matter of fact, growth not only cannot bring these comforts to everyone, but also it limits them for everyone. To assure certain comforts, inequality in private commodities is actually necessary. For instance, you can't have good servants anymore if no one is poor enough to have to be a servant.

Hirsch goes further with his analysis. The general rise in everyone's income levels under a growth economy (and philosophy) leads everyone to expect that they too will partake of the goods that were once the exclusive province of the wealthy. But if many of these goods are positional, these expectations are bound to lead to frustration. Even if one is better off, if everyone else is also proportionately better off, in terms of relative standing one is in the same position. So we have the irony that growth, which is taken to provide a promise of satisfaction and fulfillment, can itself be a cause of frustration.

We see then that the promise of growth is severely limited, and that these limits are both physical and social. Thus, the problem of distribution returns to economics with full force. No longer can economists, with any kind of good conscience, thrust it out of sight under the cover of growth and Pareto. However, limits to growth do not pose the same problem for humanistic economics as for its mainstream counterpart because the former accepts the necessity of dealing with redistribution. Indeed, this is a major concern of humanistic economics, as we have seen in previous chapters.

Material Versus Non-Material Growth

Now let us return to the discussion between the government official and the journalist, and a major theme we want to bring into focus.

Neoclassical economics, and the associated value system of a rapidly vanishing age, has led people such as the government official to look in the wrong direction for the solution to economic problems. He is looking for a material answer when the problem is one of values, spirit, and social relations—the non-material. This is the only true "noneconomic" answer. The purpose of humanistic economics is to make this answer economic. Let us quote Schumacher here, ". . . An attitude to life which seeks fulfillment in the single-minded pursuit of wealth—in short, materialism—does not fit into this world, because it contains no limiting principle, while the environment in which it is placed is strictly limited."[4] Economics has to fit itself back into the world.

Economics, which has long been the science of materialistic values, has now to move beyond materialism. The growth that we need to seek now is no longer material, but is in the realm of the fully human, i.e., the non-material or spiritual. Spiritual growth is called for, not material growth.* This is the meaning of self-actualization.

Quality as Productivity   Once we see that growth need not be looked at only in non-spiritual terms (to use this expression just once), we can easily recognize the nearsightedness of looking at productivity solely in terms of numerical material output. Today there is an increasing hue and cry over the decline in the quality of life, and a call for the renewal of this mysterious essence. But to begin to make the correct approach to this problem we need to recognize that quantity and quality are opposites, and correspond to material and spiritual.

For instance, the way we deal with material productivity is by counting; how many barrels of oil, how many automobiles, etc., but if counting becomes the be-all and end-all of existence then quality is driven out. You cannot achieve quality by counting. In order to know if quality is present you have to feel it or perceive it.**

In the area of material goods counting is quite appropriate as a measure of productivity. But the error lies in carrying the quantitative approach over to non-material areas, such as social and health services and education. The mistaken notion that you can *measure* productivity in these areas is embodied in the rise of what is called *accountability*.

---

*Our age has been so dominated by materialism that to refer to its opposite we use the negative *non-material*. In this age, the word *spiritual* has been so laden with undesirable connotations that we no longer see it simply as meaning the opposite of material. But it does mean this, and we could just as accurately refer to the material as the *non-spiritual*.

**The word *quality* is sometimes used as a synonym for *durability*; a *quality* product will last a long time. Since time can be counted, quality in this sense is quantitative, but this is a special use of the term.

While this term has the suggestion of being accountable which, within the correct perspective, is legitimate, its major meaning comes from the concept of accountancy (being countable) and here is where the damage lies. In education it results in the vulgar practice of counting class size as a measure of how much education has occurred; counting heads becomes the educational parallel of counting cars off the assembly line. An even more pervasive, but less obvious, intrusion of quantitative methods into the province of quality is the use of *output indexing*. Again, in education, this is found in what is called performance contracting, where an attempt is made to pay teachers according to pupils' scores on a given test, say a reading test.[5] Such a practice sets up an inevitable incentive to focus exclusively on the particular criterion used. All activity becomes directed to raising scores on that particular test.

Similarly, in the social- and health-service fields there is a focus on numbers. The more clients or patients herded through the clinic on one day, the more health care is presumed to have been delivered. Never mind if the haste has caused misdiagnosis, or overlooked illness, or has dissuaded numerous people from ever returning to the clinic. On a quantitative basis, productivity is up.

What occurs when counting is used to indicate quality is very ironic, the opposite of what is intended, for quality is reduced. If you are trying to deliver *good* education, or *good* medicine, then relying on counting is a likely way to fail. What is quality? It is a totality, and to reduce it to particular measures is to do just that, reduce it. There is no quantitative shortcut to the production of quality. It can only be achieved by supporting those attitudes and values in the service worker that are consistent with quality. It is a matter of encouraging the higher as against the lower.

How do people in positions of leadership do this? By developing those very attitudes and values in themselves. There is no other way. In somewhat less pointed words, quality results from establishing the proper social and attitudinal context.

The use of output indexing to enhance quality is so self-defeating because it produces insecurity. Anytime a specific target measure of production is created, all effort and apprehension centers around the attainment and failure to attain that particular target. As we have seen from our examination of Maslow's hierarchy of needs, when insecurity is high the emergence of the higher needs (values) is blocked. Quality work comes out of the conditions of security; it is not a product of the stick and the carrot. Quality depends on sensitivity, wholeness, peace of mind, all of which are generally incompatible with the attempt to achieve a quantitative goal. It is not a result of coercion, even if subtle, but a result of the process of self-actualization, a process which is nurtured by economic and emotional security.

These matters become increasingly important as more and more jobs are developed in the non-material, or service, areas. A mistaken application of quantitative concepts of productivity here will hamper quality output, and quality is precisely what is wanted. If a service of low quality has been delivered in education or health, has that service been delivered? A low-quality service may essentially be a non-service.

This is not to imply that these same kinds of considerations should be ignored in the industrial field, but they are best addressed here by the issue of industrial democracy or self-management. When these practices are more fully instituted in industry, then the matter of quality will inevitably assume its proper place. A worker who has charge of his or her own work naturally, through the process of growth, wants that work to be of the highest quality.

Time to Be For those people who, as a result of the pervasive conditioning of our materialistic culture, tend to equate social development with material growth, the following statement by two economists connected with the *Limits to Growth* study may be enlightening:

> ☐ The presence of global equilibrium (an actual steady state) could permit the development of an unprecedented golden age for humanity. Freedom from the pressures of people who would make it impossible to put substantial effort into the self-realization and development of the individual. Instead of struggling merely to keep people alive, we could employ more of our energy in developing human culture, in increasing the quality of life for the individual far above the present subsistence. The few periods of equilibrium in the past—for example, the 300 years of Japan's classical period—often witnessed a profound flowering of the arts. The freedom from ever-increasing capital—i.e., from more concrete, cars, dams, and skyscrapers—would make it possible for even our great grandchildren to enjoy solitude and silence.[6]

And it need not only be solitude and silence, although these are welcome. The point is that this kind of economy would provide leisure, something that has been in scarce supply ever since the industrial age has been upon us. Leisure provides us with what can be translated into freedom to create: to write, to paint, to play music, to make crafts, etc.; to be with friends, to spend time with children and family; or to do any of the other myriad things that make life worth living, including being in solitude and silence.

In the most concrete terms then, the activities that the humanistic economy promotes are, consequently, time-intensive rather than goods-intensive. In this kind of economy the popular statement that "time is money" will lose much of its persuasiveness. It is an economy that pays heed to the famous words of Wordsworth:

> The world is too much with us; late and soon,
> Getting and spending, we lay waste our powers.

Along with the support for quality in work, and the encouragement of self-management, the humanistic economy has the goal of making time more available.

As we have pointed out, growth in the humanistic sense is growth of the person, not the growth of things. Neoclassical, mainstream economics has concentrated on the growth of things and assumed this to be congruent, or at least consistent, with the growth of people. This was a mistaken assumption.

The great and beautiful answer to the problem of rapidly dwindling resources is to direct growth along the lines of human development, not further material development. The accomplishment of this redirection is a two-sided task. The one side is the support of those activities and values that are self-actualizing, which we have just alluded to in our discussion of quality. This must also include a new commitment to the issue of meeting basic needs, and justice in income distribution. We have tried to show in Chapter 10 that the development of an adequate welfare system and the notion of quality are consistent with each other, not contradictory as held by conventional wisdom.

The other side of the task concerns itself with the proper way to limit and control the use of resources, and it is to this that we now turn. Taking as an objective the task of imposing limits on growth is almost a complete reversal of the way economics has been accustomed to looking at things. Kenneth Boulding's statement summarizes the new situation:

> ☐ The essential measure of the success of the economy is not production and consumption at all, but the nature, extent, quality, and complexity of the total capital stock, including in this the state of the human bodies and minds included in the system. In the spaceman economy, what we are primarily concerned with is stock maintenance, and any technological change which results in the maintenance of a given total stock with a lessened throughput (that is, less production and consumption) is clearly a gain. The idea that both production and consumption are bad things rather than goods things is very strange to economists, who have been obsessed with the income-flow concepts to the exclusion, almost, of capital-stock concepts.[7]

The problem of maintaining a given total stock, or low throughput, is most easily and humanistically solved in an economy that is organized along relatively small, socially cooperative communities, as in the case of the Tanzanian *Ujamma* or the Israeli Kibbutz. In a developed, highly industrialized economy this is a much more difficult task, since these economies have been founded on the growth principle. Their productive and consumptive styles are based on growth.

The task of humanistically operating within environmental limits in the developed economies involves striking the right balance between central direction and peripheral or individual decision-making. In other words, this is the balance between public and private policy, or the macro and micro levels of the economy. Errors can be made on either side of the balance. We generally hold up the Soviet Union, and related command-type economies, as erring on the side of central direction, and we can just as easily look at the United States and other laissez-faire type economies as erring on the side of peripheral decision-making. Both kinds of economies have so far failed to come to grips with the task of developing a constant-stock, or steady-state, economy. Both economies, command and laissez-faire, are dedicatedly materialistic.

What kind of approach can meet this challenge, and strike the right balance between public and private decision-making? We are drawn to the approach described by the humanistic economist, Herman Daly, who has devoted considerable attention to the problems of growth, resource depletion, and pollution. In the following section we will sketch out Daly's solution.

The Conservation of Nonrenewable Resources: Quota Rights

Let us begin by quoting Daly's own description of the system:

☐ Let quotas be set on new depletion of each of the basic resources, both renewable and nonrenewable, during a given time. The legal right to deplete to the amount of the quota for each resource would be auctioned off by the government at the beginning of each time period in conveniently divisible units, to private firms, individuals, and public enterprises. After purchase from the government the quota rights would be freely transferable by sale or gift. As population growth and economic growth press against resources, the prices of the depletion quotas would be driven higher and higher. In the interests of conserving non-renewable resources and optimal exploitation of renewable resources, quotas could then be reduced to lower levels, thereby driving the price of the quotas still higher. In this way, the increasing windfall rents resulting from increasing pressure of demand on a fixed supply would be collected by the government through the auctioning of the depletion rights. The government spends the revenues, let us say, by paying a social dividend. Even though the monetary flow is therefore undiminished, the real flow has been physically limited by the resource quotas. All prices of resources and of goods then increase, the prices of resource-intensive goods relatively more, and total resource consumption (depletion) is reduced. Moreover, in accordance with the law of conservation of matter-energy, reduction of initial inputs will result in reduction of ultimate outputs (pollution), reducing the aggregate throughput and with it the stress it puts on the ecosystem.[8]

In Chapter 6 we discussed the problem of controlling ecological damage, and mentioned the use of pollution taxes as one way to do this (by internalizing the externalities of production). Daly's approach differs from this method in two ways that make it more direct and effective. First, Daly's approach is directed towards resource depletion, the input side of production, rather than the output end, which is pollution. Secondly, it sets *definite limits* on resource use, rather than relying on taxation. Daly's method, which can be called *depletion quotas*, can be used along with pollution taxes, if that seems desirable.

The depletion quota method imposes straightforward objective constraints on resources, and does not attempt to manipulate people's preferences through taxation or moral exhortation. These constraints provide the stability which a steady-state economy is based upon. Within these constraints a free-market pricing system could be allowed to function with individuals pursuing what they consider to be their own interest.

Since the function of the "auctioneer" for the resource market is mechanical, the whole process could be computed and should be simple and less manipulatable than the stock market. In a sense, this system would be a more basic stock market. What it does is create another market system, one that has considerable social merit. Daly envisions quota auctions which complement the ordinary market established by owners of resources. So, in order to use resource one needs *both* a quota right *and* ownership of the resources. Ownership in itself is not sufficient. Conversely, if one owned a quota right, but no resources, then one would have to buy the resources from an owner. Also, differences in quality and location of resources within the same general category of resource, though ignored at the level of the quota right market, will be reflected in price differences at the level of purchasing.

In addition to what has already been said, Daly's proposal accomplishes several desirable objectives:

1. Social decisions, based on scientific information and democratic decision, will determine the rate of depletion, and not the market itself. By our preponderant reliance on the invisible hand of the market to limit resource overuse we have been increasingly kicked ·by what Daly calls "the invisible foot" of pollution and resource scarcity.

2. With depletion made more expensive, recycling and recycling technology will become more profitable, and the more recycling, the less pollution. Here the market should work very effectively.

3. As resources are exhausted, the quotas for depletion approach zero, and recycling becomes the only source of the resource. This lends even greater incentive to recycling technology (and *efficient* technology, like the gasoline-free car).

4. Quotas for renewable and well-managed resources could be suspended.

As Daly says about his proposal: "such a policy may seem radical, but it is much less radical than attempting the impossible, which is to grow forever."[9]

Population Control

What about the issue of population control in a steady-state economy? Certainly population is one of the critical variables in being able to maintain a steady-state economy. With a growing population, resource use would have to expand. Here we part company with Daly's approach, which is based on an idea first proposed by Kenneth Boulding, in this case a proposal to once again rely on the market mechanism for solution. It involves the issuing of a certificate to each citizen to have children, say, 1.1 per person or 2.2 per couple. This certificate or a portion of it can be sold on a market by those who don't want children to those who do. Although his scheme is intriguing and challenging, from a humanistic perspective its essence appears too questionable for promotion. Instead of advocating any such kind of social policy, we leave the issue open, but not without noting that recent demographic research suggests that the meeting of basic social needs tends to go a long way towards solving the population problem. Here are several statements from a recent report:

☐ The historical record indicates that birth rates do not decline very far unless certain social needs are satisfied. Birth rates do not usually decline voluntarily in the absence of an assured food supply, literacy, and at least rudimentary health services . . .

Demographers have long known that with sufficient economic progress, as in Europe and North America, high birth rates fall sharply. Demographers also have generally recognized that widespread poverty tends to sustain high birth rates for the obvious reason that families living without adequate employment, education, or health care have little security for the future except for reliance on their children . . .

There is increasing evidence that the very strategies which cause the greatest improvement in the welfare of the entire population also have the greatest effect on reducing population growth . . .[10]

Democracy and the Steady State

We see the limits to growth as a physical reality, and the issue is whether or not a society will respond humanistically to the challenge of this reality. In this chapter we have pointed out that a humanistic perspective enables us to see physical limits as an opportunity for self-actualization rather than as a barrier to "progress." We have described some of the principles and some of the systems, such as Daly's, that meet the challenge of the steady state in this way. They show what is possible.

Whether these possibilities are actually put into practice is largely a political question. As Heilbroner and others have pointed out, the limits to growth can also be met in authoritarian ways, and the prospects for this are quite strong.[11] Note that the authoritarian solution is the *traditional* solution to scarcity; the strong get and the weak don't. This solution can be implemented regardless of the outward political form. The way this works in our society is that large economic interests exert their influence on the legislative process. For quite a long time the existence of a legislative process may cloak the fact that the democratic interests of a society are not being met.

The humanistic solution to economic problems is fundamentally a democratic solution. If real democracy is thwarted then humanistic economics won't be put into practice; it can only come about through the evolution of democratic institutions. Does governmental action lead to greater equality or greater inequality? This question applies both in conditions of physical growth or steady state. It is just that the pinch of inequality probably hurts more in the steady state. A pinch within the steady state tends to be a steady pinch.

References

1. Oka, Takasi. "Japan's Search for the Millenium." In *Christian Science Monitor*, September 20, 1977.

2. In Heilbroner, Robert L. *Business Civilization in Decline*. New York: W. W. Norton, 1976, pp. 103–104.

3. Hirsch, Fred. *Social Limits to Growth*. Cambridge: Harvard University Press, 1976.

4. Schumacher, E. F. *Small Is Beautiful*. Perennial Library Edition. New York: Harper and Row, 1973, pp. 29–30.

5. Hirsch, Fred. *Social Limits to Growth*. Cambridge: Harvard University Press, 1976, pp. 129–130.

6. Randers, Jorgen and Meadows, Donella. Cited in *Toward a Steady-State Economy*, edited by Herman E. Daly, San Francisco: W. H. Freeman, 1973, p. 127.

7. Randers, Jorgen and Meadows, Donella. Cited in *Toward a Steady-State Economy*, edited by Herman E. Daly, San Francisco: W. H. Freeman, 1973, p. 127.

8. Randers, Jorgen and Meadows, Donella. Cited in *Toward a Steady-State Economy*, edited by Herman E. Daly, San Francisco: W. H. Freeman, 1973, pp. 160–161.

9. Randers, Jorgen and Meadows, Donella. Cited in *Toward a Steady-State Economy*, edited by Herman E. Daly, San Francisco: W. H. Freeman, 1973, p. 163.

10. Brown, Lester R. *In the Human Interest*. New York: W. W. Norton, 1974, Ch. 9, pp. 112–14.

11. Heilbroner, Robert L. *An Inquiry into the Human Prospect*. New York: W. W. Norton, 1974.

Chapter Sixteen

A FINAL WORD

INTRODUCTION: THE ECONOMIC PROBLEM, YESTERDAY AND
TOMORROW

Let us return to values, the concern with which we began this book,
and the concern that is central to humanistic economics. We have seen
that mainstream economics, neoclassicism, has fostered the view that
economics is a value-free science, very much like physics. But in
reviewing the history of economics we can see that each age viewed
and defined the Economic Problem through the lenses of its values,
and that these values were too often the lowest ones in the human
hierarchy of values.

In Smith and Ricardo's day the economic problem was the problem of production, how to transform the ample available resources into
material wealth. Towards this purpose Smith and his followers relied
on the concept of the invisible hand; they said, in effect, "Let us not be
concerned with the issues of morality and justice *in our economies*,
because if each person pursues their own self-interest the public good
will ultimately be served." However there was another side to Smith's
argument, which was that he assumed moral concerns and sentiments
to be the protective and guiding social framework within which material self-interests were allowed to operate. This assumption of an
existing moral framework was appropriate for the times. Capitalism, in
its infancy, had inherited substantially intact the whole structure of
trust and fairness that was the code of feudal (pre-capitalist, pre-
industrial) life. There is consensus that early industrialism was embed-
ded in the overriding religious framework of the Northern European
Protestant Reformation. But this situation did not endure.

Economic Integration and
Social Disintegration

What Adam Smith did not foresee two centuries ago was that the implementation of his economic proposals, such as increasing the division of labor and enabling ever-widening markets, would lead to moral decay which threatens to destroy the very framework of the marketplace itself. In brief, Adam Smith was assuming a peaceful coexistence of two seemingly complementary social forces, self-interest and moral sentiments, yet history suggests that the former will gradually eliminate the latter, if given free rein. To use an analogy, it seems that there is a Gresham's Law in socioeconomic relations, as well as in the circulation of coins. Gresham's Law is an old economic axiom that states that bad money (e.g., coins of low silver content) will tend to drive good money (e.g., coins of high silver content) out of the market. The law apparently applies to the social side of economics as well; low economic values tend to drive higher economic values out of circulation.

In feudal days, whatever the drawbacks, people did know their neighbors. Moreover, they knew the people with whom they exchanged goods. Economic exchange was guided primarily by considering the basic human needs of the community. People knew each other and cared for each other. The use of money played a peripheral role, at best. During the "economic revolution," markets started to replace traditional barter and money started to circulate and become an important commodity in its own right. Yet in these early days of capitalism people still had a feeling of community. When buying bread at the baker's, the exchange was not merely economic but also social. Imagine in these days, a small-town father, rushing to the bakery to get some bread for the next day's breakfast, but discovering that the bakery had closed early that afternoon. We would expect that the initial feeling of disappointment and frustration could be to a large extent mitigated by finding out that the baker had taken a much-needed afternoon off to spend with his family in leisure. Now compare this situation with a modern supermarket or a bank that closes twenty-five seconds ahead of the actual closing time. We are furious; there is absolutely no consideration for the staff inside, and neither do they really care about the angry customer outside. People don't matter because in the marketplace they no longer know who they are dealing with.

Ever since increasing mass production has destroyed the traditional local economy, markets have grown in scope and size. Today we are on the threshold of an integrated world economy. We can expect an economic system of even greater complexity and integration in the near future. And indeed we are told by authorities that this is going to be good for us.

Yet, such an "evolution" will move people even more into the background. Interpersonal relations will give way even more to relations between things. We don't know who produces what.* The market is silent, it does not care, and neither can we. All we do know and care about is the nature of the commodity and its price. People become means, and commodities, new ends. Humanistic social values give way to pecuniary calculation and materialism. Clearly human welfare is at a low point. The Smithian hand of the marketplace has led us anywhere but to self-actualization and social harmony.

The trend is continuing. Marketization of society now is chewing away on the last human-need-oriented economy: the nuclear family. Increasingly, either involuntarily or by choice, family members follow job opportunities and careers incompatible with the social values of belongingness, loyalty and family stability.

We have to keep in mind that marketization and materialism are two sides of the same coin. Both cater to the want for things or the lust for power rather than the need for interpersonal relationships. And society becomes increasingly atomistic.

This moral and social decay cannot go on forever. Ironically, the market needs a moral framework to function properly. In the words of the late Fred Hirsch, social and moral norms "are needed not for the optimistic objective of attaining some wholly good or fully rational society, but for the more modest and limited purpose of maintaining some key under-pinnings of our existing contractual, market society."[1] By eroding higher human need satisfaction, the market increasingly becomes the victim of self-inflicted wounds. With the social and moral framework eroded and defunct, rules and regulations are necessary to ensure the working of the system, and more and more rules to enforce those rules, so that we arrive at the present point where so much of society is encased in huge bureaucratic frameworks. Modern business today is more and more the process of making and enforcing contracts and subcontracts. Anybody who visits the headquarters of a large corporation will be overwhelmed by the presence of lawyers everywhere.

Moreover, rules and regulations cost money, above all tax dollars. Yet it is precisely taxes that members of an increasingly materialistic and atomistic society are more and more reluctant to pay. As a result, individual self-interest, originally seen as freeing an economy from feudal constraints, not only eventually succeeds in stitching together its own kind of straightjacket, but is progressively cutting its own throat as well.

---

*Take the example of coffee and assume that for idealistic reasons you would not mind paying an additional dime for a cup of coffee if this would help the development of the people of Tanzania. But how do we know? The market is not likely to tell us anything more than price in terms of dollars and cents. My "moral sentiment" instead may enrich a Rhodesian absentee landowner or a Brazilian trader. Even if it goes to Tanzania, is it really going to be spent in a humanistic way?

Towards a Reformulation of the
Economic Problem

In the second half of the 1800s in England the Economic Problem changed. There was increasing concern that they would run out of coal, and that continual and unlimited growth would come to an end. It was at this time that Jevons defined economics as the science of the allocation of scarce resources. Thus, the problems of distribution and consumption rose to the forefront. Earlier, Mill envisioned what he called a stationary-state economy, and thus he was one of the first who accepted, even welcomed, such an economic goal. Let us refer to the famous quote by Mill, in order to demonstrate how remarkably pertinent and relatively humanistic his analysis was:

> ☐ It must always have been seen, more or less distinctly, by political economists, that the increase in wealth is not boundless: that at the end of what they term the progressive state lies the stationary state, that all progress in wealth is but a postponement of this, and that each step in advance is an approach to it . . . if we have not reached it long ago, it is because the goal itself flies before us (as a result of technical progress).
>
> I cannot . . . regard the stationary state of capital and wealth with the unaffected aversion so generally manifested towards it by political economists of the old school. I am inclined to believe that it would be, on the whole, a very considerable improvement on our present condition. I confess I am not charmed with the ideal of life held out by those who think that the normal state of human beings is that of struggling to get on; that the trampling, crushing, elbowing, and treading on each other's heels which form the existing type of social life, are the most desirable lot of human kind, or anything but the disagreeable symptoms of one of the phases of industrial progress. The northern and middle states of America are a specimen of this stage of civilization in very favorable circumstances; . . . and all that these advantages seem to have yet done for them (notwithstanding some incipient signs of a better tendency) is that the life of the whole of one sex is devoted to dollar-hunting, and of the other to breeding dollar-hunters.[2]

These perceptions and prescriptions of Mill were avoided by the discovery and use of a new energy supply, oil. Growth would go on after all, unimpeded, and the problems of distribution and consumption need not be faced.

But now, in the late 1900s, all our petrochemical resources are running short, as well as numerous other resources, and we find ourselves back almost at the same point as the far-sighted Mill. The technological optimists, such as our Japanese official of the last chapter, expect that, just as in the late 1800s, a new energy source will come forth. Many expect it to be nuclear power. However, by this time we should be able to see how shortsighted such a hope is, regardless of which side of the nuclear safety issue one falls on. No, oil gave the economies of the world (or, the world economy) a reprieve; it did not say you can always expect such largess. Today, amidst our increasingly strained social and physical ecology, we must look back in Mill's direction for the road that carries us to a rational future. The economic problem for the foreseeable future now becomes the attainment of a controlled-growth, or steady-state economy.

What this brief historical survey shows us is that at each stage of formulating the economic problem the ignoring of the higher human values has led us into trouble. The big push towards development did not bring us the promised social harmony, and furthermore, the vanishing moral foundation of human society has demanded that an increasingly complex, stifling, and inhumane system of rules and regulations be put in its place. Through the same ignorance we have developed an economy with an insatiable mouth that threatens to eat away the thin mineral crust of the earth's surface out from under us. It is thus folly to separate the Economic Problem from the human problem, as if we can have separate means without consideration of the ends. At all points and at all times the approach to an economic question must be undertaken in the light of the ultimate purposes of human life, the *summum bonum* of classical Greek philosophy, or *self-actualization* in the language of contemporary humanistic psychology. What this means to the steady-state economy is that the problem of economic justice must be explicitly taken as part of the economic problem. We have seen that reliance on the market by itself will not only solve this, but also most likely will make it worse.

The Goal of a New
Humanistic Economics

The needs of our times, both in practical socio-economic matters and in terms of theory, call for a more generous definition of our science. We need a new economic vision that does not limit itself to observing and explaining market behavior or to theoretical speculations about how to best satisfy a society composed of bloodless Economic Men. What we need, instead, is a science that treats people as holistic individuals with a structure of basic needs and an inborn potential to grow towards higher levels of being and more fulfilled lives. Injecting life into the mechanistic core of economics is a challenging and desperately needed task; it is the challenge of humanizing economics.

As social scientists we can no longer afford to ignore the social context when analyzing the behavior of atomistic individuals. This implies a need to introduce values, or the question of ethics. What good is a social science if it does not enable us to find a better society, a more preferable quality of life for everybody?

But let us not be misunderstood. Economic Man and his world of market mechanics is not so much wrong as it is too limited. We are not asking for a revolutionary overthrow of the present scientific edifice. Rather we aim to reconstruct the science towards a greater inclusiveness. Economic Man would still have his corner, but no longer occupy the entire stage. In a humanistic economics of the type we propose, much of the conventional theory would appear as a special case, a special case where individuals are inherently insecure and "locked into" the material world of the jungle fighter. But there is nothing intrinsically "natural" or human about such a human nature. It can be changed and should be changed. One must choose either the role of an apologist for materialism and ever worsening social decay on the one hand, or that of a promoter for a better world on the other.

In short, we have been sounding the trumpet for a new welfare economics, where "welfare" does not mean simpleminded material abundance but human well-being.

Psychology, for the most part, contradicts the economists' notion of "given" individual tastes and preferences. But things don't stop there. It's time to go deeper and to tackle the question of *how* individual preferences are formed and influenced by social variables and economic institutions. Similarly, our institutional framework, enabling and guiding economic activity, cannot be taken as a "given"; it interacts with individual preferences in a constant mutual interplay at all times. Humanistic economics seeks to study that interaction from a critical perspective in seeking not only to understand it but to guide it as well.

And it is worth repeating that the values we employ in the process are not arbitrarily chosen and imposed, but are dictated by the human organism striving for wholeness as well as observed by humanistic psychology.

By way of conclusion, humanistic economics sets out to dynamize rather than dynamite the mechanistic core of science, to supplement it rather than supplant it. This is the essence of humanistic economics, and it is by no means something radically new that we claim to have discovered. There have been most eloquent humanistic protests and admonitions going back as far as 1819, when the Swiss Count Jean Charles Leonard Simonde de Sismondi formulated his *New Principle of Political Economy*. But the masters of orthodoxy have always felt uncomfortable with the humanistic critique and preferred to pretend that it did not exist. Not surprisingly, Sismondi is one of the few economists whose principal work has never been translated into English. The alternative economic constructs of John Ruskin and John H. Hobson were also ignored by economics, even though they were written in English. And today the situation is no different with Schumacher's *Small Is Beautiful*. Yet, one most important variable is different this time. People have read Schumacher's economics in spite of the economists. In fact, *Small Is Beautiful* has turned out to be a veritable bestseller; as such it probably is the first humanistic economic book that has passed the cherished test of the academic economist, the test of the marketplace. Schumacher seems to have struck a sensitive chord, a silent force that is ready for action. After two hundred years of the (increasingly musty) economics of the traditional kind, after almost a century of being blessed with the stale welfare criterion of Vilfredo Pareto, we believe that we are ready for change. It would be tragic if our foremost scientists did not get the message.

It's time to wrap things up, but not before entering a final plea to the reader. If you are among the many who have approached economics with many hopes, *don't give up!* Economics can be something more than market mechanics. Everywhere around the country there are literally hundreds of economists busily involved in humanizing the science. Since the Second World War, at least three rival professional associations have sprung up and are challenging the long-established American Economic Association. They are the Association for Social Economics, the Association for Evolutionary Economics, and the Union of Radical Political Economics.* It is through these new associations that humanist thought gets a fair hearing and through which humanistic economics can gather strength and inspiration. But among the three it is primarily social economics that appears most intimately concerned with, if not directed by, human values.

Now that the organizational foundations have been laid, let us not waste the opportunity to actively engage in the challenging task of enlarging the economic house in which we live. Stand up and be counted among those who are willing to work for what the Great Seal of the United States refers to as NOVUS ORDO SECULORUM, a new world order!

References

1. Hirsch, Fred. *Social Limits to Growth*. Cambridge, Mass.: Harvard University Press, 1976, p. 141.

2. Mill, J. S. *Principles of Political Economy*. New York: Colonial Press, 1857, II, pp. 320–26.

---

*All three associations hold annual meetings and publish their own journals, the *Journal of Social Economy*, the *Journal of Economic Issues*, and the *Review of Radical Political Economy*, respectively.

APPENDIX ONE

QUASI-INDIFFERENCE CURVES AND LEXICOGRAPHIC ORDERS: A GRAPHICAL EXPOSITION

INTRODUCTION

We would like to introduce the interested reader to some of the most important implications of a need-based economics on the geometric analysis of choice. Figure 3-1 showed a typical utility-based indifference curve as pictured in all microeconomics textbooks. We argued in Chapter 3 that such a curve is based on the assumption of a "reducibility of wants," or the "one-dimensional" want for utility.

If, on the other hand, we assume, along with Georgescu-Roegen, irreducibility of needs, the basic principle of indifference evaporates, and with it the indifference curve. In its place we have to put something else, a geometrical construct which has been labeled *behavioral curve* or *quasi-indifference curve*. This brings us into the realm of what goes under the heading of *lexicographic orderings*, a subject that has tended to be totally out of reach of anybody not well-versed in set-theory mathematics. Yet lexicographical orderings and quasi-indifference curves are precisely what may be called the analytical foundation of humanistic economics.

To convey a general idea of what is involved, we must embark on a brief journey through graphical economics. The reader already trained in microeconomics will appreciate the difference in geometry between utility or preference analysis and human need economics.*

---

*Much of this appendix is taken from N. Georgescu-Roegen's 1954 article, "Choice, Expectations and Measurability." *Quarterly Journal of Economics*, 68 (1954): 503–34.

QUASI-INDIFFERENCE CURVES

A simple illustration of a quasi-indifference curve is given in Figure A-1. The graph shows the preferences of a beer fiend. When given the choice of beer or wine, he or she will always choose beer. The horizontal shape of the curve indicates that under no circumstances will he or she be willing to trade any beer for wine. In a sense wine and beer are not considered to be substitutes, just alternatives.

FIGURE A-1   A QUASI-INDIFFERENCE CURVE

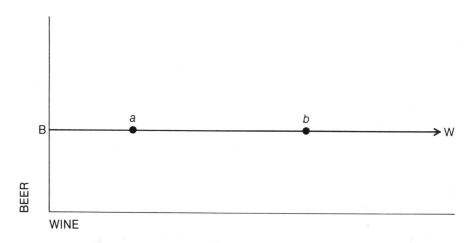

The curve resembles an ordinary indifference curve of a beer addict, but there is a key difference: If it were an ordinary indifference curve, the beer addict would have no use for wine. Specifically, he would be indifferent between having some wine (point a), or more wine (point b), given the amount of beer.

With the quasi-indifference curve, this is no longer true. Given a certain amount of beer (all he or she wishes to drink in a specific situation), *more* wine is now better than less. As a result, point b is preferred to point a. Or, more generally, all points on the horizontal curve are ordered, the more to the right, the better off the drinker is. It is this *lack of indifference* between a and b which annihilates the distinguishing quality of an indifference curve. On the other hand, we are still dealing with a *quasi*-indifference curve since it contains one important quality of a real indifference curve: Any point above it is clearly preferred to any point on it, and any point below it is clearly inferior to any point on it.

In essence, a quasi-indifference curve, such as the one in Figure A-1, is drawn with respect to a primary criteria, let us say maximization of beer consumption. But all points *on* the curve are ranked as "ordered" with respect to a secondary criteria, or less potent need (in our case, let us say the desire for a beverage of any kind).

As a result, all points in the graph are ordered by two or more criteria, or dimensions. This may be best illustrated by also drawing the curves or contour lines for the second criteria, for which, in Figure A-2, we enter the broken lines to distinguish them from the primary curves. It can now be seen that although points a and b lie on the same primary contour line BW, b does lie on a higher secondary contour line, thereby making our hypothetical consumer better off at b.

FIGURE A-2 A PRIMARY AND A SECONDARY ORDERING

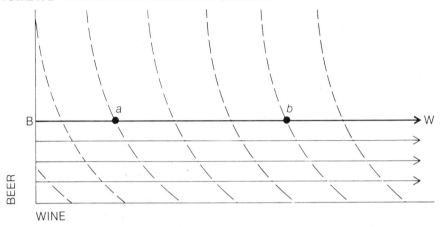

The broken contour lines would be regular indifference curves with respect to a secondary criteria like an alcoholic beverage only if there would be no other relevant criteria or needs. But the hierarchy of needs theory suggests that there is always another need which comes into play after the more urgent ones have been, at least in part, satisfied. If so, we could think of a third criteria like taste to become relevant and to "order" points on the broken lines accordingly. The broken contours would themselves now become quasi-indifference curves, implying a third map of contours, and so on.

With all this in mind let us look at an individual who is choosing between wine and beer. The individual has a certain hierarchical structure of needs (or a lexicographic ordering) which is going to affect his choice.

First, and most urgently, *thirst* is felt and has to be satisfied. Beer is assumed to be the preferred thirst-quencher.

Second in priority may be a *social* need. The individual is assumed to value wine as a more refined and socially acceptable way of drinking.

Third is the question of taste. Let us say that our individual happens to love the taste of beer; given his or her other needs, beer is preferred to wine on that aesthetic dimension.

Fourth, and least important, we assume here a concern for minimizing a potential hangover which might interfere with work the

| The corrected figure is shown below.

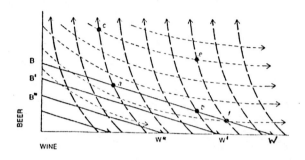

FIGURE A-3 CHOOSING BETWEEN BEER AND WINE

next morning. Excessive wine will be less harmful in this respect than excessive beer.

These various needs have been recognized in Figure A-3. The heavy lines represent the quasi-indifference curves of the first criteria: thirst. The thick broken contours represent the socially induced relative preference for wine. And the weakly drawn broken lines are the lexicographic curves ordering beer and wine according to the third criteria: taste.

We omitted the quasi-indifference map for hangover but implicitly recognized its relevance by marking the taste curves with an arrow favoring wine.

With little or nothing to drink, our individual considers beer to be (about three times) more satisfying in quenching his thirst. But, after any combination higher than *BW*, thirst no longer matters; instead our drinker is now primarily motivated by social or cultural habits and prefers wine. Above *BW* the strongly drawn broader contours now reflect the most important motivator. But in the back of the mind also lurks the less important consideration for taste, and so on.

Some Distinguishing Qualities of
Quasi-Indifference Curves

From a theoretical point of view, Figure A-3 illustrates two interesting characteristics of the quasi-indifference curves.

Until thirst is met at *BW*, the continuous lines *BW*, *B'W'* and *B''W''* are the relevant quasi-indifference curves. But above *BW* the heavy broken curves become the relevant ones. This implies that the combination of points *cabfW* now effectively becomes a quasi-indifference, but so does *efW*. Both of these curves, as well as the entire family of such curves, have a kink where they run into *BW*. At the same time, by running into *BW*, they all touch *BW and each other*.*

This illustrates two important distinguishing qualities of quasi-indifference curves. The first (i.e., existence of kinks) will make choice at times more insensitive to price changes. The second (i.e., they can touch) leads to the peculiar proposition that any point on a higher quasi-indifference curve may not be necessarily superior to another point on a lower curve. Such a possibility is pictured in Figure A-4, where *b* is preferred to *a*.

FIGURE A-4 A PROBLEM WITH QUASI-INDIFFERENCE CURVES

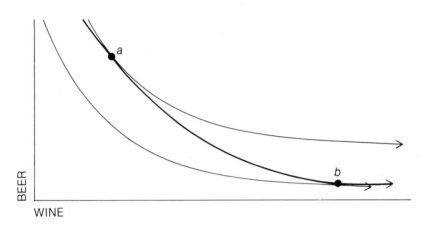

There are other peculiarities arising from the intrinsic nature of quasi-indifference curves, one of which may lead a "rational" to behave "irrationally" within a certain budget. He (or she) may behave "neurotically" by not choosing any single combination of goods. The proof is far too technical for our present exposition and purpose, but the interested reader can find it elsewhere.**

Unfortunately, mainstream economists have, not surprisingly, had a strong tendency to construct their analytical work on the assumption of the principle of indifference rather than on Georgescu-Roegen's principle of irreducibility of human needs. As a result, lexicographic orderings have been typically dealt with as a mathematical curiosity or as an instance of a helplessly lost addict of some

---

*On the other hand, quasi-indifference curves, just like regular indifference curves, cannot cut each other.

**See W. M. Gorman, "Preference, Revealed Preference and Indifference," (1955) reprinted in Chipman, John S. et al., *Preferences, Utility and Demand.* New York: Harcourt Brace Jovanovich, 1971, pp. 93–95.

sort. But lexicographic orderings are much more than that; they have to be seen as the most basic and the most relevant model of human choice and behavior. It should constitute a foremost challenge for the analytically inclined humanistic economist to develop this type of analysis further, and on a level that is more within the reach of the beginning economist.

APPENDIX TWO

HISTORY OF REVEALED PREFERENCE THEORY: A GUIDE TO THE PERPLEXED

The Revealed Preference Theory, developed by Samuelson in his famous "Note" in 1938 and further amended in 1950 by Houthakker, constitutes the climax in the search for a consumer theory liberated from any "vestigial traces of the utility concept."[1] As we mentioned in Chapter 3, this marks the entry of behaviorist psychology into economic theory, which permitted putting the law of demand on a scientific foundation without having to refer to utility maximization and such related concepts as marginal utility. Instead, all we need to do is to observe the consumer in his or her shopping behavior and from such observations (or "revealed" preferences) alone we are able to construct a preference function of the individual in question.

In this appendix we will briefly sketch the historical development of what was taken to be an analytical breakthrough and in the process indicate that the logic on which it is based is by no means as "pure" as most economists appear to take for granted. Once again, our story has been told in a more sophisticated form and long ago by Nicholas Georgescu-Roegen, and the interested reader is urged to consult his pertinent analysis directly.[2] The entire issue is so central to our critique

---

[1]Paul A. Samuelson. "A Note on the Pure Theory of Consumer's Behavior," *Economica*, N.S., V (1938). p. 62.

of Economic Man that we consider it worthwhile to reproduce a some-what diluted version here by which the more advanced student of economics may grasp the essence of the argument.

As demonstrated in the main text of our book, in the nineteenth century tradition, "utility" was the core concept of consumer behavior and welfare. It all began with Jeremy Bentham's "felicity calculus" but was soon incorporated in the work of Jevons and Walras, later to be refined by Marshall and expressed in more elegant mathematical form by Edgeworth. In a sense, Edgeworth is often regarded as the father of modern mathematical consumer analysis by first formulating the con-cept of a *utility function* in the now familiar form:

$$\text{Total Utility} = U = U\ (x_1, x_2 \ldots, x_n)$$

where the x's stand for the commodities that the consumer may pur-chase. With such a reformulation, Edgeworth was able to derive the familiar map of "indifference curves" (or better, iso-utility curves) which we encounter so frequently in the current textbooks in micro-economics.

Meanwhile, others attempted to arrive at the same concepts by avoiding Edgeworth's necessary assumption of treating utility as a cardinally measurable quantity. First attempts in this direction were made in Italy by Antonelli (1866), but his work was not understood even by his Italian contemporaries and has only recently been trans-lated into English.[3]

Much better known is Vilfredo Pareto's pioneering work on the subject. Instead of assuming measurable utility he chose to take con-sumer *choice*, or actual preference as the foundation of law of demand. All that was necessary was to simply ask the consumer what he or she liked when confronted with two commodities: "What do you prefer? Ten cherries and ten dates or nine dates and eleven cherries?"[4] Equip-ped with sufficient answers and certain assumptions, particularly tran-sitivity, we can construct the map of indifference curves by means of a mathematical procedure called "integration."[5]

However, the eminent mathematician Volterra was quick to point out that such a technique of integration typically only works in situa-tions of binary choice, and not for choice among three or more com-modities. Ever since, the question of how to assure integrability in the

---

[2]See for example: Nicholas Georgescu-Roegen: "Utility", *International Encyclopedia of the Social Sciences*, 17 vols., (New York, 1968), 16, 235–67, and (perhaps even more illuminating the core of the issue) the recent essay "Vilfredo Pareto and his Theory of Ophelimity" reprinted in Nicholas Georgescu-Roegen, *Energy and Economic Myths*, Pergamon Press Inc., New York, 1976, Ch. 13.

[3]See J. Chipman, L. Hurwicz, et al., eds. *Preferences, Utility, and Demand.* New York: Harcourt Brace Jovanovich, 1971, pp. 333–60.

[4]Pareto, quoted in Georgescu-Roegen. *Energy and Economic Myths*, Pergamon Press Inc., New York, 1976, p. 329.

(more general) situation of more than binary choice has preoccupied the minds of mathematical economists. It was felt that once this problem was solved, the way was cleared for a more elegant analytical basis of consumer choice no longer dependent on comparing utilities in constructing the fundamental "law of demand."

Samuelson, in his 1938 "Note" presented an alternative method of constructing a preference function in a purely behavioristic manner. Instead of questioning the consumer in a Pareto-type laboratory, all that was needed was to observe the consumer while shopping. Such "spying" alone would "reveal" the orders of preference in the real world of non-binary choices. Moreover, Samuelson claimed that in this new axiomatic approach, labeled *"The Weak Axiom of Revealed Preference,"* the issue of integrability was finally settled and no longer an obstacle to deriving a family of indifference curves.

Samuelson's *Weak Axiom of Revealed Preference* not only claimed to have settled the question of integrability but also had the great merit of making it possible to derive the convexity property indifference curves in a more persuasive and more transparent manner, which no longer necessitated the assumption of diminishing marginal rate of substitution. Furthermore, it promised to greatly facilitate the research methods necessary to obtain actual and honest preferences from an individual.

Yet, in spite of these undeniable merits, there remained a basic flaw. Two years before the Weak Axiom was first articulated, Georgescu-Roegen had already demonstrated that more integrability was not sufficient for constructing a preference index.[6] The problem is that we have to assume consistency in the preference field *before* attempting to arrive at indifference curves through revealed preference theory.

More specifically, Georgescu-Roegen had pointed to the possibility of so-called "spirals" and other "singularities" among integral lines which deny the alleged powers of Samuelson's axiom. A stronger axiom was needed.

In 1950 Houthakker put forward the *Strong Axiom of Revealed Preference* in order to eliminate Georgescu-Roegen's counter-example of

---

[5]To be more specific, the procedure is explained by Georgescu-Roegen as follows: "For the case of two commodities, by a mathematical operation called the integration of the linear elements we can construct a family of 'integral curves,' such that the tangent to any curve at any of its points is the linear element of that point." (Nicholas Georgescu-Roegen, "Utility," *International Encyclopedia of the Social Sciences*, 17 vols., (New York, 1968), 16, 256.

[6]N. Georgescu-Roegen, "The Pure Theory of Consumer's Behavior," *Quarterly Journal of Economics*, L. (1936), pp. 545–93.

[7]Paul Samuelson. "The Problem of Integrability in Utility Theory." *Economica* N.S., XVII (1950), p. 369.

asymptotic "spirals." The ground seemed finally cleared of all obstacles. The optimistic mood prevailing in the profession is well articulated in Samuelson's claim that Houthakker's contribution enables us "to complete the programme begun a dozen years ago of arriving at the full empirical implications for demand behavior of the most ordinal utility analysis."[7] Yet, the victory trumpet had been sounded too soon. A few years later, in 1954, Georgescu-Roegen proved that even the Strong Axiom is not sufficient to warrant the existence of a preference function.[8] The remaining snag is the singularity called "poles." It prevents us from assuming comparability among commodity baskets.[9]

But even if we succeed in axiomatically destroying all singularities, including poles, in a new "Strongest" axiom of revealed preference, one final—and insurmountable—barrier remains. Georgescu-Roegen recently proved that even in a world of no singularities, it will be impossible to regard the map of integral curves as reflecting preferences.[10] In essence, preference maps can be revealed only if they are *assumed* to exist in the first place. If we see a shadow, we cannot necessarily assume it reveals a tree without prior familiarity with a tree.

This is the Behaviorist paradox. In order to establish truth behavioristically one has to leave the behaviorist trails and *assume* that there is a preference map in people. Any procedure to get rid of metaphysical entities by showing the effects of metaphysical entities is contradictory and doomed to failure. Yet, the behaviorist's plight is the humanist's light.

[8]N. Georgescu-Roegen. "Choice and Revealed Preference." *Southern Economic Journal*, XXI, (1954) pp. 119–130, reprinted in *Analytical Economics*, Cambridge, Mass.: Harvard University Press, 1966, Ch. 4.

[9]A graphical explanation of poles and their effects on revealed preference can be found in N. Georgescu-Roegen, *Energy and Economic Myths*, Pergamon Press Inc., New York, 1976, p. 336–337.

[10]See N. Georgescu-Roegen, *Energy and Economic Myths*, Pergamon Press Inc., New York, 1976, pp. 344–346.

APPENDIX THREE

A READER'S GUIDE
TO THE LITERATURE

As we all know by now, humanistic economics is not a new field, quite the contrary. But as with Sleeping Beauty, it may have taken one hundred years or even more to be finally recognized.

Our book has attempted to introduce the reader to some of the key ingredients of humanistic economics. But we do not pretend to have fully uncovered the richness of ideas contained in this alternative economic vision, we encourage the interested student to go directly to the source. In order to facilitate such self-study, it may be well worthwhile to provide the novice with additional information on some of the available literature.

1. General Works. A good starting point, both easy and pleasurable reading, is E. F. Schumacher's *Small is Beautiful* (Harper and Row, New York, 1973). Slightly more demanding but perhaps more pleasing to the intellectually minded student are three books: Eugene Loebl's *Humanomics* (Random House, New York, 1976), Walter Weisskopf's little gem, *Alienation and Economics* (Dell Publ. Co., New York, 1973) and the Yugoslav Mihailo Markovic's *From Affluence to Praxis* (University of Michigan Press, Ann Arbor, 1974). For a more analytically oriented psychological approach we recommend Erich Fromm's classic masterpiece, *The Sane Society* (Holt, Rinehart and Winston, N.Y., 1955), as well as its revealing but challenging critique written by the Soviet Marxist V. I. Dobrenkov, *Neo-Freudians in Search of "Truth"* (Progress Publishers, Moscow, 1976).

Finally, the sophisticated student should attempt to read the more philosophical argument presented in Nicholas Georgescu-Roegen's,

The Entropy Law and the Economic Process (Harvard University Press, Cambridge, 1971). Understanding this book is not easy, but as a reward for having successfully completed the struggle, we promise instant illumination.

2. History of Humanistic Economics.   We assume the reader has some basic familiarity with the history of economics. Otherwise, an excellent introduction can be found by Robert L. Heilbroner, *The Worldly Philosophers* (Simon and Schuster, New York, 1972). Perhaps more to the point but somewhat more technical is Ray Canterbery's *The Making of Economics* (Wadsworth, Belmont, 1976).

Thomas More's *Utopia* (London, 1516) is one of the oldest and best books in the humanistic tradition (and perhaps even overall). Originally written in Latin, it is now available in numerous translations. We strongly recommend the translation by Paul Turner (Penguin Books, Baltimore, 1965). It is simply amazing how strongly the alternative Latin translation affects the readability of the book.

For the nineteenth century humanistic contributions the interested student should start with available material of J. C. Simonde de Sismondi. Most of his pioneering thought has not yet been translated into English, but many college libraries carry a collection of his writings: *Political Economy and the Philosophy of Government*, (1847, reprinted by A. M. Kelly, New York, 1966).

Karl Marx's early writings, particularly his *Economic and Philosophical Manuscripts of 1844* constitute a classic attempt to relate economic phenomenon to human needs. We recommend as a starting point Erich Fromm's *Marx's Concept of Man* (New York, 1961) which reprints and explains to the layman key paragraphs of the *Manuscripts.*

John Ruskin is well known for his brilliant command of the English language. A sample of his economics is provided by his *Unto This Last* (London, 1888). For a comprehensive and thoughtful evaluation of his economic work, the student should consult J. C. Sherbourne's *John Ruskin or the Ambiguity of Affluence* (Harvard University Press, Cambridge, 1972).

John Hobson published more than a dozen books, but especially two stand out: *Work and Welfare: A Human Valuation* (London, 1914), and his textbook *Economics and Ethics* (London, 1927). The latter is unfortunately extremely difficult to get a hold of. We also recommend his entertaining autobiography *Confessions of an Economic Heretic.* (Allen and Unwin, London, 1938).

Last but not least, any student of humanistic economics should read R. H. Tawney's classic, *The Acquisitive Society* (1920, now available in paperback by Harcourt, Brace, Jovanovich, New York, 1948). More than 50 years have passed since it was originally published, yet its message appears to be even more relevant today than it was back then.

3. Humanistic Methodology.   On a more general level, we recommend as two introducing books, M. Polanyi's *Personal Knowledge*

(University of Chicago Press, 1958) and A. Maslow's *The Psychology of Science* (Henry Regnery Company, Chicago, 1966). The student may also look up Abraham Maslow, editor, *New Knowledge in Human Values* (Henry Regnery Company, Chicago, 1959).

For an eloquent and highly illuminating survey about the rise of a humanist perspective in psychology and social science, as well as a review of the developments in modern physics, the student should read F. Matson, *The Broken Image* (George Braziller, New York, 1964).

Finally, a general and philosophical critique of logical positivism can be found in the recent book by W. Barrett, *The Illusion of Technique* (Anchor Press, New York, 1978).

4. Humanistic Economic Policy: Industrial Economies. Little work has been published on systematically relating modern policy issues to human values. One exception is Sidney Hook, editor, *Human Values and Economic Policy* (New York University Press, New York, 1967), but the book assumes some background in economic theory.

In contrast, there are innumerable books on poverty and security. Yet, probably still the most stimulating work on the subject is J. K. Galbraith's bestseller, *The Affluent Society* (Signet, New York, 1970).

The literature on the quality of jobs and organization of work also abounds and stretches far beyond the boundaries of conventional economics. We recommend the study edited by James O'Toole, *Work in America* (MIT Press, Boston, 1973), for an excellent summary of studies in the field.

The developments abroad in industrial democracy are surveyed in a book edited by Solomon Barkin, *Worker Militancy and Its Consequences, 1965–1975* (Praeger, New York, 1975). For an eloquent argument for worker management we recommend J. Vanek, *The Participatory Economy* (Cornell University Press, Ithaca, 1971).

The issues of competition and welfare are reconsidered in Fred Hirsch's *Social Limits to Growth* (Harvard University Press, Cambridge, 1976), and Tibor Scitovsky's new book, *The Joyless Economy* (Oxford, New York, 1977), the latter approaching the subject by means of more conventional psychology. For a thought-provoking neo-marxian analysis on the subject the reader should turn to P. Baran and P. Sweezy, *Monopoly Capital* (Monthly Review Press, New York, 1954).

In our book we have not emphasized the highest virtue of socioeconomic organization: justice. Instead we have implicitly equated a just economy with a fully humanized one. Yet, the student interested in a direct discussion of the concept should turn to John Rawls' *Theory of Justice* (Harvard University Press, Cambridge, 1971) as well as to the helpful and critical commentary by R. P. Wolff, *Understanding Rawls,* (Princeton University Press, Princeton, 1977). For a more inclusive treatment of justice see also the excellent new book by David L. Miller, *Social Justice,* (Calendron Press, Oxford, 1976).

5. Humanistic Economic Policy: Third World. The Interna-

tional Labor Office has published an excellent survey of the situation and some of the political remedies in *Employment, Growth and Basic Needs: A One World Problem* (Praeger, New York, 1977). Gunnar Myrdal has devoted much of his work to analyzing this crucial problem. Among his books on the subject we recommend most *The Challenge of World Poverty* (Random House, New York, 1971).

We also point to the many books by Tanzania's president, Julius Nyerere, of which his *Man and Development* (Oxford University Press, New York, 1974) provides a representative but brief sample.

Finally, the interested student may want to consult Michael Harrington's new book: *The Vast Majority* (Simon & Schuster, New York, 1977).

6. The Future of the World from a Humanistic Perspective. No survey on humanistic economics would be complete without referring to the work of H. Daly. His recent book, *Steady-State Economics* (Freeman and Company, San Francisco, 1977), is a nontechnical and beautiful attempt to explore our alternative futures.

Any student who has read and digested most of the material listed here is ready for the Big One: Rene Guenon's *The Reign of Quantity and the Signs of the Times*, (Penguin Books, Baltimore, 1972). You'll see why.

Index

France
  and restructuring of jobs,
    223, 224
  and work councils, 234
Fraser, Douglas, 241
Free trade
  and corruption, 120–122
  and Pareto Optimum, 92, 93
  and victims, 98, 99
Freedom in economics, 127–139
  and choice, 135–137
  and government, 133–135
Frei, H., 220
Freudian psychology, 6, 7
Frictional unemployment, 184
Friedman, Milton, 60, 67, 73, 88,
    128–130, 133–135, 137, 318
Fringe benefits, 217, 218
Fromm, Erich, 5, 35, 79, 328
Full employment
  and competitive wage theory,
    151, 152
  Keynesian policies, 183, 184
  and minimum wage, 188
  and poverty, 181–189

Galbraith, John Kenneth,
    112–123, 130, 186, 255, 267,
    268, 329
Gambs, John S., 15, 24
Gandhi, Mahatma, 40, 51, 52,
    280–282, 287, 290, 291
Garson, G. D., 236
General case, 70
General Foods Corporation,
    238, 239
Georgescu-Roegen, N., 51, 59,
    66, 68, 73, 89, 163, 317–323,
    325, 326, 328
Gift giving, 81
GNP
  among advanced economies,
    215–217
  of China, 292
  and freedom, 137
  and happiness, 94, 95
  and marginal utility, 84
  and Pareto Optimum, 161
  and social services, 199
  in Tanzania, 288
  taxes and social security
    contributions as percentage
    of, 207
  for underdeveloped countries,
    271, 273, 274
Gordon, David, 177
Gorman, W. M., 321
Government
  big government concepts, 168
  and freedom, 133–135, 138
Graves, maintenance of, 206
Great Britain. See England

Great Depression and welfare
    system, 194
Greeks and economics, 26
Greenberg, 211
Gresham's Law, 310
Greznutzen, 44, 45
Gross National Product. *See* GNP
Grossman, Gregory, 258
Growth limits, 297–308
Guénon, René, 20, 24, 330
Gurley, John, 276
Gyllenhammar, Pehr, 222, 223

Hamilton, Alexander, 132
Happiness capacity, 84, 85
  and GNP, 94, 95
  Robbins on, 85–87
Harman, Willis, 152
Harrod, Roy, 85, 86, 91, 101,
    128, 163
Hart, Phillip, 266
Hartlib, Samuel, 180
Having-oriented rationality, 79
Hawthorne experiment, 227
Health care, 196, 201–203
  and individual expense
    sharing, 202
  and national insurance,
    202, 211
  and sickness cash benefits, 203
Hegel, George, 34, 146
Heilbroner, Robert, 29, 307, 328
Heisenberg, Werner, 8, 24
Helco, Hugh, 220
Heyne, Hall, 24
Hierarchy of needs, 10–2, 44
  and democracy, 170
  and fixations, 79
  and labor, 142
  support of theory, 162, 163
  and work groups, 146–148
Hirsch, Fred, 300, 311, 329
History
  of economics, 25–55, 309–313
  of lobbying, 132
  of poverty, 179–181
  of revealed preference theory,
    323–329
Hitachi Company, song of, 225
Hobson, John A., 40–43, 49,
    51–53, 59, 149, 150, 182,
    183, 194, 280, 281, 314, 328
Holesovky, V., 260
Hollis, Martin, 62, 66
Hook, Sidney, 329
Housing
  government programs for, 201
  and old age assistance, 204–206
Houthakker, Hendrik S., 323, 325
Hua Kuo-feng, 292
The Human Side of Enterprise,
    229–232

Humanistic management,
    226–232
Humphrey-Hawkins Full
    Employment Act, 183

Illegality of shared
    monopolies, 112
Illiterate adults, 273
Imperfect competition, 109–112
Imperial Chemical Company in
    Great Britain, 222
In Praise of Folly, 4
Income tax
  optimal income tax, 164–166
  and redistribution, 167, 168
Increasing immiseration,
    law of, 36
Indifference curve,
    71–73, 317
Indigent persons. *See* Poverty
Individual preferences, 314
Industrial democracy, 153–155,
    232–242, 245–268
Industrial Reorganization
    Act, 266
Industrial work, 148, 149
Inflation rate, 218
  and full employment, 184
  and minimum wage, 188, 189
Input, work as, 142
*An Inquiry into the Wealth of
    Nations*, 27
Insecurity for jobs, 193, 213
Institutional economics, 25
Intermediary technology, 283,
    284, 288
Internalization of market, 107
Interpersonal relationships, 11
Invalidity insurance, 204
Invisible hand idea, 28
Irrationality and Veblen, 50
Irreducibility of human needs,
    317, 321
Isolated jobs, 148, 149

Japan
  Nenko, 224, 225
  Rengi, 224, 226
Jeans, Sir James, 8
Jefferson, Thomas, 132
Jevons, Stanley, 44–46, 51, 52,
    103, 312, 324
Jobs. *See* Work
Journal of Humanistic
    Psychology, 5

Kaldor, N., 99
Kamata, 257, 259
Kaufman, Roger, 213, 220
Kelso, Louis, 263, 264
Keynes, John Maynard, 52,
    183, 184